THE Allergy
Self-Help
COOKBOOK

THE Allergy Self-Help COOKBOOK

Over **350** natural food recipes, free of *All* common food allergens

MARJORIE HURT JONES, R.N.

RODALE

Notice
While self-help is vital to effective relief of allergies, many readers will also need medical guidance. In infants and children, for instance, food allergy may be hard to distinguish from a serious infection without medical help. The information in this book can help you control your food allergies; however, it is not meant to replace medical diagnosis or treatment. If you are under the care of a physician for your allergies, be sure to inform him or her of any major changes you make in your diet or environment. In some cases, your medication may need to be adjusted.

Cover and Interior Designer: Carol Angstadt
Cover Photographer: John Kelly/Stone and Rodale Images

The recipes for Kamut-Grain Bread on page 131 and Wheat-Free Oat-Bran Bread on page 132 are adapted from *Easy Bread Making for Special Diets* by Nicolette Dumke. Reprinted with permission. To obtain a copy of this book, call (303) 666-8253.
The recipes for Marjorie Fisher's Venison Stew with Carrots on page 150 and Fruit Gelatin Cutouts on page 299 are reprinted with permission from Nutrition for Optimal Health Association (NOHA): www.nutrition4health.org.
The recipe for Oven-Fried Fillets with Cashews on page 246 is reprinted with permission from Dr. Sally Rockwell: www.drsallyrockwell.com.

Library of Congress Cataloging-in-Publication Data

Jones, Marjorie Hurt.
    The allergy self-help cookbook : over 350 natural food recipes, free of all common food allergens / by Marjorie Hurt Jones.
        p.   cm.
    Previously published: New York : Wings, 1994 with subtitle: Over 325 natural foods recipes, free of wheat, milk, eggs, corn, yeast, sugar and other common food allergens.
    Includes index.
    ISBN 1–57954–276–X   paperback
    1. Food allergy—Diet therapy—Recipes.   I. Title.
RC588.D53 J65   2001
641.5'631—dc21   00–012347

Distributed to the book trade by St. Martin's Press
2   4   6   8   10   9   7   5   3   1   paperback

Visit us on the Web at www.rodalecookbooks.com, or call us toll-free at (800) 848-4735.

WE **INSPIRE** AND **ENABLE** PEOPLE TO IMPROVE
THEIR LIVES AND THE WORLD AROUND THEM

This book is

lovingly dedicated

to my dear friend

Gail Olsen Meyer,

whose asthma took her

from this world

too soon.

Contents

Useful Tables and Charts

Acknowledgments

I want to thank the following people who have shared their expertise and time with me. It is no exaggeration to acknowledge that without the help of these valued friends and professional colleagues, this book would not have happened. My thanks and appreciation go to each and every one of them.

William G. Crook, M.D., of Jackson, Tennessee, an environmental medicine physician, who helped me understand how *Candida albicans* and other microorganisms may be the culprits when food allergies fail to respond to dietary adjustments alone.

Marjorie Fisher of Evanston, Illinois, who provided me with the information about the botanical families for foods, which is the basis for the Rotary Diversified Diet.

David Frazier of Hayden, Idaho, owner-manager of a health food store, who willingly special-ordered whatever flours and other supplies I needed and dispensed his wisdom in the process.

Stan Jones of Hayden, Idaho, my husband, who ate without question all manner of meals while this book was in the making and who rescued me repeatedly when my computer became adversarial.

Betty Mulkey of Hayden, Idaho, owner-manager of a health food store, who willingly consulted with me about nutrition issues for this book and supported my efforts.

Carol Munson, editor, and the Rodale editorial and research team, who worked many long hours to fit together all of the pieces needed to produce a book of this caliber.

Kenneth Patchen of Trevor, Wisconsin, who introduced me to amaranth in 1980 and initiated my ongoing quest for "new" ancient foods to incorporate into the diets of folks with food allergies.

Barbara Peter of Lake Forest, Illinois, a professional home economist who helped educate me about the value and versatility of tofu and other soy foods.

Larry Walters of Naperville, Illinois, owner of Nu-World Amaranth, who supplied me with amaranth flour for testing recipes in this book and introduced me to puffed quinoa.

Introduction

Allergies wear many faces. Some start as sneezy-wheezy reactions to pollens, molds, or even common house dust and the invisible but ever-present dust mites. After some years, people who experience these reactions may notice that certain foods don't agree with them, or perhaps that perfume or gasoline fumes give them headaches or other symptoms. This is called the spreading phenomenon. And it often, though not always, follows an upheaval in the person's life.

I followed that pattern myself. Hay fever appeared in my early teens and only got worse through the years. After my second child (a major life event), my skin became supersensitive to soaps and cosmetics. Sometimes this manifested as a rash, or tiny cuts and raw places on my hands, or a strong sensation of burning. I found relief mostly through trial and error, learning what products I had to avoid to minimize my symptoms.

I coasted along through the next decade, coping with the hay fever and sensitive skin, without too much change in either. Then, after menopause (hormones in turmoil), food allergies reared their ugly heads. For me, fumes (the chemical aspect of allergies) were the least apparent, but this is not always the case.

In today's world, we are all immersed in a chemical soup that pollutes to a greater or lesser extent our air, food, and water. Many people—even healthy people with no history of reacting to any aspect of their environment—may start to notice symptoms associated with chemical exposures. Almost always,

they are followed in short order by allergies to foods and inhalants.

So, there you have it, the big three of allergy: food allergies, inhalant allergies, and multiple-chemical sensitivities. I should point out that, for the purposes of this book, I use the word *allergy* broadly to cover three different reactions to food: allergies, sensitivities, and intolerances. The exact definition of a true allergy is explained in detail on page 35. However, my criteria for a food "allergy" is entirely empirical, straightforward, and easy to understand: If eating a food causes you distress, or if you discover any clear cause-and-effect symptoms that are relieved by avoidance of specific foods, you are dealing with some type of food allergy.

FINDING HELP

When I was diagnosed with food allergies, like any good bookworm, I headed for the public library for help. I was sorely disappointed. That was in 1976. (Today's libraries are much better sources of allergy information, particularly if they have access to the Internet.) In any case, because of limited storage space, I cleaned out my cupboards, gave away the foods that I would be avoiding, and made room for new, alternative foods with which I had yet to become acquainted.

Naturally, I wanted to keep notes on my experimental cooking and baking. If I thought that I could improve a dish with more or less of this or that, I wanted to note that for the next time. And for sure, if I hit it right with something we really enjoyed, I wanted to know how to duplicate it. Eventually, my notes filled a whole kitchen drawer, and I began to think about turning them into a book. I wanted to share my recipes with others so that they wouldn't have to go through the same trial-and-error process of discovery.

ABOUT THE RECIPES

I set out to create recipes that would be health-enhancing in the broadest sense of those words. Here's what I mean: Those who have food allergies may also experience a wide variety of other ailments, as well as hereditary health risks. For example, my family all died of cardiovascular "events" that followed years of hypertension, heart attacks, strokes, or aneurysms. So I decided to keep my recipes moderately low in fat. But they are not fat-free or extremely low in fat.

I kept some fat in my recipes because everyone—including people with allergies—needs good fat in their diets, in moderation of course. I'm talking about flax seeds and flax oil, hemp seeds and hemp oil, nuts and nut oils (if you don't react to them), soy oil (if it doesn't bother you), as well as mono-unsaturated canola, olive, and avocado oils. These are heart-healthy fats that nutritionists recommend including in any health-enhancing diet.

Likewise, I use salt conservatively in my recipes, often ¼ teaspoon for every cup of flour, ½ teaspoon to a pound of meat, or 1 teaspoon to 1 pound of dry beans—that's just enough to enhance the flavor of the foods without dominating the taste. This is about half the amount of salt called for in many standard cookbooks, but if you need to use even less than that, cut the amount in half again. Under no circumstances should a recipe in this book actually taste salty.

Your family history may involve different health challenges, but whatever they are, I think you will find them compatible with the recipes in this book. You or someone in your family may have diabetes, hypoglycemia, obesity, or other diagnoses that require certain dietary adjustments. With a little juggling, I think you will find that your special diet meshes very nicely with what you will find in these pages. Several recipes use alternative sweeteners such as agave nectar, alternative milks such as soy milk and nut milk, and alternative grains such as quinoa. Plus, most recipes can be easily adjusted to incorporate the ingredients that agree with you. By substituting appropriately, your total percentages of meat, fish or poultry, vegetables, fruits, and whole grains (or grainlike foods) can remain right where they should be.

The point, of course, is that those of us with food allergies must learn to adapt our selection of foods to compensate for our allergies. So if we have other medical conditions with dietary requirements, we just do more of what we are already doing: adapting.

GETTING IT TOGETHER

Of course, it's not easy to change the way you eat. But the payoff for making changes can be very great: feeling better, thinking brighter, and having energy and enthusiasm for life rather than dragging through it. This book picks up where the doctor's diagnosis leaves off, when you leave the office with a new name for your problems—food allergies—and a list of forbidden foods. You find yourself wondering what in the world you're going to eat! I hope you darted into a bookstore on your way home and purchased this book early on—it can help in so many ways.

For example, if you are allergic to wheat, milk, and eggs, your usual breakfasts and most of your usual sandwich-based lunches may be off-limits now. You can brood about that and rail against the injustices, or you can take the situation as a challenge and embark upon a journey of discovery.

What other foods are out there? How do you use those new foods? Can you possibly make fare tasty enough so that the family will enjoy it too? What will birthdays and holidays be like without your favorite foods? (Turn to page 350 to find out.)

Fortunately, there are many terrific flours and foods to choose from. And you're about to discover that life can and does go on after eliminating wheat, milk, and eggs. In fact, I've devoted the whole first chapter to introducing new and less-common ingredients. Nothing is as frustrating as buying a new flour, getting it home, and not having any idea how to use it. I help you avoid that by giving you enough information about each ingredient so that you will have a good idea of how different flours will behave.

Rather than rushing you into the recipes, I've included several chapters of basic information that will help explain the various aspects of food allergies. You'll find tips for deep-cleaning your kitchen and house, hints for successful dining out, and guidelines for dealing with children who have allergies. Because your food choices are so important to your health now (or your loved one's health), I've included a crash course in nutrition, suggestions for lunches, and a chapter explaining the Rotary Diversified Diet, should you decide to try that therapeutic tool.

While the information in this book will make your food allergies easier to manage, this book cannot take the place of a caring, nutritionally oriented environmental physician who can help you rebuild your health. As I mentioned earlier, this book starts where your doctor stops. He will do the professional testing you need, arrive at a diagnosis, and design a treatment plan. Then it's up to you to implement that plan. The diagnosis will tell you what it is you need to avoid, and it may be quite a list. The treatment plan, though individual, should help you find different foods to eat. Because I've done so much work in the field of alternative, less-allergenic foods, I'm proposing that you and your doctor include this book in your treatment plan.

With food allergies, the doctor can't make you well; he can only point out your path to wellness. Think of him as your health consultant. He can help you sort out your problems, guide you in making food and lifestyle choices, and hand you a road map to recovery. But you're the one who will be taking that journey.

Getting better from food allergies can be a daunting task and may take 2 to 3 years. It's well worth your trouble to find a doctor with whom you're comfortable, even if you have to travel an hour or two to get to the doctor's office. If you haven't found the right physician yet, check the Food Allergy Network referred to on page 381. Keep searching until you find a doctor you're happy with.

With this book in one hand and your doctor's road map in the other, bon voyage! You're off on a journey of discovery, with lots of great-tasting food along the way.

PART

I

Getting Started

Exploring New Ingredients

Once you know which foods you're allergic to, the next step is to make the most of what you *can* eat. In developing recipes for this book, I've concentrated on finding alternatives to the common allergens—milk, eggs, wheat and other common grains, sugar and corn sweeteners, and fruits and vegetables such as citrus, green beans, and legumes. Although I've included eggs and soy occasionally in the recipes, they are not used frequently. And I've introduced recipes for little-used but less allergenic foods such as lamb, rabbit, spaghetti squash, and several alternative flours.

In exploring new ingredients, it pays to be an optimist. I've found that cooking and eating are most enjoyable when I approach my diet with a sense of adventure and stay open to trying new or less familiar foods.

MILK ALTERNATIVES

Milk is difficult to avoid when buying commercially prepared foods, but it's one of the easier foods to sidestep when cooking from scratch. There are lots of substitutes for cow's milk: rice milk, soy milk, zucchini milk, and so on.

Stock up on soy milk. For infants and toddlers who are not breastfeeding and are allergic to cow's milk, most allergy doctors recommend soy milk. Likewise, many older children and adults can use soy milk with cereal, in cooking and baking, and as a beverage. Excellent-quality prepared soy milk is available in health food stores everywhere and in many supermarkets, although flavor and palatability vary from product to product. Every soy milk that I have seen is ivory in color. Typical flavors include original (plain), vanilla, and chocolate. Some brands add calcium and other nutrients to make their product more comparable to cow's milk. Always read the label; some products contain a sweetener, and vanilla and chocolate themselves can elicit allergic reactions. If soy agrees with you, try several brands of soy milk to find the one you like best. And why not check out some of the great soy ice creams and soy-based cheeses that are available?

If you can eat soy freely, that's great. However, soy is an increasingly common food allergen in its own right, and many milk-allergic people complain that they're just plain tired of soy. So if you use soy milk, ration it to intervals of 4 or more days, which may help prevent you from becoming food-sensitive to it.

Try zucchini milk. In cooking and baking, you can often substitute Zucchini Milk (page 302) for cow's milk. Because it's somewhat thicker than cow's milk, cut back on the flour or increase the liquid in baked goods when using it.

Or use goat's milk. Allergy doctors and patients alike have discovered that some infants and children who can't tolerate cow's milk thrive on goat's milk. Although both cows and goats belong to the Bovid family, evidently their milk differs enough from each other so that goat's milk can be tolerated by some who can't drink cow's milk. Part of the reason may be that fat globules in goat's milk are smaller, making it easier to digest. Consequently, goat's milk—and goat's-milk products—are worth a try. Fresh goat's milk is widely available in supermarkets as whole milk or low-fat (1%), usually "ultra-pasteurized" and in aseptic packaging for a shelf life of a month or more. Canned and powdered goat's milk are available in many health food stores, but the widely available fresh milk has a lighter, more pleasant flavor.

Chèvre, or goat's-milk cheese, is a welcome alternative for people who are allergic to cow's-milk cheeses. (Watch out for blends of cow's milk and goat's milk, called michèvres, or blends mislabeled as "100 percent goat cheese." Call the distributor if you must to be sure.) Depending on its age and, therefore, moisture content, goat's-milk cheese may be creamy, smooth, and soft or crumbly, dry, and hard. As with most cheeses, the flavor intensifies with age. I have found some chèvres that resemble Cheddar cheese and others that are much like cream cheese. If it's new to you, start with mild, "young" goat's-milk cream cheese until you get accustomed to its distinctive flavor and texture.

As the dairy industry experiments further, you can expect to find still other goat's-milk products available—ricotta, yogurt, cottage cheese, and Camembert, for example. I've developed recipes for goat's-milk cheese and yogurt that I think you'll enjoy if cow's-milk cheeses are off-limits.

Sheep's milk makes a tasty alternative. Sheep's-milk feta cheese and yogurt are sometimes available, usually in health food stores, sometimes in supermarkets. The sheep's-milk feta cheese I've found in supermarkets is imported from France, and the yogurt is from Canada. In both, the flavor is mild and delicious.

Use juice or water for baking. In some recipes, you can substitute unsweetened juice or water for milk, which is what I've done in many recipes. To make up for the omission of milk solids, use about ¾ cup juice or water for each cup of milk called for.

Try nut milks. Almond milk and other nut milks are available in supermarkets these days. You can also make your own using the recipe in this book (page 302). I have also developed beverages from fruit and herbal teas to broaden your choices.

Avoid nondairy creamers and toppings. I do not recommend that people with milk allergies use nondairy creamers or toppings. Some of those milk substitutes contain whey, lactose, or caseinate—all milk derivatives. In addition, nondairy substitutes are usually made from corn, soy, or coconut and contain flavor additives and petroleum-based chemicals, all of which are potential allergens. Further, they contain trans fatty acids, which have been shown to be harmful to cardiovascular health. (See Nutrition Basics in Brief on page 52.)

To match the nutritional makeup of cow's milk, stick with goat's milk, sheep's milk, or fortified soy milk as an alternative. If you use any of the other milk substitutes on a regular basis, it's smart to check the label for calcium content and, if need be, take a calcium supplement. (See Nutrition Basics in Brief on page 52.)

WHEAT AND GRAIN ALTERNATIVES

Wheat intolerance—and grain allergy in general—is probably one of the most perplexing of all food allergies. Our diet relies so heavily on wheat-based bread and baked goods that other flours are practically unheard of (or, like rye, usually used in combination with wheat flour). Corn, which often appears on labels as cornstarch and corn syrup, is also widely used and is a prime allergen.

My aim is to help you discover the wealth of other grain options available. Many people who are allergic to wheat can tolerate related grains, especially if they don't eat them every day. Rice, rye, barley, oats, and millet may or may not be part of the answer for you, or perhaps some of the other available grains— Kamut brand grain, spelt or teff, or the grainlike grass called quinoa—will agree with you. Initially, buy grains in small quantities, then taste them to see which ones you prefer. (See Planning a Rotary Diversified Diet on page 35.) Spelt and Kamut brand grain are types of wheat and should be avoided by people with celiac disease.

Teff contains no gluten and is the least like wheat. Even though Kamut brand grain and spelt are genetically quite similar to wheat, they are different enough that many wheat-sensitive people have hailed them as "lifesavers." Researchers speculate that controlled genetic breeding has made wheat less easy to digest, while Kamut brand grain and spelt are genetically the same readily digestible ancient grains that our ancestors ate.

Gluten-Free Flours

For those allergic to gluten, here are two handy lists: flours that contain gluten and flours that are essentially gluten-free.

Flours That Contain Gluten
Spelt flour
Wheat flour
Kamut brand flour
Rye flour
Oat flour
Barley flour

Essentially Gluten-Free Flours
Amaranth flour
Arrowroot flour
Brown rice flour
Buckwheat flour (100%)
Chickpea flour
Legume flours
Nut and seed flours
Potato flour
Potato starch flour
Quinoa flour
Soy flour
Tapioca starch flour
Teff flour

To eat well without wheat, I've borrowed recipe ideas from Middle Eastern, Indian, and other Asian cuisines in which rice, chickpeas, lentils, potatoes, tapioca, arrowroot, and other plant foods (usually grains or legumes) are ground or mashed to produce flours, meals, or starchy bases with wonderfully diverse flavors and textures.

Because I'm allergic to wheat, I've had a strong interest in developing recipes using alternative flours. I quickly discovered that each flour has its own set of cooking properties. The information below will save you hours of experimentation and frustrating results when you want to make grain-free versions of your family's favorite baked goods. And it will help you understand the options given in my recipes. For example, oat flour and chickpea flour are both excellent thickeners, but oat flour gives milk-free sauces a grayish tinge, so golden chickpea flour is a better choice visually. You can buy any of these alternative flours in health food stores or ethnic markets or from catalog distributors. (See "Foods," on page 383.)

COOKING AND BAKING WITH ALTERNATIVE FLOURS

If you're allergic to wheat, you can substitute other starches and flours to make breadings, sauces, or baked goods. Each flour has certain strengths and weaknesses. Here are details on which alternatives work best in each case.

Amaranth Flour

Flavor and Color   Flavor is grain-like, mild, and almost nutty. Color varies from off-white to nearly black. Most common varieties are the color of mild honey. If flour gets old, it will smell of rancid oil and have a strong "off" flavor. Discard and buy fresh.

Flavor mixes well with other foods, especially spices, carob, and nuts.

Breading   Flour does an adequate job of breading. Results are even better when you grind puffed amaranth in a blender and use the resulting powder as breading. Browns quickly. Use medium or medium-low heat. If breaded food browns before it is cooked through, finish cooking in a 350°F oven for 10 to 20 minutes, or until food is done.

Herbs may be added for flavor: tarragon or Italian Seasoning (page 210) for chicken; dill or Pizzazz Seasoning (page 210) for fish.

Thickening   Each variety of amaranth differs slightly in its thickening ability.

To test your flour: Combine 1 cup cool water with 2 tablespoons amaranth flour; bring to boil over medium heat, stirring. Should thicken within 15 minutes. Increase or decrease the amount of flour for a thicker or thinner sauce.

Baking   Excellent, especially in combinations.

Substitute for 25 to 50 percent of total flour, and use quinoa, buckwheat, or any tolerated grain flour for the remainder.

For grain-free baked goods with nice flavor, substitute amaranth flour and quinoa flakes in equal amounts and add 1 tablespoon arrowroot or tapioca starch flour per cup of flour replaced (the starch is an optional enhancement for a slightly improved texture). Or use ⅓ part each of amaranth flour, quinoa flakes, and white buckwheat flour (for example, ½ cup each for a total of 1½ cups).

Comments   An ancient grainlike food, amaranth is not related to wheat or other grains and is well-tolerated by many people. Used in the proportions suggested, amaranth produces baked goods that are moist, with excellent flavor and texture. When used for 100 percent of the flour for a cake, cookie, or bread, it retains so much moisture that the center remains pudding-like, even when the exterior is very brown. For best results, use amaranth flour in combinations. Most health food stores carry the flour, though you may want to ask about freshness. If the store keeps it on an open shelf, suggest that it be kept in a cooler. If the flour is ground on the premise, find out when it's ground. Whenever possible, buy it that day. If you're uncertain about freshness, you may prefer to order puffed or freshly ground flour by mail. The higher cost is worth it.

This flour is vulnerable to rancidity, so store it in a tightly covered container in the freezer. Or keep it at room temperature in glass canning jars sealed with a food saver home vacuum packaging system (a home appliance that creates a vacuum in jars by removing the oxygen).

Puffed amaranth may be used as a ready-to-eat cereal but becomes mushy quickly. This makes it perfect for infants and young children. Puffed amaranth also makes a delightful caramel-coated confection, somewhat like those you find in health food stores. (See Caramel-Coated Puffed Amaranth and Glazed Puffed Amaranth, page 287.)

Home grinding is difficult. Whole-seed amaranth is very hard and about the size of a poppy seed, so it slips right through many grinders. Small nut and seed or coffee grinders usually work well for small quantities—about 2 tablespoons at a time. You may be able to grind 1 to 2 cups of the seeds in a powerful home grinder such as a Vita Mix.

Rich in nutrients and higher in protein and fiber than any grain. Contains B vitamins and a good supply of minerals, including calcium and iron.

Amaranth is essentially gluten-free.

Arrowroot Flour

Flavor and Color Flavorless and snow white in color. Can be used "anonymously" in baked goods. Add herbs or spices for flavor.

Breading Browns quickly and well, producing an attractive golden, crisp coating. Again, add seasonings or combine with other flours for flavor.

Thickening Excellent. Substitute for equal amount of cornstarch. Or dissolve 1 tablespoon per cup of cool liquid for a medium-thick sauce. Add ½ teaspoon for a thicker sauce. Bring to boil and allow to bubble for 2 to 3 minutes only; prolonged cooking causes the starch to break down and the sauce to thin.

To thicken stew: Dissolve arrowroot in cool liquid and add to boiling stew during last 5 minutes of cooking; stir until thick and clear. Remove from heat. May need to re-thicken leftovers with additional arrowroot.

Baking Substitute for up to 25 percent of total flour or use as little as 1 to 2 tablespoons per cup of flour to lighten dense or heavy baked goods. Use in combination with other wheat alternatives.

Usually interchangeable with tapioca starch flour.

Comments Silky powder, much like cornstarch. Buy in bulk—by the pound—in health food stores. Available in the spice aisle of grocery stores, but four to five times more expensive in those little jars.

Store in tightly sealed jar to prevent moisture absorption.

Offers little nutrition; use small amounts only to produce quality baked goods.

Arrowroot is gluten-free.

Brown Rice Flour

Flavor and Color Mild flavor enhanced by spices, herbs, and ingredients such as honey, cinnamon, or maple syrup. As flour ages, oils become rancid and flavor deteriorates. Off-white.

Breading Not good. Gets mushy instead of crisp. Instead, use finely ground crumbs of Rice-Flour Pancakes (page 93).

Thickening Satisfactory. Produces light, off-white sauces.

Use 25 percent more than wheat flour (2½ tablespoons brown rice flour for each 2 tablespoons of wheat flour). Texture is somewhat grainy, but not offensive. For smoother sauces, let flour stand in the liquid for 1 to 2 hours to soften.

Baking   Excellent for cookies and pie crust. Color will be off-white.

Cakes and breads tend to be dry unless mixed with other flours, starches, or ground nuts. Substitute 10 to 25 percent arrowroot or tapioca starch, up to 25 percent ground nuts, and the remainder brown rice flour.

As a flour substitute: $\frac{7}{8}$ cup rice flour (1 level cup less 2 tablespoons) = 1 cup wheat flour. But remember, rice flour lacks gluten, so it will never behave exactly like wheat flour.

Good bet: Use 30 to 50 percent brown rice flour with other flours. For example, in place of 1 cup wheat flour use $\frac{1}{2}$ cup rice flour plus $\frac{1}{2}$ cup oat flour, or use $\frac{1}{3}$ cup each of brown rice, oat, and barley flours.

Comments   Contains no gluten; considered the least allergenic of the grains. White rice flour has a longer shelf-life than brown rice flour, but it lacks fiber and some nutrients.

To avoid dry baked goods: Substitute a starch or ground nuts for part of the flour and add dates or other dried fruits that have been soaked until plump. Or use a puree of fresh, unsweetened canned, or stewed dried fruit for all or part of the liquid. Or add grated vegetables, such as carrots or zucchini, and increase the amount of oil (don't increase oil if using nuts).

Brown rice and its flour are gluten-free.

Buckwheat Flour, Dark (ground from roasted groats)

Flavor and Color   Most common kind of buckwheat flour available. Has a strong characteristic flavor. Often blended with milder flour or starch to moderate flavor. Tan with dark speckles.

Breading   Very good. Crisp, dark brown coating.

Thickening   Not good. It thickens only as it cools, and its flavor dominates the dish. Not practical for sauces.

Baking   Satisfactory when blended with another (usually wheat) flour but flavor is still strong; white (unroasted) buckwheat flour has a milder flavor. (See Buckwheat Flour, White, page 10.)

Comments   Commercial buckwheat flour may contain a small amount of wheat flour. Look for 100 percent buckwheat flour on label.

Dark buckwheat groats and flour are essentially gluten-free. But check commercial products that may contain wheat. Buckwheat "soba" noodles, for example, may contain wheat flour; buckwheat pancakes may have 20 to 40 percent dark buckwheat flour, the rest being wheat.

Buckwheat Flour, White (ground from unroasted whole groats)

Flavor and Color	Mild and mellow. Seems totally different from dark flour. Groats have a faint greenish cast; the flour is very light tan.
Breading	Excellent. Crisp, dark brown coating, with mild flavor; may be seasoned with herbs or spices.
Thickening	Not good. Same as dark buckwheat.
Baking	Excellent. Very similar to brown rice flour: light with a tendency to be dry. To avoid dryness, try the "Baking" suggestions under Brown Rice Flour (page 8).
Comments	Mild flavor appeals to many people, especially when using it for 100 percent of the flour.

One of the least expensive and most satisfactory alternatives to wheat flour. High in rutin, a bioflavonoid, which may cause a reaction in a small percentage of allergics. Not refined as white wheat flour is.

Easy to grind in a blender. To grind your own flour: Buy white, unroasted whole groats. Grind ½ cup at a time in a blender, for 1 to 2 minutes. Pour into sifter or sieve and shake. Repeat grinding, adding any groats that didn't sift through. Repeat process until you have as much flour as you need. (It takes about 7 minutes to grind and sift 2 cups of flour.)

Store whole groats at room temperature in a tightly covered container for up to a month. Store in the freezer for up to a year.

White buckwheat groats and flour are essentially gluten-free.

Chickpea (garbanzo bean) Flour

Flavor and Color	Mild. Blends well with other flours (not "beany" tasting). Produces a yellow, rich-looking sauce.
Breading	Fair. Doesn't get crisp. Better when mixed with ground seeds.
Thickening	Excellent. Approximates wheat for this function. Good choice to thicken soups or stews.

Baking	Excellent. Use 25 percent with other flours for high-protein baked goods. For totally grain-free pancakes, try using ⅓ part each amaranth, buckwheat, and chickpea flours or ⅓ part each chickpea flour, either amaranth *or* buckwheat flour, and ground nuts.
Comments	Sometimes packaged as "gram" flour—not to be confused with graham flour, which is a wheat flour. Read labels carefully. Use commercial flour only. Dry chickpeas are so hard that they break the average nut and seed grinder, and they will dull the blades of a blender. As with any legume, there may be a problem with digestibility. Start with 1½ tablespoons chickpea flour in a measuring cup and fill the cup with the flour of any grain (this is approximately 5 percent chickpea flour). If that percentage proves comfortable, double to 3 tablespoons (approximately 10 percent) for improved protein in finished product. Found in Indian and Middle Eastern groceries, as well as in most health food stores and some supermarkets. Chickpea flour is gluten-free.

Kamut Brand Flour

Flavor and Color	Delicious earthy, whole-grain flavor. Grains are light tan in color; flour is more golden than wheat.
Breading	Similar to wheat; browns and crisps nicely.
Thickening	Similar to wheat; use 2 tablespoons to thicken 1 cup of liquid for medium consistency.
Baking	Excellent. Similar—though not identical—to whole wheat pastry flour. In most applications can be used interchangeably with wheat, in equal measure. Yeast breads are fairly dense and crumbly. For best results, use a specially developed recipe.
Comments	Closely related to wheat genetically, but more easily digested. As many as 86 percent of people allergic to wheat can tolerate Kamut brand flour very well. Sometimes called "Egyptian wheat," Kamut brand grain is descended from 32 grains found in an Egyptian pyramid. A true "natural" food, in its ancient digestible form. Kamut brand flour contains gluten.

Legume Flours (other than soy and chickpea)

Flavor and Color   Mild flavor. Color varies with legume used.

Breading   Same as chickpea flour.

Thickening   Not suitable; mashed or pureed beans that have been soaked and cooked do a better job.

Baking   Same as chickpea flour. In combination with other flours, red lentils and lentil flour make attractive and appetizing baked goods.

Comments   Uncooked, unsoaked beans ground for flour may cause intestinal distress. Therefore, do not grind beans for flour; use commercially prepared legume flours instead. Two exceptions to this rule: lentils, especially the red variety, and yellow split peas. To grind these: Place ½ cup lentils or peas in a blender; process on high for about 5 minutes. For some baked goods, pureed cooked lentils can replace lentil flour.

Legume flours are gluten-free.

Nut, Peanut, and Seed Flours

Flavor and Color   Excellent flavor that varies with nut or seed.

Grinding tends to release the flavor, as does light dry roasting. Color depends on nut or seed.

Breading   Excellent nutty flavor; works best when mixed with a flour.

Thickening   Cashews work best.

Baking   Excellent. Use for up to 25 percent of grain flour. Reduce oil in recipe to compensate for high oil content of nut flour.

Good replacement for wheat germ in recipes.

Comments   May use raw or toasted nuts and seeds; toasting provides richer flavor.

Buy fresh, whole, unsalted nuts and seeds (organic, if possible). Store nuts in a tightly closed container in a cool place—an unheated pantry, freezer, or refrigerator.

Grind small amounts for immediate use. Do not store after grinding, as ground nuts and seeds readily turn rancid. Before grinding walnuts, pecans, or other soft and oily nuts, toss with 1 or 2 tablespoons of arrowroot or another starch to reduce clumping.

To grind all nuts: Grind about 2 tablespoons at a time in a small nut and seed grinder. Or grind up to ½ cup at a time in a blender. (Food processors don't chop nuts finely enough to make a flour.) Process briefly using on/off pulses. Strain or sift. Return chunks to blender, add more nuts, and process. Particles should be fine enough to pass through the strainer. Do not overprocess, as nuts will turn into nut butter. For pancakes, muffins, or cookies, nuts can be coarsely ground or chopped.

If you are allergic to nuts, replace the amount of nut flour in a recipe with an equal amount of another flour or starch.

Nut and seed flours are gluten-free.

Oat Flour

Flavor and Color	Flavor is mild and does not dominate. Color is light tan; color of baked goods is brown and appetizing. Color of sauce is gray, unless curry, paprika, or other high-color seasoning is added.
Breading	Browns nicely.
Thickening	Very good. Use same proportions as wheat flour (2 tablespoons to 1 cup liquid). Stone-ground oat flour makes a smoother sauce than ground rolled oats, but either is satisfactory.
Baking	Excellent in cookies and pancakes—may be used for 50 to 75 percent of flour called for. Too heavy by itself for cakes, but quite satisfactory when used 50-50 with barley or rice flour. May also add 1 to 2 tablespoons arrowroot or tapioca starch flour to lighten and retain moisture.
Comments	Stone-ground oat flour is available commercially and can be used in equal measure for wheat flour, though baked goods will be heavier than with all wheat. For best results, combine with one of the lighter flours, such as rice or barley. To make 1 cup of flour: Grind 1¼ cups rolled oats into fine powder. Oats and oat flour contain gluten.

Potato Flour

Flavor and Color	Bland. White.
Breading	Not suitable.

Thickening	Can be used to make some sauces. Contributes potato flavor to sauces, so not always desirable.
Baking	Substitute ½ to ⅝ cup potato flour for each cup of wheat flour. Combines well with brown rice flour to add body to cookie dough. Let batter stand a few minutes before baking to allow flour to absorb liquid.
Comments	Made from cooked potatoes. Do not confuse with potato starch. Note that potato flour has a high gylcemic index number. Potato flour is gluten-free.

Potato Starch Flour

Flavor and Color	White. Bland. Add herbs or seasonings.
Breading	Browns quickly. Crisps well.
Thickening	Poor—turns to glue.
Baking	Suitable for cakes but not breads. Needs eggs, baking powder, or other leavening.
Comments	Made from raw white potatoes. Do not confuse with potato flour. Looks and feels like cornstarch. Note that potato starch has a high glycemic index number (See Potato Flour, page 13.) Potato starch is gluten-free.

Quinoa Flour

Flavor and Color	Flavor is pleasant, nutty, and somewhat assertive. Pale seeds, with occasional black or red ones.
Breading	Not good.
Thickening	Not practical to wet-grind seeds; flour thickens satisfactorily.
Baking	Satisfactory, when flour is fresh. Baked goods can be dry; add applesauce or soaked, moist raisins and a little arrowroot or tapioca starch to help retain moisture.
Comments	Flavor varies with freshness and thoroughness of rinsing. If flour is ground from unwashed seeds, flavor will be bitter. In commercially produced quinoa flour, saponins are mechanically removed before grinding takes place.

To clean seeds and remove bitter saponins: Place the seeds in a sieve and run under cold water. Stir the grains with your hand or a spoon until the water drains clear. Washed whole seeds can be cooked and used like rice; flavor is mild.

Quinoa is a member of the Goosefoot family.

Quinoa is gluten-free.

Soy Flour

Flavor and Color	Bland to slightly beany. Flavor easily camouflaged by other flavors. When mixed with fruit, spices, carob, or nuts, the other tastes dominate. Makes golden to tan soy milk.
Breading	Good. Makes a crisp coating. Add herbs for flavor. Can mix with a starch or flour.
Thickening	Does not thicken liquids.
Baking	Use 2 to 4 tablespoons per 1 cup of grain flour. In this combination, it produces baked goods with high quality protein. Mixes successfully with amaranth, buckwheat, ground nuts and starches, and other grains. Baked goods have a good texture and retain moisture.
Comments	Commercial processing of soybeans for flour isn't standardized. Soy must be cooked to be digested. When and how this is done influences the flavor and quality of the flour. Least satisfactory is grinding dry beans (as is done with grain) and dry roasting the flour. (Some flour is even marketed raw.) Fearn's Soya Powder, made of cooked soy beans, dried and then ground, is finer than other flours and usually tastes better. Fearn's Soya Powder contains all the natural oil of the soybean. Oil content of a recipe you are converting may be reduced by 1 teaspoon for each ¼ cup of soya powder used. Soy is a common allergen; use it no more than once every four days, if you tolerate it. Soy flour is gluten-free.

Spelt Flour

Flavor and Color	Wonderful whole-grain flavor. Tan whole grains and flour.
Breading	Similar to wheat; browns and crisps nicely.

Thickening	Similar to wheat; 2 tablespoons thicken 1 cup liquid.
Baking	Excellent. Similar, though not identical, to wheat. Produces great cookies, cakes, and pie crust. Yeast bread rises well, though will be more crumbly than whole wheat bread.
Comments	Available in health food stores as whole grain flour and white spelt flour. The white version is achieved by fine sifting, not bleaching. Nutritionally, the white flour contains less fiber and nutrients than the whole grain version.
	Is also available as unbleached white flour, which will produce somewhat lighter baked goods than whole grain spelt flour. If you have a very fine sieve or sifter, you can sift whole spelt flour to make your own white flour. Save the resulting bran to use in muffins or pancakes.
	Spelt flour contains as much gluten as wheat, sometimes more. Therefore, it should be avoided by people with celiac disease.

Tapioca Starch Flour

Flavor and Color	Silky and flavorless, like arrowroot.
Breading	Very good, like arrowroot.
Thickening	Excellent. Dissolve 1 tablespoon starch in 2 tablespoons cold water and stir into 1 cup boiling liquid; thickens in 1 to 2 minutes. Remove from heat as soon as liquid has thickened and become clear.
	Substitute for equal amount of cornstarch. Or use half as much in place of wheat flour to thicken a sauce. (One tablespoon starch thickens 1 cup liquid.) As with arrowroot, add during last 2 to 3 minutes of cooking. When cooked too long, tapioca flour first takes on a rubbery consistency, then breaks down and loses its thickening ability as the liquid returns to its original thin consistency.
Baking	Excellent. Substitute for 25 to 50 percent of total flour. Will lighten wheatless baked goods. See "Baking" tips under Arrowroot Flour on page 8 for more suggestions.
Comments	Do not confuse tapioca starch with tapioca granules (which are commonly used to thicken desserts such as puddings or pies).
	Store in a tightly sealed jar.
	Tapioca starch flour is gluten-free.

Teff Flour

Flavor and Color Flavor is distinctive and pleasing. The variety most widely available in the United States is dark brown, although it also exists in reddish-tan and ivory.

Breading Satisfactory.

Thickening Absorbs more liquid than wheat flour. Use 1½ tablespoons to thicken 1 cup liquid to a medium consistency.

Baking Teff is essentially gluten-free and handles much like rice flour; therefore, yeast breads made with it will fail to rise much. Works well in brownies, cakes, and pancakes.

Comments Very hard, tiny seeds; many home grinders allow some of the seeds to pass through unbroken. Look for fresh commercially ground flour.

Quite low in fat, so baked goods may be dry, especially if overbaked.

Nutritionally, teff is impressive; it is five-fold richer in iron, calcium, and potassium than any other true grain! It is an ancient grain native to Ethiopia and other parts of Africa. It hitch-hiked to the United States via an American who was working as a public health worker in Ethiopia, who now grows it in southern Idaho.

Teff is essentially gluten-free.

ALTERNATIVE SWEETENERS

White table sugar is usually made from cane (a grass related to wheat, and a prime allergen), corn (a common allergen), or beets—or a blend of all three. You can't tell which is which since all look like white table sugar, and labeling ranges from poor to nonexistent. Most allergic people are best off using honey, maple sugar or syrup, stevia extract, agave nectar (extracted from a cactus), date sugar, fruit juice concentrates, or dried fruits. These alternative sweeteners don't behave like white sugar, though, so it's important to understand how they work before substituting them freely in baked goods.

Honey. It's sweeter than sugar, so experts recommend using ⅔ or ¾ cup honey to replace 1 cup of sugar. But I often cut it by half. Also, honey changes the proportion of liquid-to-dry ingredients—a critical factor in producing light, finely textured baked goods. To adapt your own recipes, you will need to add a little flour. Or decrease the total amount of liquid called for by ½ cup for every cup of honey used. To further ensure lightness in baked goods, add an additional ½ teaspoon baking soda per cup of honey used, and reduce the oven temperature by 25°F to prevent overbrowning. (My recipes have already taken these factors into account; no adjustment is necessary.)

Some other helpful tips for cooking with honey:

* To measure honey, use the same cup you used to measure oil in a recipe. The honey will slip out easily.

* If you are using a recipe that calls for eggs, gradually pour the honey into well-beaten eggs in a thin stream, beating continuously. That step dramatically increases the volume of baked goods, so you won't end up with a heavy, dense product.

* Do not overheat honey—its flavor and color may change. There's nothing wrong with granulated honey. But if you want to reliquify it, place the jar in a bowl of warm (not hot) water. It may take an hour or longer to liquify, depending on the amount of honey.

* Store honey in a tightly covered container, preferably in a cool, dark place. Freezing or refrigeration is not harmful but will thicken or granulate the honey.

Maple syrup. Pure maple syrup has a very distinct flavor, so you can't substitute it in just any recipe. It's best used in breakfast breads and certain desserts. Be sure to avoid maple-flavored syrups—they're usually made of corn syrup, and many contain sodium benzoate, a common allergen for asthmatics. Further, they may contain sugar to bolster their level of sweetness.

Maple syrup is not quite as sweet as honey. It can be substituted in equal measure for sugar—or perhaps 75 to 80 percent, depending on your taste for sweets. When baking with maple syrup, I find I need to de-crease the total amount of liquid ingredients in a recipe by nearly the full amount of syrup used. In other words, for each cup of maple syrup used, omit at least ⅔ to ¾ cup of the other liquids (usually water, juice, and/or oil).

Maple sugar is simply dehydrated maple syrup granules. It is sometimes available in health food stores or by mail order and can be used in equal measure like brown sugar, but it is expensive. (See "Foods," page 383.) Because maple sugar tends to form hard lumps, I usually press it through a strainer before baking with it.

Date sugar. This sweetener looks like brown sugar but doesn't dissolve quite as well. And it's expensive. Both maple and date sugar come in handy for birthday cakes, holiday cookies, and other special treats that need to look and feel as much like regular fare as possible.

Fruit juice. Some of my recipes are sweetened with dried fruit, fruit juice, fruit juice concentrate, or a combination of those foods. The results are fantastic. (See Spicy Date Drops on page 292 and Elegant and Easy Fruitcake on page 360.) The recipe for Two-Step Carrot Cake (page 316) contains dried fruit and a small amount of honey. Buy dried fruits from stores that keep them refrigerated, especially if you are allergic to molds and other fungi. In the course of being dried, fruits pick up minuscule spores of otherwise harmless yeasts and molds, but it may be enough to cause symptoms in sensitive individuals. To minimize growth and reproduction of molds on food, always store dried fruit in the refrigerator. Rinse raisins and currants before using. Incidentally, fresh fruits make good sweeteners, too, and I've used them liberally as the basis for various snacks, smoothies, and desserts.

Molasses. Because it is made from sugar cane, I include molasses in just a few recipes (sorghum or dark agave nectar is listed as an alternative).

Grain-based sweeteners. Sorghum, rice syrup, and barley malt originate from grains, so they may trigger allergies in grain-sensitive people. An interesting sweetener, sorghum tastes very sweet and is derived from milo, a seldom used grain. Like molasses, it has a distinctive flavor. Although available in many health food stores, sorghum may be difficult to find, especially in the northern United States. Rice syrup and barley malt are both much less sweet than sugar, honey, or sorghum. They are usually available separately, though occasionally they appear in a combined sweetener. Be sure to read labels.

Agave nectar. Organically grown in Mexico, this sweetener is extracted from the Blue Agave cactus. Agave nectar is sweeter than sugar, so you can replace 1 cup sugar with ¾ cup agave—but you must also reduce liquids by ⅓ cup or more. Its composition is 90 percent fructose and only 10 percent glucose, so it isn't likely to cause wide spikes in blood sugar, as cane sugar does. Agave is available in both light and dark versions. The dark syrup has a heavy, distinctive flavor, not unlike molasses and sorghum. The light syrup, which has been filtered to remove minerals, is the color of light honey and is thinner than honey. It has a neutral sweet flavor. If honey doesn't agree with you, substitute agave in recipes for

muffins, cookies, and cakes. (See Carob Crispy Crunch, page 297.)

Stevia. This herbal sweetener has been used safely in South America for centuries. Stevia extract is refined from the leaves of the *Stevia rebaudiana* plant. It is an extremely concentrated pure white powder—a tiny pinch can sweeten a cup of tea (that's about ¹⁄₃₂ of a teaspoon!). You might use ⅛ teaspoon to sweeten pancake or waffle batter for 4 servings, or as much as 1 teaspoon to sweeten a loaf of nut bread or a dozen muffins. These estimates are based on recipes calling for 1½ to 2 cups of flour. White stevia powder is usually added to the dry ingredients rather than dissolved in the liquid, but that can vary.

CITRUS ALTERNATIVES

Avoiding citrus in cooking isn't much of a problem, except when lemon juice is needed to help leaven baked goods or to give tang to certain dishes. Sometimes you can substitute vinegar—if you're not sensi-

---

Ingredient Alternatives in Recipes

The recipes in this book offer several ingredient alternatives. I've given alternatives so that you can rotate ingredients in and out of your diet or use the ones that are most agreeable to you. In many cases, additional alternatives can be found among the ingredient options given in this chapter.

---

tive to fermented foods (which may contain yeast). For people who are allergic to both citrus and yeasts, I suggest pure vitamin C crystals as an alternative. (Vitamin C crystals are powdered—not tablets, not capsules.) Use unbuffered crystals or powder (the label will tell you if the product is buffered) made from sago palm rather than corn, available from health food stores and mail order catalogs. (See "Nutritional Supplements," page 386.)

To convert your own recipes, substitute ¼ teaspoon unbuffered vitamin C crystals for each tablespoon of lemon juice. In many recipes, I use vitamin C crystals equal to half the amount of baking soda (½ teaspoon baking soda to ¼ teaspoon vitamin C crystals, for example.)

Cream of tartar is another acid product that will react with baking soda to leaven baked goods (an acid substance plus an alkaline substance, usually baking soda, provides the leavening action). I've had excellent results using it in equal measure with baking soda; that is, 1 teaspoon baking soda along with 1 teaspoon cream of tartar. Cream of tartar is derived from grape, though it is highly refined and may not bother you even if eating grapes does. Test with caution, if grapes bother you.

OILS AND FATS

Margarine is a potential problem for allergic people. It may contain either milk solids or soy oil as well as artificial colors and flavors. (See Nutrition Basics in Brief, page 52.)

Butter is out for people who are allergic to milk, although some allergics do tolerate ghee, which is made by melting butter in a saucepan over low heat, then separating the liquid (oil of butter) from the milk solids. (Simply pour the liquid ghee into a jar, taking care that the milk solids remain in the bottom of the pan.) Ghee will solidify and can be used like butter, and its smoke point is higher, so it works well for sautéing.

For baked goods, your best bet is to keep various bottled vegetable, nut, and seed oils on hand. Unless a particular type of oil is listed in a recipe, choose from olive, avocado, canola, sunflower, sesame, almond, and walnut oil (depending on what you tolerate best). Canola is best for baking because it has the mildest flavor. Always read labels to be sure the oil that agrees with you is not combined with other oils to which you may react.

MEAT ALTERNATIVES

There are more than 25 different families of mammals, so if you're allergic to beef or pork, you still have plenty to choose from—lamb, rabbit, venison, and a wide variety of other game meats. Similarly, people who are allergic to chicken and turkey are likely to be able to eat Cornish hen, pheasant, quail, or duck with no problem. Fish offer more than 30 commonly eaten families to choose from. With all those options, you should be able to cook and tolerate several forms of meat, fish, or fowl. (See Planning a Rotary Diversified Diet, page 35.) I've developed a number of recipes for lamb, venison, and rabbit. To incorporate other, more exotic game and wild fowl in your menu, keep in mind that undomesticated game and birds need to be braised or stewed rather than broiled or baked, because their meat is leaner and less tender. Marinating the meat before cooking also helps. Incidentally, compared to that of domesticated animals, the meat in wild game tends to be higher in sought-after omega-3 fatty acids.

Even if you can eat pork, you may not be able to eat ham or bacon because of a possible reaction to nitrites or other preservatives or to unspecified curing agents (such as sugar) or seasonings. On the other hand, additive-free pork sausage is okay, as long as it's cooked well and drained of fat. To reduce fat further, pat both sides of cooked sausages with double layers of paper towels.

CHICKEN AND TURKEY ALTERNATIVES

As a nation, our consumption of both chicken and turkey has increased dramatically—especially since both birds are now available ground. In this form, they are easily and quickly prepared for burgers, meat loaf, sloppy joes, chili, and many dishes we usually associate with beef. Problem is, much of the ground turkey, and some chicken, is laced with monosodium glutamate (MSG), though it may not be mentioned by name. Beware of ground meats that admit to enhancing taste and juiciness with "natural flavorings"; the product most likely contains MSG. I contacted Foster Farms, a maker of ground turkey and turkey sausages, and their spokesperson assured me that there is no MSG in any of their products. The spice in their ground turkey is black pepper, the fla-

voring is rosemary. That's fine for my family, but it might be cause for someone else to reject their products. The key is to know, so check the package label.

UNUSUAL FRUITS AND VEGETABLES

If you're allergic to citrus fruits, bananas, berries, melon, or other commonly eaten fruit, a whole world of exciting options awaits you. Try kiwi, mangoes, pineapple, currants, figs, and a number of other choices to satisfy your cravings for sweet, juicy fruit.

If you're allergic to peas, tomatoes, green beans, or celery, introduce yourself to artichokes, Chinese cabbage, bok choy, or Japanese radishes (daikon). Unusual fruits and vegetables are available in many stores—you may have simply overlooked them until now. I've given brief "personality profiles" of several in the table on pages 22–33, to help you make their acquaintance.

The recipes in this book are in no way restricted to odd or exotic produce. Instead, I give enough options to accommodate individual tastes and tolerances. If it agrees with you, you can still eat everyday produce. Try to buy organic and vary the produce you choose to prevent new allergies from developing.

Incidentally, some people think they're allergic to pineapple because it burns their mouth or tongue. That irritation is caused by an enzyme that can be destroyed by boiling fresh pineapple and its juices for 2 minutes. If pineapple still bothers you, it may indeed be a true allergen (but this would be unusual).

UNUSUAL FRUITS AND VEGETABLES

Make a clean break with allergies to common fruits and vegetables. Try these alternatives.

Fruits

FOOD	DESCRIPTION
Cherimoya	Size of a grapefruit. Irregular brown surface looks like hand hewn wood. Flesh is creamy white with nonedible seeds dispersed throughout the fruit (as in watermelon).
Currants	Small red or black fruit in tiny grapelike clusters. Look for fresh in farmers' markets in late summer and fall. Dried currants are similar to raisins.
Kiwifruit	Approximate size and shape of a lemon. Skin is greenish brown and fuzzy. Flesh is green with tiny black edible seeds.
Mango	Green, gold or rosy. Oval, about the size of small cantaloupe, but irregularly shaped. Skin may have streaks of pink. Flesh is golden.
Papaya	Pear-shaped, but larger than a pear. Skin is green, sometimes with streaks of yellow. Flesh is golden. Center contains a clump of easily removed black seeds.
Persimmon	Size and shape vary. Skin is flame orange and very smooth. Flesh is also orange. Roughly the size of a small, slightly squashed orange.

PURCHASE AND STORAGE INFORMATION	COMMENTS
Shipped and sold underripe. Ripen at room temperature until it yields to gentle pressure. Store in refrigerator up to 1 week. Remove from the cold about 1 hour before eating.	Fruit is not sprayed or dusted. Cut halves or wedges, like a melon. Very sweet and juicy—cross between a very sweet pear and a pineapple or papaya. Discard seeds. Limited availability in spring.
Dried are more common than fresh. Look in health food store for organic.	Terrific alternative to raisins. Work well in baked goods, with less tendency to sink than raisins. May be plumped by soaking in liquid.
Usually purchased when firm. Ripen at room temperature. When soft to touch, eat or refrigerate until needed. For best flavor, let stand at room temperature for 1 hour before eating.	When ripe and soft, flavor is both tangy and sweet. If eaten too soon it's less sweet. Cut in half crosswise and eat with a spoon, like a miniature melon. Or peel and cut crosswise into 1/4" slices.
Buy green, ripen at room temperature. Ripe fruit yields to gentle pressure and will have a pink blush.	When ripe and soft, it is very sweet, juicy, and golden like premium peaches. Flesh adheres tightly to large stone. To eat, cut flesh away from stone, working over a dish to catch the juices. Score the flesh into cubes, then invert and cut cubes away from skin. One mango may serve 2 or more people.
Usually purchased when firm. Softens and turns yellow as it ripens at room temperature.	Available in many supermarkets as well as specialty shops. When soft and ripe, flavor is mildly sweet. Cut in half lengthwise and eat with a spoon. Contains an enzyme that aids digestion and tenderizes meat, especially game. (See Tender-Meat Marinade, page 205.) Though seeds are edible, they are not commonly eaten. (See Peppy, page 211.)
Firm or partially soft when purchased. Ripen at room temperature until very soft and sweet.	Flavor is sweet but with a bite that causes the mouth to pucker. Eat peeled or unpeeled.

(continued)

Fruits (cont.)

FOOD	DESCRIPTION
Pomegranate	Size of an orange. Skin ranges in color from brownish yellow to red. Interior is full of seeds, each surrounded by a bit of juicy, bright red flesh. Like citrus fruit, sections are divided by a membrane, which is not eaten.

Vegetables

Bean sprouts	Slender shoots. Pale off-white in color.
Bok choy **(Chinese celery; Chinese chard)**	A member of the cabbage family; resembles a cross between celery and Swiss chard. Stalks are pale, almost white, while leaves are dark green.
Celeriac (celery root; parsley root)	This strain of celery is cultivated for the root, not the top. It's about as big as your fist and brown and tough-looking.

PURCHASE AND STORAGE INFORMATION	COMMENTS
Purchase when firm. Ripen at room temperature until fruit yields to gentle pressure, but is not soft.	To eat, cut through the skin surface only and pull apart with your hands. Seeds should be bright red; discard any that are dark. Because the seeds are difficult to separate from the juicy flesh, many people eat the flesh, seeds and all. Otherwise, you can suck the flesh from the seeds. (Pomegranates take patience to eat.) Another approach: separate the seeds from the membrane and place them in a sealable plastic bag. Go over the whole thing with a rolling pin to separate the fruit from the seeds. Strain, and use the juice and pulp in a nut bread, salad dressing, or dessert.
Choose fresh-looking sprouts. The tips should not be dry or brown. Short sprouts are younger and more tender. Commercial sprouts may be bleached. Sprout your own for more color. Store in refrigerator in vegetable crisper or in a glass jar.	Crisp and delicate in flavor, sprouts have been around for centuries in Asia and are associated with Asian food, stir-fries, and vegetable salads. Cook only briefly: Blanch for 2 minutes, steam for 3 to 5 minutes, or stir-fry during last 2 minutes of cooking.
Look for crisp, fresh-looking leaves and firm stalks.	May be used like Swiss chard. Slice stalks as you would celery, and use in stir-fry dishes. Tear greens from center rib and toss them into the stir-fry for last 2 minutes.
Smaller roots are more desirable; large, mature ones may be woody. A sprouted root also denotes age. Press firmly to detect soft spots of decay. Trim roots and tops and store in vegetable crisper of refrigerator.	Primarily used in soups and stews. Can also be braised, steamed, or used in salads. Peel before cooking and cut into bite-size pieces. Discolors when exposed to air, so drop directly into a boiling pot or plunge into water with vinegar, lemon juice, or vitamin C crystals immediately after cutting.

(continued)

Vegetables (cont.)

FOOD	DESCRIPTION
Chayote (chi-OH-tee) squash	Green, about the size of summer squash. Flesh is pale green like honeydew. Single seed.
Chile peppers	Many varieties. Come in many sizes, shapes, and colors—green, yellow, and red. Flesh is usually the same color as the skin.
Collard greens	Large, broad-leaved greens.
Daikon (Japanese radish; winter radish)	Large, white radish. Usually several inches in length, perhaps over 1 foot. (Some markets cut them into pieces.)
Fennel (Florence fennel)	Resembles celery with a large root and fernlike top.
Globe artichokes	Pear-shaped, but larger. Rough exterior with "leaves" or petals. Green in color, sometimes with a few brown spots (from frost), which seem to enhance flavor.

PURCHASE AND STORAGE INFORMATION	COMMENTS
May be eaten when young and tender or when dark green and hard. Refrigerate like zucchini.	Use tender squash in salads and firmer ones cooked in soups, main dishes, or as a vegetable. To steam, wash well and cook whole until tender. Peel while still hot. Split, remove seed, and serve. Allow 1 per person, if small.
Look for bright, shiny skins; avoid any that are shriveled. Store in refrigerator (unless drying them intentionally).	Range from mildly hot to very hot. Skin is thin but tough. To remove, spear chile with a fork and char the skin over a stove burner or under broiler. Rotate until the skin is black and blistered. Enclose in a paper bag for 15 minutes, then slip skin off. Wear gloves and handle with great care. *Do not touch face or eyes while handling chiles.* The juice irritates and burns skin.
Should be fresh and crisp, not limp or wilted.	A traditional vegetable in the South, but regarded as unusual north of the Mason-Dixon line. See Swiss chard (page 32) for preparation.
Choose a firm root, free of nicks and with no signs of decay. Store in refrigerator in vegetable crisper until ready to use.	Grate, slice, or cut into matchsticks. Add to salads or a stir-fry. Eat raw or cook briefly— perhaps 3 to 5 minutes, depending on the size of the pieces. Flavor is radishlike.
Look for crisp stalks and fresh leaves. Store in vegetable crisper of refrigerator.	Labeling can be confusing. Fennel is often marked "sweet anise" because of the licorice flavor. Trim, wash, and slice as you would celery. Eat stem raw, like celery, or slice and cook as a hot vegetable.
Select artichokes that are plump and heavy. Avoid those with signs of decay or petals that have begun to spread.	Flavor is delicate, so usually served with tangy sauces or fillings. Boil or steam whole until tender, about 20 to 40 minutes, depending on size. To eat, remove leaves one at a time, dip the thick end into a sauce of your choice, and pull through your teeth. Remove hard fuzzy "choke," using a spoon. This will expose the tender heart; quarter, dip, and eat. Allow 1 per person.

(continued)

Vegetables (cont.)

FOOD	DESCRIPTION
Jerusalem artichokes (sunchokes)	Knotty brown tubers. Size of new potatoes, but irregular in shape.
Jicama (HEE-kah-mah)	Brown, round, disk-shaped tubers. Can grow very large. A small one weighs between 1 and 2 pounds. Larger ones may be woody.
Kale	Green or purplish-green; deeply frilled, curly leaves. Doesn't form head.
Kohlrabi	Small globes with leaves. Color is white, pale green, or purple.

PURCHASE AND STORAGE INFORMATION	COMMENTS
Should be firm with no soft spots. Store in a cool place or refrigerate.	Scrub well with a vegetable brush. Discolors rapidly if not used quickly. Eat raw or cook in water for 20 minutes or until tender.
Select as you would potatoes, looking for firmness. If they are too large, ask for halves or quarters. (Many markets oblige.) When stored in a cool, dry place, jicama keeps well for 10 days or more.	Mild, slightly sweet flavor and super-crisp texture are their greatest assets. Remains snow white long after cutting. Raw, crisp sticks are excellent with dips and spreads. Or dribble thin slices with lemon juice. (Mexicans sprinkle chili powder over the lemon juice.) Dice or shred in salads. May cut into sticks and use in place of water chestnuts or bamboo shoots in stir-fry: Add during last 2 minutes of cooking time so they just heat through. They retain their crunch when only cooked briefly.
Look for thin ribs and stems and crisp, healthy-looking leaves.	Will keep up to 5 days in a plastic bag, refrigerated. When ready to use, wash well. Strip leaves from center ribs and discard the stems and ribs. Steam briefly and serve by itself; chop and drop into soups; or blanch and use in place of spinach in casseroles. Highly recommended for its nutritional attributes: rich in vitamins, minerals, and phytochemicals.
Should be very firm with fresh-looking leaves. Globes 3 to 4 inches across are most desirable.	Young leaves may be cooked like spinach, but primary use is for globes. If vegetable is very fresh, steam without peeling, and peel after cooking. If more mature, peel thick fibrous covering, quarter or slice, and steam or boil in a little water until tender. Or peel, slice thinly, and add to stir-fries in place of water chestnuts and bamboo shoots for last 3 to 5 minutes of cooking, depending on their thickness. They add terrific "crunch."

(continued)

Vegetables (cont.)

FOOD	DESCRIPTION
Lamb's-quarters	Grows as a weed. Pick fresh. Not in most markets. Be certain "found" specimens haven't been sprayed with pesticides.
Leeks	Look like huge green onions (scallions).
Nappa cabbage (Chinese cabbage)	Pale white-green, shaped like romaine lettuce. Averages 10 to 12 inches long.
New Zealand spinach	Resembles spinach growing on a short stalk.
Parsnips	Size and shape of thick carrots, but cream-colored.
Rutabaga	Size similar to a large Spanish onion. Often waxed. Outer skin color is pale yellow to orange.
Shiitake (shee-TAH-kay) mushrooms	Larger and flatter than regular mushrooms. Creamy color with hints of brown.

PURCHASE AND STORAGE INFORMATION	COMMENTS
Ideally, cook the same day. However, may be washed, dried, rolled in a towel, and stored in the crisper for 1 or 2 days.	Steam briefly, like spinach. Flavor is similar to that of spinach, but more delicate. A little lemon juice adds a pleasing touch.
Choose small to medium leeks with fresh-looking green ends.	Related to onions, but more delicately flavored. Tricky to clean because dirt is caught in the inner layers: Split them lengthwise and rotate under running water. Drain and thinly slice. Very versatile—bake, broil, braise, puree, stew, or add to soups, salads, appetizers, or stews. Almost always eaten cooked, even in salads.
Look for fresh-looking outer leaves; avoid browning edges. Store in vegetable crisper of refrigerator. Smaller heads tend to have more delicate flavor.	Very versatile; sweet and crisp. Outstanding in salads, stir-fries, and as a vegetable by itself. Available all year. Enjoy raw or cooked. (No cooking odor.)
Look for fresh leaves. Best cooked the day of purchase, but can refrigerate in a plastic bag for 1 to 3 days. Pull leaves off stalks and wash well before using.	New Zealand spinach is not in the same food family as "regular" spinach. Leaves are thicker, less suitable for salads. Stalks, which are usually discarded, are edible and may be chopped into bits and cooked in the same way as peas.
Should be firm with no sprouting. Store in refrigerator.	A member of the carrot family, parsnips have a distinctive sweet flavor. Scrub well and steam. When tender, skin peels off easily. Add to soup or stew.
Avoid those with many sprouts. Waxing seems harmless. Firm vegetables retain freshness best.	Peel heavy outer wax coating with potato peeler or paring knife. Dice and steam, or boil in ½ cup of water in a heavy pot with a tight lid. Serve as is, or mash like potatoes, moistened with cooking water; or add a small one, diced, to soup or stew.
A little browner than regular mushrooms. Avoid signs of decay. Store in a brown paper bag in refrigerator	Discard tough stems. Slice cap into matchsticks and sauté to serve as a side dish, or add to stir-fry or other combination dishes.

(continued)

Vegetables (cont.)

FOOD	DESCRIPTION
Snow peas	4- or 5-inch-long flat pods. Eaten for the crisp pods (which contain only token, underdeveloped peas). Light green in color.
Sugar snap peas	Fuller, rounder, heavier than snow peas.
Swiss chard	Large green leaves on tall stalks.

OTHER HELPFUL OPTIONS

I've found the following foods to be very helpful in diversifying my diet and adding interest and flavor to my meals.

Carob powder. This is made by grinding pods of carob (also called St. John's bread), a subfamily of the Legume family. Carob is usually available in health food stores as roasted or toasted dry powder. Occasionally, I've seen it available as a raw powder, but the flavor is much better when it's been roasted or toasted. Carob tastes much like chocolate, minus the fat and bitterness of chocolate. It has a natural, mild sweetness and is high in fiber.

I don't use carob chips in this book because the ingredients are not standardized: Different manufacturers combine carob with any of a variety of ingredients, often including soy lecithin, corn sweeteners, fats, and even sugar. It's not always easy to find out what's in carob chips. That makes them a potential problem for people with food allergies. But feel free to use any carob chips that you think you can trust.

Kombu (kelp). A sea vegetable with a nat-

PURCHASE AND STORAGE INFORMATION	COMMENTS
Available frozen, but fresh are best. Avoid soft, droopy, or wilted pods. Should look fresh and be free of blemishes. Refrigerate until ready to use.	Wash. Remove end stem and string from 1 side. Pat dry for a stir-fry, where they require only 3 or 4 minutes to cook and change from light green to bright green. Do not overcook (or color fades again, eventually becoming almost gray). Or add to stews or mixed-vegetable dishes for last few minutes of cooking.
Same as snow peas.	Remove stem and string. May eat pod and all, raw or cooked briefly. Steam 4 to 5 minutes or stir-fry.
Select fresh-looking greens and red or white, firm ribs. Avoid chard with spongy ribs. Best eaten the day you buy it but can be refrigerated in plastic bag for up to 3 days.	Wash leaves thoroughly. Delicious lightly steamed. Use as you would cooked spinach. Leaves and stems may be cooked together for interesting contrast, or strip greens from stems and steam them alone. Either or both may be torn or chopped to add to a stir-fry in last 2 minutes of cooking. If serving steamed chard as a side dish, add a little lemon juice or vinegar (or sprinkle with vitamin C crystals) to enhance flavor.

urally salty flavor, kombu can be used as a salt substitute. It's high in trace minerals, especially iodine. About 3 percent of the population is allergic to high concentrations of iodine, so beware. However, kombu is no problem for most people when used in moderation as a condiment. Like most sea vegetables, you can add it to soups.

Miso. This is a fermented soybean paste, varying in flavor and degrees of saltiness. Use miso the same way you would bouillon cubes: Dissolve a small amount in just boiled water to make a flavorful broth or soup or use to enhance the flavor of a dish. You can reheat miso soup gently, but it is best not to boil it. There are dozens of varieties of miso, with hundreds of subtypes, so shop around and try different kinds of miso from different sources. Some miso contains barley or rice, so check labels if you are allergic to those grains. Salt content of miso ranges from 6 percent for sweet, light-colored varieties to 14 percent for dark red and brown miso. The midrange is usually labeled "mellow" and contains 8 to 10 percent salt.

To use miso: Place 1 or 2 tablespoons of

miso in a cup (Asian recipes may call for more). Remove your finished soup from the heat and ladle a little of the hot liquid over the miso. Mix well, then stir back into the pot. Don't boil the soup after adding miso. (See Vegetable-Miso Soup, page 138.) Highly flavorful, miso does not contain MSG.

Wheat-free tamari. Tamari soy sauce is another fermented soy food. In the process of fermentation, tamari develops a deep, rich flavor that tastes saltier than it is. Each teaspoon contains 267 milligrams of sodium, compared to 2,132 milligrams of sodium in

a teaspoon of salt. However, you can use less tamari—about ¼ to ½ teaspoon—to get the same degree of salty flavor and flavor enhancement imparted by a whole teaspoon of salt.

When buying tamari, read labels. Ordinary fermented tamari soy sauce (or shoyu) is a mixture of soybeans and wheat and may also contain caramel coloring, corn syrup, MSG, and preservatives. Several companies offer a wheat-free tamari that's also free of other additives. It's available in most health food stores.

Planning a Rotary Diversified Diet

People with food allergies are most likely to be allergic to foods they eat every day—milk, wheat, eggs, corn, yeast, and citrus fruits, among others. Eight foods account for about 90 percent of all allergic reactions—peanuts, tree nuts (walnuts, pecans, and so forth), fish, shellfish, eggs, milk, soy, and wheat.

When I use the word "allergy" in this chapter, I mean a food sensitivity, not true allergy. If you have a true allergy, one that is caused by an allergic antibody called IgE (Immunoglobulin E), you will get symptoms even if you eat a very small amount of the food. In this case, a rotary diversified diet will not help your condition. If you think you might have anaphylaxis due to a certain food, do not use the rotary diet.

For folks with food sensitivities, avoiding allergy-producing foods for a while and then spacing consumption of those foods by four or more days may allow your body to once again tolerate allergenic foods. Further, rotating all the foods you eat helps prevent new allergies from developing.

How long you initially need to avoid foods that you're sensitive to depends on your physician's protocol and the severity of your symptoms. Since not all doctors agree

on this diet for treating food allergies, you may want to search out an alternative-medicine physician with a specialty in environmental medicine to coach you. To find one in your region, contact the American Academy of Environmental Medicine at 7701 East Kellogg, Suite 625, Wichita, Kansas 67207, call them at 316-684-5500, or locate them on the Web at www.aaem.com.

Food rotation is an approach to allergy developed in 1934 by Herbert J. Rinkel, M.D., which for the most part went ignored. Over the past few years, the Rotary Diversified Diet has been resurrected by a small number of allergists both in the United States and abroad. The results have been excellent. The diet can be used to diagnose, treat, and prevent food allergies. It works well for what are known as "cyclic" food allergies, the kind that tend to fade if you avoid the food for a period of time. For example, following a Rotary Diversified Diet has taught me that I can eat wheat once a week without reacting to it. If I eat it more often than that, I become groggy and lethargic.

For me, wheat is a "cyclic" allergy. In contrast, my skin itches and I break out in hives each and every time I eat shrimp or crab, no matter how infrequently. Those are "fixed" allergies, and they are not going to disappear. So I avoid shrimp and crab.

Because most food allergies are cyclic, food rotation is a tremendous help to many people. Used along with a diary of symptoms, a Rotary Diversified Diet can also help detect hidden food allergies. Surprisingly, it may even help you deal with inhalant allergies, such as to pollen or dust. That's because food and inhalant allergies produce a cumulative effect, called the "allergic load." The fewer allergens of all types that you're exposed to, the better you'll feel. (See The Allergy-Free Home, page 60.)

BASIC GUIDELINES

In addition to recommending that you rotate each food every four or more days, doctors who've used the Rotary Diversified Diet have established six other basic guidelines:

Eat only foods to which you are not allergic. That may seem obvious, but why include a food that you know makes you itch, sneeze, or experience other discomfort until you have time to build up your tolerance? Later, you can cautiously reintroduce some of those foods, one at a time.

Rotate food families. This concept requires some familiarity with the biologic classification of foods. (See "Food Families," page 41.) As you follow the Rotary Diversified Diet, allowing at least a four-day interval between ingestions of each food, keep in mind the role of "first cousins." It works like this: Say you eat oranges for breakfast Monday morning, and plan to do the same four days later, on Friday. On Wednesday, you may eat another type of citrus fruit. Perhaps you'll choose grapefruit, tangerine, or lemon. These related foods in the same family, or "first cousins," may be eaten on the second day—unless you're dealing with a major offender. For instance, if wheat is your nemesis, you may be instructed by your physician to abstain from it, plus its first cousins rye, barley (and malt), and oats. Maybe spelt and Kamut brand grain, as well. Other "cousins" don't seem as similar to the body, so perhaps you can have teff, millet, rice, or milo/sorghum. To be sure, you'd have to experiment, or be tested, to see how you tolerate each of these alternatives. Even if you strike out for every single grain you try, perhaps amaranth, buckwheat, or quinoa will agree. They are similar to grains in the diet, but genetically quite different and not true grains at all. Because allergies are so individual, you can see why Rotary Diversified

Diets are also individual. No single diet fits everyone.

Learning about food families is fascinating—and full of surprises. For example, almonds, walnuts, cashews, and pine nuts are all members of different food families, even though we refer to them collectively as "nuts." Following a Rotary Diversified Diet, you might eat almonds on Monday, walnuts on Tuesday, cashews on Wednesday, and pine nuts on Thursday without repeating a food family (provided you're not allergic to any one of those foods). You may be equally surprised to learn that foods bearing little or no resemblance to each other are "siblings under the skin." For example, tomatoes, eggplants, potatoes, chiles, and peppers are all members of the Nightshade family. Certain other foods, such as amaranth, pineapple, and sesame seeds, are "loners," unrelated to other foods that we customarily eat, so you can rotate them without concern for closely related foods.

Design a plan that works for you. To set up your own Rotary Diversified Diet, first choose 28 foods that you know you can eat without experiencing symptoms. (If necessary, you can include a few foods that seem to cause only minimal reactions.) Arrange those foods into a menu of three meals a day, plus snacks, for four days. For the first four days, your diet will be very simple. (See "Sample Rotary Diversified Diet for 1 Week," page 50.) Because choices are somewhat limited at first, you can eat as much as you want of each food to feel satisfied. During the second four days, add one additional food or ingredient each day or to each meal, depending on how cautious you need to be. Take care to rotate all beverages, oils, garnishes and even seasonings such as onions and black pepper.

Only pure sea or earth salt (available in health food stores), water, and baking soda are "freebies." (See "Cooking and drinking water," page 64.)

What's the big deal about a four-day interval? It generally takes your body about three days to digest and utilize food and to excrete the residue, so allowing for a rest day, the four-day interval meets the needs of most people. But not always. If you are often constipated, which indicates a slow passage of intestinal contents, you may need a five- to seven-day interval. Rarely, a person may require a ten-day interval. For me, four days seems to work just fine, except for wheat. Rather than design a seven- or eight-day plan, it has been much easier to adopt a four-day plan and indulge in wheat only every other cycle.

As you work with the Rotary Diversified Diet, you'll learn how to rotate cooking oils, spices, sweeteners—in short, anything you include in a dish. To help you rotate ingredients, most recipes in this book offer several alternative ingredients—choices between two or three flours, oils, sweeteners or herbs. Why all the alternatives? Because each of the alternatives comes from a different plant. For example, soy oil, safflower oil, sunflower oil and canola oil are each a product of a different plant. You'll also find a number of recipes with foods from only one, two or three food families, so can you prepare stews, salads and desserts yet remain true to your diet. (See Index to Recipes for a Rotary Diversified Diet, page 388.)

Why, you ask, don't I just write the recipes to reflect a master rotated diet? If only it were that simple! There is no *one* Rotary Diversified Diet. There are so many ways to implement the basic concepts that every diet differs from every other. The only way to master the diet and implement it correctly is to learn the basic concepts.

Keep a diet diary. Write down every food you eat and note any symptoms you experience. Should a specific symptom recur a few times, you can then look back over your notes to find out what foods eaten may have triggered the reaction. If you get headaches every so often, for instance, you may discover by checking your diary that your headaches always follow meals that contain green beans or some other specific food. If that happens, drop the food in question from your Rotary Diversified Diet for 2 or 3 months, then try it again. If the symptom does not reappear, you can reintroduce that food into your diet. Observe how you feel, and evaluate whether you can eat that food on a regular basis. Jotting down what you eat and how you feel helps you detect foods to which you may be allergic *and* helps you to plan your next few meals.

Diversify your diet. Eating the same few foods day in and day out causes and reinforces food allergies. Conversely, eating a wide variety of foods decreases exposure to common allergens and prevents new food allergies from developing. To diversify your diet, rethink traditional meals. People who are allergic to milk, eggs, and grains may have to get used to breakfasts of, say, honeydew melon and walnuts or salmon and cantaloupe. Also, try foods from families you're not accustomed to eating, and choose less commonly eaten members in each food family. For example, a salad might consist of spinach or cabbage (greens not related to lettuce), beets instead of tomatoes, and avocado instead of cucumbers.

When choosing protein sources, use less common members of the poultry, meat, and fish families. Many people who are allergic to chicken find they can tolerate Cornish hen, pheasant, and quail, which are eaten far less frequently. Many people who are allergic to beef can eat lamb, buffalo, or venison with no trouble whatsoever. Because there are so many different families of fish, allergic people often find that they can eat fish frequently, sometimes even daily, as long as they choose different kinds.

Luckily, less common produce and meats are readily available in many supermarkets and health food stores. (See "Foods," page 383.)

Eat whole, uncomplicated foods. Single ingredient foods are much easier to rotate than combination foods, which may contain an array of ingredients and additives to which you may be allergic. For example, a baked or boiled potato may be fine, but potato chips and potato salad are not good choices, at least initially. Steak may be okay, but hot dogs are not. Orange juice may be fine, but sweetened orange drink is not. Eating whole foods is especially important when you're still finding out which foods agree with you and which cause reactions.

TIPS AND SHORTCUTS

Here are a few tips and shortcuts that have helped me follow a Rotary Diversified Diet.

Label everything. Nothing is more frustrating than not being able to recognize a food. But labeling is especially important for people on a Rotary Diversified Diet. It isn't enough to know a muffin is a muffin—you need to know what kind of flour, sweetener, nuts, and oil it contains. Hint: Use labels large enough to list all the information you need.

Double recipes and freeze the extra. This saves precious time and works especially well when you're rotating foods.

Group frozen foods together. Use wire or plastic bins in the freezer and label them with the contents—chicken, turkey, lamb, burgers (specify kind), stock, stews (list contents), and casseroles (list contents). Assign the day (Day 1, Day 2, Day 3, or Day 4) or identify your packages with color-coded dots. Indicating the day of rotation makes it a cinch to plan meals. And you can quickly tell which staples are in short supply.

Remember to rotate snacks. Nuts, seeds, and fruits are popular snack foods that are easy to rotate. In addition, you can make snacks from recipes in this book.

To help children rotate snacks, make a game of it. Number each day of the calendar one through four, repeating the sequence for the whole month. Number all snacks accordingly. That way, children can tell at a glance which snacks they're allowed to eat each day. For children too young to read, color-code the calendar and corresponding snacks with self-adhesive colored dots, sold in stationery stores.

PERSONALIZING YOUR ROTARY DIVERSIFIED DIET

Because no two people have exactly the same set of food allergies, no one Rotary Diversified Diet suits everyone. To establish your own plan, exclude any foods to which you are allergic. Allow an interval of four days or more before repeating a specific food. When you are free of symptoms, you can begin to reintroduce marginally allergenic foods—foods to which you think you

may have been allergic but aren't sure about, or foods that you can tolerate sometimes. Test only one food at a time. And test only when you're feeling normal, not when you already have a headache or are unusually fatigued. If you have a severe allergy that may cause anaphylaxis, do not use this method with the foods to which you are allergic.

Ideally, anyone with food allergies should adopt a Rotary Diversified Diet for life. If you return to repetitious, monotonous eating patterns, your food allergies will probably recur and you'll have to start all over. However, food rotation is demanding, so many doctors concede that people with mild to moderate food allergies need only follow a strict Rotary Diversified Diet—rotating *all* their foods—periodically, to reestablish their tolerance to certain foods or to help weather allergic "bad times."

For instance, I strictly rotate my diet during hay fever season only (from mid-August to the first killing frost). That's when all my allergies seem to be at their worst. If you're allergic to tree pollen, you may find that following a Rotary Diversified Diet in spring helps to relieve both your food allergies and your pollen allergies. Or you may choose to rotate your foods after the winter holidays. During the rest of the year, you may be able to choose foods more freely, perhaps rotating only major food allergens rather than everything you eat.

Because food rotation can limit consumption of major sources of important nutrients, certain deficiencies are not uncommon. (See Nutrition Basics in Brief, page 52.) Also, be aware that allergic reactions are not limited to itching, sneezing, wheezing and gastrointestinal complaints. Allergy can produce headaches, depression, fatigue, irritability, and other mental and emotional symptoms as well.

BUT I'M NOT BETTER

If followed conscientiously, a Rotary Diversified Diet usually leads to fewer allergic symptoms and an increase in energy. However, some people may experience little if any change in their symptoms. If you don't improve, review your diet with your environmental medicine doctor. You may be overlooking something.

More than once, I remember the late Dr. Theron Randolph saying, "The best diet in the world can't make a person well if their natural gas appliances—the stove, furnace, and water heater—are making them ill." (See The Allergy-Free Home, page 60.) Or you may be one of the few people whom doctors call "universal reactors"—people who are allergic to virtually all foods commonly eaten in the typical American diet. If that's the case, you can take the Rotary Diversified Diet one step further and try rotating a "rare foods" diet. By eating unusual meats, vegetables, fruits and grains—such as rabbit, parsnips, kiwifruit, and amaranth—for three to six months, you may be able to clear your system of food allergies. Then gradually reintroduce more familiar foods one at a time, in rotation.

Other rare foods include pheasant, venison, duck, beaver or other wild game, rutabaga, turnips, jicama, artichokes, Brazil nuts, and macadamia nuts, to name a few. To incorporate new foods into your diet, learn as much as you can about using them. (See Exploring New Ingredients, page 3, and "Foods," page 383.)

If you still don't feel better, consider the possibility that intestinal yeasts, such as *Candida albicans*, may be contributing to your health problems. While yeasts are common inhabitants in the healthy human digestive system, problems can arise after you take antibiotics, birth control pills, or steroids, which allow yeasts to multiply wildly. Here's a typical scenario: Your doctor prescribes a potent antibiotic. It wipes out not only the bacteria making you ill, but also the beneficial bacteria in your system, such as *Lactobacillus acidophilus*, *L. bifidus*, and others, which had been keeping the yeasts in check. Left without opponents, yeasts grow like crazy.

Yeast-connected symptoms include chronic and overwhelming fatigue, fuzzy thinking, depression, headache, and complaints related to the reproductive and digestive systems, such as vaginal yeast infections and intestinal gas and bloating. Some physicians recognized the importance of candida in allergic disorders in the 1970s. Since then the word has slowly been spreading among enlightened practicing physicians, though agreement is still far from universal.

Avoiding yeast-containing foods is only part of the solution. The biggest dietary change is the need to limit sweets and the number of grams of carbohydrates in the diet because the candida organism thrives on simple carbohydrates. Charles T. Hinshaw, M.D., president of the American Academy of Environmental Medicine, headquartered in Wichita, Kansas, suggests to his women patients with this condition that they eat 60 to 80 grams of carbohydrates spread throughout the day.

William G. Crook, M.D., author of *The Yeast Connection*, says that when candida is brought under control—by diet and anti-fungal medication—the immune system has a chance to heal, and severe allergies may diminish into minor annoyances. For more information, read Dr. Crook's book *The Yeast Connection Handbook* as well as *The Yeast Connection Cookbook*, which I co-authored with him. The handbook will offer guidance regarding lifestyle and dietary changes; the cookbook will help plan meals.

And finally, if your illness persists, talk to your doctor about the possibility of hormone imbalances or intestinal parasites. Chronic allergies, especially when they have gone on for decades, can have a debilitating effect on total health. When this is the case, it takes more than a corrective diet to influence how you feel.

Remember, controlling food allergy is not a cure-all. But it is one very big step on the road back to robust health.

FOOD FAMILIES

To prevent reactions to foods that bother you, you may also need to avoid foods to which they are closely related. This chart can also help you plan your own personalized Rotary Diversified Diet. Botanical family names of plants appear in parentheses after the common names.

FAMILY	PLANT FOODS
Agave *(Agavaceae)*	Agave nectar, yucca
Algae *(Algae)*	Agar-agar, carrageen, kelp (kombu)
Apple (subfamily of *Rosaceae*)	Apple, crab apple, pear, quince
Arrowroot *(Marantaceae)*	Arrowroot
Banana *(Musaceae)*	Banana and plantain
Beech *(Fagaceae)*	Beechnut and chestnut
Berry (subfamily of *Rosaceae*)	Blackberry, boysenberry, dewberry, loganberry, raspberry, rose hips, strawberry
Birch *(Betulaceae)*	Filbert or hazelnut, oil of birch (wintergreen flavor)
Brazil Nut *(Lecythidaceae)*	Brazil nut
Buckwheat *(Polygonaceae)*	Buckwheat, garden sorrel, rhubarb
Caper *(Capparidaceae)*	Caper
Cashew *(Anacardiaceae)*	Cashew, mango, pistachio

(continued)

❀

FOOD FAMILIES (cont.)

FAMILY	PLANT FOODS
Chocolate (*Sterculiaceae*)	Chocolate (cocoa), cola, gum karaya
Citrus or Rue (*Rutaceae*)	Citron, grapefruit, kumquat, lemon, lime, orange, pomelo, tangelo, tangerine
Coffee (*Rubiaceae*)	Coffee
Composite† (*Compositae*)	Globe artichoke*, chamomile, chicory, dandelion greens, endive, escarole, lettuce, safflower, sunflower seeds, tarragon
Conifer (*Coniferae*)	Juniper berry (used to make gin) and pine nuts
Custard-Apple (*Annonaceae*)	Pawpaw and cherimoya
Ebony (*Ebonaceae*)	Persimmon
Flax (*Linaceae*)	Flaxseed
Fungus†† (Fungi)	Mold in certain cheeses, mushroom, truffle, yeast
Ginger (*Zingiberaceae*)	Cardamom, ginger, turmeric
Gooseberry (*Saxifragaceae*)	Currant and gooseberry
Goosefoot or Beet (*Chenopodiaceae*)	Amaranth, beet, chard, lamb's-quarters, spinach, sugar beet, quinoa
Grain (cereal or grass) (*Gramineae*)	Bamboo shoots, barley, corn, Kamut brand grain, lemongrass, millet, oats, rice, rye, sorghum/milo, spelt, sugarcane/molasses, teff, wheat, wild rice
Grape (*Vitaceae*)	Grape
Heath (*Ericaceae*)	Blueberry, cranberry, huckleberry, bilberry
Honeysuckle (*Caprifoliaceae*)	Elderberry
Iris (*Iridaceae*)	Saffron
Kiwi (*Actinidiaceae*)	Kiwiberry (kiwifruit)
Laurel (*Lauraceae*)	Avocado, bay leaf, cinnamon, sassafras

FAMILY	PLANT FOODS
Legume *(Leguminosae)*	Alfalfa, bean (adzuki, broad or fava, kidney, lentil, lima, mung, navy, pinto, runner or scarlet runner, soy, string), carob, gum acacia, kudzu, licorice, pea (black-eyed or cow pea, chickpea, green), peanut
Lily *(Liliaceae)*	Asparagus, chive, garlic, leek, onion, sarsaparilla, shallot
Macadamia *(Protea)*	Macadamia nuts
Mallow *(Malvaceae)*	Cottonseed, hibiscus, okra
Maple *(Aceraceae)*	Maple syrup and maple sugar
Melon or Gourd *(Cucurbitaceae)*	Cantaloupe, cucumber, gherkin, honeydew, muskmelon, pumpkin, summer squash, winter squash, watermelon, zucchini
Mint *(Labiatae)*	Basil, catnip, horehound, lavender, lemon balm (melissa), marjoram, mint, oregano, peppermint, rosemary, sage, savory, spearmint, thyme
Morning-Glory *(Convolvulaceae)*	Jicama** and sweet potato
Mulberry *(Moraceae)*	Breadfruit, fig, mulberry
Mustard *(Cruciferae)*	Horseradish, mustard, radish, rutabaga, turnip, watercress, and varieties of cabbage: broccoli, brussels sprouts, cabbage kraut, cauliflower, Chinese cabbage, collards, kale, kohlrabi
Myrtle *(Myrtaceae)*	Allspice, clove, guava
New Zealand Spinach *(Tetragoniaceae)*	New Zealand spinach
Nightshade or Potato *(Solanaceae)*	Eggplant, potato, tobacco, tomato. This family includes all foods called "pepper" (except black and white peppercorns), such as cayenne, chile pepper, green pepper, hot pepper sauce, paprika, pimiento, red pepper
Nutmeg *(Myristicaceae)*	Nutmeg and mace
Olive *(Oleaceae)*	Olive
Orchid *(Orchidaceae)*	Vanilla
Palm *(Palmaceae)*	Coconut, date, sago palm starch
Papaya *(Caricaceae)*	Papaya

(continued)

PLANNING A ROTARY DIVERSIFIED DIET

FOOD FAMILIES (cont.)

FAMILY	PLANT FOODS
Parsley *(Umbelliferae)*	Carrot, celeriac, celery, lovage, parsley, parsnip. Also these spices: angelica, anise, caraway, celery seed, coriander (cilantro), cumin, dill, fennel
Pepper *(Piperaceae)*	Peppercorns
Pineapple *(Bromeliaceae)*	Pineapple
Plum (subfamily of *Rosaceae*)	Almond, apricot, cherry, nectarine, peach, plum, prune, wild cherry
Pomegranate *(Punicaceae)*	Pomegranate (also, grenadine syrup)
Poppy *(Papaveraceae)*	Poppyseed
Purslane *(Portulacaceae)*	Purslane
Sedge *(Cyperaceae)*	Chinese water chestnuts
Sesame *(Pedaliaceae)*	Sesame seed
Soapberry *(Sapindaceae)*	Litchi nuts
Spurge *(Euphorbiaceae)*	Tapioca
Tea *(Theaceae)*	Tea
Walnut *(Juglandaceae)*	Black walnut, butternut, English walnut, hickory nut, pecan
Yam *(Dioscoreaceae)*	Chinese potato and yam

FAMILY	MAMMALS
Bear	Bear
Beaver	Beaver
Bovid (Bovine)	Beef cattle (including veal), buffalo, goat, sheep (lamb and mutton), bison, and their milk and milk products
Camel	Camel and llama
Cat	Mountain lion
Deer	Caribou, deer (venison), elk, moose, reindeer
Hare	Hare and rabbit

FAMILY	MAMMALS
Hippopotamus	Hippopotamus
Horse	Horse
Opossum	Opossum
Pronghorn	Pronghorn (also called pronghorn antelope)
Squirrel	Squirrel
Swine	Hog (pork)

FAMILY	BIRDS
Dove	Dove and pigeon (squab)
Duck	Duck, goose, and their eggs
Grouse	Ruffed grouse (partridge)
Guinea Fowl	Guinea fowl
Pheasant	Chicken, Cornish hen, pheasant, quail, peacock, and their eggs
Turkey	Turkey and their eggs

FAMILY	FISH
Anchovy	Anchovy
Anglerfish	Monkfish
Bass	White perch and yellow bass
Bluefish	Bluefish
Catfish	Catfish, minnows, carps
Codfish	Cod (scrod), cusk, haddock, hake, pollack, whiting, toadfish, codfish, and allies
Croaker (freshwater)	Freshwater drum or croakers
Croaker (saltwater)	Croaker, drum, sea trout, silver perch, spot, weakfish (spotted sea trout)
Eel	American eel

(continued)

PLANNING A ROTARY DIVERSIFIED DIET

FOOD FAMILIES (cont.)

FAMILY	FISH
Flounder	Dabs, flounder, halibut, plaice, sole, turbot
Harvestfish	Butterfish and harvestfish
Herring (freshwater)	Shad (roe)
Herring (saltwater)	Pilchard (sardine) and sea herring "anchovies"
Jack	Amberjack, pompano, yellow jack (family *Carangidae*)
Mackerel	Albacore, bonito, mackerel, skipjack, tuna
Marlin	Marlin and sailfish
Minnow	Carps, chubs
Ostariophysi	Catfish, minnows, carps
Mullet	Mullet
Perch	Sauger, walleye, yellow perch
Pike	Muskellunge, pickerel, pike
Porgy	Northern scup (porgy)
Salmon	All salmon species and all trout species
Scorpionfish	Rosefish (ocean perch)
Sea Bass	Grouper and sea bass
Sea Catfish	Ocean catfish
Shark	Shark, skates, rays
Silverside	Silverside (whitebait)
Smelt	Smelt
Sturgeon	Sturgeon (caviar)
Sucker	Buffalofish and sucker
Sunfish	Black bass, crappie, sunfish
Swordfish	Swordfish
Tilefish	Tilefish

PLANNING A ROTARY DIVERSIFIED DIET

FAMILY	FISH
Tuna	Mackerel, tuna
Whitefish	Whitefish

FAMILY	SHELLFISH
Abalone	Abalone
Clam	Clam and quahog
Cockle	Cockle
Crab	Crab
Lobster	Crayfish, langostinos, lobster
Oyster	Oyster
Scallop	Scallop
Shrimp	Prawn and shrimp
Snail	Snail
Squid	Squid

FAMILY	AMPHIBIANS
Frog	Frog

* According to Theron Randolph, M.D., sunflowers and Jerusalem artichokes are members of the Composite family, but they are so unlike lettuce and other members of that family that they may be rotated separately, as though they were a family in themselves.

† All foods in this family are related to ragweed and may bother those extremely reactive to ragweed pollen.

††Fungi are technically a plant division, not a single family, but doctors using the Rotary Diversified Diet regard them as one family for purposes of dietary planning.

** Botanists differ in their classification of jicama. Some consider it a legume; others relate it to the sweet potato. Doctors using the Rotary Diversified Diet prefer to relate jicama to the sweet potato, putting it in the Morning-Glory family.

SETTING UP YOUR ROTARY DIVERSIFIED DIET

The 1-week menu plan shown in the "Sample Rotary Diversified Diet" (page 50) is an example of how to plan a nourishing diet while rotating foods. I'll explain the reasons for my choices and show you how to plan a diet of your own, based on the same principles.

To begin, make a list of 12 foods to which you are not allergic. Then arrange them into a basic "skeleton" diet of 1 food per meal for four days. For Days 1 through 4 on the Sample Rotary Diversified Diet, I've chosen honeydew melon, carrots, lamb, peaches, broccoli, turkey or pheasant, apples, zucchini, salmon, plums (or dried prunes, soaked), cabbage, and chicken or grouse, shown in capital letters. If some of these don't agree with you, substitute other fruits, vegetables, and protein sources. Use game meats if you need to. Be sure that foods from the same food family are no closer than two days apart. (See "Food Families," page 41.) Honeydew melon and zucchini, for example, are both members of the Gourd family and appear on Days 1 and 3 in the Sample Rotary Diversified Diet. The late Dr. Theron Randolph and others who have treated thousands of people with the Rotary Diversified Diet have said that members of the same food family may be rotated every two days to avoid daily exposures to similar foods. That pattern controls symptoms and prevents new food allergies and sensitivities from developing.

Whatever foods you choose, you can eat them at any time of the day. Eating fruit in the morning, vegetables at noon, and meat, fish, or poultry in the evening is purely arbitrary. Note that in the early stages of the diet—when the number of foods permitted in one meal is limited—typical portion size is meaningless. You can eat as much of each food as necessary to feel satisfied. For example, you might eat a whole honeydew melon, or most of one, and maybe four peaches and so on. Also, when eating all one food, remember that you can vary the preparation. For example, raw peaches and poached peaches, or raw apples plus baked apples or unsweetened applesauce. Remember, everything should be simple—no fancy combo dishes.

Because many people plan and shop for a week's worth of meals at a time, I've continued this diet plan for Days 5, 6, and 7. I've chosen cantaloupe, parsnips, scrod or buffalo, nectarines or apricots, cauliflower, duck or Cornish hen, apples, butternut squash, and whitefish, shown in capital letters. That shows that the menu for Day 5 doesn't have to be identical to Day 1. In fact, they *shouldn't* be identical. Doctors who prescribe this diet encourage people to eat as wide a variety of foods as possible, both to prevent new allergies from developing and to help ensure a better intake of essential nutrients. And, of course, the cardinal rule of food rotation, as explained above, is that you *do not repeat any one food more often than every fourth day.* In the Sample Rotary Diversified Diet, for instance, apples appear on Days 3 and 7, four days apart. And it's fine for pears to appear on Days 1 and 5, illustrating that related foods may be eaten at two-day intervals.

At this point, the "skeleton" diet—foods shown in capital letters only—can serve either of two purposes: to help the few people who have so many food allergies that they need to stick to a minimum number of foods (monomeals), at least until they feel better, or to help you test yourself for food allergies. To conduct a test, substitute a *different* single food for a test meal and evaluate how you feel afterward. Later when you're through testing, you can add one new food and then another that you appear to tolerate. In this manner, you can expand the list of foods in your diet plan fairly quickly.

Because the diet is initially very limited, and doctors often prohibit nutritional supplements during testing, try to ensure intake of at least modest amounts of calcium, magnesium, vitamin C, and other essential nutrients. As soon as you are finished testing, you may wish to add the purest forms of nutritional supplements you can find. (See Nutrition Basics in Brief, page 52, and "Nutritional Supplements," page 386.)

If your food allergies are not very severe and you can eat a wide range of foods, you can add 1 new food per meal, after eating the basic 12, 24, or 36 foods for one cycle. For Days 1 through 4, I've chosen walnuts, sole, white potato, macadamia nuts, butterfish, sweet potato, pecans, flounder, beets, almonds, grouper or catfish, and lima beans, shown in lowercase letters. If you then add a sweetener, a cooking oil, and another food for snacks each day, you build up to 36 different foods for four days. I've added honey, sunflower seeds and oil, pureed peaches or agave nectar, olive oil, cashews, unsweetened apple juice (or apple-juice concentrate) or white stevia powder, sesame or canola oil, sesame seeds or pine nuts, maple syrup, avocado and avocado oil, and Brazil nuts. I've chosen nuts for snacks because they're easily carried to school or office, and their high fat content can help you feel satisfied. But there's no reason you can't choose other foods such as dried fruit or raw vegetables. Again, be sure that related foods belonging to any given food family are eaten two days apart.

Eventually, you can add still more foods to your menu, as illustrated by foods listed in parentheses in the Sample Rotary Diversified Diet, giving you a total of 48 food choices within any four-day period. I've omitted grains, but if you can eat them, your options will be even wider.

You can also test yourself for seasonings—adding only one at a time to see your response. Some seasonings are rather potent

> ## Getting Ready to Bake
>
> At some point, you'll want to test yourself for arrowroot and tapioca starch flours. Then you can reserve them for baking something special instead of assigning them to specific days. Here's how I suggest testing: On Day 1, combine amaranth, walnuts, honey, and arrowroot for muffins; on Day 3, mix apples, pecans, quinoa, and tapioca starch flour for a tasty coffee cake. When you get to Day 5, if you don't feel like baking, you can eat the foods plain, keeping the arrowroot in reserve for another occasion.

allergens. They include black pepper, cinnamon, and cumin, but any herb or spice can be a problem.

When you're ready for simple recipes, combine related foods into a single dish. For example, combine apples, pecans, and quinoa into a simple coffee cake for breakfast on Day 3 of the Sample Rotary Diversified Diet. Similarly, you can prepare delicious stews and chowders by combining foods from only a few families. Basic Beet Borscht (page 142) for example, is made primarily with foods in the Goosefoot family.

When implementing this diet, remember that it is both rotated and diversified. Let's say you want to incorporate spinach into your diet. You see that spinach is in the Goosefoot family along with beets and chard. So you simply insert spinach in place of either beets or chard wherever they appear in the plan. And when you're doing very well, you might try having both beets and spinach in the same meal.

PLANNING A ROTARY DIVERSIFIED DIET

SAMPLE ROTARY DIVERSIFIED DIET FOR 1 WEEK

This is an example of a Rotary Diversified Diet, in which no food is eaten more frequently than every fourth day. In this case, beef, citrus, shellfish, egg, grains, cane sugar, milk, yeast, and all members of the Composite family (lettuce, sunflower, and other foods related to ragweed) have been omitted. I have chosen 12 basic foods to which I am not allergic. These appear in capital

	DAY 1	DAY 2	DAY 3
Breakfast	HONEYDEW MELON walnuts (amaranth)	PEACHES OR BING CHERRIES macadamia nuts (buckwheat)	APPLES pecans (quinoa)
Sweetener	honey	pureed peaches or agave nectar	unsweetened apple juice or apple juice concentrate or white stevia powder
Lunch	CARROTS sole (pears)	BROCCOLI butterfish (persimmon)	ZUCCHINI flounder (grapes)
Oil	sunflower oil	olive oil	sesame or canola oil
Dinner	LAMB white potato (papaya)	TURKEY OR PHEASANT sweet potato (fresh figs, or dried)	SALMON beets (kiwi)
Snack	sunflower seeds	cashews	pine nuts

letters. Foods in parentheses may be added to or substituted for the primary foods listed. To set up a Rotary Diversified Diet based on your food allergies, use this sample as a guide and make substitutions as necessary. (See "Setting Up Your Rotary Diversified Diet," page 47.)

DAY 4	DAY 5	DAY 6	DAY 7
PLUMS (OR PRUNES) almonds (chickpeas)	CANTALOUPE walnuts (amaranth and puffed amaranth)	NECTARINES (OR APRICOTS) macadamia nuts (buckwheat)	APPLES pecans (quinoa)
maple syrup	honey	pureed nectarines or agave nectar	unsweetened apple juice or apple juice concentrate or white stevia powder
CABBAGE grouper (blueberries)	PARSNIPS OR CARROTS venison or goat's-milk cheese (pears)	CAULIFLOWER tuna (pineapple)	BUTTERNUT SQUASH pork (grapes)
avocado or almond oil	walnut oil	olive oil	sesame or canola oil
CHICKEN OR GROUSE lima beans (banana)	SCROD OR BUFFALO asparagus (mango)	DUCK OR CORNISH HEN sweet potato (raspberries)	WHITEFISH Swiss chard (watermelon or grapes)
Brazil nuts	walnuts or sunflower seeds	cashews	pine nuts or filberts

Nutrition Basics in Brief

People with food allergies have special nutritional needs. That's no surprise, really. If you have to avoid one or more essential sources of nutrients such as milk, bread, or citrus for long periods of time, you run the risk of one or more deficiencies. And you need to make up those deficits to stay healthy. In other words, you don't want to solve one problem—food allergy—and at the same time set yourself up for another—nutritional deficiencies. If you decide to take supplements to offset a dietary shortfall, check with the manufacturer to be sure the product you are considering contains nothing to which you are allergic. (Supplement labels often include an address or a toll-free customer service phone number.) Here are some common food allergens and alternative ways of getting the nutrients they provide.

Beef, poultry, and other protein sources. Animal foods such as beef, poultry, fish, game, milk, eggs, and cheese each contain a full complement of 20 amino acids approximating the protein makeup of our own bodies. Amino acids are called the building blocks of our bodies. Foods that contain adequate amounts of those amino acids are the protein sources we can use most efficiently.

However, if you must omit any of those foods, or if you are rotating them at four-day intervals, you can match the protein efficiency of animal foods with vegetable sources of protein. Simply mix legumes—beans, peas, or peanuts—with grains, dairy products, or nuts. Legumes supply lysine and isoleucine, the amino acids that are not in high supply in grains and nuts. Grains and nuts supply methionine and tryptophan, which are not high in legumes. Combining these foods means that your body can fully use their available protein. Nutritionists used to recommend eating those complementary proteins together at the same meal. Today, they've relaxed those guidelines and simply say it's important to eat a variety of these foods through the course of the day.

For people who are allergic to grains and legumes (which is not uncommon), amaranth, buckwheat, and quinoa have much to offer. They contain lysine and a healthful assortment of the other amino acids—enough that they can either complement the protein of grains and nuts or, if enough is eaten, provide adequate protein by themselves. In fact, the National Academy of Sciences has called quinoa "the best source of protein in the vegetable kingdom." Quinoa provides almost eight grams of protein in a two-ounce serving (measured before cooking). The same amount of buckwheat provides almost the same protein and amaranth has just a little more protein. All three grains are good sources of protein.

"Mixing and matching" vegetable sources of protein pays an added nutritional dividend: It fits in perfectly with advice to cut down on saturated fat and eat more whole grains. The recommendation to reduce your intake of saturated fat comes from the Dietary Guidelines for Americans, and it is intended to reduce the incidence of heart disease among Americans. Between 1980 and 1991 our average intake of saturated fatty acids as a percentage of calories dropped only 1 percentage point. Many of the recipes in this book combine complementary sources of vegetable protein to help you get the most nutritious diet possible.

Milk. Anyone who avoids milk, cheese, yogurt, and other dairy products is likely to fall short of calcium requirements and possibly vitamin D requirements, which we need to use calcium properly. Most nondairy sources don't quite measure up: Three-and-a-half ounces of dry amaranth contains approximately 150 milligrams of calcium—about as much as a half-cup of low-fat milk or 1 cup of 2 percent low-fat cottage cheese. And who wants to eat a half cup of dry amaranth seeds? Some beans, greens, and other vegetable sources contain between 30 and 125 milligrams of calcium per half-cup serving. However, we need between 800 and 1,500 milligrams of calcium a day to prevent brittle bones and other health problems. That's hard to achieve by diet alone, even if you can drink

milk and eat cheese. If you can tolerate soy, use fortified soy milk. It has as much calcium as cow's milk. If you can't tolerate soy, I recommend supplements of calcium aspartate and citrate, especially for growing children and pregnant, nursing, or postmenopausal women, whose calcium needs are greatest of all. (Calcium lactate may be a problem for people with milk allergy, because it contains lactose, a milk fraction. The previously mentioned supplements provide calcium in a form the body can use more readily than calcium gluconate or calcium carbonate.)

Fortified cow's milk also happens to be our main source of vitamin D, second only to sunlight. In the northern hemisphere, the probability of getting enough vitamin D from natural sunlight is very slim during the darkest six months of the year. Good nondairy sources of vitamin D include fortified soy milk, fatty fish (such as mackerel), egg yolks, liver, and butter. If those foods are off-limits to you, or if you eat them infrequently, you might consider taking vitamin D supplements. Most people need an average of 400 International Units (IU) a day. The government recommends that people older than 70 should get as much as 600 IU to help prevent osteoporosis.

As with many supplements, vitamin D capsules may contain artificial colors, flavors, or preservatives to prevent rancidity. Yet, some brands of supplements have been designed specifically to be hypoallergenic. The staff of any good health food store should be able to help you find supplements that you can tolerate. Otherwise, your best bet may be preservative-free cod liver oil (provided you're not allergic to it) or a dry form of vitamin D in capsules.

Citrus fruits. Fresh orange juice and

grapefruit juice provide plentiful amounts of vitamin C. Tomatoes, peppers, and strawberries are also rich sources. If you are allergic to any of those foods, get your vitamin C from cantaloupe, white potatoes, sweet potatoes, bell peppers, cabbage, broccoli, brussels sprouts, spinach, and other green, leafy vegetables. Vitamin C builds good health in a number of ways: It helps to fight infections, speeds wound healing, and improves absorption of iron and folate (a B vitamin). For people with allergies, getting enough vitamin C is of special importance because it counteracts the release of histamine, a major factor in allergic reactions such as itching, runny nose, sneezing, and hives. According to Drs. Emanuel Cheraskin, Marshall Ringsdorf, and Emily Sisley, authors of the out of print book *The Vitamin C Connection*, "[Vitamin C] counteracts food allergies. The antihistaminic action of vitamin C can enable people to tolerate foods they otherwise could not eat."

If you have to omit citrus and other foods listed above, vitamin C supplements become even more important. Because many vitamin C supplements are based on corn or citrus fruit, people who are allergic to those foods may be better off buying pure vitamin C crystals or powder made from sago palm. (Read labels carefully because some powders and crystals on the market come from corn, carrots, or beets.) Whether you're relying on food or supplements for vitamin C, remember that vitamin C is water soluble—the body does not store it. You need to replenish the supply every day.

How much vitamin C is enough? Tough question. Even the experts don't agree. However, they all seem to agree on one thing: the Daily Value of 60 milligrams is too low. The government has set the Daily Reference Intakes at 75 milligrams for women, 90 for men. Most alternative practitioners believe that is not adequate for people with allergies and other special needs. However, the American Academy of Allergy, Asthma, and Immunology has found no published evidence for a possible role of antioxidants in treatments of allergies and asthma.

Suggested targets range from 500 milligrams to 1,000 milligrams. Here's a tip to help you find your own optimal dose: Any time your body receives more vitamin C than it needs, the excess will act as a laxative. So if this happens, reduce your dose gradually until you're on a comfortable, well-tolerated dose. However, if you start to come down with a cold, flu, or other infection or illness, your need for vitamin C increases and you will find that your tolerance has suddenly increased as well. So be open to fluctuating doses.

Wheat and other grains. Wheat germ and wheat-germ oil are two of the most concentrated sources of vitamin E. Whole-grain cereals and bread are fairly good sources of both vitamin E and B vitamins, along with fiber, minerals, and other nutrients. So people who cannot eat wheat and other grains—or those who eat them only once every four days or longer—can miss those B vitamins if they're not careful. You can probably meet your minimum requirement for vitamin E by eating nuts, seeds, and using cold-pressed vegetable oils such as walnut, sunflower, canola, peanut, and olive oils, among others. However, many health professionals feel strongly that the Daily Value for vitamin E for adults—30 International Units (or 20 alpha-tocopherol equivalents)—is far too low, and that 100 to 400

International Units (IU) is much closer to a truly healthful level. Among other functions, vitamin E acts as an antioxidant. That is, vitamin E protects against cancer by preventing polyunsaturated fats we eat from turning into peroxides, substances that can damage cells or promote tumors. Vitamin E also shields cells against the effects of pollution. However, just to be safe, people with high blood pressure or heart disease should check with their doctor before taking *high* doses of vitamin E. It's usually best to begin at a low dose, perhaps 100 IU a day for a few weeks, and then increase the dose gradually to the desired strength.

For people who want to consume protective amounts of vitamin E but wish to avoid wheat germ oil, soy-based supplements are an available source. (See "Carlson Laboratories," page 386.) Some of those supplements are purified to the point where little soy remains. (Synthetic forms of vitamins A and E are derived from petroleum and may cause reactions in people who are allergic to petroleum products of all kinds.)

As for B vitamins, if you can eat brown rice, you're in luck—it can contribute fair amounts of these important vitamins. Spelt, Kamut grain, teff, barley, rye, and millet all also offer a wide array of nutrients and fiber. If you're allergic to all grains, try to eat beans, nuts, seeds, eggs, pork, organ meats, buckwheat, quinoa, and amaranth to get your supply of Bs. Or take a supplement. (See "Food Sources of B Vitamins," below.)

FOOD SOURCES OF B VITAMINS

Many of the richest sources of B vitamins happen to be common food allergens. Choose food sources carefully to avoid a deficiency. (See "Nutritional Supplements," page 386.)

VITAMIN	FOOD SOURCES	COMMENTS
Thiamin (B₁)	**Brewer's yeast, chicken livers, oats, pork, fish, legumes, whole grain flours, enriched breads and cereals, peanuts, pine nuts,** brown rice, rice bran, legumes, walnuts	Without grains, may be hard to get adequate supply. Thiamin may also be in short supply if you don't eat meat and legumes fairly frequently. Pork is the highest nongrain source.
Riboflavin (B₂)	**Brewer's yeast, liver, meat, tongue and other organ meats, milk and dairy products, almonds, eggs, green leafy vegetables,** whole grain or enriched breads and cereals	If you avoid yeast, milk and other dairy foods, organ meats, and eggs, you may be at high risk of deficiency. If you are allergic and vegetarian too, that risk increases. Signs of deficiency often manifest as cracks in the corners of the lips, sore and inflamed tongue, or other mouth sores.

(continued)

FOOD SOURCES OF B VITAMINS (cont.)

VITAMIN	FOOD SOURCES	COMMENTS
Niacin (B₃)	**Brewer's yeast, fish, lean meats, organ meat, peanuts, poultry, rice bran, avocados,** mushrooms, asparagus	Niacin supplements come in two forms: niacinamide and niacin (nicotinic acid). Both forms can be used to treat pellagra, but they do have differences: The nicotinic acid form of niacin can help lower cholesterol, but may cause flushing. Discuss with your doctor.
Vitamin B₆ (Pyridoxine)	**Bananas, poultry, fish, meats (especially organ meats), green soybeans,** cooked dried soybeans and other legumes, walnuts, whole grains and flours	Omitting meat would eliminate a lot of B₆ from your diet. And wheat, soy, and yeast are all common allergens. So most allergics who avoid meat run the risk of deficiency.
Vitamin B₁₂ (Cobalamin)	**Meat (especially organ meats), milk, cheese, eggs, fish, shellfish**	If your diet excludes meat, fish, eggs, and dairy products, deficiency is possible. Some people may not absorb B₁₂ from their food properly and may require injections. Discuss your options with your doctor. Vitamin B₁₂ is easily destroyed by microwave cooking.
Pantothenic Acid	**Avocados, brewer's yeast, broccoli, organ meats, salmon, egg yolk, milk,** mushrooms, whole grain flours	Essential to a healthy immune system and considered beneficial to people with allergies.
Folate or Folic Acid	**Liver, asparagus, brussels sprouts, broccoli, oranges,** avocado, banana, beets, cantaloupe, legumes, romaine, seeds, spinach, and other green leafy vegetables	Requirements are small and sources diverse. If your allergies limit food sources of folate in your daily diet, do consider supplements. Research associates a deficiency with neural tube birth defects and cardiovascular disease.
Biotin	**Kidney, liver, egg yolk, fish, legumes, whole grains, and whole grain flours**	Although some of the best sources of biotin are common allergens, requirements are small and it can be produced by intestinal bacteria.

Note: Boldface type indicates major sources of vitamins; regular type indicates modest sources.

Yeast. Nutritional yeasts, such as brewer's yeast, are excellent sources of B vitamins. If you're allergic to yeast, be sure to include other sources of those nutrients in your daily diet. You may have to restrict the amounts of tyramine in your diet if you are taking mono-amine oxidase inhibitors (MAO inhibitors). Tyramine interacts with MAO inhibitors, which are prescribed to treat certain forms of severe depression. Products made with baker's yeast are allowed in a tyramine-controlled diet, but brewer's yeast is not allowed.

Soy. Soybeans and soy products are the richest, least-expensive sources of vegetable protein. Lecithin is a soy product, which in turn is a product of choline, a little-known nutrient that is essential to the brain and nervous system; some research hints that it may help to sharpen memory. For people who are allergic to soy, alternative sources of choline are beef liver, milk, eggs, and peanuts—all known allergens.

OTHER ESSENTIAL NUTRIENTS

Here are a few other essential nutrients to look for:

Vitamin A. This fat-soluble vitamin helps to fight infection and maintains the health of our eyes, skin, and tissues that line the body. Most yellow and orange food and deep green, leafy vegetables are respectable sources of beta-carotene, which is the precursor to vitamin A. That includes apricots, broccoli, cantaloupe, carrots, kale, nectarines, peaches, pumpkin, spinach, squash, sweet potatoes, and Swiss chard. If you can eat those foods and do so regularly, you can probably meet your basic requirement for vitamin A quite easily.

Some nutrition-oriented doctors recommend large amounts of vitamin A—up to 10,000 IU for adults—to help prevent cancer and other diseases. Fish liver oil is the most common source of concentrated vitamin A, a problem for people who are allergic to fish. Also, fish oil perles, or soft-gels, usually contain preservatives to retard spoilage. The capsules themselves may be made of either beef or pork gelatin, may contain preservatives, and may contain artificial colors or flavors. If you're allergic to any of those and need an extra source of vitamin A, look for liquid cod liver oil. Most of all, try to eat yellow and green foods to meet your need for beta-carotene.

Zinc. The Daily Value for this trace mineral is 15 milligrams for adults. Zinc is considered helpful for taste perception, prostate health, and making of sperm. Because it is involved in vitamin A metabolism, zinc is helpful in clearing up eczema and other skin problems, sharpening night vision, healing wounds, and fighting infection. Three ounces of lean beef supplies a little over 5 milligrams of zinc. Toasted wheat germ contains almost 1 milligram per tablespoon. Whole wheat flour also contributes some zinc. If you're allergic to beef or wheat, other good sources of zinc include Brazil nuts, cashews, chickpeas, lentils, oysters, pumpkin seeds, and soybeans. Supplements of zinc gluconate can also help ensure adequate intake.

Iron. Meat is by far the richest source of iron. If you can't eat meat of any kind—or if you eat it sparingly for one reason or another—it may be tough to get the 9 to 18 milligrams of iron needed for rich, red blood, strong immunity, and peak energy levels. Amaranth, dried beans, dark green leafy vegetables, tofu, and blackstrap molasses are good plant sources of iron.

However, few health professionals would suggest taking iron supplements without a blood test to determine an actual deficiency. The reason is that excessive iron can lead to polycythemia, a serious blood disorder. Infants, children, and menstruating females are the most likely candidates for iron supplementation. Men and post-menopausal women are less likely to need a supplement.

Phytochemicals. Researchers have compelling evidence that these substances in fruits and vegetables are very beneficial to good health, and some actually appear to prevent cancer and other degenerative diseases. Not vitamins and minerals, phytochemicals are simply beneficial "food factors" that help keep us well. Broccoli and other members of the cabbage family are especially good sources—but all fruits and vegetables contain phytochemicals.

Co-enzyme Q-10. This is thought by some experts to be another beneficial "food factor." First recognized for its ability to boost the immune system, it later was found to strengthen the heart muscle, and current research suggests that it may play a role in fighting cancer. Dosages tend to fall into the 60 milligram-a-day range. You may want to discuss dosage with your doctor.

FATS

Obesity has been called a growing national epidemic. Currently, about 55 percent of the American population is overweight or obese. Despite the flood of fat-free and low-fat products in grocery stores, Americans seem to be gaining more weight than ever.

Should we cut back on fat even more? If less fat in our diet is good, is no fat even better? Absolutely not! Fat is an essential nutrient.

The problem is this: The American diet is too high in total fats and especially too high in saturated fats, which are found mostly in red meats and dairy products. The typical American diet is also too high in hydrogenated fats, which form when liquid oils are processed into margarines and shortenings that are solid at room temperature. To eat more healthfully, experts recommend reducing our intake of all fats and replacing most of the saturated and hydrogenated fats with monounsaturated fats (found in olive and canola oils) and omega-3 fatty acids (found in cold water fatty fish such as salmon, mackerel, and tuna and in walnut oils and flax seeds).

Let's translate that into action you can take: Using the Rotary Diversified Diet, plan menus that help you ease into eating meat every other day or less, rather than every day. Fill menu gaps with fish, poultry, and vegetarian alternatives. Steer clear of high-fat dairy products and choose low-fat and fat-free varieties of milks, cheeses, and yogurts in rotation, if you're not allergic to them.

Good fats. Using the Rotary Diversified Diet, incorporate at least four oils, not just one, into your diet (four or more is an important part of diversity). For starters, try olive oil. It's monounsaturated and has been embraced by the medical community as a heart-healthy choice.

Also considered beneficial are cold-pressed oils from nuts such as walnuts and seeds, especially flax, because they're good sources of omega-3 essential fatty acids (EFAs). In theory, very high doses of EFAs may contribute to our well-being by bolstering our immune system and reducing our reactivity to allergens. Tip: Flax oil doesn't stand up well to heat, so use it in salad dressings or drizzle it over cooked vegetables. EFAs should be included in your diet as substitutes for other less healthful fats.

We also need omega-6 and omega-9 fatty acids, but they are so broadly distributed in nature that most of us get plenty.

Not-so-good fats. Fats to avoid include lard, butter, other animal fats; solid white shortenings; and hydrogenated and partially hydrogenated margarines. The trouble with hydrogenation is that it creates trans fatty acids, which our bodies don't break down properly. These fats raise total cholesterol, reduce HDLs (good cholesterol), and raise LDLs (harmful cholesterol). Researchers also say that trans fats end up being deposited in internal organs and on artery walls. Trans fats can, therefore, significantly raise a person's risk of cardiovascular disease.

If you truly want a margarine-type spread, try Spectrum Spread by Spectrum Naturals, Inc. It contains no hydrogenated oil. Original Spread is made with canola oil, water, sea salt, xanthan and guar gums, soy protein isolate, annatto, citric acid, sorbic acid (at $\frac{1}{10}$th of 1 percent, to protect from mold), natural butter flavor (nondairy, soy-based) and turmeric for color. It has a pleasing, natural-tasting flavor and is available in most health food stores.

This basic guide should help you cover the essentials of good nutrition on a limited diet. If you decide to consult a doctor for more detailed nutritional information, keep two things in mind: Recommendations for one family member don't necessarily apply to others. Also, when it comes to supplements, more is not necessarily better. Especially with infants and small children, avoid guesswork. For the best nutritional guidance, find a qualified registered dietitian or nutritionally savvy holistic or environmental doctor.

The field of nutrition in general is relatively new. The study of nutrition as it applies to food allergy is even newer. Research has proven that nutritional needs increase under many forms of stress or illness, and allergy certainly qualifies as an ever-present stress and, at times, as an illness, too. Whatever symptoms you're trying to relieve, it's probably safe to say that a well-nourished body is better able to cope than one that is chronically deficient in essential nutrients. Hopefully, as more health professionals investigate this area, we can look forward to even more information to help us stay well and manage food allergies successfully.

The Allergy-Free Home

Bah, humbug!" I confess that this was my first reaction to the idea of trying to minimize my food allergies by cleaning my home. I had been keeping a fairly clean place—or so I thought. However, I reluctantly decided to try de-cluttering it and giving everything a thorough scrub down. My symptoms didn't ease immediately. Rather, it seemed as if the more I cleaned, the better I felt. To see how much difference cleaning could make, I launched a really extensive cleanup. It worked. I felt better. And here's what I found.

THE ALLERGY-FREE KITCHEN

Anyone with food allergies faces two challenges in the kitchen. First, you must stock food you can eat. Second, you need to store it, prepare it, and clean it up in ways that keep you feeling well. Even if you pay careful attention to what you eat, you won't feel completely well if something else in the room, such as molds or gas fumes, is making you ill.

Few of us realize that the kitchen can be one of the densest pockets of pollution we encounter, indoors or out, city or country—even if it's always scrupulously clean. To illustrate my point: A government worker in Washington, D.C., wore a portable pollution monitor throughout a typical day as part of a study on environmental health. In the course of the day, he commuted to his office, following closely behind a smoky diesel truck, sat among smokers in the cafeteria, was exposed to cigar smoke later in the day, and breathed in the exhaust from a mass transit bus on his way home. Yet, he was exposed to the most pollution while cooking dinner in his kitchen. Here's a quick snapshot of how to keep your kitchen from becoming an allergy trap.

Minimize cooking odors. Believe it or not, even cooking odors can trigger reactions in highly sensitive people. Fish, eggs, and onions are common offenders, but any food can do it.

I learned this firsthand after moving to a community where, at that time, Sara Lee products were being baked. Whenever I stopped at a certain red light, that wonderful baking aroma engulfed me. Then, without having eaten a thing, I'd drive straight home, desperate to take a nap!

To help minimize reactions in your kitchen, install a vent over your stove to draw cooking odors out of doors.

Avoid gas appliances. Gas-burning appliances give off nitrogen dioxide, a major irritant and pollutant. Gas stoves are the primary offenders, although gas hot-water heaters, gas dryers, and unventilated gas and kerosene space heaters give off offending fumes, too.

Avoid molds, dust, and plastics. Aside from cooking odors and gas fumes, kitchens often harbor molds, dust, formaldehyde, plastics, and other petroleum products as well as household cleaners—all common irritants to the eyes, nose, and throat. You may be surprised to see formaldehyde among those irritants, but a study in 1985 showed that among 230 people with asthma-like respiratory problems, 12, or about 5 percent, reacted adversely to formaldehyde. If you're one of those people, you can suffer headaches, eye-ear-nose-and-throat symptoms, or other respiratory reactions.

AN ALLERGY INVENTORY

Let's take a detailed cook's tour of the kitchen to examine potential problem areas and provide solutions. Chances are you won't need to make all of the changes discussed. That will largely depend on what you discover is bothering you or your family.

Kitchen cabinets. One of the biggest sources of formaldehyde, especially in new or remodeled kitchens, is particle board cabinets, constructed with formaldehyde-containing glues. Sherry Rogers, M.D., an internationally known environmental allergist whose clinic is in Syracuse, New York, says that there are two things you can do about them. One is to paint the cabinets with a coat or two of latex paint to seal in the formaldehyde. (The paint fumes take a few weeks to die down, so have it done while you're away on vacation.) Or you can install one of the air filters capable of dealing with formaldehyde fumes. One is the Foust. (See "Household Goods and Cleaning Products," page 381.) Check with the manufacturer to confirm that the model you are considering will get rid of formaldehyde.

If you plan to build a new home or have your kitchen remodeled, ask the cabinetmaker to use real wood (not particle board) and formaldehyde-free glue. Metal cabinets are okay, too. If you've been in your present kitchen for several years or longer, chances are good that formaldehyde is no longer a problem.

The stove. If you have a gas stove, replacing it with an electric range is a major stride toward removing irritants—particularly if you react to petroleum products and gas fumes. In a study of 137 homes in one Wisconsin community, levels of nitrogen dioxide—a major by-product of gas combustion—averaged five times that of outdoor levels in kitchens with gas stoves. Kitchens with electric stoves had nitrogen dioxide levels below outdoor levels. But if for some reason you can't get rid of your gas stove, vent the fumes outdoors by having an adequate exhaust system installed. (Gas furnaces should also be vented.)

Very rarely, an individual may react to fumes of heated metal coils on an electric range. I know one woman who overcame that by buying a ceramic-top range. These are widely available.

Cookware. The wisest choice in cookware for people with food allergies is pots and pans (and bowls, pie plates, and casseroles)

made of enamel, enamel-coated iron, lined copper, glass, glazed ceramic (such as Corningware), stainless steel, or aluminum bonded to stainless steel (the stainless will touch the food). None of those materials seem to migrate into food. Iron migrates slightly, but that's acceptable, so uncoated cast iron cookware is fine, too.

Uncoated aluminum presents a potential problem: Traces of aluminum can leach into food, especially into acidic foods like citrus, cherries, tomato dishes (such as spaghetti sauce), and rhubarb. The same goes for aluminum pie plates. The symptoms of aluminum toxicity mimic senility. Just how big a threat this may be is highly controversial. Nevertheless, the fact remains that some people may be more vulnerable to aluminum exposure than others because of the individual differences in the way our bodies handle the metal. However, aluminum is an excellent heat distributor. Aluminum pots bonded to an outer surface of stainless steel are the perfect answer, combining aluminum's excellent heat-conducting properties with an impervious, noncorrosive stainless steel finish. If you already own uncoated aluminum cookware and don't care to switch, be sure to use it to cook nonacidic foods only. That applies to aluminum pie plates as well.

Nonstick coatings are a boon to people who are allergic to dairy products because they allow you to cook without butter. And they are safe, according to several studies. However, a minority of people with chemical sensitivities claim to react to food cooked in a nonstick pan. I personally enjoy the convenience and easy cleaning of nonstick cookware and have felt no ill effects. In fact, one scientist states that there has never been a case reported in which a person became ill from normal cooking with nonstick cookware. But everyone—allergic or not—should be aware that some nonstick coatings scratch fairly easily. Because many people with allergies react to plastic utensils, I advise using wooden utensils with nonstick pans. (Note: Soft plastics are more likely to bother people who are chemically sensitive than hard plastics.) For cleaning nonstick pans, avoid harsh scrapers and steel wool; they, too, will damage the coating. Use soft scrub brushes and a firm hand. If your pan does become scratched and nicked, replace it. A further word of caution: Don't use pans with nonstick coatings in the broiler or heat them empty on the stove-top. When overheated, the finish can break down more easily.

Clay cookers are a bit expensive, but they're a wonderful replacement for plastic roasting bags for cooking roasts, poultry, and potatoes. Enamel roasting pans also work well—and usually cost less than a clay pot.

Individual-serving-size ceramic au gratin dishes (such as Corningware's) are convenient to "freeze, heat and eat" foods. They usually have plastic lids, but glass lids are also available. If you have plastic, place waxed paper, parchment, or cellophane between the food and the lid. That way, you'll block the transfer of chemicals in the plastic to your food during storage. Remove the paper and plastic lid before heating the food in the oven.

Food storage. I can't discuss food storage without talking about plastic. Because it's so versatile, it's everywhere. Food scientists at Rutgers University have found that the plasticizers in the polyvinyl chloride (PVC) film

Picnic Basket Supplies

For camping or picnics, use inexpensive stainless steel flatware, rather than disposable plastic versions. Flatware with plastic handles should pose no problem, as long as the bowls of the spoons and tines on the forks are stainless steel. The plastic handles don't come in contact with your food. But if you're extremely chemically reactive, you might want to avoid plastic handles.

Thermos bottles are ideal for carrying your own food and beverages so you don't have to rely on soda machines or fast-food eateries. Look for glass-lined, stainless steel bottles, not plastic versions. You're most likely to find the preferred type in camping supply departments, well-equipped hardware stores, and sometimes discount stores.

used to wrap meats in most supermarkets do eventually migrate into the meat. One of the most common migrants is DEHA. That's also true of "clingy" plastic food wraps. And studies have found that vinyl chloride in PVC-type containers can leach into vegetable oils such as olive oil as well. The plasticizers in PVC migrate into fat-containing foods. Fortunately, there are safe alternatives to plastic. Here are my suggestions for avoiding harmful plastics:

✳ Buy meat from a butcher who uses cellophane or butcher's paper to wrap your meat, and use the same materials to store meat at home. Of the two, butcher's paper is thicker and better for wrapping frozen

food. For long-term freezing, place paper-wrapped food in a sealable plastic food storage bag, to prevent loss of moisture.

✳ Use cellophane, which comes in sheets and bags of various sizes. You can buy it at specialty stores, some health food stores, and mail-order firms. It punctures easily and isn't impervious to air, so use cellophane only for short-term storage of foods. (See "Food Storage and Equipment," page 383.)

✳ Choose glass over plastic bottles. Whenever you have a choice, buy spring water, oils, nut butters, ketchup, and any other packaged foods in glass bottles, rather than plastic.

✳ Store leftovers in glass wide-mouth canning jars. They're a safe, no-waste way to hold not only soups and sauces but solid foods like leftover casseroles; cooked broccoli, carrots, and other vegetables; and raw carrot or celery sticks.

✳ Select stoneware or glass dishes and cups over plastic versions.

Even if it takes you a year or two to completely phase out plastic, it's worth it. A physician friend of mine told me about a woman who had a stubborn nagging cough for 20 years. She went to a number of specialists and underwent several tests, yet no one could help her. After a 45-minute investigation of the woman's home environment, the doctor concluded that the woman was allergic to plastics. She says that after the woman cleared all of the plastic from her kitchen, her cough disappeared.

So many paper products, including lunch bags and paper towels, contain formaldehyde that these articles can be a problem for formaldehyde-sensitive people. If that's the case in your family, carry lunches in cellophane bags, cloth tote bags, or insulated lunch boxes. Use a clean, absorbent cotton towel instead of paper towels to dry salad greens, fish, meat or poultry.

Cooking and drinking water. If you or someone in your family has a problem with chlorine, formaldehyde, or something else in your household water supply, you may have to choose an alternative source of water for cooking and drinking. When buying bottled water, choose brands packaged in glass, not plastic bottles.

If you can't find suitable bottled water, consider installing a water filter. There are a variety of methods to consider: whole house or point-of-use models which include countertop models, under-the-counter models, and filters right on the faucet head. Several types of home water purification filters are available, including solid carbon block, cellulose impregnated with carbon, and granulated active carbon (GAC). Carbon block can be either a solid tube of carbon, with a hollow center which provides increased surface area, or thin film extrusion. Another method is reverse osmosis, but it's relatively expensive and filters at a slower rate. Studies show that these filtering methods effectively remove some or all of the following: chlorine, industrial chemicals, disagreeable taste, and bad odors.

Uncontaminated well water may be the least expensive solution if you have access to it. I am comfortable drinking water from our well and strongly prefer it to "city" water. When you have your own well, remember to have it tested regularly to ensure its ongoing safety.

CLEANING UP

Cleaning up is an unavoidable part of cooking—and is equally fraught with allergy pitfalls.

Oven spills and soil. Of all the offensive cleaning compounds that allergic people find in their kitchens, oven cleaners are by far the worst. Any chemicals that can dissolve baked-on grease and grime must be potent and are often highly irritating to asthmatics and other people with sensitive airways or skin. Instead of commercial cleaners, use the following method (a bit harder on your elbows, but easier on your lungs): Sprinkle greasy or sugary spills with salt. After 20 minutes or so (or when the oven cools down), scrape off the burnt food and wipe the area with a damp sponge. Wearing rubber gloves, use a scouring soap pad to finish the job. Use this method to clean wire racks, too.

Are self-cleaning ovens safe for those with food allergies? That will depend on your sensitivity to fumes. If you have a self-cleaning oven, open a window and put on the exhaust fan to help move out the fumes.

Mold. Mold threatened to ruin Leonardo da Vinci's *The Last Supper.* And molds can ruin your meals, too. I don't necessarily mean molds on forgotten leftovers. Molds and bacteria that grow surreptitiously in the refrigerator drip-pan and garbage pail, especially in warmer, humid months of the year, can trigger respiratory allergies such as hay fever or asthma. A microbiologist at Indiana-Purdue University has found that the drip pans in self-defrosting refrigerators harbor a certain type of bacteria that can easily slip past the sweeping action of bronchial cilia in the airways and lodge in the lungs, triggering respiratory allergy. Here are some ways to reduce kitchen molds and bacteria.

✳ Clean the refrigerator drip pan at least once a month. Hot soapy water should do it. And follow the manufacturer's directions.

✳ Get rid of the garbage pail. If you don't already have one, invest in a garbage disposal. Or if you're into composting, take scraps out regularly, or let them accumulate in a covered coffee can in the refrigerator.

✳ Take precautions when composting. Compost heaps can harbor lots of nasty molds. So if you're allergic to mold, wear a mask when carrying vegetable trimmings out to the pile. Or ask someone else to do it for you. And for sure, delegate the turning of the compost to someone else.

✳ Check for mold growth on indoor plants. If you grow herbs or ornamental plants in wicker baskets in your kitchen, check for mold growth that can proliferate in moisture-laden wood. Find new containers and discard the moldy wicker.

✳ Wipe down every square inch of your kitchen twice a year with a solution of either Clorox, borax, vinegar, or baking soda diluted in water (depending on which of those you can best tolerate).

✳ Install a dehumidifier to help reduce mold growth if your kitchen sits partially below ground level or adjoins the basement.

Cutting boards. Cutting boards (and countertops, for that matter) that are rough or made with a porous material are a potential hideout for molds and bacteria, a health hazard regardless of allergy. From that standpoint, maple (a hardwood) or plastic cutting boards may be safest and most sanitary. If you're bothered by plastics, be sure to buy the hardest plastic cutting board you can find. One doctor told us that harder boards are less likely to bother sensitive people. I find that harder boards are easier to keep clean and less subject to stains and odors. Just run them through the dishwasher regularly. Clean your cutting board well after every use- wash and sanitize it. Consider using two separate boards—one for fish, poultry, and meats and another for foods you'll eat raw, like salads.

Soiled dishes and pots and pans. If you have sensitive skin, wash dishes with a hypoallergenic all-purpose cleaner such as Bi-O-Kleen's All Purpose Cleaner or a similar product. Better yet, wear either cotton-lined rubber gloves or cotton gloves under an unlined pair, whenever you put your hands in water—to scrub walls, woodwork, floors, countertops, or appliances.

Dish towels. The fabric in dish towels, like many other fabrics, is steeped in formaldehyde and can trigger dermatitis. That's because formaldehyde reacts readily with skin protein. Formaldehyde can also trigger various other reactions in sensitive people. Wash new towels several times before using them. And stick with all-cotton or Irish linen towels.

General soil and grime. Ammonia and ammonia-based cleaners are great for sponging off fingerprints and smudges, but ammonia fumes can trigger violent reactions in asthmatics and other people with sensitive airways. Instead, use borax, baking soda, or white distilled vinegar and water as nontoxic alternatives. Here are some other general cleaning tips:

* Shine appliances with club soda, rubbing alcohol, or vinegar and water instead of commercial, petroleum-based waxes. (Hospitals often use rubbing alcohol to clean and shine stainless steel equipment.)

* Clean windows and metal appliances with a solution of white vinegar and water or a nonaerosol, pump-style window cleaner.

* Mop no-wax floors with borax and water. Floor wax has been known to give some

people headaches and to trigger other unpleasant reactions. If you must wax the floor, run the exhaust fan and open the windows. Afterwards, leave the house for a few hours while the fumes die down.

Air fresheners. Both the aerosol and "stick-up" types usually contain formaldehyde, which doesn't freshen the air at all but numbs your sense of smell (permanently, in some cases). And aerosol products often contain hydrocarbons, a petroleum derivative. So if you're allergic to formaldehyde or petroleum products, air fresheners don't belong in your kitchen. Here are some better, safer alternatives.

* Eliminate the source of odors—be it trash, old food, or spills.

* Keep pets clean at all times.

* Sprinkle odor-absorbing baking soda in cat litter and trash pails. Leave an open box of baking soda in the refrigerator.

* Empty the trash daily so discarded cans and cartons don't start to smell bad.

* Open a window and turn on a fan. Ventilation is the only true source of fresh air.

To get rid of cooking odors, smoke, and other airborne offenders, you'll need a good kitchen exhaust fan. Aside from a fan, an air filter of some type can help purify the air you breathe while you cook and eat, and it prevents cooking odors and other fumes from traveling to other areas of the house, too.

Air-conditioning acts like an air filter, since air is whisked out of the house and replaced with outdoor air, which is presumably less contaminated. If you don't have central air-conditioning, you'll need an extra-large room unit for the kitchen to deal with the heat generated by cooking.

If your home is located near traffic, industry, or farms that are sprayed with pesticide, your air conditioner must have a charcoal filter or other means of purifying incoming air. Also, be sure the air intake is not located near a garage, chimney, or other source of fuel exhaust.

Air filters themselves come in different types and don't all work equally well. Electronic air cleaners rid the air of numerous larger particles, but many give off ozone, which can aggravate asthma, especially when they're new. A number of allergy doctors recommend HEPA (High Efficiency Particulate Air) filters, which are more efficient, but some may have formaldehyde from the sealants. Formaldehyde is tough to get out of the air, one doctor explains, because, as in many gases, the particles are so small. The best way to remove the formaldehyde is to run the filter.

KITCHEN DECOR

Not everything in a kitchen is purely utilitarian. Many decorative items may be fine for most people but not for those with allergies. Here's a list of possible offenders.

Flooring. If you're thinking of carpeting your kitchen, think again. Carpeting complicates life for people with allergies because it's hard to keep clean, it harbors molds when wet, and it's usually installed with petroleum-based glues. All-cotton, washable scatter rugs are a better alternative from the standpoint of allergies, though they may be safety hazards from the standpoint of slipping and falling.

Ceramic tile makes a wonderful, durable floor. But it's expensive and hard on the feet, back, and legs. It's also very slippery when wet. One solution is to buy commercial rubber mats to stand on—they significantly reduce back and leg strain, they're easy to clean, and they last a long time. The only downside is that new mats have a strong chemical odor, so air them out for a few weeks before using.

Another possibility: hardwood floors. The problem with them is they require finishing and, sometimes, waxing and polishing to keep them looking lovely. In the long run, it pays to figure out your method of finishing the floor (varnish, sealers) and its upkeep before investing.

Knickknacks. Plastic flowers, woven baskets, and other ornaments collect dust, the nemesis of many allergic people. And the plastic itself can trigger subtle reactions. Crockery and wrought iron trivets are among the safer alternatives. Keep in mind that practical, frequently used items collect less dust than idle ornaments.

Table linens. Again, plastic can cause problems for the allergy-prone. Use cotton or linen tablecloths or place mats whenever possible. For easy maintenance, choose cotton terry or some other minimal-care cotton. Terry cloth finger-tip guest towels make excellent carefree napkins. Before using new table linens, wash them several times to remove all traces of formaldehyde.

Candles. These can make dinnertime special or romantic. For people who react to fragrances or petroleum products, beeswax candles are a better bet than regular petroleum-based candles. So are floating candles—these have special wicks that float in vegetable oil in attractive glass vessels.

At the risk of sounding like a broken record, I want to emphasize that any changes you make in your kitchen will depend on what you're allergic to and how bad your symptoms are. Until you make some of these changes, you will never know how significantly your symptoms might be reduced.

THE ALLERGY-FREE BEDROOM

Environmental physicians believe that the presence of irritating inhalants such as dust, dust mites, seasonal pollens, pet dander, and many strains of molds increases a person's allergic load, which in turn increases a person's level of reactivity to everything that bothers them. This concept is called the "total allergic load."

I can say from experience that when my inhalant allergies were worse, my food reactions occurred more often and more severely. During hay fever season, I had to be very careful and had to eat only plain food. I eliminated all spices and herbs, even favorites such as cinnamon and black pepper. For those two months every year, I seasoned food only with sea salt. Be assured that anything you do to reduce inhalant irritants may significantly minimize your food allergies—even if you can't immediately implement every aspect of my recommendations.

When it comes to the bedroom, environmental physicians suggest that it be set up as an "oasis," a place where common environmental allergens are held to an absolute minimum. Here's what to do to create that special spot in your home:

Simplify. First, strip an allergic person's room of all soft goods that aren't essential: extra blankets, off-season clothing and, for a child, most of the soft toys. If you de-clutter the room as one of your first cleaning steps, you will find it easier to keep that room dust-free and allergy-clean.

Change the floor covering. Do you have hardwood floors with throw rugs? Ideal! Remove the rugs for now, at least in the bedroom, and run a slightly dampened mop over the floor daily. If you have carpeting, seek out a good nontoxic carpet cleaner and use it on the carpeting not only in the bedroom but also in the whole house. Then vacuum and damp-dust the allergic person's room often—daily if possible.

If the problem is life-threatening asthma, replace carpets with something smooth and easily damp-mopped, such as vinyl, linoleum, or hardwood. Be sure to investigate each type of flooring as well as the products needed to maintain it before purchasing anything.

Replace drapes. Remove heavy drapes and replace them with metal miniblinds or washable curtains. Then clean the blinds or launder the curtains weekly. After the allergic symptoms diminish, try cleaning every other week and watch to see if the symptoms worsen during the second week—a sign you need to go back to the weekly interval.

Pick favorite toys. If it's a child's room you are working with, select two or three of your child's favorite washable soft toys. Look for loose buttons, glued eyes, and other trimmings that might come off during laundering, and either secure or remove them. Put the toys in a pillow case, tie shut, and machine wash and dry on a "gentle" setting. Launder weekly, at least until the symptoms are under control. Gather blocks, cars, dolls, and other wooden or hard plastic toys and wash them once or twice a week with something nontoxic. I like to wash toys in dishwashing detergent, one of the new fruit and vegetable cleaning products, or white vinegar and water; then let them air dry.

Provide fresh air. Consider getting an air cleaner for any allergic person's bedroom as well as a larger one for the rest of the house. Or open the windows as often as possible.

Ban pets. Getting rid of pets may or may not help, but in any case, you should prevent close contact, such as hugging and kissing, between a pet and the person who has allergies, and don't allow the pet into that person's room.

Have heating ducts cleaned. If you have forced air heat, the ducts are full of dust, dust mites, molds, and animal dander, some of which is circulated every time the blower goes on. Once the ducts have been cleaned, use efficient air cleaners to help keep the ducts cleaner longer. Those two steps alone will help reduce allergy symptoms to some degree across the board. If you should decide to find another home for your pets, you may only notice minimal reduction in allergic symptoms until you have the ducts power-vacuumed to remove dust-dander build-up.

Damp-dust furniture. Wipe the furniture in the bedroom with a damp cloth every other day or two. Keep furnishings simple and uncluttered so this can be done quickly and easily. Avoid letting books or magazines accumulate in this room. Damp-dust the rest of the house two or three times a week.

Select hypoallergenic bedding. Choose pure cotton sheets, pillow cases, and blankets because the synthetic material in "perma-pressed" fabrics is irritating to many people with allergies. If dust mites are high on the list of allergens, use hypoallergenic

covers on the mattress and pillow. Read labels; not all covers seal in mites. And be sure the cover completely envelopes the mattress like a giant pillow case and closes with a zipper. Such covers are widely available in department stores, bed linen shops, and discount stores.

Another idea: Get a new bed pillow annually and wash the cover for the new pillow so you're starting fresh. Hypoallergenic linens are also available for an infant's room.

Take extra care with laundry. For laundering bed linens and other items, choose an unscented, mild soap or detergent, preferably one labeled "fragrance-free." In the past decade, many environmentally friendly products have hit the market, but many have a strong "natural" scent, such as citrus. Keep looking until you find one that you like. If you or your child has skin problems, always use an extra rinse when laundering clothing, linens, and soft toys.

Unfortunately, dust mites survive gentle laundering using warm water. And hot water (135°F or higher) can ruin special-care, delicate items. What to do? Dry those special items outdoors in direct sunlight.

You may also want to try adding Grapefruit Seed Extract (GSE) to the laundry. Nontoxic and odorless, GSE may be effective against some strains of bacteria, some viruses, yeasts, fungi, molds, mites, and even some parasites. Since it's very concentrated, you need only 30 drops per laundry load in the wash cycle. An extra rinse is optional but still a good idea. Another 30 drops of GSE may be added to the extra rinse for diapers as well as sheets and towels when there is illness in the house. GSE is available in many health food stores.

Allergies and the Workplace

Okay, so you've made dietary changes. And you've done a thorough environmental cleanup at home. But you still feel sick. It may be that some factors in the workplace are affecting you.

Some workers suffer from what is known as "sick-building syndrome," a condition caused by tight buildings with poor ventilation systems and windows that don't open. In such buildings, fumes from formaldehyde-soaked carpeting, particle board furnishings, glues, and other adhesives, paints, stains, sealers, waxes, and other finishes have no place to go.

As a result, they create a chemical soup workers must breathe in day after day. When the building is the problem, usually more than one person is affected. And those who are affected often feel better whenever they are away from the building.

If you find yourself working in such a building, determine if your employer is willing to make some changes, such as installing an adequate ventilation system or providing air cleaners for affected employees. If changes aren't possible, consider finding employment elsewhere.

THE ALLERGY-FREE BATHROOM

Because of dampness, your bathroom can be a haven for mold. If you see mildew (those annoying black spots) growing on the grout between tiles in your bathroom, mold is present. Fortunately, there are ways to eliminate it, but you must be diligent.

Ventilate the room. First and foremost, install an exhaust fan (or inspect and clean your current one), and make sure it's properly vented to the outside. If buying a new one, choose a powerful model. In nice weather, open the window after showers are finished.

Keep things dry. Spread wet towels and wash cloths, rather than fold them, over a towel bar so they dry as quickly as possible. If drying space is limited, use an old-fashioned wooden rack that will allow the whole family to spread out their wet towels. If feasible, put the rack in the laundry room or, in nice weather, on a porch or patio to get that moisture out of the bathroom.

After showers are done, dry the tiled splash area around the tub (or the shower walls) to reduce moisture. By reducing bathroom moisture, you are very effectively reducing the mold population in the air and on fixtures.

Clean up visible mold. Removing existing mildew requires strong chemicals, and you may have to try two or three products before you find one you're comfortable working with. When using any mildew-removing product, always open the window and run the exhaust fan.

Is an environmental clean-up worth the time, effort, expense, and inconvenience if you are trying to target food allergies? You'll have to try it to evaluate the results for yourself. Doing so made a believer out of me!

Eating Away from Home

When you have food allergies, it may seem best to eat all your meals at home. I know, I've been there. But I've learned to resist the temptation. Dining out, restaurant-style, can be a fun and rewarding experience. After all, the average American spends about 40 percent of his or her food budget for food eaten away from home. Relaxing on a park bench with a sack lunch or enjoying a dinner party with special friends can be equally rewarding. All it takes to make dining away from home pleasurable is confidence and a game plan.

Before I discuss specific tactics for each outing—breakfast, lunch, dinner, party—I'd like to share a few guidelines that help me dine well on restaurant cuisine.

Select a good, independent restaurant. The better the restaurant, the more choices you'll have. I've found that to avoid major food allergens—corn, wheat, milk, soy, eggs, and yeast—I have to eat in fairly good restaurants, which prepare food to order, rather than chain and fast-food restaurants, which prepare each meal the same way.

Call ahead. Find out what's offered, how it's prepared, and whether the chef can adapt a dish for you. Ask for the no-smoking sec-

tion. If calling ahead isn't feasible, request the information as soon as you arrive. If an airline meal is on your agenda, arrange for it when you make your reservations. You can also call at least 24 hours ahead for a special meal. Regardless of those arrangements, I suggest that you carry food that could satisfy you for a meal, if necessary (such as fruits, nuts, or a sandwich).

Order plain fare. Your safest policy is to order unadorned food—preferably baked, broiled, or steamed. Sauces, toppings, marinades, casseroles, and other mixed dishes may have a number of hidden ingredients.

Be flexible. If you're rotating foods once every four days, your menu choices may be limited. But it's wiser to break rotation and eat a food you had yesterday than to eat something that may cause an allergic reaction. Simply resume your Rotary Diversified Diet as soon as possible.

Carry Alka-Seltzer Gold or other alkaline salts with you. These over-the-counter medications may help neutralize a reaction if you happen to eat something that doesn't agree with you. That emergency remedy has helped me out many times. Of course, this will not stop an immune allergic reaction. If you might be having an anaphylactic reaction do not use Alka-Seltzer Gold. You must get immediate medical help.

BREAKFAST

If you can't eat eggs, milk, wheat cereal, toast, muffins, biscuits, pancakes, or waffles, your breakfast choices at a restaurant boil down to fruit, fruit juice, and oatmeal. For fruit, you can often find grapefruit or melon and maybe fresh strawberries, bananas, or peaches. Be sure to ask if the fruit has been frozen or prepackaged. If so, strawberries, peaches, citrus, or melon may include sugar. That may leave only fruit juice and oatmeal (assuming you can eat oats). You could combine the two—a workable plan and a great idea if you can't have milk. Honey will also

perk up oatmeal, but ask if it's pure; I've seen some honey that's extended with corn syrup. The same is true for maple syrup. Restaurants rarely carry the more expensive, pure maple syrup; most serve maple-flavored corn syrup.

Most waffles and pancakes, as you probably know, are little more than wheat flour, milk, and eggs. If you're allergic to any of those foods, pancakes and waffles will be off-limits. Be careful if you're considering buckwheat pancakes—they usually contain about 30 percent buckwheat. The rest is wheat flour.

Enjoy hash-brown potatoes? Remember to ask whether they're cooked in butter or oil. And has anything been added, such as onions or green peppers? To be safe, order a baked potato; many restaurants can prepare it in 10 to 15 minutes in a microwave oven.

Which brings us to another way around the limitations of restaurant breakfast menus: Think beyond traditional breakfast fare. If you can eat beef, order a small steak or hamburger patty. Or ask the server if the kitchen has any turkey or other plain, roasted meat on hand.

If you'd like a hot beverage but prefer to avoid coffee and tea, especially the caffeinated versions, the easiest thing to do is to carry your own herbal tea bags and order a pot or cup of boiling water. Of course, you may have to pay for a cup of tea, even though you'll use your own tea bag. Most headaches associated with drinking coffee and tea are caused by withdrawal from caffeine, but a few people may be allergic to coffee.

Sometimes, the only breakfast place for miles is a doughnut shop or fast-food restaurant, in which case your food choices will be quite limited. My suggestion: Carry dried fruit, nuts, and maybe a muffin from your freezer. Such a backup plan will prevent you from finding yourself with nothing to eat.

MID-DAY MEAL

For those of us who truly enjoy a mid-day meal but have to contend with food allergies, the time has come to think beyond the traditional sandwich. Here are my suggestions for the best-ever meals, whether you're lunching out or carrying a sack lunch.

Restaurant lunches. You can easily sidestep the ubiquitous burger and fries routine with any of these ideas.

✳ Order sandwich fixings without bread and eat them with a knife and fork. Or bring a small package of pancakes or other flat bread from home, and make a sandwich with the fillings you order.

✳ Take advantage of luncheon specials that feature plain broiled fish, chicken, or beef with a cooked vegetable on the side. These are usually quite good. Be sure to ask about any seasonings or sauces used in preparation. (See "Dinner," page 75.)

✳ In a pinch, order a steaming bowl of oatmeal and supplement it with a cooked vegetable.

✳ Select fresh fruit from the appetizer list for a refreshing dessert. If you order something, such as fresh strawberries, peaches, or banana, be sure to tell them, "No cream, no sugar, no surprises."

Sack lunches. I am a big proponent of the sack lunch. I never feel deprived when feasting on lunch. Try the ideas below and you'll always have a satisfying mid-day meal, whether at home or on-the-go.

Make a flat-bread sandwich. Stack tortillas or other tasty flat breads for healthful sandwiches. If allergy to yeast or grains prevents you from eating commercially baked bread, take heart: A number of breads in this book make excellent sandwiches. I specifically devised the Zesty Loaf (page 248) with the lunch-carrying crowd in mind. People who can eat yeast but not wheat will find the few yeast-raised breads that I include a close second to any wheat loaf. My pancakes, tortillas, and flat breads made from a variety of alternative flours can also pinch-hit for sliced bread.

As for fillings, sliced home-cooked meats and poultry make tasty choices for people limited to eating fairly plain foods. For more elaborate fillings, make poultry and fish salads with the mayonnaise alternatives given in the Salad Dressings, Sauces, and Condiments chapter (page 190), or use a commercial mayonnaise, if the ingredients agree with you. Baked-Chicken Salad with Apricots (page 220), Tofu Salad (page 258), Better Burgers (page 254), and Tuna Burgers (page 245), all do well as sandwich fillings. So do bean spreads, including South-of-the-Border Sandwich Spread (page 272).

Love peanut-butter-and-jelly sandwiches but you're allergic to peanuts or sugar? Try nut or seed butter (available in many markets) with Simple-Simon Jam (page 279) or Old-Fashioned Fruit Butter (page 280). Or use a commercial all-fruit spread that agrees with you.

Stir up a hot and hearty soup. Nothing revives you on a cold, damp day like a steaming bowl of soup, stew, or chowder. Minestrone (page 145), Chickpea-Potato Soup (page 146), and Kidney-Bean Vegetarian Stew (page 152) are so substantial, they're meals in themselves. Double the recipes and freeze in single-serving-size containers to use as needed. Or take them with you and reheat them in a microwave oven. If a soup or stew is too chunky for your thermos bottle, puree it in a blender or food processor before you go.

Toss together a simple salad. Homemade salads can make lunch time a feast. Choose from New Potatoes with Basil Vinaigrette (page 173), Four-Bean Salad (page 184), Cauliflower-Dill Salad (page 186), Spicy Jicama Slaw (page 188), Hold the Lettuce Salad (page 185), and Confetti Rice Salad (page 252). Pack in a wide-mouth jar with a tight-fitting lid.

To make tossed salads, think beyond lettuce, tomato, and cucumber. By adding leftover cooked beans, peas, meat, poultry, or fish, you can turn a simple salad into a robust meal. Some, like tuna salad, you can dress at home, but for those based on tender greens, you may want to pack the dressing separately so the salad doesn't get soggy as it sits. Supplement your salad with an appropriate muffin, pancake, flat bread, crackers, or Oat and Barley Scones (page 117).

Bag your favorite fruit, nuts, and seeds. Fruit-nut-seed combinations make crunchy agreeable meals. They're also great for anyone who's on the Rotary Diversified Diet and trying to eat from just one or two food families. Why? Almonds, apricots, cherries, nectarines, peaches, plums, and prunes, for example, all belong to the same family. By combining almonds with any of those fruits, you've got a tasty meal and you've met your one-food-family requirement. Mix the fruit with seeds (from pumpkin, squash, or sunflowers if you're allergic to nuts), and you've still used only two food families.

I often carry Brazil nuts and dried pineapple or papaya for lunches away from home. And I leave those foods out of my diet rotation so I can enjoy them whenever I want (which averages once a week).

Grab dinner extras. For the ultimate in creative lunches, be on the lookout for dinner foods that have lunch-box potential, especially if there's a stove, microwave, or hot plate to reheat food where you work. I often cook extra portions of dinner (planned-overs) for just such purposes. If you bake a whole chicken for dinner, wrap and freeze the legs for future lunches. Then, you can pack them along with a few Pancakes (pages 88–93) from breakfast and some fruit. Leftover Vegetarian Chili (page 250), Versatile Meatballs (page 230), and Turkey Meatloaf (page 224) are other examples of dinner entrees that add variety to lunches. Don't forget to bring a knife, fork, and spoon!

Plan a sweet ending. Many of the baked goods in this cookbook make portable desserts that will round out your lunch. Plus, they're high in protein and can be used to augment a meatless or dairy-free lunch. Try a piece of Banana Bread (page 120), Grain-Free Gingerbread (page 317), or Two-Step Carrot Cake (page 316). Either of the Steamed Breads (pages 122–123) also travels well. Or tuck a handful of Cookies on Parade (page 289), Dream Cookies (page 290), or Hidden Treasures (page 363) into your lunch-to-go. Most of those recipes call for whole grains.

Drink to your health. The simplest hot beverage is a cup of herb tea, made with tea brought from home. Or pack a thermos of Berry-Good Tea Punch (page 307), Herbal Iced Tea (page 308), Melon Cooler (page

306), Sweet Nut Milk (page 302), Pineapple-Nut Shake (page 303), or Banana-Orange Milk-Free Shake (page 304).

Keep foods cold until lunchtime. If you pack your lunch the night before, refrigerate overnight, and refrigerate again at work, or pack food in an insulated lunch bag with an ice pack or in a glass- or stainless-steel-lined vacuum flask such as a wide-mouth Thermos™ bottle. These precautions will help prevent bacteria from replicating wildly in lukewarm food.

DINNER

Many of the tricks that get you through a lunch menu will also get you through dinner, with a few added strategies. Some restaurant menus are detailed; others consist of a few scrawled phrases on a chalkboard. Either way, you'll need to know how the food is prepared. Let's say you're considering getting the broiled chicken or fish. Here are a few things to ask, depending on what foods you're allergic to:

✳ Has the chicken or fish been marinated in anything? If so, what?

✳ Is the chicken or fish brushed with butter or oil? If you're allergic to milk, butter should be omitted. If oil is used, what kind is it? Has the butter or oil already been applied or can this step be omitted? If your server seems uncertain, order "dry broil."

✳ Is paprika or any other seasoning used?

✳ Are crumbs or herbs added to the chicken or fish? (Don't worry about the skin on the chicken. It helps keep the meat moist, and you can remove it yourself.)

✳ Is lemon juice used in preparation?

Considering a broiled beef entree? Find out if it's been tenderized with monosodium glutamate (MSG). Even in tiny amounts, MSG has been known to trigger migraine headaches, asthma, and other allergic-type symptoms in some people. It may be used in combination dishes, such as meatloaf, gravy, and sauces.

When it comes to potatoes, go for a whole, uncut baked potato. I find that it's necessary to specify "uncut." Otherwise, the cook may slit it open and automatically dress it up with sour cream or butter—both problems if you're allergic to milk products. Similarly, ordering a potato baked in the half shell doesn't guarantee that the cook won't scoop out the center and mash it with milk. Of course, if you can have milk products, stuffed potatoes are fine. Scalloped potatoes usually contain (wheat) flour and milk, and french fries and hash browns are cooked in hot cooking oil. Parsley potatoes are usually dipped in butter or margarine before being

---

Getting Help for a Severe Allergic Reaction

It's easy to mistake anaphylactic shock for a heart attack or choking episode, unless a fellow diner realizes that the problem started with a reaction to food. If someone collapses at dinner, call 911 or rush the victim to the nearest emergency room. Be sure to mention the possibility of allergy so the person gets the right treatment. If you have severe food allergies, wear an identification bracelet or necklace that says so. (See "Allergy Safety Measures," page 379.)

---

rolled in minced parsley. Find out what the restaurant uses, and then decide.

As for margarine, I don't recommend it for potatoes—or anything else. If you must use margarine, look for the "trans-free" kind in a tub, which does not contain any trans fatty acids. (See Nutrition Basics in Brief, page 52.) You can also bring salad dressing from home to use on a baked potato.

For many people, wine, candles, and flowers make a dinner very special. But for some, those niceties can put a real damper on the occasion. Wines often contain sulfites and other additives, which could give you a headache or other discomfort. Most candles contain petroleum, so if you know that you're bothered by petroleum products, don't light the candles on your table. Flowers are rarely a problem, unless they're a very pungent type such as lilacs, hyacinths, or marigolds. But if they bother you, have them removed.

When the only salad available is a house version, inquire about all fixings, including garnishes and dressing ingredients. Ask the server to omit anything you can't eat. If the items appear in your salad, send it back for another.

Other potential trouble spots are combination salads—potato salad, cole slaw, Waldorf salad, pasta salad. Plain garbanzo beans (chickpeas) are a good choice if they're available, but a three-bean salad with a sugar-vinegar dressing may not be.

As for salad dressings, be aware that many contain egg, cornstarch, milk, stabilizers, sugar, or flavor enhancers, such as MSG. You're best off choosing the simple oil-and-vinegar option or a squeeze of fresh lemon juice. When I'm dining close to home, I usually carry a homemade dressing in a small, tightly sealed bottle, secured in a plastic bag.

How to Send Back Food

No matter what restaurant you're dining in, if you make clear, specific requests, yet receive the wrong food despite your efforts, don't hesitate to send it back. You need not be rude, merely firm. Simply remind the server of what you had originally requested. Most restaurants are more than happy to meet your requests. After all, they are in business to please customers. And sometimes the server may have made an honest mistake by picking up the wrong order.

While it pays to be specific and direct, it also pays to reward excellent service and cooperation at tip time.

If speaking up makes you uneasy, consider taking a class in assertiveness training. Once you get past the "I'm dying of embarrassment" stage, you'll enjoy meals away from home much more. It's important to be able to take control and still feel good about yourself.

PARTIES AND OTHER SOCIAL OCCASIONS

For family get-togethers and visits with friends, your best bet is to explain your situation to the hostess ahead of time. Then offer to bring your own food. Anyone who sincerely cares about you will not be insulted; nor will they encourage you to "try just a little" of some food that you're allergic to. He or she may even offer to prepare something that you can eat. Once at the get-together, focus on the pleasure of being with family and friends. Remember, you can enjoy these occasions so much more when you're feeling well.

The tougher situations are those social occasions with strangers, as in a business setting or when a friend wants you to meet his or her family. These times are often stressful enough without food allergies to cope with. If you can bring food easily and comfortably, fine—it's never improper when your health is at stake. However, packing your own food may invite unwanted attention and can make things more complicated. If that's the case, simply eat before you go, and then decline the food by saying you've already eaten. Bring an herbal tea bag and sip tea slowly throughout the meal. If you are pressed for an explanation, simply say you have food allergies; there's no need to elaborate. Other times, you may be able to politely sidestep the situation by joining the party after dinner.

ENTERTAINING AT HOME

The flip side to dining out is entertaining at home. Inviting a crowd for dinner, an informal Super Bowl party, or a barbecue takes effort and planning, but the advantage is that you control what's served. There's no need to fear that your guests will not like the food. There are plenty of delicious, allergy-free party foods that everyone can enjoy. (See Holiday Foods, page 350.)

SNACKING AT THE MALL, BALL PARK, AND ELSEWHERE

As I mentioned earlier, carrying homemade snacks is the best way to avoid snacking on risky foods. Can't eat franks, popcorn, or soda, for example? Then take your own treats to the ball park. I even bring food and water with me when I shop or run errands. A small glass- or stainless-steel-lined vacuum bottle such as Thermos full of ice cubes and water serves as a beverage. For "refrigeration," take a small ice pack. And a damp washcloth in a plastic bag is ideal for washing sticky fingers after savoring a juicy snack of fresh peaches, plums, or pears.

Fact is, it has never been easier to carry food safely. Insulated lunch boxes are available in supermarkets and department stores. Large coolers are ideal for weekend trips. You can even buy battery-operated car refrigerators at most stores that sell van and RV equipment. On several four-day trips, I've carried breakfast (including flat bread) for two people by replenishing the ice in the mornings and evenings. I sometimes supplement the chilled food in my cooler with purchases of fresh fruit, vegetables, nuts, and rice crackers. (Trying to find wheat-free bread away from home is usually a frustrating task, so plan ahead and carry your own.) If you happen to find plenty of options available in restaurants, just save the food in your cooler for later.

Packing your own food may seem troublesome at first. But the rewards are well worth it: You'll feel good, stay nourished, and enjoy yourself even when you're away from home.

Helping Allergic Children

When your children suffer from allergies, your goal is simple: Help them feel better. Here's a game plan for dealing with allergies and limiting your child's contact with common allergens, whether they're caused by food, environmental conditions, or a combination of the two.

Keep in mind that when I use the word "allergy" in this chapter, I mean a food sensitivity, not true allergy. If your child has a true allergy, one that is cause by an allergic antibody called IgE (Immunoglobulin E), he will get symptoms even if he eats a very small amount of food.

BABIES

Even when both parents have allergies, it may be possible to minimize a baby's risk for food allergies. The key is to reduce the baby's contact with major food allergens *before* birth. To do that, mom-to-be must eliminate her major allergens and rotate the remaining foods in her diet during pregnancy. After giving birth, mom must continue to rotate foods in her diet throughout her baby's first year of life if she's nursing.

(See Planning a Rotary Diversified Diet, page 35.)

Nevertheless, some infants show signs of allergies very soon after birth. Here's how to handle these potential allergies. (Be certain to discuss these strategies with your family doctor, pediatrician, or environmental medicine specialist before implementing them.)

Check for Food Allergies in Nursing Babies

A few simple steps will tell you if your baby is allergic to the foods that you are eating.

Keep a food diary of your diet. The most common offenders in the mother's diet are cow's milk and milk products like cottage cheese, other cheeses, yogurt, ice cream, etc. After milk, the next two foods to suspect are eggs and peanuts, followed by spices and sometimes herbs, according to John Gerrard, M.D., Professor Emeritus in the Department of Pediatrics at University Hospital in Saskatchewan, Canada. While these are the top five suspect foods, some nursing moms may have to give up pizza, chili, and salsa for several months in order to have a happy baby. In your diary, carefully write down what you eat from meal to meal. Also jot down when your baby seems content and when she seems fussy (especially note when the baby's cheeks or ear lobes get very red or when a rash develops around the mouth). These notes will make it much easier to pinpoint the problem food or foods. Even if you have a colicky baby or your baby develops eczema, the solution can often be found in the mother's diet, according to Dr. Gerrard.

Test for reactions. Finding the food or foods causing your baby's symptoms is a process of trial and error. To find out if your baby is allergic to a specific food, eliminate the suspect food from your diet for 5 days. Then eat a fairly large portion, such as 2 or 3 oranges if you are testing citrus, or 2 full glasses of milk if you are testing dairy. If your baby doesn't fuss in the next few hours after nursing, the suspect food is most likely not the culprit.

When you eliminate cow's milk and milk products from your diet for months, you'll need to make up lost nutrients, especially cal-

cium. During those months, eat plenty of green leafy vegetables such as spinach, chard, beet greens, mustard greens, or kale. Also choose whole grains (if you don't react to them), meat, fish, or poultry, and fresh fruits (except citrus fruits if they are a suspect allergen).

Try a Rotary Diversified Diet. If there are many food allergies in the family, consider putting yourself (and your nursing baby) on a rotary diet. Such a move may forestall food-allergy problems. Discuss this strategy with your doctor before implementing.

How to Introduce New Foods

When it's time to introduce solid foods to your baby, here's how to keep food allergies at bay:

Wait to try eggs, meats, and grains. Not all babies should eat cereal at 6 weeks of age or meat at 5 months. Introducing those foods that early will not guarantee that your baby will be exceptionally strong or smart. And it may increase your baby's chances of developing allergies or developing more serious allergies.

Most babies can wait until the age of one year before they try these foods. A baby who is fed only fruits and vegetables may get hungry sooner than a baby who is also being fed cereal, but if your priority is to avoid or minimize allergies, withholding hard-to-digest grains, meats, and eggs may be well worth the additional feedings. Instruct daycare staff or outside caregivers not to give your baby cereal or teething biscuits (which otherwise could be your infant's first exposure to grains). Be sure to discuss this gradual approach with your doctor.

> ## Freezables for Infants
>
> Infants eat only 1 or 2 tablespoons of food at a time. Because it's impractical to make such small portions of single foods, prepare extra and freeze the unused portions in an ice cube tray. When the cubes are frozen, place them in a jar or plastic bag and label. Then simply reheat individual portions in the microwave or on the stovetop.

Give your baby organic produce. When your baby is ready for fruits and vegetables, choose organic versions to avoid exposing your baby to pesticides. Then, simply steam fruits and vegetables until tender. Do not add seasonings or sauces. Use a blender or mini-processor to puree foods until they're the consistency of applesauce. Early on, avoid giving your baby cabbage, broccoli, dried beans, and other known gas-forming foods. But take advantage of the enormous variety of fruits and vegetables available in today's markets.

Of course, you can also purchase organic baby food. But commercial baby food often comes in food combinations—a real no-no for an allergic child. Initially, introduce all foods individually. That way, if your baby reacts to a food, you'll know which one to eliminate. Avoid that food for three to six months, then try introducing it again.

Hold off on common allergens. Wait to test your baby's tolerance for corn and peanuts until he is 2 to 4 years old. At the very least, wait until just before the child enters day care or nursery school. When you do introduce new foods, be sure to do it yourself so you can watch for a reaction.

Avoid balanced meals for infants and toddlers. Many pediatricians say that if your baby is content with only breast milk, there's no need to introduce solid food of any kind until one year of age. Even then, don't try to create balanced meals for your child. When your baby is most hungry, offer several bites of a single food such as squash or spinach. Then let the baby fill up by nursing. It's not necessary to offer meat or dessert. Overall, be guided by your baby's contentment and your doctor's advice.

Environmental Allergies

Another way to reduce your infant's reactions to food is to lessen the baby's exposure to environmental allergens. Here are a few strategies:

* Dress infants in 100 percent cotton clothing that's been laundered with unscented soap or detergent. Avoid fabric softeners.

* Clean the nursery often. (See The Allergy-Free Home, page 60.)

* Keep the home environment free of molds and dust. (See The Allergy-Free Home, page 60.)

Tips for Teething Babies

Many new moms ask: "If I can't use wheat-based teething biscuits, what will I use when my baby's teething?" Surprise! Baby doesn't need teething biscuits at all. In fact, it's probably not a good idea for babies and toddlers to get into the habit of constantly munching on food between meals. Instead, offer your baby a hard rubber teething ring or toy to satisfy her urge to chew.

If you still want to offer an occasional biscuit or dessert treat, look for wheat-free biscuits in health food stores. Be sure your baby can tolerate the grains listed on the label (for instance, many wheat-free biscuits contain barley).

---

* Choose a good water filter, which will also benefit the whole family. (See The Allergy-Free Home, page 60.)

TODDLERS AND PRE-SCHOOLERS

As children age, their eating habits change as they become more physiologically mature. Children aged 2 to 4 years can chew food better and their digestive, immune, and enzyme systems are more developed. At this age, it is appropriate to carefully introduce highly allergenic foods such as corn, white potato, tomato, green pepper, eggplant, and peanuts. It's a good idea to expose your child to these possible allergens *before* the child enters day care, pre-school, or kindergarten. That way, you avoid risking a serious reaction from first-time exposure when your child is away from home. If necessary, make arrangements for special snacks and treats in school.

SCHOOL-AGE CHILDREN

For the school-age child, the social ramifications of food allergies can be just as important, if not more important than, the diet itself. It is essential that a child of 8 or 10 years be comfortable saying "No, thank you" to certain trigger foods—even in the absence of a parent. For this to happen, parents must be supportive and prepare the child from the earliest years.

For instance, birthday parties can be a disaster. The most common party menu for school-age children includes pizza, ice cream, cake, and candy—in other words, wheat, dairy, tomato, and lots and lots of sugar. Truly, an allergic child's nightmare.

Such situations call for creative coping skills! The most successful solution I know is for parents to prepare one of their child's favorite treats in advance and send it along to the party. It helps, too, to explain the situation to the host so he or she can handle the treat without fuss. Possible substitutes include a frozen rice-based treat or frozen soy dessert. Both are dairy free, often sweetened with something other than sugar, and are available at many health food stores and supermarkets. A substitute cake or pizza will more likely need to be prepared at home. Either way, it's important to involve your child in the planning and to provide food that he or she perceives as a treat.

For your child's own birthday party, as well as holidays, allow your child to select a few favorite foods and perhaps participate in preparing them. Such efforts can help your child accept the presence of tempting-but-forbidden foods with grace rather than a tantrum. (See Holiday Foods, page 350, and Desserts, page 311.)

TEENS

No longer little children, no longer totally dependent on their parents, but not yet adults—teenagers are betwixt and between. Their behavior reflects this ambivalent position. One minute your teen may be goofing off with friends, the next minute she might be surprising you by making a very adult-like decision. Teens often handle food allergies the same way—it tends to be inconsistent, to say the least.

Almost always, when a dietary indiscretion occurs at this age, it isn't because the youngster didn't know better. It usually happens because the teen wanted so badly to be like his friends that he was willing to suffer the consequences of eating pizza or ice cream with them.

The best thing a parent can do is to help the teen see cause-and-effect between consuming a no-no food and the resulting headache or rash. Then the youngster can ask himself if eating a reactive food is worth the misery. Giving your teen this choice is very empowering. And, in most cases, your teen will respect that they have been given the choice. It gives him the ability to decide if and when to feel bad—or good.

To get through the teen years, make sure your child has accurate information about allergies and options. Give praise when your teen makes good choices. And avoid overreacting when the choices are not so good. Nagging will only reinforce the idea that selecting healthful foods is still mom's or dad's responsibility, rather than the teen's responsibility.

By age 14, allergic teenagers should learn how to shop for groceries. They must learn to read labels to spot their allergens and to recognize the code names for common allergens, such as whey and casein, which are derived from milk. Teenagers should also be able to get the information they need when it is not provided on the label: that means calling toll-free consumer hotlines to inquire about suspect ingredients.

Cooking (or at least preparing food) is another must-do for allergic 13- and 14-year-olds. Get a head start by involving your allergic child in the kitchen when he is a toddler or school-age child. Children can easily snap the ends off asparagus or stir ingredients. Even if they just hold a wooden spoon and an empty bowl, they'll feel involved. If your teen is "in the kitchen" for the first time, start with something simple, like showing them how to whip up a smoothie. Gradually work up to things like easy dinner entrees. Remember to let them practice. There may be a few inedible disasters, but your child has to start somewhere. More important, doing things in the kitchen with a parent helps empower a teen. It takes the mystery out of food preparation, and it helps your teen feel more in control of their health instead of feeling like a victim of circumstance. Best of all, your teens will learn to prepare healthful foods . . . by themselves.

When does parental responsibility end? Or at least slack off? There's no denying that raising allergic children is a time-consuming task. The special needs of such children may keep you involved in their lives longer than you anticipate. But, eventually, your twenty-something children will be able live on their own—and you'll heave a sigh of relief.

STUDENTS AWAY AT COLLEGE

By the time a student reaches college age, most allergies are nothing new. But how much will they influence the choice of schools and affect college life? That depends on the severity of the allergies, of course. Before selecting a school, find out all you can about eating on campus and the dormitory environment. Here's a sampling of questions to ask the admissions staff of a prospective school and issues to discuss with your child:

✳ Does the cafeteria serve plenty of fresh fruits and vegetables? And is organic produce available? Are organic markets nearby?

✳ Are fish and poultry often baked, or are they always served breaded and deep fried?

✳ Is soy or goat's milk ever available at the cafeteria? If not, are they open to including one or both of these foods on the menu?

✳ Are health-food stores with supplies of fresh fruits and acceptable snacks located nearby?

✳ Can students have small refrigerators in their dormitory rooms? Check all rules and regulations to be sure that amenities, such as a small air cleaner, are permitted in your child's room.

✳ How are dorms cleaned? What products are used? And who does the cleaning—

staff or students themselves? Can less toxic products be used?

✳ Is cleaning done on a fixed schedule? Is the schedule flexible?

✳ Are the dorms or grounds sprayed with pesticides? When? Only during breaks?

✳ What big industries in the area contribute to air pollution?

✳ Can freshmen live off-campus in nearby apartments for medical reasons? Usually, off-campus living is restricted to upperclassmen and married students. How does your child feel about living off-campus versus on-campus?

✳ Is your child willing to shop for groceries and prepare food? Is this necessary, or can your child make do with cafeteria food?

✳ Is your child mature enough to live away from home and to handle a restricted diet without supervision? Or would a local community college be a better choice for the first year or two?

✳ Has your child been tested for molds, especially library molds? If not, consider testing and entering into a program of desensitization shots if test results warrant action.

Once your student is established on campus, you may want to send care packages of allergy-free goodies. What better way to express your love and to ensure that your student has access to healthful treats? Definitely send food during frenzied exam-time when eating patterns become erratic, to say the least. Pack boxes chock-full of ready-to-eat, good-for-you snacks.

PART

II

Recipes

Best-Ever Breakfasts

Breakfast no longer has to be the toughest meal of the day to plan, even if you're allergic to wheat, milk, or eggs. Here you'll find pancakes and waffles made of rice, teff, spelt, Kamut brand grain, barley, rye, and oats. For those who must avoid or rotate grains, there are breakfast breads and cereals made with amaranth, quinoa, buckwheat, pumpkin seeds, coconut, and carob.

Don't stop with breads and cereals, though. One of the things that helps allergic people most is to break out of the rut of eating the same old foods, day after day. Once you realize that breakfast doesn't have to consist of toast and eggs or cereal and milk, the possibilities are nearly endless. For example, consider having a leftover chicken leg or a piece of roast, reheated, if you wish. Or quickly cook a pork chop, lamb patty, or

piece of fresh fish, and add a few vegetables. I have also learned to relish soup in the morning.

For those mornings when time will be short, cook ahead the evening before. These dishes are great for make-aheads: Best Grain-Free Breakfast Bars, Oatmeal Patty Cakes, Rice Pudding with Apricots and Almonds, Instant Rice Pudding, and the slow-cooker version of Breakfast Oats Plus. In the morning, you can grab a couple of the bars and be eating within seconds. Another option: Reach into your freezer for something you made on a more leisurely day, when you doubled a recipe. Pancakes and waffles, for instance, reheat especially well in a toaster oven.

With all those options, breakfast can be as nutritious, satisfying, and easy to plan as the rest of the day's meals.

Whole Grain Pancakes

Relatively quick to whip up and cook. Sturdy enough to go brown-bagging, too.

1½ cups Kamut brand, spelt, or teff flour
1 teaspoon baking soda
1 teaspoon cream of tartar
¼ teaspoon salt
1½ cups soy milk or water
3 tablespoons vegetable oil
1–2 teaspoons agave nectar or maple syrup (optional)

PREHEAT A NONSTICK GRIDDLE or large skillet.

In a large bowl, whisk the flour, baking soda, cream of tartar, and salt.

In a 2-cup measure, combine the milk or water, oil and agave nectar or maple syrup. Pour into the flour mixture, and whisk just until combined. Don't beat or overmix.

Drop by spoonfuls (2 per cake) onto the griddle or skillet. Cook until the tops are bubbly and edges are brown. Turn and cook until light brown.

Makes about 12

COOK'S TIPS

✳ Other milks that I often use in this recipe include nut, rice, and goat's milk.

✳ If the batter thickens, add liquid, 1 tablespoon at a time, as needed.

Variation
Barley Pancakes: Substitute 2 cups barley flour for the flour and increase the water or milk to 2 cups. Makes about 14 pancakes.

Grain-Free Pancakes

Delicious and grain-free, these pancakes are sturdy enough to toast
(in an oven or toaster oven) and make into sandwiches for lunch.
For a real treat, use them as a grain-free bread for a nut butter sandwich.

½ **cup amaranth flour**

½ **cup white buckwheat flour**

½ **cup quinoa flakes or flour**

1 **teaspoon baking soda**

1 **teaspoon cream of tartar**
  or ½ teaspoon unbuffered
  vitamin C crystals

½ **teaspoon salt**

1⅓ **cups soy milk or water**

2 **tablespoons vegetable oil**

½ **tablespoon maple syrup or agave**
  nectar

PREHEAT A NONSTICK GRIDDLE or large skillet.

In a medium mixing bowl, combine the amaranth flour, buckwheat flour, quinoa flakes or flour, baking soda, cream of tartar or vitamin C, and salt.

In a small bowl, whisk the milk or water, oil, and maple syrup or agave nectar. Stir into the flour mixture and combine well.

Drop by spoonfuls onto the griddle or skillet. Cook until the tops are bubbly and edges are brown. Turn and cook until lightly brown. Serve at once.

Makes about 12

COOK'S TIPS

✳ To make white buckwheat flour, grind ½ cup white, unroasted whole groats at a time in a blender for 1 to 2 minutes. Pour into sieve. Repeat grinding, adding any groats that didn't go through the sieve.

✳ You can use quinoa flour instead of the flakes; if you do, increase the liquid to 1½ cups.

✳ Other milks that I often use in this recipe include nut, rice, and goat's milk.

✳ If you'd like to sweeten your pancakes with honey instead of maple syrup or agave nectar, combine it with ½ cup of the milk or water in a small pan. Heat the mixture, stirring, until the honey is thin. Add the oil and remaining milk or water.

✳ Thin the batter with water as needed.

Variation

Spiced Grain-Free Pancakes: Add 1 teaspoon ground cinnamon, ginger, or pumpkin pie spice.

Buckwheat Pancakes

People who love the flavor of buckwheat will enjoy these at breakfast,
topped with fruit, maple syrup, or Uncooked Fruit Sauce (page 208). Make enough to use
a few for sandwiches at lunch. They will happily go brown bagging!

1½ cups white buckwheat flour
1 teaspoon baking soda
1 teaspoon cream of tartar
½ teaspoon salt
1½ cups soy milk or water
3 tablespoons oil

PREHEAT A NONSTICK GRIDDLE or large skillet.

In a large bowl, whisk together the flour, baking soda, cream of tartar, and salt.

Make a well in the flour and pour in the water or milk and oil. Whisk just until the ingredients are combined.

Drop by spoonfuls onto the griddle or skillet. Cook until the tops are bubbly and edges are brown. Turn and cook until lightly brown. Serve at once.

Makes about 12

COOK'S TIPS

✳ To make white buckwheat flour, grind ½ cup white, unroasted whole groats at a time in a blender for 1 to 2 minutes. Pour into sieve. Repeat grinding, adding any groats that didn't go through the sieve.

✳ Other milks that I often use in this recipe include nut, rice, and goat's milk.

Variations

Spiced Buckwheat Pancakes: Add one of the following spices: 1 teaspoon of cinnamon or ginger (or ½ teaspoon of each), ½ teaspoon nutmeg, ⅛ teaspoon cloves, or 1½ teaspoons pumpkin pie spice. Or you can add 1 tablespoon grated fresh ginger; combine it with the other liquids in a blender first.

Sweet Buckwheat Pancakes: Add 1 to 2 teaspoons maple syrup along with the other liquids.

Coconut-Carob Pancakes

These unusual breakfast treats are sure to please. Children think
they are getting chocolate for breakfast and regard them as special treats. Make only
what you'll use for breakfast; they're too fragile to go brown bagging.

1 cup grated unsweetened coconut

1¼ cups water

1 tablespoon arrowroot or tapioca starch

3 tablespoons carob powder

⅓ cup chickpea flour

½ teaspoon baking soda

⅜ teaspoon white stevia powder

1 teaspoon vanilla extract (optional)

¼ teaspoon vitamin C crystals or ½ teaspoon cream of tartar

Maple syrup, all-fruit jam, or Goat's-Milk Yogurt (page 266) (optional)

PREHEAT A NONSTICK GRIDDLE or large skillet and mist with cooking spray.

In a small saucepan, combine the coconut with 1 cup of the water. Cook on medium-low heat for 10 minutes.

In a blender or food processor, combine the arrowroot or tapioca, carob powder, chickpea flour, baking soda, white stevia powder, coconut mixture, and the remaining ¼ cup water. Process on highest setting for 2 minutes. Add the vanilla and vitamin C crystals or cream of tartar and process for 5 to 10 seconds.

Pour batter into a small bowl and drop by spoonfuls onto the griddle or skillet and use the back of the spoon to spread the pancakes. Cook until brown on bottom and wait 3 to 5 minutes after bubbles appear before turning.

Turn and cook until brown. (Test for doneness by breaking a pancake in half. Slight moisture is okay.)

Serve topped with the syrup, jam, or yogurt.

Makes 2 servings

Pumpkin-Seed Pancakes

These simple milk-free, wheat-free, egg-free pancakes are a big help to people on a Rotary Diversified Diet. Make the pancakes very small so they will be thin and crisp and easy to turn. Eat them out of hand or top with fresh fruit, Pumpkin Butter (page 277), or mashed bananas.

½ **cup pumpkin seeds**
½ **cup boiling water**

COAT A NONSTICK GRIDDLE or large skillet with cooking spray and preheat.
   Grind the seeds to a fine powder in a blender. Add the water, and process for 30 seconds. Allow to rest for 5 minutes.
   Drop a scant tablespoon onto the griddle or skillet. Cook until bubbly on top and brown underneath. Turn and cook until brown and crisp. Serve at once.
Makes 1 serving

Three-Seed Pancakes

No wheat, no other grain flour, either. And no cow's milk or eggs. Are they still pancakes? You bet. Their texture is different—they are thinner, crisper, and a bit more fragile than traditional pancakes, almost cookie- or crackerlike. You may wish to eat them out of hand— I often do. Serving ideas: Spread with Hummus Bean Spread (page 271), Soft Goat's-Milk Cheese (page 262), or an all-fruit jam. Or lay a slice of banana, nectarine, or other fresh fruit on the pancake just before taking each bite.

¾ **cup pumpkin seeds**
2 **tablespoons anise seeds**
2 **tablespoons flax seeds**
2 **tablespoons of arrowroot or carob flour**
1 **tablespoon vegetable oil**
¼ **teaspoon salt**
1 **cup soy milk or water**

MIST A NONSTICK GRIDDLE or large skillet with cooking spray and preheat.
   In a small bowl, combine the pumpkin seeds, anise seeds, flax seeds, and arrowroot or carob flour. Process the seed mixture, half at a time, in a blender until ground. Stop the blender and scrape the sides and bottom. Process again.
   In the blender, combine the ground seed mixture, oil, salt, and ¾ cup of the milk or water. Process for 2 minutes. Scrape the sides, and process for 1 minute more. Pour into a

bowl. Pour the remaining ¼ cup of milk or water into the blender and process for 10 seconds. Stir into the seed mixture and let batter rest for 10 minutes.

Drop by spoonfuls onto the griddle or skillet. Cook until the tops are bubbly and edges are brown. Turn and cook until lightly brown. Serve at once.

Makes about 18

COOK'S TIPS

✳ Instead of the arrowroot or carob flour, you can use chickpea flour, kudzu starch (break up chunks first),

tapioca starch flour, or 1 tablespoon plus 1 teaspoon chestnut flour.

✳ Other milks that I often use in this recipe include nut, rice, and goat's milk.

✳ Batter may rest overnight in a covered contain in the refrigerator.

Variation
Sweet Seed Pancakes: Add ¼ to ½ teaspoon white stevia powder. Don't substitute any other sweetener, or these pancakes will scorch before they are done in the middle.

Rice-Flour Pancakes

Rice flour produces good tasting, tender baked goods and lovely pancakes.
Because they're a bit fragile, don't make these pancakes too thin. They make terrific sandwiches
and great go-alongs for soup or salad at home, but unlike Buckwheat Pancakes (page 90)
or Grain-Free Pancakes (page 89), they aren't sturdy enough for brown-bag sandwiches.

1 cup brown rice flour
1 teaspoon baking soda
1 teaspoon cream of tartar
1 teaspoon date or maple sugar
¼ teaspoon salt
¾ cup cooked brown rice
1 cup soy milk or water
2 tablespoons vegetable oil

OIL AND PREHEAT a nonstick griddle or skillet. In a large bowl, combine the rice flour, baking soda, cream of tartar, date or maple sugar, and salt. Stir in the rice and toss to coat.

In a 2-cup glass measure, combine the milk or water and oil. Pour into the flour

mixture, and mix just until combined. Do not beat or overmix.

Spoon onto the griddle or skillet. Cook until the tops are bubbly and edges are brown. Turn and cook until light brown. Serve at once.

Makes about 16

COOK'S TIPS

✳ Other milks that I often use in this recipe include nut, rice, and goat's milk.

✳ Maple syrup can replace the date or maple sugar; use 2 teaspoons of the syrup.

Variation
Rice-Flour Pancakes with Wild Rice: Substitute cooked wild rice for the brown rice.

Perfect Pancakes and Waffles

Here are a few pointers for wonderful waffles and pancakes every time.

For pancakes:

Allow ½ cup flour for each adult serving. If you want leftovers, add another ½ cup flour per adult. Based on the amount of flour required, you can estimate the amounts needed for other ingredients. Usually, the flour and liquids are added in equal or near-equal amounts. Record your ideal quantities for future reference.

Get a second pancake griddle. Using more than one griddle speeds up cooking and lets you cook the pancakes before the bubbles in the batter deflate from sitting too long.

Consider using a sweetener. Pancake recipes often call for 1 or 2 teaspoons of maple syrup or another sweetener. Though not necessary, the sweetener facilitates browning.

Wait for a little dance. Heat the griddle until a drop of water dances around before evaporating. If the drop just sits still, the griddle isn't hot enough; if the drop goes "poof!" into steam, the griddle is too hot.

Keep liquid and dry ingredients separate. Combine them when the griddle is hot, not before. Whisk the liquid and dry ingredients together just until combined, then quickly spoon onto the hot griddle. Batter that stands for too long will finish bubbling in the mixing bowl—and your pancakes won't rise.

Keep them warm. Wrap pancakes in a few layers of clean dish towel, but don't hold them for more than 10 to 15 minutes.

Spread them on a rack. To use pancakes as bread, place them on a wire rack right away, without keeping them warm. When cool, wrap in foil or waxed paper. Use within 24 hours, or freeze.

For waffles:

Oil the waffle iron. You can use an oil or a cooking spray to lubricate the grids of your waffle iron. If you prefer oil, use a pastry brush to spread the oil more easily. If necessary, repeat oiling after cooking the first waffle.

Always preheat. To avoid disappointment—and a messy cleanup—never pour batter into a waffle iron that isn't fully preheated. I find that setting my waffle iron on medium works best.

Mix quickly. Mix the liquid and dry ingredients just until combined; often about 10 stirs will do the trick. And bake promptly after combining those ingredients. If the batter sits too long, it will lose its leavening power.

Thin it out. Waffle batter is usually a little thicker than pancake batter, but if it thickens too much, stir in a tablespoon or two of water.

Use a glass 1-cup measure. Use 1 cup batter for each waffle in a 9" × 9" iron. An 8" round iron might need only ⅔ to ¾ cup batter. Don't use too much; the overflow may cement the top and bottom of the iron together.

Don't peek. Avoid opening the lid while baking; the waffle's top and bottom might separate. When it's done, it will stop steaming.

Be speedy. Work quickly when the waffle iron is open so it won't lose too much heat. Use a fork and knife to remove the waffle; then immediately pour in more batter (relubricating the iron if needed).

Save extras. Use within 24 hours, or freeze and use within a few weeks. Heat in a moderately hot oven for 2 to 5 minutes.

Whole Grain Waffles

These delicious waffles can be made with any of four different flours. But for best results, you'll need to vary the amounts of flour and liquid. See "Flour and Milk for Whole Grain Waffles" for the amount. And see Cook's Tips for ideas on milk.

Flour

1½ **teaspoons baking soda**

1½ **teaspoons cream of tartar or ¾ teaspoon unbuffered vitamin C crystals**

½ **teaspoon salt**

Milk

3 **tablespoons oil**

COOK'S TIPS

✳ Any of these milks works here: soy, rice, nut, or goat's milk. Both soy and rice milk come in vanilla flavor, which I found pleasant when testing. If you want to add a little vanilla to the nut or goat's milk, 1 teaspoon would be good.

✳ If batter thickens, stir in 1 or 2 tablespoons of water.

MIST A WAFFLE IRON with cooking spray, and preheat to medium according to the manufacturer's directions.

In a large bowl, whisk together the flour, baking soda, cream of tartar or vitamin C, and salt. In a 4-cup measure, combine the milk and oil. Pour into the flour mixture and mix just until combined. Don't overmix.

Using a 1-cup glass measure, pour into the prepared waffle iron and quickly close the lid. Cook until done; follow the waffle iron manufacturer's directions or watch for steaming to stop. Remove promptly. Repeat until all the batter has been used.

Makes about 4

Flour and Milk for Whole Grain Waffles

Choose a flour and the appropriate amount of milk; follow the Whole Grain Waffles recipe.

FLOUR		MILK
3 cups rye	*requires*	3½ cups milk
3 cups spelt	*requires*	2 cups milk
3 cups Kamut brand	*requires*	3 cups milk
4 cups barley	*requires*	3 cups milk

Grain-Free Waffles

These flours make waffles that are quite crisp, perfect for sandwiches on "toast."

1½ cups amaranth flour
¾ cup quinoa flour
¾ cup quinoa flakes
½ teaspoon salt
1½ teaspoons baking soda
1½ teaspoons cream of tartar
2½ cups soy milk or water
3 tablespoons vegetable oil

MIST A WAFFLE IRON with cooking spray, and preheat to medium-light according to the manufacturer's directions.

In a bowl, combine the amaranth flour, quinoa flour, quinoa flakes, salt, baking soda, and cream of tartar.

In a 4-cup measure, combine the milk or water and oil. Pour into the flour mixture and mix just until combined. Don't overmix.

Using a 1-cup glass measure, pour into the prepared waffle iron and quickly close the lid. Cook until done; follow the waffle iron manufacturer's directions or watch for steaming to stop. Remove promptly. Repeat until all the batter has been used.

Makes about 4

COOK'S TIPS

* Other milks that I often use in this recipe include nut, rice, and goat's milk.

* For a softer waffle, substitute 2 tablespoons of arrowroot or tapioca starch for 2 tablespoons of the amaranth flour.

Carob-Buckwheat Waffles

When my grandchildren were younger, they used to beg me to make these "chocolate" waffles—adults love them, too.

2 cups white buckwheat flour
¾ cup + 2 tablespoons toasted carob powder
2 tablespoons tapioca starch or arrowroot
1½ teaspoons baking soda
1½ teaspoons cream of tartar or ¾ teaspoon unbuffered vitamin C crystals

½ teaspoon salt
¼ teaspoon white stevia powder (optional)
2⅔ cups soy milk or water
¼ cup vegetable oil
1½ teaspoons vanilla extract (optional)

MIST A WAFFLE IRON with cooking spray, and preheat to medium according to the manufacturer's directions.

In a bowl, combine buckwheat flour, carob, tapioca or arrowroot, baking soda, cream of tartar or vitamin C, salt, and stevia if using.

In a 4-cup measure, combine the milk or water, oil, and vanilla if using. Pour into the flour mixture and mix just until combined. Don't overmix. Using a 1-cup glass measure, pour into the waffle iron and quickly close. Cook until done; follow the manufacturer's directions or watch for steaming to stop. Remove promptly. Repeat to use all the batter.

Makes about 4

COOK'S TIPS

* To make white buckwheat flour, grind ½ cup white, unroasted whole groats at a time in a blender for 1 to 2 minutes. Pour into sieve. Repeat grinding, adding any groats that didn't go through the sieve.

* Other milks that I often use in this recipe include nut, rice, and goat's milk.

Variation

Carob Waffles with Nuts: Add ½ cup chopped pecans and increase the white stevia powder to a scant ½ teaspoon.

Oatmeal Patty Cakes

We served this to a teenager who's allergic to milk, and he was delighted to be able to enjoy breakfast cereal again. It takes just 15 minutes to prepare.

1⅔ **cups water**
½ **cup rolled oats**
⅓ **cup oat bran**
¼ **teaspoon salt**
¼ **cup raisins (optional)**
2 **teaspoons flax oil (optional)**
2–4 **tablespoons Old-Fashioned Fruit Butter (page 280)**
4 **tablespoons chopped pecans**

IN A SAUCEPAN, combine the water, rolled oats, oat bran, salt, and raisins if using. Bring to a boil. Reduce the heat, cover, and cook for 10 minutes, stirring, or until very thick. Remove from heat. Stir in the oil if using.

Spoon a mound onto each of 2 plates. With the back of a spoon, flatten the mounds into patties, about ¾" thick. Top with fruit butter and sprinkle with nuts.

Makes 2 servings

COOK'S TIP

* You can use steel-cut oats instead of the rolled oats. Increase the cooking time to 30 minutes.

Variation

Fried Breakfast Oat Cakes: Cook the oats ahead (up to 10 hours) and omit the oil. Scrape onto an oiled pie plate. Cover and chill. To serve, cut into wedges and cook in vegetable oil in a nonstick skillet for 5–6 minutes. Turn and cook for 3 to 4 minutes more.

Breakfast Shortcake

I didn't even realize this had become my house special until a house guest asked if I would be serving "the house special" for breakfast while she was visiting. I had to ask what she meant but had no trouble complying. People do tend to regard eating shortcake for breakfast as something special.

1 **Country-Style Quick Bread (page 121)**
1 **pound frozen peaches**
¼ **cup maple syrup**
1¼ **cups water**
1½ **tablespoons arrowroot or tapioca starch**
   Goat's-Milk Yogurt (page 266) (optional)

WHILE THE QUICK BREAD is baking, combine the peaches, maple syrup, and 1 cup of the water in a saucepan. Bring to a boil. Reduce the heat, and cook for 8 to 10 minutes, or until softened. Cut the fruit into bite-size pieces.

Dissolve the arrowroot or tapioca starch in the remaining ¼ cup of water. Add to the peaches, and cook, stirring briskly, for 1 minute, or until the sauce is thick and clear. Remove from the heat.

Let the bread cool in the pan for 10 to 15 minutes. Cut into 6 pieces, and split each piece in half horizontally. Top the halves with the fruit sauce and the yogurt if using.

Makes 3 servings

COOK'S TIPS

* Other fruits I'm especially fond of using in this recipe include sweet black (pitted) cherries and fresh or frozen blueberries.

* Honey and light agave nectar also work very nicely in the sauce.

* To serve 4, use 1½ pounds of fruit.

* Make the Country-Style Quick Bread with 1 to 1½ teaspoons minced fresh or dried ginger.

Variation

Breakfast Strawberry Shortcake: Replace the peaches, maple syrup, water, and arrowroot with 5 cups of strawberries. Slice 4 cups of the berries and place in a bowl. Combine 2–3 tablespoons honey or light agave nectar and the remaining 1 cup strawberries in a blender. Process until liquefied. Pour over the sliced berries.

Banana-Buckwheat Breakfast Cake

Unroasted buckwheat's mild flavor is enhanced by banana and maple. Serve this breakfast cake plain or shortcake-style, with Pineapple Preserves (page 277).

1½ cups white buckwheat flour

2 tablespoons arrowroot or tapioca starch

1 teaspoon baking soda

1 teaspoon cream of tartar

½ teaspoon salt

½ teaspoon white stevia powder

1⅓–1½ cups mashed bananas

⅓ cup walnut oil

½ cup maple syrup

PREHEAT THE OVEN to 350°F. Oil an 8" × 8" baking pan.

In a large mixing bowl, whisk together the flour, arrowroot or tapioca starch, baking soda, cream of tartar, salt, and white stevia powder.

In another bowl, combine the bananas, oil, and maple syrup. Pour into the flour mixture and mix just until combined.

Pour into the prepared pan and bake for 20 to 22 minutes, or until the top is brown and a cake tester inserted in the center comes out clean. Cool in the pan on a rack. Serve warm or at room temperature.

Makes 1

COOK'S TIP

✳ To make white buckwheat flour, grind ½ cup white, unroasted whole groats at a time in a blender for 1 to 2 minutes. Pour into sieve. Repeat grinding, adding any groats that didn't go through the sieve.

Variations

Banana-Brazil Nut Breakfast Cake: Add ⅓ cup chopped Brazil nuts and ½ teaspoon freshly grated nutmeg if you wish.

Banana-Buckwheat Bread: Omit the maple syrup and compensate for the reduction of liquid by adding ⅓ cup water.

Breakfast Oats Plus

This hot and hearty cereal combines oats with amaranth and quinoa for a high protein dish. It's supremely satisfying with or without milk. When prepared in a slow cooker overnight, this dish becomes the ultimate in ready-to-eat cereal.

⅔ **cup rolled oats**

¼ **cup oat bran**

¼ **cup quinoa flakes or soy grits**

¼ **cup toasted amaranth flakes or soy grits**

½ **cup raisins, dates, or currants (optional)**

4 **cups water**

½ **teaspoon salt**

Sweet Nut Milk (page 302); soy, rice, or goat's milk (optional)

Date sugar, agave nectar, or maple syrup (optional)

IN A 3-QUART PAN, combine the rolled oats, oat bran, quinoa flakes or soy grits, amaranth flakes or soy grits, and raisins, dates, or currants. Stir in the water and salt. Cover, and cook over low heat for 30 minutes, stirring every 10 minutes.

Serve with the milk and a sweetener.

Makes 4 servings

COOK'S TIPS

* If you're in a hurry, you can cook this cereal for just 10 minutes. For this option, don't use the soy grits, which require 30 minutes of cooking.

* If you have either amaranth or quinoa flakes, but not both, double up on the one you've got (use ½ cup).

* To make this cereal in a slow cooker, combine all the ingredients—except the fruit—in a 5-cup cooker. Cover and cook for 8 hours on low. Add the fruit right before serving, and mix well.

* If you're not serving the cereal with milk, add ½ cup more water for a creamier consistency.

* You can keep the cereal warm over low heat for up to half an hour. Add water as needed and stir occasionally.

Best Grain-Free Breakfast Bars

Looking for a quick yet satisfying breakfast-on-the-go? Look no further. These bars, which freeze beautifully, pack plenty of flavor and protein—thanks to nuts, seeds, and fruits.

¾ **cup amaranth flour**

¾ **cup white buckwheat flour**

½ **cup quinoa flakes**

½ **cup walnuts, chopped**

¼ **cup sunflower seeds**

¼ **cup sesame seeds**

1 **teaspoon baking soda**

1 **teaspoon cream of tartar**

1½ **teaspoons pumpkin pie spice**

½ **teaspoon salt**

¾ **cup chickpeas**

⅔ **cup soy milk**

1 **banana, broken into 1" pieces**

⅓ **cup walnut oil**

½ **cup maple syrup or honey**

1½ **teaspoons vanilla extract**

⅔ **cup raisins or dates or ⅓ cup currants (optional)**

PREHEAT THE OVEN to 350°F. Oil an 11" × 7" baking pan.

In a large bowl, mix the amaranth flour, buckwheat flour, quinoa flakes, nuts, sunflower seeds, sesame seeds, baking soda, cream of tartar, pumpkin pie spice, and salt.

In a blender or food processor, combine the chickpeas, milk, banana, oil, maple syrup or honey, and vanilla. Pour into the flour mixture and stir to mix well. (Mixture will be quite thick and heavy.) Stir in the raisins, dates, or currants if using.

Spread in the prepared pan. Bake for 20 minutes or until set. Cool in the pan on a rack. Cut into 12 bars. Store wrapped in plastic wrap.

Makes 12

COOK'S TIPS

✳ To make white buckwheat flour, grind ½ cup white, unroasted whole groats at a time in a blender for 1 to 2 minutes. Pour into sieve. Repeat grinding, adding any groats that didn't go through the sieve.

✳ Other milks that I often use in this recipe include nut, rice, and goat's milk.

✳ Feel free to use any other favorite nuts in this recipe: almonds, Brazil nuts, pecans.

✳ If you want, you can use light agave nectar in place of the syrup or honey.

Variations

Carob Breakfast Bars: Reduce the amaranth flour by ¼ cup and add ¼ cup of carob powder. Omit the pumpkin pie spice.

Dark Breakfast Bars: Use dark agave nectar instead of the maple syrup or honey and use raisins.

Spicy Breakfast Bars: Replace the pumpkin pie spice with ½ teaspoon ground cinnamon, ½ teaspoon ginger powder, and ¼ teaspoon freshly ground nutmeg. Use singularly or in combination. If using singularly, double the amount of the spice.

High-Protein Granola

*Combining a grain with a legume, seeds, nuts, and quinoa or amaranth gives you
a high-protein breakfast dish. That's a plus if you can't drink milk or eat eggs.
Try this with Goat's-Milk Yogurt (page 266) and a sliced banana
or with Pineapple Milk (page 305).*

      3 **cups rolled oats**
      1 **cup quinoa flakes or toasted
         amaranth flakes**
   ½–¾ **cup halved Brazil nuts, almonds, or
         filberts**
      ½ **cup sunflower seeds**
      ½ **teaspoon salt**
      ⅓ **cup almond or sunflower oil**
      ½ **cup honey, agave nectar, or maple
         syrup**
      1 **teaspoon vanilla extract (optional)**
   ½–¾ **cup raisins (optional)**

PREHEAT THE OVEN to 350°F. Oil a jelly-
roll pan or line it with parchment paper.

In a large bowl, combine the oats, quinoa
or amaranth flakes, nuts, seeds, and salt.

In a small saucepan, combine the oil and
honey, agave nectar, or maple syrup. Heat
for 1 to 2 minutes, or until the honey is thin
(don't boil). Remove from heat and stir in
the vanilla. Pour over the oat mixture. Toss
to coat.

Spread in a thin layer in the prepared
pan. Bake for 30 minutes, stirring every 10

minutes. Turn off the oven and leave the
door ajar. Let the mixture cool slowly in
the oven.

Stir in the raisins if using. Spoon into a
container with a tight-fitting lid. Store at
room temperature and use within 2 weeks.
For longer storage, refrigerate.

Makes about 7 cups

COOK'S TIPS

* Instead of 1 cup of quinoa flakes or toasted
  amaranth flakes, you can use ½ cup of each.

* Instead of ½ cup sunflower seeds, you can use ¼
  cup sunflower seeds and ¼ cup sesame seeds.

* Dried fruits such as apricots, bananas, pineapple,
  apples, peaches, and pears can replace the raisins
  if you wish. Chop large pieces of fruit.

Variation

Fruit-Sweetened Granola: Omit the honey, agave
nectar, or maple syrup. Instead, combine the
oil, 1 large ripe banana (broken into 1"
pieces), ¾ cup pineapple juice (one 6-ounce
can), and ¾ teaspoon white stevia powder in
a blender. Process for 1 minute, or until
smooth, and pour over the oats mixture.

Traditional Swiss Muesli

This is a very chewy Swiss-style breakfast-in-a-bowl that's enormously satisfying.
Choose tart-sweet apples and top with more apple juice, if you like.

¾ **cup rolled oats, toasted**
1 **apple or pear, chopped**
½ **cup chopped walnuts or pecans**
4 **tablespoons sunflower seeds**
4–6 **tablespoons raisins or currants**
½ **cup thawed apple-juice concentrate**
    Goat's-Milk Yogurt (page 266) or
    store-bought yogurt (optional)

DIVIDE THE OATS, apple or pear, nuts, seeds, and raisins or currants between 2 cereal bowls. Toss to combine and pour in the juice concentrate. Top with the yogurt if using.

Makes 2 servings

COOK'S TIP

✳ To toast the oats, spread them in a nonstick skillet. Cook, stirring often, over medium heat for 5 minutes, or until lightly browned and fragrant.

Creamy Breakfast Cereal

This cereal is ideal for infants, toddlers, and convalescents. The consistency is similar to a heavy cream soup, and you can prepare it in 8 to 10 minutes. Soaking the grain overnight and then whisking the cereal as it cooks produces a very smooth, lump-free porridge. And the variations that follow give you a wide choice for rotating foods.

1 cup water
⅓ cup brown rice, oat, or rye flour
1 tablespoon maple syrup
Pinch of salt (optional)
1–2 teaspoons flax oil

EIGHT HOURS AHEAD: Pour the water into a small saucepan. Sift or strain the flour into the water, whisking until smooth. Discard particles remaining in the sieve. Cover, and allow to stand for 8 to 10 hours.

Bring to a boil. Add the maple syrup and salt if using. Reduce the heat to medium. Cook, whisking constantly for 8 to 10 minutes, or until thickened. Remove from the heat and stir in the oil.

Makes 1 serving

COOK'S TIPS

* Other grains that work quite nicely in this recipe include millet, white buckwheat, spelt, Kamut brand grain, teff, or amaranth flour; quinoa flakes; or ½ cup barley flour.

* You can also sweeten this recipe with a fruit juice concentrate; omit the maple syrup if you wish.

* For a thicker cereal, add 1 tablespoon of flour.

* Infants may lack the enzymes necessary to digest gluten-containing foods. Therefore, check with your pediatrician before offering your infant or young child foods containing spelt, Kamut brand grain, oat, barley, wheat, or rye.

Variation

Creamy Breakfast Cereal with Milk: Replace all or part of the water with soy or goat's milk.

Mix-and-Match Breakfast Pudding

*The formula for this dish is quite simple: Take a starchy food, and add a fruit,
a sweetener, and some kind of nuts. The recipe offers many choices—you could eat it
every day for a week without repeating yourself!*

**1 cup cooked starch: millet or brown
rice**

½–⅔ cup pureed fruit: apricots or peaches

**2 tablespoons thawed juice
concentrate: orange or apple**

**¼–⅓ cup coarsely chopped unsalted nuts:
almonds or Brazil nuts**

PLACE THE MILLET or brown rice in a
large cereal bowl.

In a blender, combine the fruit and juice
concentrate and process until smooth. Pour
over millet or brown rice. Top with nuts.

Makes 1 serving

COOK'S TIPS

✳ In place of the millet or brown rice, I also like to use
any of the following: chopped cooked sweet potato,
chopped cooked winter squash, cooked whole
quinoa, hulled barley, or unroasted buckwheat
groats.

✳ Other favorite fruits that work nicely in this pudding
include fresh or canned pineapple chunks with juice,
bananas, kiwifruits, pears, applesauce or apple
butter, and berries. Use singularly or in combination.

✳ Instead of the orange or apple juice, I often use one
of the following concentrates to sweeten the
pudding: white grape juice, pineapple juice, or
lemonade. Other times I use a little maple syrup,
honey, or agave nectar.

✳ Four other nuts that are great here include
hazelnuts, pecans, pine nuts, and walnuts. These
can be used raw or toasted.

✳ To toast small nuts and seeds, spread them in a
small nonstick skillet. Cook, stirring often, over
medium-low heat for 5 minutes, or until lightly
browned and fragrant.

Instant Rice Pudding

Similar to Mix-and-Match Breakfast Pudding (page 105), this quick breakfast-in-a-bowl is nicely satisfying and supplies lots of vitamins, minerals and fiber. It's a great alternative to ready-to-eat cereals and milk. Adding nuts or seeds boosts the protein content.

¾ **cup unsweetened pineapple juice**

8–10 **pitted dates, quartered**

1½ **cups warm or cold cooked brown rice**

⅓ **cup almonds, peanuts, or sunflower seeds (optional)**

Goat's-Milk Yogurt (page 266) or store-bought goat's-milk yogurt (optional)

IN A BLENDER or mini-food processor, combine the juice and dates. Pulse for 20 seconds, or until the dates are chopped.

Divide the rice between two large cereal bowls. Pour the date mixture over the rice. Top with nuts or seeds if using and yogurt if using.

Makes 2 servings

COOK'S TIP
---

* Looking for something quick and hot? Warm this pudding briefly in your microwave oven.

Rice Pudding with Apricots and Almonds

Try this pudding in place of hot or cold cereal. It's milk-free and delicious.

8 **ounces low-fat tofu, drained and crumbled**

¾ **cup unsweetened apple-apricot juice**

2 **tablespoons apple-juice concentrate**

Pinch of salt

1½ **cups hot or cold cooked brown rice**

⅔ **cup chopped dried apricots, softened in hot water**

Chopped toasted almonds

IN A BLENDER or food processor, combine the tofu, juice, juice concentrate, and salt. Process until smooth.

Divide the rice between two cereal bowls and top with the apricots, tofu mixture, and nuts.

Makes 2 servings

COOK'S TIPS
---

* To toast nuts, cook in a nonstick skillet, stirring often, over medium-low heat for 5 minutes, or until lightly browned and fragrant.

* For a warm pudding, heat the tofu mixture over medium heat, stirring constantly. Do not boil.

* To save leftover tofu, place it in a wide-mouth pint jar and cover it with cold water. Refrigerate for up to a week, changing the water every couple of days.

Sweet-Potato Delight

When I was eating a fairly restricted diet, this simple dish was my favorite grain-free breakfast or lunch fare—along with a bit of leftover meat, fish, or poultry to provide just a bit more protein. I often bake or steam an extra sweet potato at dinner, wrap, and save it just for this dish. It's a big help for people who follow a Rotary Diversified Diet because it's nearly a meal in itself.

1 teaspoon vegetable oil

1 banana, halved lengthwise

1 sweet potato, cooked, peeled, and cut into ½" slices

2–4 tablespoons chopped pecans or pine nuts, toasted

1 tablespoon maple syrup or agave nectar (optional)

HEAT THE OIL in a large skillet over medium heat. Add the banana, flat sides down, and sweet potato in a single layer. Cover, and cook for 2 minutes. Uncover, and cook for 5 minutes more, or until heated through and browned on one side.

Arrange on a plate, browned sides up. Scatter nuts over the top and drizzle with syrup or agave nectar if using.

Makes 1 serving

COOK'S TIP

---

* To toast small nuts and seeds, spread them in a small nonstick skillet. Cook, stirring often, over medium-low heat for 5 minutes, or until lightly browned and fragrant.

Poached Eggs in Zucchini Nests

A great Sunday morning option. For a totally grain-free breakfast, omit the rice layer and serve the eggs with crisply toasted Grain-Free Pancakes (page 89).

1 **cup cooked brown rice (optional)**

1 **large zucchini, shredded**

2–4 **eggs**

 Salt

2 **teaspoons capers or chopped black olives (optional)**

⅔ **cup Tomato Sauce (page 199) or Creamy Mustard Sauce (page 197), warmed**

PREHEAT THE OVEN to 300°F. Oil poaching cups.

Divide the rice between 2 oven-safe bowls or plates. Place the bowls or plates in the oven, and turn off the heat.

Steam the zucchini over boiling water for 3 or 4 minutes.

Meanwhile, cook the eggs for 6 minutes in poaching cups or barely simmering salted water until the egg whites are set.

Top the rice with the zucchini, 1 or 2 eggs, and the sauce. Sprinkle with the capers or black olives if using.

Makes 2 servings

COOK'S TIP

＊ Capers are very salty; rinse and drain them before using them.

Eggs Florentine

This spectacular breakfast or brunch dish is lovely with brown rice or quinoa and a fruit cup.

1–1½ **cups Creamed Spinach (page 175)**

4 **eggs**

 Salt

 Pepper

¼ **cup grated goat's- or sheep's-milk Cheddar cheese or soy cheese (optional)**

PREHEAT THE OVEN to 375°F.

Prepare the creamed spinach in a large oven-safe skillet. Make 4 depressions in spinach mixture. Break an egg into each depression. Season the eggs with the salt and pepper to taste. Sprinkle with the cheese if using.

Bake for 10 minutes, or until the egg whites are set. Serve immediately.

Makes 4 servings

COOK'S TIP

＊ You can also prepare and serve this dish in oiled individual ramekins.

Better Breads

Bread is the single greatest concern for people with wheat and yeast allergies. Your quest for suitable bread may even be what prompted you to buy this book. You made the right decision—many wheat-free and yeast-free breads are possible if you think beyond the pre-sliced, airy loaves sold in grocery stores. After all, people met their bread needs very well for thousands of years by simply combining whatever flour was available with water; patting the dough into a flat, round shape; and cooking it quickly on hot rocks at a fire's edge. The various tortillas given here use that same idea. (Crackers are simply a variation of flat breads and are found in the Snacks chapter on page 281.)

Skillet bread, too, is a very simple yet satisfying alternative to sliced bread. Quick Skillet Bread can be made with any one of five different flours. Surely there's at least one version for you.

Fresh Apple Muffins

Spelt and Kamut brand grains offer nutrition and flavor
and need be sweetened only with fruit juice and a little white stevia powder.

2 cups whole grain cold cereal flakes

1 cup soy or goat's milk

½ cup thawed apple juice concentrate

3 tablespoons sunflower oil

1 cup coarsely chopped apple

2 cups spelt or Kamut brand flour

2½ teaspoons Corn-Free Baking Powder (page 212)

½ teaspoon baking soda

½ teaspoon salt

½ teaspoon ground cinnamon (optional)

¼ teaspoon freshly ground nutmeg (optional)

½ teaspoon white stevia powder

PREHEAT THE OVEN TO 400°F. Oil and flour a 12-cup muffin pan.

In a bowl, combine the cereal, milk, juice concentrate, and oil. Stir in the chopped apple.

In another bowl, whisk together the flour, baking powder, baking soda, salt, cinnamon if using, nutmeg if using, and white stevia powder. Add to the cereal mixture and mix just until moistened.

Spoon into the prepared muffin cups, filling them almost full. Bake for 16 to 18 minutes, or until brown and firm when touched in the center. Cool in the pan on a rack for 5 minutes. Remove to the rack and cool completely.

Serve warm or at room temperature.

Makes 12

COOK'S TIPS

✳ In health food stores, you can find spelt flake and Kamut brand flake cold cereals, as well as other multigrain cereals. Read labels carefully. If you wish to avoid cane sugar, stay away from organic sugar and evaporated cane juice as well.

✳ If you want, you can make these muffins with water instead of the milk.

✳ Tightly wrapped, these muffins will retain their quality for at least 2 days at room temperature. They also freeze well.

Grain-Free Banana-Nut Muffins

By using plenty of bananas, you'll get a rich banana flavor in these grain-free muffins.

¾ cup white buckwheat flour

¾ cup quinoa flour

½ cup amaranth flour

1½ teaspoons baking soda

½ teaspoon unbuffered vitamin C crystals

¼–½ teaspoon freshly grated nutmeg (optional)

⅔ cup chopped Brazil nuts

5 bananas (2 cups, about 1½ pounds)

¼ cup canola oil

¼ cup agave nectar, maple syrup, or honey

PREHEAT THE OVEN to 375°F. Oil a 12-cup muffin pan.

Sift the buckwheat flour, quinoa flour, amaranth flour, baking soda, vitamin C, and nutmeg if using into a large bowl. Stir in the nuts.

Break 4 of the bananas into 1" pieces and place them in a blender. Process for 30 seconds, or until smooth. Add the remaining banana if needed to make 2 cups and process until smooth. Add the oil and agave nectar, maple syrup or honey, and process until mixed. Pour into the flour mixture and mix just until combined. Don't overmix.

Spoon into the prepared muffin cups, filling them almost full. Bake for 17 to 20 minutes, or until firm when touched in the center and a cake-tester inserted in the center comes out clean.

Makes 12

COOK'S TIP

* To make white buckwheat flour, grind ½ cup white, unroasted whole groats at a time in a blender for 1 to 2 minutes. Pour into sieve. Repeat grinding, adding any groats that didn't go through the sieve.

* Substitute other nuts if you wish.

Pineapple-Cranberry Muffins with Quinoa

Including a sweet fruit with the cranberry provides a nice balance in the flavor.

2 cups quinoa flour

2 tablespoons tapioca starch or arrowroot

1½ teaspoons baking soda

½ teaspoon salt

⅓ cup chopped toasted walnuts or pecans (optional)

1 cup fresh cranberries, chopped, or ⅔ cup dried

½ cup warm water

½ cup thawed pineapple juice concentrate

Grated peel of 1 orange (optional)

¼ cup walnut oil

¼ cup agave nectar or honey

PREHEAT THE OVEN to 375°F. Oil a 12-cup muffin pan or line with paper cups.

In a large bowl, whisk the flour, tapioca or arrowroot, baking soda, and salt. Stir in the nuts if using.

In a small bowl, combine the cranberries, water, juice concentrate, orange peel if using, oil, and agave nectar or honey. Pour into the flour mixture and mix just until combined. Don't overmix.

Spoon into the prepared muffin cups, filling them almost full. Bake for 17 to 19 minutes, or until firm when touched in the center and a cake-tester inserted in the center comes out clean. Cool in the pan on a rack for 5 minutes. Remove to the rack and cool completely.

Makes 12

Variation

Orange-Cranberry Muffins: Replace the pineapple juice concentrate with orange juice concentrate.

Pumpkin Spice Muffins

Easy to make—and great flavor!

1¼ cups barley flour

¾ cup rye flour

¼ cup maple or date sugar

2 teaspoons pumpkin pie spice

1½ teaspoons baking soda

¾ teaspoon unbuffered vitamin C crystals

½ teaspoon salt

½ cup raisins or dried cranberries

1 cup pumpkin puree

¾ cup goat's or soy milk

¼ cup sunflower oil

¼ cup maple syrup or light or dark agave nectar

PREHEAT THE OVEN to 375°F. Oil a 12-cup muffin pan or line with paper cups.

In a bowl, whisk the flours, maple or date sugar, pumpkin pie spice, baking soda, vitamin C, and salt. Stir in the raisins or cranberries.

In another bowl, whisk the pumpkin, goat's or soy milk, oil, and maple syrup or agave nectar. Pour into the flour mixture and mix just until combined. Don't overmix.

Spoon into the prepared muffin cups, filling them almost full. Bake for 16 to 18 minutes, or until firm when touched in the center and a cake-tester inserted in the center comes out clean. Cool in the pan on a rack for 5 minutes. Remove to the rack and cool completely.

Makes 12

COOK'S TIP

* If milk bothers you, make these muffins with water instead.

Grain-Free Blueberry Muffins

These grain-free muffins are quite light with excellent texture.

1 cup buckwheat flour

1 cup quinoa flour

¾ cup amaranth flour

2 tablespoons tapioca starch

½ teaspoon xanthan gum

2¼ teaspoons baking soda

1 teaspoon vitamin C crystals

¾ teaspoon salt

1 cup water

⅓ cup canola oil

½ cup agave nectar, maple syrup, or honey

1 cup fresh or frozen blueberries

PREHEAT THE OVEN to 375°F. Oil a 12-cup muffin pan or line with paper cups.

In a bowl, whisk the buckwheat flour, quinoa flour, amaranth flour, tapioca starch, xanthan gum, baking soda, vitamin C, and salt.

In a 2-cup glass measure, whisk the water, oil, and agave nectar, maple syrup, or honey. Pour into the flour mixture and mix just until combined. Don't overmix. Fold in the blueberries.

Spoon into the prepared muffin cups, filling them almost full. Bake for 15 to 17 minutes, or until firm when touched in the center, lightly browned, and a cake-tester inserted in the center comes out clean. Cool in the pan on a rack for 5 minutes. Remove to the rack and cool completely.

Makes 12

COOK'S TIP

* If using frozen blueberries, scatter them on a plate to partially thaw.

Variation

Sweet Grain-Free Blueberry Muffins: Add ½ teaspoon white stevia powder to the flour mixture.

Oat Bran Muffins

Each muffin contains 2 tablespoons of oat bran—yet their texture is light.

¾ cup brown rice flour

1 tablespoon tapioca starch

½ teaspoon xanthan gum

2 teaspoons baking soda

½ teaspoon salt

1½ cups oat bran

⅓ cup raisins or currants

1 cup pureed banana

¾ cup pineapple juice

½ teaspoon unbuffered vitamin C crystals

⅓ cup canola oil

2 tablespoons maple syrup

PREHEAT THE OVEN to 400°F. Oil a 12-cup muffin pan or line with paper cups.

In a small bowl, whisk the brown rice flour, tapioca starch flour, xanthan gum, baking soda, and salt.

In a large bowl, combine the oat bran and raisins or currants. In a blender, combine the banana, pineapple juice, vitamin C, oil, and maple syrup. Process for 30 seconds and pour into the oat bran mixture. Stir to mix. Allow to soak 5 or 10 minutes. Add the flour mixture and mix just until combined. Don't overmix.

Spoon into the prepared muffin cups, filling them almost full. Bake for 15 to 17 minutes, or until firm when touched in the center, lightly browned, crusty, and a cake-tester inserted in the center comes out clean.

Makes 12

Rhubarb Oat-and-Rice Muffins

*Oat and rice flours work well together and produce muffins
that are tender and a little crumbly.*

1 cup oat flour

1 cup brown rice flour

2 teaspoons baking soda

½ teaspoon salt

1½ cups chopped rhubarb, fresh or
frozen

½ cup apple or white grape juice
concentrate

¼ cup water

¼ cup canola or other oil

PREHEAT THE OVEN to 375°F. Oil a 12-
cup muffin pan or line with paper cups.

In a large bowl, whisk the oat flour, rice
flour, baking soda, and salt.

In a saucepan, combine the rhubarb, juice
concentrate, and water. Bring to a boil, and
cook for 15 minutes, or until the fruit starts
to fall apart when stirred. Strain, reserving
the juice. Measure the juice, and if necessary,
add water until the liquid measures ¾ cup.
Stir into the fruit and whisk in the oil.

Pour into the flour mixture and mix just
until combined. Don't overmix. Fold in
rhubarb with its juice.

Spoon into the prepared muffin cups,
filling them almost full. Bake for 18 to 20
minutes, or until firm when touched in the
center and a cake-tester inserted in the
center comes out clean. Cool in the pan on
a rack for 5 minutes. Remove to the rack
and cool completely.

Makes 12

Variations

Spiced Rhubarb Muffins: Add ½ teaspoon
ground allspice, ¾ teaspoon ground cinnamon, or ½ teaspoon grated nutmeg.

Sweet Rhubarb Muffins: Use ¾ cup fruit juice
concentrate and omit the water.

Pineapple Muffins: No stovetop cooking is
necessary. Drain two 8-ounce cans of
crushed pineapple, reserving the juice. Replace the water with pineapple juice. Use
1½ cups of the drained pineapple.

Quick Breads without Wheat, Milk, Egg, and Cane Sugar

Making a successful quick bread without the traditional ingredients—wheat, milk, eggs, and cane sugar—presents a challenge. But I've found six possible solutions, offered in this chapter.

Use a different pan. By moving the batter (with alternative ingredients for wheat, milk, eggs, and refined sugar) out of a loaf pan and into a flat container, such as a pie plate or an 8" pan, you can bake a crumbly corn-style bread that's delightful as well as quick and easy to make. Country-Style Quick Bread (page 121) has the texture of cornbread and the flavor of whatever grain you choose.

Experiment with xanthan gum. Though this product is a little pricey, one bag usually lasts me at least two years—and I bake a lot. It takes very little xanthan gum in a recipe to work its magic, and I've learned to use the least amount that will enhance baked goods: The amount I use ranges from ½ teaspoon per cup of flour in gluten-free or low-gluten yeast breads to ½ teaspoon in a whole recipe. More is *not* better. If you put too much xanthan gum in a bread recipe it imparts a wet, gummy texture. But here's what it does well when used in miniscule amounts: It provides structure for nongluten or low-gluten breads and enables them to rise with either yeast or baking soda leavening. It binds ingredients together in breads and muffins much as eggs do and reduces the tendency of egg-free baked goods to crumble and fall apart (try the Banana Bread on page 120 to see proof of how beautifully and cleanly an egg-free bread can be cut!). And it helps hold moisture so baked goods will still be tender two or three days after baking and will survive freezing with a nice texture.

Get acquainted with steamed breads. These breads are a delightful egg-free treat. But they do require about 2 hours for steaming. I've only included a few steamed breads.

Focus on muffins. The muffin recipes in this book are so light and good-tasting, it's hard to believe they're made without wheat, milk, or eggs. And they taste sweet without using cane sugar. At our house, where sweet desserts are the exception rather than the rule, muffins have been known to take the place of cake, cookies, or pie. Or we eat them as a snack, with a cup of herb tea. I always feel ahead of the game when I have several muffins stored in the freezer. For top quality, use frozen muffins within a few weeks.

Try tortillas. After chatting with several people who had allergies, I discovered that many were using a handy-dandy electric appliance called the Tortilla Chef for making made-to-order flour and water breads. Somewhat reluctantly, I ordered one for about $50. It's great! All the cook has to do is mix a little flour and water and add salt, if desired. It makes short work of pressing and baking tortillas. Of course, you can make tortillas without the appliance, too; I did for years.

Become a fan of pancakes and waffles. Recipes for these quick breads appear in the Best-Ever Breakfasts chapter on page 87. I use leftover pancakes or waffles for sandwiches, heat them in a toaster oven for toast, and chop them for breadcrumbs.

Oat and Barley Scones

Traditionally, scones were the backbone of Scottish and English tea parties and were usually eaten with butter, "clotted cream," or jam. But I created these to be tasty enough to enjoy plain. Good as they are warm from the oven, we like them even better the next day.

⅓ cup Spectrum Spread

⅓ cup light or dark agave nectar,
   or a mixture

¾ cup oat flour

¾ cup barley flour

¼ cup tapioca or arrowroot starch

½ teaspoon salt

¾ teaspoon baking soda

⅜ teaspoon unbuffered vitamin C
   crystals

⅓ cup currants

1 cup rolled oats

PREHEAT THE OVEN to 325°F. Line a baking sheet with parchment paper.

In a bowl, combine the spread and agave nectar.

In a small bowl, combine the oat flour, barley flour, tapioca or arrowroot, salt, baking soda, and vitamin C. Set aside ½ cup of the mixture. Stir the currants into the remaining flour.

Stir the flour mixture (with the currants) into the agave nectar mixture. Beat for 10 to 20 strokes. Add the reserved flour, half at a time, stirring just until combined. Mixture should form a ball.

Scatter ⅔ cup rolled oats over an 18" piece of waxed paper. Cut the ball of dough in half. Put one ball of dough on top of the rolled oats and roll to coat.

On the prepared baking sheet, scatter the remaining ⅓ cup rolled oats into two 8"-diameter circles. Place the ball of dough in the center of one circle of oats. Using a rubber spatula, flatten into an 8"- or 9"-diameter circle, about ½" thick. Repeat with remaining ball of dough.

Using a pizza cutting wheel or a thin sharp knife, cut each circle of dough into 8 wedges, but do not separate the wedges.

Bake for 18 minutes, or until slightly puffy, with tiny cracks, and golden brown at the edges. Re-cut into the 8 wedges. Separate the wedges slightly and allow to cool on the baking sheet for 15 to 30 minutes before serving.

Makes 16

Variation

Citrus Oat Scones: Add 1 to 2 teaspoons lemon, lime, or orange zest. Stir into the flour with the currants.

COOK'S TIPS

* Although professionally milled oat flour is very fine, you can improvise oat flour by grinding rolled oats in a blender until fine. You'll need about 1 cup rolled oats to make ¾ cup oat flour.

* If you want to substitute honey for the agave nectar, use a 3-quart saucepan instead of a bowl, and heat over low heat just until the honey melts. Remove from heat, and stir in the spread.

Rye and Barley Drop Biscuits

Drop biscuits are one of the quickest of the quick breads.
Top them with your favorite all-fruit spread.

1 cup rye flour

1¼ cups barley flour

½ teaspoon salt

1½ teaspoons baking soda

¾ teaspoon unbuffered vitamin C crystals

⅓ cup Spectrum Spread

¾ cup 1% goat's milk

PREHEAT THE OVEN to 400°F. Line a baking sheet with parchment paper.

In a bowl, whisk the rye flour, barley flour, salt, baking soda, and vitamin C. Using a fork, cut the spread into the flour mixture until it resembles very coarse meal.

Add the milk and mix for about 10 strokes. (Mixture will be a very soft dough.) Spoon into 4 or 6 equal mounds on the prepared baking sheet.

Bake the 4 large biscuits for 12 minutes or the 6 medium biscuits for 10 minutes, or until the tops are brown and firm to touch. Biscuits will be crisp on the outside and soft on the inside.

Makes 4 large or 6 medium

Variation

Rye and Barley Dessert Shortcakes: Add 2 tablespoons of maple or date sugar or ½ teaspoon of white stevia powder.

Spelt Drop Biscuits

2½ cups whole spelt flour
½ teaspoon salt
1½ teaspoons baking soda
¾ teaspoon cream of tartar
⅓ cup Spectrum Spread
⅔ cup 1% soy or goat's milk

Preheat the oven to 400°F. Line a baking sheet with parchment paper.

In a bowl, whisk the spelt flour, salt, baking soda, and cream of tartar. Using a fork, cut the spread into the flour mixture until it resembles very coarse meal.

Add the soy or goat's milk and mix for about 10 strokes. (Mixture will be a very soft dough.) Spoon into 4 or 6 equal mounds on the prepared baking sheet.

Bake the 4 large biscuits for 12 minutes or the 6 medium biscuits for 10 minutes, or until the tops are brown and firm to touch. Biscuits will be crisp on the outside and soft on the inside.

Makes 4 large or 6 medium

Variation

Spelt Dessert Shortcakes: Add 2 tablespoons of maple or date sugar or ½ teaspoon of white stevia powder.

Kamut Drop Biscuits

2 cups Kamut brand flour
½ teaspoon salt
3 teaspoons Corn-Free Baking Powder (page 212)
⅓ cup Spectrum Spread
1 cup soy or goat's milk

PREHEAT THE OVEN to 400°F. Line a baking sheet with parchment paper.

In a bowl, whisk the Kamut brand flour, salt, and baking powder. Using a fork, cut the spread into the flour mixture until it resembles very coarse meal.

Add the milk and mix for about 10 strokes. (Mixture will be a very soft dough.) Spoon into 4 or 6 equal mounds on the prepared baking sheet.

Bake the 4 large biscuits for 12 minutes or the 6 medium biscuits for 10 minutes, or until the tops are brown and firm to touch. Biscuits will be crisp on the outside and soft on the inside.

Makes 4 large or 6 medium

Variation

Kamut Dessert Shortcakes: Add 2 tablespoons of maple or date sugar or ½ teaspoon of white stevia powder.

Banana Bread

For breakfast or snacking, there's nothing like banana bread.
People who are allergic to wheat, milk, or egg can enjoy this loaf freely.

3 cups Kamut brand flour

¼ cup maple sugar

2 teaspoons baking soda

¾ teaspoon salt

½ teaspoon xanthan gum

½–⅔ cup chopped black walnuts (optional)

5 very ripe bananas (2 cups, about 1½ pounds)

¼ teaspoon unbuffered vitamin C crystals

¼ cup oil or Spectrum Spread

¼ cup maple syrup

¼ cup water

1 teaspoon pure vanilla extract (optional)

PREHEAT THE OVEN to 350°F. Oil and flour an 8½" × 4½" loaf pan.

In a large bowl, whisk the Kamut brand flour, maple sugar, baking soda, salt, and xanthan gum. Stir in the nuts if using.

In a blender, combine 4 bananas and the vitamin C. Process for 10 to 20 seconds, or until pureed. Add banana and process until they measure 2 cups. Add the oil or spread, maple syrup, water, and vanilla if using. Process 20 seconds. Pour into the flour mixture, and mix just until combined. Don't overmix.

Pour into the prepared pan and bake for 30 minutes. Cover loosely with a foil tent and bake 25 to 30 minutes more, or until a cake tester inserted in the center comes out clean.

Cool in the pan on a rack for 10 minutes. Remove to the rack and cool completely. Wrap well and store at room temperature or freeze.

Makes 1 loaf

Variations

Banana Cake: Omit the water and increase the maple syrup to ½ cup.

Banana Bread with Fruit: Replace the nuts with ½ cup currants, raisins, or dried cranberries.

Country-Style Quick Bread

*Like traditional cornbread, this bread is baked in a flat pan—an 8" square or a 9" pie plate—
and is cut into squares or wedges. While not for sandwiches, this fragrant, golden bread
is a winner with salad, soup, or stew—or (my favorite) for breakfast, topped with fruit,
like a shortcake. (See Breakfast Shortcake, page 98.) It can contain no sweetener,
a little bit, or it can be quite sweet, as you might expect a sweet bread to be.*

1½ **cups spelt, buckwheat, or rye flour**

1½ **teaspoons baking soda**

1½ **teaspoons cream of tartar
or ¾ teaspoon unbuffered vitamin C
crystals**

½ **teaspoon salt**

2–4 **tablespoons maple or date sugar
(optional)**

⅔ **cup plain or vanilla 1% soy milk,
1% goat's milk, or water**

¼ **cup maple syrup or light or dark
agave nectar**

3 **tablespoons sunflower oil**

PREHEAT THE OVEN to 375°F. Oil and
flour a 9" pie plate or an 8" × 8" baking dish.

In a bowl, whisk the spelt, buckwheat, or
rye flour; baking soda; cream of tartar or vitamin C; salt; and maple or date sugar if
using.

In a 2-cup measure, combine the milk or
water, maple syrup or agave nectar, and oil
and whisk to blend. Pour into the flour mixture and mix just until combined. Pour into
the prepared pan and smooth. Bake for 18 to
20 minutes, or until brown and a cake tester
inserted in the center comes out clean. Cool
in the pan on a rack for 10 minutes.

Makes 1

COOK'S TIP

✱ Other flours also work very well in this recipe. You
might try 1½ cups Kamut brand flour or 1¾ cups
barley flour. If you'd like to use a combination of
flour, try one of these four combos:

½ cup each amaranth, buckwheat, and quinoa flours
¾ cup each oat flour and brown rice flour
¾ cup each Kamut brand flour and whole grain or
white spelt flour
¾ cup + 2 tablespoons barley flour and ¾ cup rye flour

Variations

Barely Sweetened Quick Bread: Omit the ¼ cup
maple syrup or light or dark agave nectar and
add ¼ cup more soy or goat's milk or water.

Spiced Quick Bread: Add 1½ teaspoons
pumpkin pie spice, cinnamon, or ginger. (Especially good when baked as a sweet bread.)

Spiced Nut Bread: Add ½ cup of chopped nuts
(walnuts, almonds, or pecans) along with one
of the spices listed in Spiced Quick Bread.

Nut Bread: Add ½ cup of chopped nuts
(walnuts, almonds, or pecans).

Quick Coffee Cake: Reduce the water or milk
by ¼ cup. Combine the liquids in a blender
and add ⅓ cup mashed sweet potato, or one
jar (4 ounces) baby food (applesauce, green
peas, winter squash, sweet potato, carrots,
pears, or prunes).

Steamed Apricot Bread

Steamed breads are firm, dense, and moist without the addition of eggs to the batter.
And they're just right for soup and salad luncheons.

¾ cup rolled oats

⅔ cup brown rice flour

¼ cup amaranth flour

2 teaspoons Corn-Free Baking Powder
(page 212)

½ teaspoon salt

½ cup almonds

¾ cup boiling water

⅓ cup dark agave nectar, sorghum,
or honey

½ teaspoon almond extract

⅔ cup chopped dried apricots

OIL A 1-QUART MOLD or 1-pound can.

In a large bowl, combine the oats, rice flour, amaranth flour, baking powder, and salt.

Place the almonds in a blender and process to a fine powder. Gradually add enough water to bring the level up to 1 cup. With the machine running, add the agave nectar, sorghum, or honey and almond extract. Add the apricots and pulse until chopped. Pour into the flour mixture and stir to mix. Turn out into the prepared mold or can. Cover with foil or waxed paper; tie waxed paper securely with string.

Place on a wire rack in a Dutch oven or large pot. Add enough boiling water to come halfway up the sides of the mold. Cover the pot, and steam over medium-low heat for 2 hours. Do not remove the cover during the cooking time.

Remove the mold from the pot. Cool the bread in the mold on a rack for 15 minutes. Remove to the rack to cool completely. For easiest slicing, use a serrated knife and a sawing motion.

Makes 1 loaf

COOK'S TIP

* If you want, you can replace the amaranth flour with ¼ cup soy flour, white buckwheat flour, or quinoa flour.

Steamed Apple-Raisin Bread

A gluten-free, egg-free loaf. Dense and moist, it can be sliced without crumbling and goes brown-bagging very well.

1 cup brown rice flour

¼ cup ground sunflower seeds or amaranth flour

1½ teaspoons Corn-Free Baking Powder (page 212)

½ teaspoon salt

¾ teaspoon ground cinnamon

½ cup walnuts or almonds

¾ cup boiling unsweetened apple juice

¼ cup light or dark agave nectar, sorghum, or honey

1 tablespoon lemon juice or ¼ teaspoon unbuffered vitamin C crystals

½ cup chopped dried apples

½ cup raisins

OIL A 1-QUART MOLD or 1-pound can.

In a large bowl, combine the rice flour, sunflower seeds or amaranth flour, baking powder, salt, and cinnamon.

Place the walnuts or almonds in a blender and process to a fine powder. Add the apple juice, and process for 20 seconds. (If necessary, add more juice as needed to make 1 cup of the mixture.) Add the agave nectar, sorghum, or honey and lemon juice or vitamin C. Process briefly. Add the apples, and pulse until coarsely chopped.

Pour into the flour mixture and mix just until combined. Stir in the raisins. Don't overmix. Turn into an oiled 1-quart mold or 1-pound can. Cover with waxed paper or foil and tie it securely with string.

Place on a wire rack in a Dutch oven or large pot. Add enough boiling water to come halfway up the sides of the mold. Cover the pot, and steam over medium-low heat for 2 hours. Do not remove the cover during the cooking time.

Remove the mold from the pot. Cool the bread in the mold on a rack for 15 minutes. Remove to the rack to cool completely. For easiest slicing, use a serrated knife and a sawing motion.

Makes 1 loaf

Grain-Free Boston Brown Bread

A milk-free, egg-free, and—yes—even grain-free version of a traditional New England bread. Very good, very moist.

1 cup + 2 tablespoons amaranth flour
¼ cup arrowroot
1 teaspoon baking soda
½ teaspoon salt
¾ teaspoon powdered ginger
½ cup currants
½ cup Brazil nuts
¾ cup boiling unsweetened fruit juice or water
¼ cup agave nectar, honey, or sorghum
1 tablespoon lemon juice or ¼ teaspoon unbuffered vitamin C crystals

OIL A 1-QUART MOLD or 1-pound coffee can.

In a large bowl, combine the flour, arrowroot, baking soda, salt, and ginger. Stir in the currants.

In a blender, process the nuts to a fine powder. Add the fruit juice or water, and process for 20 seconds. If necessary, add more juice or water to reach 1 cup. With the blender running, add the agave nectar, honey, or sorghum and lemon juice or vitamin C.

Pour into the flour mixture and mix just until combined. Don't overmix. Pour into the prepared mold. Cover with foil or waxed paper; tie waxed paper securely with string.

Place on a wire rack in a Dutch oven or large pot. Add enough boiling water to come halfway up the sides of the mold. Cover the pot, and steam over medium-low heat for 2 hours. Do not remove the cover during the cooking time.

Remove the mold from the pot. Cool the bread in the mold on a rack for 15 minutes. Remove to the rack to cool completely. For easiest slicing, use a serrated knife and a sawing motion.

Makes 1 loaf

COOK'S TIP

✳ You can make any of these changes for variety: Substitute ground cinnamon or grated nutmeg for the ginger. Use pecans or walnuts instead of Brazil nuts. Instead of the currants, use dried unsweetened pineapple, apples, or prunes and use the corresponding juice as the liquid.

Quick Skillet Bread

Resembling a large crepe, this is the easiest bread you'll ever make. There's no rolling, patting, or cutting. And with so many flours to choose from, you'll be able to eat it no matter what your allergies may be. Serve it warm with a hearty soup.

⅔ **cup water**
½ **cup chickpea flour**
¼–½ **teaspoon salt**
2 **teaspoons olive oil**

IN A BOWL, combine the water, flour, and salt. The batter will be very thin.

Heat a 12" nonstick skillet over medium-high heat until a drop of water dances on the surface. Add 1 teaspoon of the oil, and swirl the pan to distribute.

Stir the flour mixture and pour into the skillet. Cover, and cook for 2 minutes. Drizzle with the remaining 1 teaspoon oil, and, using the back of a spoon, spread over the surface. Cook, uncovered, for 5 minutes.

When the bread appears dry around the edges, loosen it with a spatula. Flip over, and reduce the heat to medium-low. Cook, uncovered, for 5 minutes more. (For especially crisp bread, cook for 5 minutes more, turning every minute or so.)

Serve immediately.

Makes 2 servings

COOK'S TIPS

＊ If you want, you can replace the chickpea flour with one of the following: oat flour, white buckwheat flour, amaranth flour (use medium heat instead of medium-high), or ⅓ cup brown rice flour.

＊ To make 1 serving, divide the ingredient amounts in half and cook the batter in a 10" skillet. To serve 4, make 2 separate breads in the 12" pan.

Wheat-Free Tortillas

These tortillas are a tasty alternative to traditional tortillas, which are made from corn or wheat flour. Simple as they are, they have myriad uses. Go Mexican by topping them with well-seasoned beans and guacamole, or tear into bite-size pieces and crown them with salad fixings, chicken salad, or roast turkey. Another plus is that they freeze well after they're cooked, so you can keep a supply on hand.

1 cup barley, brown rice, or buckwheat flour
¼–½ teaspoon salt
½ cup water

IN A SMALL BOWL, mix the flour and salt. Stir in the water. The dough should be soft but not wet and should hold its shape when you pinch it. The dough will likely form a ball as you stir it. If necessary, add more flour or water, 1 tablespoonful at a time, to achieve the proper consistency.

Pinch off balls of dough the size of golf balls. Roll in flour to coat well. Knead each ball as you pat or roll it into a 5"- to 6"-diameter circle, ⅛" thick.

Heat a heavy skillet or griddle. Place each tortilla in the hot pan, and cook about 3 minutes on a side, or until lightly brown and just starting to appear dry. Longer cooking will make the tortillas crisp. Wrap in a cotton towel to keep warm, or cool on a rack.

Store in the refrigerator for up to 1 week, or freeze. Reheat in a toaster or warm oven.

Makes about 4

COOK'S TIPS

✳ You can also make these tortillas from a variety of other flours, including 1 cup oat, rye, or teff flour; 1¼ cups amaranth or spelt flour; or 1¼ cups quinoa flour + ⅓ cup tapioca starch flour.

✳ To bake with a Tortilla Chef: Preheat for 8 to 10 minutes. Place the balls of dough, one at a time, on the hot surface and follow the directions to flatten them into tortillas. Leave the lid down for 1 to 2 minutes. Using a plastic pancake turner, loosen from the lid and turn. Cook for 30 to 60 seconds. (For crisp, crackerlike tortillas, cook longer.)

Variations

Sweet Tortillas: Add ⅛ teaspoon white stevia powder and ½ teaspoon ground cinnamon. Or try a pinch of grated nutmeg, powdered ginger, or ground allspice.

Sesame Tortillas: Add 1 tablespoon Savory Seed Seasoning (page 209).

Using a Bread Machine

If you do lots of baking, as I do, you'll find a bread machine can come in handy. Here are a few tips for working with your machine and alternative ingredients:

Assemble your machine. It's best to follow the manufacturer's directions. All yeast bread recipes in this book were tested in a DAK bread machine.

Be flexible. Contrary to the directions that came with my machine, I find it best when using alternative flours and xanthan gum to combine all dry ingredients in a bowl and whisk them. Likewise, I combine and, if necessary, warm the liquids first. (When combining the ingredients in this way, I don't use the timer feature.)

Know the right order. Follow your machine's directions for the order to put ingredients in the canister (either dry ingredients first, then liquids, or vice-versa).

Program to suit the recipe. If you program your bread machine with specific time settings (many bread machines lack this feature), these are the approximate times used for the yeast breads in this book:

1st mix: 15 minutes
Fermentation: 60 minutes
2nd mix: 18 minutes
Fermentation: 20 minutes
Loosening the paddle: 3 seconds
Fermentation: 75 minutes
Baking: 50 minutes
Cooling: 20 minutes

Wrap it up. Most machines take about 4 hours to make bread. And most will beep or otherwise signal you when the bread is baked and ready to be removed from the machine. Cool on a rack. (Some machines have a cooling cycle so you don't have to be there to remove the bread.) As soon as it's cool, wrap your preservative-free bread to help it stay fresh longer.

Spelt Yeast Bread

People who can eat yeast but not wheat will welcome this recipe with open arms.
Wait (if you can!) until the bread is nearly cool before slicing it.
Make by hand or in a bread machine.

1½ **cups warm water (120°–125°F)**
2 **tablespoons fruit juice concentrate, maple syrup, or honey**
2¾ **teaspoons quick rising yeast (1 package of yeast + ½ teaspoon)**
3 **cups white spelt flour**
1 **teaspoon salt**
2 **tablespoons olive oil**
1¾ **cups whole grain spelt flour**

POUR ¼ CUP of the water into a large bowl and add the juice concentrate, maple syrup, or honey and yeast. Stir to dissolve.

In a large bowl, whisk the white spelt flour and salt. In a 2-cup measure, combine the oil and remaining 1¼ cups water. Pour 1 cup of the oil-water mixture into the flour mixture. Beat well. Add the remaining ¼ cup oil-water mixture and beat well. Beat for 3 minutes by hand or for 5 minutes by mixer. Add the whole spelt flour, ½ cup at a time, beating well after each addition.

Turn the dough out onto a lightly floured work surface, and knead for 15 minutes, or until smooth and elastic.

Oil a large bowl and place the dough in it. Turn so the top is lightly oiled (or mist with olive oil cooking spray). Cover with oiled plastic wrap and place in a 70° to 80°F, draft-free place, to rise for 1½ to 2 hours, or until doubled in bulk.

Oil two 8" × 4" loaf pans. Oil or flour your hands and punch the dough down. Divide in half and shape each half into an elongated roll. Fit into the prepared pans. Brush lightly with vegetable oil or mist with olive oil cooking spray.

Preheat the oven to 350°F. Cover the loaves with oiled plastic wrap, and allow to rise in a warm (70° to 80°F), draft-free place for 45 minutes, or until the dough is ½" above the pan tops.

Gently remove the plastic wrap and bake for 40 to 45 minutes, or until light brown.

Makes 2 loaves

COOK'S TIP

* Spelt flours vary in their moisture and gluten contents. Usually, Purity Foods brand, which is available in health food stores, is fairly consistent.

Variation

Bread-Machine Spelt Yeast Bread: Place the ingredients in the bread machine in the order recommended by the manufacturer's directions. Select the basic white bread cycle. If you can select the darkness of the crust, choose light or medium. Makes one 1½-pound loaf.

Bread Machine Troubleshooting Tips

Okay, you just baked your first loaf of bread and it's not up to your expectations. Here's how to tweak the next one to perfection.

Add more water. Depending on your machine, the flour, and humidity, you may need to add 1 or 2 (occasionally even 3) tablespoons of water. The primary signs for needing to do this include the following: The dough looks dry; it crumbles or splits in half (instead of coming together in a smooth ball), and the machine sounds as if it's laboring. Add the water, 1 tablespoon at a time. Wait a minute or two after each addition to see if it's enough. As the dough gets close to being smooth and elastic, add water by the teaspoon.

Add more flour. In this case, the machine sounds are normal because it does the mixing easily. But when you peek after it's been mixing for 5 minutes, you see what appears to be a heavy batter rather than dough.

Within those first 5 minutes, the dough should have gathered itself into a ball. To help it do just that, add flour 1 or 2 tablespoons at a time.

Have patience. Whenever you need to add anything to dough after the machine is working, do so cautiously and a little at a time. Always wait a minute or two to see how the dough looks before adding more.

Don't sweat a collapse. Until you can figure out when the dough needs more flour (especially when using low-gluten or gluten-free flours), you may find that your bread rises beautifully with a nice dome on top—only to collapse to a flat-top, or perhaps even dip down into a saucer-shaped top. Add flour as directed. Take heart—it will still taste great.

Have fun. Don't be afraid to experiment. Like anything else that you do repetitively, you will become better at judging the dough, and your breads will get better, too.

Pumpernickel Bread

If you must avoid gluten, or all grains, you'll treasure this easy machine-bread recipe (I do!).
The texture, while dense and moist, is pleasing—much like any pumpernickel or
other type heavy bread. The carob may surprise you, but it's just cosmetic, to darken the bread.
Like most people who have tasted it, I enjoy this bread best when it's toasted.

1¾ cups buckwheat flour

1¾ cups quinoa flour

1 cup amaranth flour

2 tablespoons carob powder

2 packages quick rising yeast
(about 4½ teaspoons)

2¼ teaspoons xanthan gum

2 teaspoons caraway seeds

¾ teaspoon salt

1¾ cups warm water (120°–125°F)

1½ tablespoons olive oil

1½ tablespoons sorghum, maple syrup,
or honey

PLACE THE BUCKWHEAT FLOUR,
quinoa flour, amaranth flour, carob powder,
yeast, xanthan gum, caraway seeds, salt,
water, oil, and sorghum, maple syrup, or
honey in the bread machine in the order
recommended by the manufacturer's directions. Select the basic white bread cycle. If
you can select the darkness of the crust,
choose light or medium.

Makes one 1½-pound loaf

COOK'S TIPS

* Look at the dough 5 to 10 minutes after the bread
  machine starts. If there is a protrusion of dough
  sticking up that appears much drier than the rest of
  the dough, press it down (use a rubber spatula) into
  the softer dough. Scrape down the sides of the
  canister, too.

* Because these alternative flours don't contain
  gluten, you must add that little bit of xanthan gum,
  which enables gluten-free flours to rise (to a limited
  extent).

Slicing Round Loaves

Most bread machines produce square
or rectangular bread; however,
some older machines produce round loaves,
like small towers of bread. To slice the round
loaves, place a cooled loaf on its side, and
using a serrated bread knife, gently saw the
bread in half. (Don't press too hard or you'll
compress the fresh bread.) Put the cut side
down on a cutting board and slice the bread
into half-circle slices about ½" thick. To
freeze sliced bread, place waxed paper between the slices so you can remove one
slice at a time for toasting.

Kamut-Grain Bread

You'll love this nutritious loaf. Kamut brand flour produces pretty golden baked goods, so children turned off by brown whole grain breads may be delighted with this one.

2¾ teaspoons active dry or quick rising yeast (1 individual package + ½ teaspoon of yeast)

4 cups Kamut brand flour

1 teaspoon salt

1 tablespoon liquid lecithin

2 tablespoons olive oil

¼ cup thawed apple or white grape juice concentrate

1¼ cups warm water

PLACE THE YEAST, KAMUT FLOUR, salt, lecithin, oil, juice concentrate, and water in the bread machine in the order recommended by the manufacturer's directions. Select the basic white bread cycle. If you can select the darkness of the crust, choose light or medium.

Makes one 1½-pound loaf

COOK'S TIP

✳ Lecithin is a soy product. If you react to soy, substitute an equal measure of oil.

Dinner Rolls

You can make dinner rolls from any of the machine- or hand-kneaded yeast doughs in this book (though a heavy bread, like the pumpernickel, will make heavy rolls). Simply follow the recipe until after the first rise.

Then, punch down the dough and divide it among 24 oiled muffin cups. (If you wish, scatter ¼ teaspoon sesame seeds in the bottom of each cup.) Or if you prefer one loaf of bread and 12 dinner rolls, shape half of the dough to fit an 8" × 4" loaf pan and fill 12 muffin cups.

Preheat the oven to 375°F. Cover the cups with oiled plastic wrap and let them rise in a warm, draft-free place for 30 to 40 minutes, or until almost doubled in size. Remove the plastic wrap and bake for 16 to 18 minutes, or until lightly brown.

Wheat-Free Oat-Bran Bread

This is a good light-colored bread with nice flavor. Super for sandwiches; terrific for toast.

¾ **cup oat bran**
3 **cups white spelt flour**
2¼ **teaspoons active dry yeast**
¾ **teaspoon salt**
½ **tablespoon liquid lecithin**
1 **tablespoon vegetable oil**
¼ **cup thawed apple or white grape juice
   concentrate**
1 **cup water**

PLACE THE OAT BRAN, spelt flour, yeast, salt, lecithin, oil, juice concentrate and water in the bread machine in the order recommended by the manufacturer's directions. Select the basic white bread cycle. If you can select the darkness of the crust, choose light or medium.

Makes one 1½-pound loaf

COOK'S TIP

* Lecithin is a soy product. If you react to soy, substitute an equal measure of oil.

Sticky Buns

You can make sticky buns from any of the machine- or hand-kneaded yeast doughs in this book, except the Pumpernickel Bread. Here's what to do:

Add 1 teaspoon ground cinnamon to the flour and knead in ⅓ cup of raisins or currants if you want them. Follow the recipe until after the first rise.

Oil 24 muffin cups (or mist them with cooking spray) and place 1 teaspoon dark agave nectar, sorghum, or honey in the bottom of each cup. Add 1 teaspoon coarsely chopped pecans or 3 pecan halves.

When the dough has doubled in bulk (first rise), punch it down. Turn and punch it down again. Turn the dough out onto a piece of waxed paper, and, using a sharp knife, cut it into 24 pieces. Shape the pieces into balls and place in the cups.

Preheat the oven to 350°F. Cover the cups with oiled plastic wrap and let the dough rise in a warm, draft-free place for 30 to 40 minutes, or until nearly doubled in size. Carefully remove the plastic wrap and bake for 16 to 18 minutes, until light brown.

Waldorf Stuffing with Buckwheat

A grain-free stuffing that's great for poultry or wild fowl.

2 cups cooked unroasted buckwheat groats

1½ cups chopped apples

1 cup chopped celery

½ cup raisins or dried cranberries

¾ cup chopped walnuts or pecans

2 tablespoons lemon juice

½ teaspoon poultry seasoning

½ cup Cashew Spread (page 195) or Tofu-Dijon Spread (page 194)

1 cup unsweetened apple juice or chicken broth (optional)

IN A BOWL, mix the buckwheat, apples, celery, raisins or cranberries, nuts, lemon juice, and poultry seasoning. Stir in the spread.

Use to stuff a 5- or 6-pound chicken (do not pack tightly).

Or bake the stuffing separately: Add the apple juice or chicken broth. Bake, covered, at 350°F for 45 to 50 minutes in an oiled 1½-quart casserole dish. Uncover for the last 10 to 15 minutes of cooking time.

Makes about 6 cups

COOK'S TIPS

＊ If you want, you can use ½ teaspoon unbuffered vitamin C crystals dissolved in 2 tablespoons water instead of the lemon juice.

＊ If you don't have one of the spreads on hand, use an additional ½ cup apple juice or chicken broth to moisten.

Variation

Waldorf Stuffing with Quinoa: Replace the buckwheat with 2 cups of cooked quinoa.

Easy Bread Crumbs

These crumbs are like an ace up your sleeve for spur-of-the-moment cooking.
You can make them at your leisure, then store in the freezer for use on casseroles,
in puddings, and in meat loaves. Unless you plan to use the crumbs on sweet dishes,
you may wish to omit any spices from the pancake recipe you choose.

12 Grain-Free Pancakes (page 89)
**½ teaspoon poultry seasoning or sage
(optional)**

PREHEAT THE OVEN to 300°F.

Arrange the pancakes in a single layer on one or more baking sheets. Bake for 15 minutes, or until almost dry and brittle. (For very crisp pancakes, turn them over and turn off the oven, allowing them to cool gradually.)

Let cool thoroughly. Break into pieces and place, about 1 cup at a time, in a blender or food processor. Add the poultry seasoning or sage if using, and process into crumbs.

Place in jars or cellophane bags, label, and store in the freezer. To use, remove what you need while the crumbs are frozen.

Makes about 2¾ cups

COOK'S TIP

✳ Omit the sage if you'll be using the crumbs in a sweet dish such as pudding.

Italian Crumbs

Use these crumbs instead of cheese on any Mediterranean-style casseroles.

1 tablespoon olive oil
½ cup Easy Bread Crumbs (above)
½ teaspoon dried oregano
½ teaspoon dried basil
⅛ teaspoon onion powder
Pinch of garlic powder

HEAT THE OIL in a skillet over medium heat. Add the crumbs and cook for 3 minutes. Stir in the oregano, basil, onion powder, and garlic powder. Cook, stirring, for 3 min-

utes, or until the seasonings are well distributed and the crumbs are well-coated with oil.

Makes ½ cup

COOK'S TIPS

✳ You can also make crumbs by drying and grinding dry or overly crisp tortillas or crackers.

✳ If you want to, substitute 1½ teaspoons Italian Seasoning (page 210) for the oregano, basil, onion powder, and garlic powder.

✳ To use the crumbs as a casserole topping, cook them only briefly in a little oil.

Super Soups, Stews, and Chowders

Soups and stews are much more than cold-weather comfort food. They're a versatile and appetizing way for allergic people to combine foods to maximize flavor. Eating plain, steamed vegetables next to unadorned meat can easily grow tiresome. But toss those same vegetables, meat, poultry or fish into some seasoned stock, and you have a delightful soup or stew.

When you want a cream soup without milk, try Asparagus Soup, Garbanzo Garden Stew, Zucchini Bisque, or Creamy Mushroom Soup. Blending brings out the "body" in these soups. To thin or thicken these cream-style soups, vary the amount of liquid used.

Whatever type of stock or soup you make, be sure to label it clearly, listing all ingredients. That's especially helpful if you will be freezing portions for later use. And labeling is essential if you are rotating ingredients such as chicken, meat, or fish or if members of your family are allergic to different foods.

I usually keep a few pints of homemade chicken and turkey stock in my freezer. But it also helps to have canned broth in the pantry for last-minute soups and sauces. Be sure to read ingredient labels carefully when buying canned broth.

Basic Stock

*Homemade stock is essential to people with allergies who can't always rely on
store-bought broth or other soup bases. Most stock recipes call for vegetables to be included,
but you can vary the ingredients of any stock to fit your own needs, including
a Rotary Diversified Diet. If you can't have onions, carrots, celery, and parsley,
just simmer the meat, fish, or fowl in plain water.*

1 **pound meaty bones**

2 **quarts water**

1 **teaspoon salt**

2 **tablespoons vinegar or lemon juice or
½ teaspoon vitamin C crystals**

1 **onion, quartered (optional)**

1 **large carrot, sliced (optional)**

¼ **cup celery or lovage leaves (optional)**

IN A STOCKPOT or Dutch oven, combine
the bones, water, and salt with the vinegar,
lemon juice, or vitamin C. Add the onion if
using, carrot if using, and celery or lovage
if using.

Cover and cook for 6 to 8 hours over low
heat. Remove the lid and bring to a boil
over high heat. Cook for 20 to 40 minutes,
or until the liquid is reduced to about 3½
cups (about half the original volume).
Strain through a colander into a large bowl.
Strain again through a sieve.

Use at once. Or refrigerate, tightly covered, for up to 5 days. For longer storage,
freeze.

Makes 3 to 4 cups

COOK'S TIPS

✳ You may want to collect chicken, meat, or fish bones
in a labeled plastic bag in your freezer until you have
enough to make stock. If you're in a hurry, buy
inexpensive soup bones or chicken wings or backs.
(If you do this, remove the bones after an hour of
cooking and pick the meat off. Save the meat and add
it to the soup later. Return the bones to the stock.)

✳ Salt and vinegar (or lemon juice or vitamin C) will
make the stock cloudy looking—with minerals!

✳ Other optional ingredients include 4 large parsley
sprigs, 1 or 2 bay leaves, 2 sprigs fresh thyme or ½
teaspoon dried, and/or giblets. Remove and discard
bay leaves before using stock.

Simple Asian Soup

I'd forgotten how good simple broth and vegetables could be, until I saw this soup prepared by a "pro" at a dinner party featuring Chinese food. The cook had the clear broth simmering while he made the stir-fry, rice, fish course, and poached pears for dessert. When everything else was ready, he dropped a few thinly sliced mushrooms and the thinly sliced white portions of the scallions into the broth. He served the soup just a few minutes later, in small Asian-style bowls. Utter simplicity—and excellent flavor.

1 quart chicken stock or broth
4 small mushrooms, thinly sliced
2–3 slender scallions, thinly sliced

HEAT THE STOCK or broth in a saucepan over medium heat. Three minutes before serving, add the mushrooms and white portions of the scallions, reserving the green portions. Cook for 2 minutes. Divide among 4 bowls and top with the green scallions.

Makes 4 servings

Variations

Asian Soup with Chicken: Add ¾ cup diced cooked chicken to the stock or broth. Heat through. Add the mushrooms and scallions 2 minutes before serving.

Asian Soup with Noodles: Add ¾ cup cooked thin noodles to the stock or broth. Heat through. Add the mushrooms and scallions 2 minutes before serving.

Asian Soup with Rice: Add ¾ cup cooked rice to the stock or broth. Heat through. Add the mushrooms and scallions 2 minutes before serving.

Vegetable-Miso Soup

A delicious Japanese-style soup. In Japan, this is served for breakfast!

2 tablespoons olive oil

1½ cups sliced carrots

1½ cups sliced celery

1½ cups finely shredded cabbage

½ cup finely chopped onions

4 thin slices fresh ginger root

1–2 cloves garlic, minced

8 cups chicken or vegetable stock or broth or water

1–2 tablespoons Oriental rice vinegar or ¼–½ teaspoon unbuffered vitamin C crystals

1 tablespoon wheat-free tamari sauce

1 teaspoon honey

⅛ teaspoon ground red pepper (optional)

2 tablespoons light miso

2 scallions, chopped (optional)

Toasted sesame seeds (optional)

HEAT THE OIL in a Dutch oven or stockpot over medium heat. Add the carrots, celery, cabbage, onions, ginger, and garlic, and cook for 10 minutes. Remove the ginger slices.

Add the stock, broth, or water; rice vinegar or vitamin C; tamari; honey; and red pepper. Cover and cook for 10 minutes.

In a small bowl, dissolve the miso in a few tablespoons of the hot vegetable mixture, stirring until well blended. Remove soup from heat. Stir miso mixture into the soup.

Serve topped with scallions and sesame seeds if using.

Makes 3 quarts

Variations

Tofu-Vegetable Soup: Add up to 8 ounces of drained, cubed tofu. (Simply add the tofu. Or brown it first, if you want, in 1 tablespoon vegetable oil over medium heat.)

Fish-Miso Chowder: Add 8 ounces of cod, flounder, catfish, or other mild fillets. Before serving, break the fish into bite-size pieces.

COOK'S TIPS

✳ To toast small nuts and seeds, spread them in a small nonstick skillet. Cook, stirring often, over medium-low heat for 5 minutes, or until lightly browned and fragrant.

✳ Traditionally, miso is not boiled to preserve its beneficial enzymes. To reheat leftovers, heat over medium heat, stirring, only until steam starts to rise.

Asparagus Soup

A light, velvety green soup made primarily from members of the Lily family.

1 **pound asparagus stalks, trimmed**
1 **tablespoon olive oil**
2 **leeks, thinly sliced**
2 **cups vegetable or chicken stock or broth or water**
½ **teaspoon dried dillweed (optional)**
1 **clove garlic, crushed**
  Pinch of grated nutmeg

SLICE OFF THE ASPARAGUS TIPS about 2" from the end. Cut them into ½" pieces and reserve them. Cut the remaining stalks into 1" pieces.

Heat the oil in a saucepan over medium heat. Add the leeks and cook for 5 minutes, or until soft. Add 1½ cups of the stock, broth, or water. Stir in the dill if using and sliced asparagus. Cook for 8 minutes. Add the garlic and cook for 2 minutes, or until the asparagus is tender.

Remove from the heat and add the remaining ½ cup stock, broth, or water. Pour into a blender, 2 cups at a time, and process until pureed. Return to the pot, add the reserved asparagus tips, and

cook for 1 minute, or until hot throughout.

Divide among 4 bowls. Top each portion with the nutmeg.

Makes about 1 quart

COOK'S TIPS

* Instead of the leeks, you can use 4 to 6 large shallots or 1 medium onion.

* The easiest way to trim asparagus stalks is to snap them at the point where the tender portion begins.

* If you want, you can use ½ teaspoon of dried savory, tarragon, or thyme instead of the dill.

Variations

Chicken-Asparagus Soup: Add ½ cup diced cooked chicken to the soup after it has been pureed. Or you can use cooked Cornish game hen.

Turkey-Asparagus Soup: Add ½ cup diced cooked turkey to the soup after it has been pureed.

Scallop-Asparagus Soup: Add ½ cup quartered cooked sea scallops to the soup after it has been pureed.

Creamy Mushroom Soup

This creamy soup is milk- and cream-free. It tastes rich, is delightfully aromatic,
and has good body, even without flour to thicken it.

½ cup raw cashews

3 cups boiling vegetable stock or broth
  or water

2 tablespoons olive oil

1 large Spanish onion, chopped

½ pound mushrooms, sliced

1 tablespoon Hungarian paprika

1½ teaspoons dried dillweed

½ teaspoon salt

  Dash of ground red pepper

1 tablespoon lemon juice
  or ¼ teaspoon unbuffered vitamin C
  crystals

PLACE THE CASHEWS in a blender and
process until finely ground. Scrape bottom
of the container and grind again. Add 1 cup
of the stock, broth, or water, and process
for 30 seconds. Add the remaining 2 cups
stock, broth, or water and process for 30
seconds more.

Heat the oil in a 3-quart saucepan over
medium heat. Add the onion and cook for 5
minutes, stirring occasionally. Add the
mushrooms and cook for 10 minutes, or
until the vegetables are soft. Stir in the paprika, salt, dill, and red pepper.

Stir in the cashew mixture and cook, stirring often, for 15 minutes or until hot and
thickened. Just before serving, stir in the
lemon juice or vitamin C.

Makes 5 to 6 cups

Quick Spinach Soup

*The trick to getting a beautiful green soup is to
remove it from the heat as soon as the spinach wilts.*

1½ tablespoons olive oil

½ pound mushrooms, sliced

3 cups chicken stock or broth or water

8 ounces spinach, torn

1 tablespoon lime or lemon juice
or ¼ teaspoon unbuffered vitamin C
crystals

½ teaspoon salt

¼ teaspoon freshly grated nutmeg

HEAT THE OIL in a stockpot or Dutch
oven over medium-high heat. Add the
mushrooms and cook for 5 minutes, or until
tender. Add the stock, broth, or water;
spinach; lime or lemon juice; salt; and
nutmeg. Bring to a boil. Reduce the heat
and cook for 2 minutes, or just until the
spinach wilts.

Makes 4 servings

Zucchini Bisque

A delicious creamy no-milk, no-wheat soup.

1 tablespoon olive oil

1 cup chopped onions

1–2 cloves garlic, minced

3 cups chicken stock or broth or
vegetable broth

1 large zucchini, shredded
(about 3 cups)

1–2 tablespoons minced fresh basil
or 1 teaspoon dried

¼–½ teaspoon grated nutmeg

½ teaspoon salt

Freshly ground black pepper
(optional)

1 tablespoon lemon juice
or ¼ teaspoon unbuffered vitamin C
crystals

HEAT THE OIL in a 2-quart saucepan over
medium heat. Add the onions and cook,
stirring occasionally, for 5 minutes, or until
soft but not brown. Add the garlic and cook
for 1 minute. Add the stock or broth, zucchini, basil, nutmeg, salt, and pepper if
using, and cook for 15 minutes. Let cool for
5 to 10 minutes.

Ladle half into a blender or food
processor, and process until pureed. Return
to the saucepan. Repeat with the remaining
half. Reheat. Adjust the seasonings to taste.
Stir in lemon juice or vitamin C.

Makes 4 servings

Basic Beet Borscht

*This is a good example of combining vegetables from one family
into a dish that suits a Rotary Diversified Diet. The basic recipe calls for a meaty shin bone,
but you can use a little chicken or fish instead.*

2–3 **small beets**

   3 **cups water or vegetable stock
   or broth**

   1 **meaty shin bone**

1–2 **cups chopped beet greens, chard,
   or spinach**

IN A LARGE POT, combine the beets; water,
stock, or broth; and meaty bone. Cook for 1
hour, or until the beets and meat are tender.
Remove the bone, chop the meat, and return the meat to the pot. Discard the bone.

Remove the beets from the pot and slip
off their skins. Place in a blender or food
processor, and process until pureed. (Or let
them cool so you can shred them finely
using a grater.) Return to the pot. Add
more water if the mixture is too thick.

Bring to a boil. Add the greens. Cook for
5 minutes.

Makes 1 quart

COOK'S TIP

＊ Top each serving with a dollop of Dairy-Free "Sour
Cream" (page 194) in place of traditional sour
cream.

Variations

Beet Borscht with Chicken: Replace the shin
bone with the wings, neck, and back of a
chicken.

Beet Borscht with Fish: Replace the shin
bone with 4 ounces boneless fish. Cook
the fish for 10 minutes, breaking it up as
it cooks; the fish will become pink from
the beets.

Beet Borscht with Vegetables: Add ½ cup each
of chopped carrots, celery, celery root,
parsnips, onions, or leeks. Or add 1 cup
shredded cabbage. Season with ½ teaspoon
dried marjoram or fennel seeds or 1 tablespoon lemon juice.

Kale-Lentil Soup

Kale is a highly nutritious but underused member of the cabbage family—
and well worth becoming acquainted with. Allow about an hour and 10 minutes
to pull this soup together.

2 tablespoons vegetable oil

1 large onion, chopped

2–3 ribs celery, sliced

1 can (14–16 ounces) diced tomatoes (in juice)

1½ cups lentils

8 cups water

1 small butternut squash, peeled and cut into 1" cubes

½ bunch (about ½ pound) kale, ribs removed and leaves chopped into bite-size pieces

1 teaspoon salt

2 cloves garlic, pressed or minced

1–2 tablespoons lemon or lime juice

Freshly ground black pepper or drops of hot-pepper sauce (optional)

HEAT THE OIL in a 5-quart saucepan over medium heat. Add the onions and celery and cook for 10 minutes, or until softened, but not brown. Add the tomatoes, lentils, and water. Bring to a boil. Reduce the heat, partially cover, and cook for 15 minutes. Add the squash and cook for 15 minutes.

Add the kale and garlic and cook for 10 minutes, or until the lentils, squash, and kale are tender. Just before serving add the salt, lemon or lime juice, and pepper or pepper sauce if using. Adjust seasoning to taste.

Makes about 6 servings

COOK'S TIPS

∗ Instead of the water, you can use half water and half vegetable broth if you wish.

∗ You can use 1 tablespoon cider vinegar or ¼ teaspoon unbuffered vitamin C crystals if you want instead of the lemon or lime juice.

∗ This soup freezes well. Store in a tightly covered container for up to 1 month.

∗ For a quicker soup with a yellow color, use red lentils instead of the usual brown variety. Reduce cooking time by 10 to 15 minutes.

Variation

Spicy Kale-Lentil Soup: Add ½ teaspoon turmeric or ground cumin (or both) to the onions and celery. (Or add a whole or half small jalapeno pepper, finely minced, or a 4-ounce can of mild chopped chiles with the tomatoes.) Stir in ½ cup raisins along with the kale, if you wish.

30-Minute Bean Soup with Bok Choy

This is a hearty, nourishing meal that can be put together from scratch when you need a hot lunch in a hurry. Vary the vegetables and seasonings to suit your diet.

½ cup chickpea or red-lentil flour

3 cups vegetable or chicken stock or broth or water

1–2 small turnips, cut into ½" cubes

1 cup chopped bok choy

½ cup chopped leeks or onions

1 tablespoon vegetable oil

1 clove garlic, crushed (optional)

¼ teaspoon vitamin C crystals

½ teaspoon salt

⅛ teaspoon ground dried rosemary

Freshly ground black pepper or 2–4 drops of hot-pepper sauce (optional)

IN A 3-QUART SAUCEPAN, combine the bean or lentil flour; stock, broth, or water; and turnips over medium-high heat.

Heat the oil in a large skillet over low to medium heat. Add the bok choy (reserving the greens) and leeks or onions and cook for 10 minutes, or until tender. Add the garlic, and cook for 2 minutes.

Add to the turnip mixture. Stir in the bok choy greens, vitamin C, salt, rosemary, and pepper or hot-pepper sauce. Cover, and cook for 15 minutes. The soup will be thick; if desired, thin with a little water.

Makes 1 quart

COOK'S TIPS

✳ The secret to making this soup in 30 minutes is to have the chickpea or lentil flour ready ahead.

✳ You can replace the bok choy with finely chopped spinach, cabbage, chard, or beet greens.

Minestrone

*This "big soup" is great for people with allergies because it offers
a wide choice of ingredients that can be changed or omitted as desired.*

2 tablespoons olive oil

2 cups chopped onions or leeks

1½ cups sliced celery

2 cups sliced carrots

1–2 teaspoons dried oregano

1–2 teaspoons dried basil

1 teaspoon chili powder or ⅛ teaspoon
ground red pepper

6 cups water or stock

3 cups cooked pinto beans or 2 cans
(14–19 ounces each), rinsed and
drained

4 cups stewed tomatoes

¾ teaspoon salt

⅔ cup chopped green bell peppers

½ cup chopped parsley

1 tablespoon lemon juice

1 teaspoon light agave nectar or honey

3 cloves garlic, crushed

2 cups cooked wheat-free macaroni or
brown rice

HEAT THE OIL in a Dutch oven or
stockpot over medium heat. Add the onions
or leeks, celery, and carrots and cook, stirring occasionally, for 10 minutes, until soft
but not brown. Add the oregano, basil, and

chili powder or ground red pepper. Cook
for 2 minutes.

Add the water, beans, tomatoes, and salt.
Cook for 30 minutes. Add the peppers,
parsley, lemon juice, agave nectar or honey,
and garlic. Cook for about 5 minutes.

To serve, place a spoonful of pasta or rice
in bowls. Ladle soup over it.

Makes 8 servings

COOK'S TIPS

＊ To cook beans, soak them in cold water for 8 hours,
then discard the water. Rinse the beans and cover
them with water an inch deeper than the beans.
Cook for 1 to 2 hours, or until tender. Drain. If you
want, you can reserve the cooking liquid and use it
to make the soup.

＊ If you want to use fresh basil, chop and add 8
leaves during the last 10 minutes of cooking time.

＊ Other favorite beans that I like to use in this soup
include kidney beans, black beans, limas, Great
Northern beans, adzuki beans, chickpeas, and
soybeans. Use singularly or in combination.

＊ If you wish, 2 cups of tomato puree plus 2 cups
water can be substituted for the stewed tomatoes.

＊ One tablespoon cider vinegar or ¼ teaspoon
unbuffered vitamin C crystals can replace the lemon
juice if you want.

＊ This soup freezes well in a tightly covered container.
Use within a month.

Chickpea-Potato Soup

Try this thick soup with waffles or pancakes and a green salad.

3 potatoes, peeled and diced

3 cups water

¾ teaspoon salt

2 tablespoons vegetable oil

1 yellow bell pepper, chopped

½ teaspoon rosemary, crushed

2 cups cooked chickpeas or 1 can (14–19 ounces), rinsed and drained

1 tablespoon lemon or lime juice or ¼ teaspoon unbuffered vitamin C crystals

   Freshly ground black pepper (optional)

IN A 2-QUART SAUCEPAN, combine the potatoes, water, and salt. Bring to a boil. Reduce the heat, cover, and cook for 15 minutes, or until tender.

In a 3-quart saucepan, heat the oil over medium heat. Add the peppers and rosemary and cook for 12 minutes, or until the peppers are tender. Remove and reserve 4 tablespoons of peppers. Add the remaining peppers to the potatoes and their cooking water, stirring to mix.

Combine 1 cup of the chickpeas and the lemon juice in a food processor or blender. Ladle in half of the potato mixture and process until pureed. Pour into the 3-quart saucepan. Ladle the remaining potato mixture into the food processor or blender and process until smooth. Pour into the 3-quart saucepan.

Stir in the remaining 1 cup chickpeas. Season to taste with the pepper if using. Bring to a boil over medium-high heat, stirring often. Serve at once. Garnish each serving with a portion of the reserved peppers.

Makes 4 servings

Variations

Creamy Chickpea Soup: Substitute white turnips, peeled and diced, or 4 cups cauliflower florets for the potatoes.

Spicy Chickpea Soup: Add ½ to 1 small jalapeño pepper, finely minced. Cook it along with the bell peppers.

Fruit Soup

*This fruit soup is perfect as a light summer lunch or a refreshing
first course at dinner. For optimum flavor, choose a cantaloupe that smells sweet.
Because cantaloupe, watermelon, and honeydew are all members of the Gourd family,
this recipe can easily be adapted for a Rotary Diversified Diet.*

1 large cantaloupe, cut into cubes

6 mint leaves (optional)

1 cup watermelon balls

1 cup honeydew balls

1 cup blueberries or sliced strawberries (optional)

1 cup chopped peaches, nectarines, or plums (optional)

PLACE THE CANTALOUPE in a food processor or blender. Process for 1 minute, or until pureed. Add the mint if using and process in 2 or 3 short bursts. Set aside.

Combine the watermelon, honeydew, blueberries or strawberries if using and peaches, nectarines, or plums if using in a bowl. Pour the cantaloupe mixture over them and stir gently.

Serve at once or chill a few hours.

Makes 8 servings

COOK'S TIP

* If you prefer, you can puree one of the other melons. Simply increase the amount of the melon to be pureed and reduce the cantaloupe to 1 cup. Watermelon will give you a rosy-pink soup, honeydew a very pale green. For a bright green color, include mint leaves when pureeing the honeydew.

Pork and Pepper Stew

To save time, I buy lean pieces of pork labeled "stir-fry pork strips" for this recipe,
which is outstanding served over sweet potatoes, rice, or wheat-free pasta.

1 tablespoon vegetable oil

1½ pounds of lean pork, cut into 1" pieces

1½ cups chopped onions

2 large red bell peppers cut into short thin strips

½ cup sulfite-free white wine

3½ cups water

½ teaspoon salt

Black pepper or 6 drops hot-pepper sauce (optional)

1 package (10 ounces) frozen green beans

1 large clove garlic, crushed (optional)

½ cup quinoa flakes

HEAT THE OIL in a Dutch oven or large pot over medium heat. Add the pork, onions, and peppers. Cook, stirring often, for 10 minutes or until the meat is no longer pink and the onions are soft. Stir in the wine, water, salt, and pepper if using. Reduce the heat, cover, and cook over low heat for 1½ to 2 hours. Ten minutes before serving, add the green beans and the garlic if using. Sprinkle the quinoa flakes over the stew and cook, stirring constantly, until the mixture thickens and the beans are tender.

Makes 4 servings

COOK'S TIPS

* Instead of the white wine, you can use 2 tablespoons lemon or lime juice plus water to make ½ cup, or ½ teaspoon unbuffered vitamin C crystals dissolved in ½ cup water.

* If you don't have quinoa flakes on hand, use ½ wheat-free flour and ⅓ cup water to thicken the mixture. Simply stir the flour into cool water until smooth, then stir into the stew.

Lamb Stew

Thickened with vegetables only and ready in less than an hour!

1 pound extra-lean ground lamb

1 cup chopped onions

10 small new potatoes

5–6 carrots, cut into chunks

3–4 celery ribs, cut into 1" pieces

2 parsnips, cut into 1" pieces

1 teaspoon dried rosemary, crushed

ON A SHEET of waxed paper, pat the lamb into a large flat square about ½" thick. Cut into 1" cubes, and brown in a 4-quart saucepan. Drain off the fat.

Add the onions and cook for 5 minutes. Add the potatoes, carrots, celery, parsnips, rosemary, and water to barely cover the vegetables. Cover and cook for about 15 minutes, or until the vegetables are tender.

With a slotted spoon, place about 1½ cups of the vegetables in a blender or food processor. Process until smooth, and stir back into the stew. Cook for 10 minutes, or until thickened.

Makes 4 servings

Variation

Lamb Stew over Sweet Potatoes: Omit the new potatoes and steam 4 sweet potatoes. Mash slightly and top with the stew.

Rabbit-Vegetable Stew

You can buy frozen domestic rabbit in most supermarkets. Rabbit is all white meat, fine-grained, mild-flavored, and low in fat. Preparing it is very much like working with chicken.

- **1 young frying rabbit, cut into serving pieces (about 3 pounds)**
- **2 cups sliced peeled sweet potatoes**
- **2 celery ribs, cut into ¾" chunks**
- **10 pearl onions or ½ cup chopped onions**
- **1 clove garlic, crushed**
- **¼ cup chopped parsley**
- **2 tablespoons lemon juice or ¼ teaspoon unbuffered vitamin C crystals**
- **1½ teaspoons Hungarian paprika (optional)**
- **½ teaspoon salt**
- **⅛ teaspoon ground red or black pepper (optional)**
- **⅓ cup quick-cooking tapioca**
- **2 cups water**
- **1½ cups frozen peas**

PREHEAT THE OVEN TO 350°F. Arrange the rabbit, sweet potatoes, celery, onions, garlic, and parsley in a small roasting pan. Sprinkle with lemon juice or vitamin C, paprika if using, salt, pepper if using, and tapioca. Pour in the water.

Cover the pan, and bake for 1 to 1½ hours, or until the rabbit is tender, stirring once or twice during baking to distribute the seasonings and tapioca. Add the peas 10 minutes before the end of the cooking time.

Makes 4 servings

COOK'S TIPS

✳ If you want, you can replace up to ½ cup of the water with sulfite-free white wine.

✳ To avoid foods in the Nightshade family, replace the paprika and cayenne with 2 bay leaves and 3 or 4 cloves garlic. Discard bay leaves before serving.

✳ For a 4- or 5-pound mature rabbit, add 50 percent more vegetables and increase the baking time by 50 percent.

Variation

Slow-Cooker Rabbit Stew: Place the onions and celery in the bottom of the pot. Top with the tapioca, and add the rabbit, sweet potatoes, garlic, and parsley. Sprinkle with the lemon juice or vitamin C and seasonings. Pour water over all. Cover, and cook for 10 to 12 hours on low. Stir in the peas for the last 10 minutes of cooking time.

Marjorie Fisher's Venison Stew with Carrots

*As past president of Nutrition for Optimal Health Association, as well as the
Chicago Chapter of the Human Ecology Action League, Marjorie Fisher is very knowledgeable
about Rotary Diversified Diet and teaches classes on it in the north suburbs of Chicago.
She follows the diet herself, and this is one of her tried-and-true recipes. Because wild game
is lean and muscular, it responds well to long, slow cooking.*

2 **pounds venison loin roast, cubed**

2 **quarts water**

¼ **teaspoon unbuffered vitamin C
   crystals**

  Salt (optional)

4 **carrots, sliced**

6 **celery ribs or a few handfuls of
   lovage foliage, sliced**

PLACE THE VENISON in a Dutch oven or
large pot. Add the water and vitamin C.
Cover and cook for 4 to 5 hours, or until
tender. Season with the salt if using to taste.
Add the carrots and celery or lovage, and
cook for 20 minutes, or until the vegetables
are tender.

Makes 4 servings

Variations

Venison Stew with Beets: Replace the carrots
and celery or lovage with diced red beets
and sliced beet tops. Serve with a spinach
salad to keep the vegetables confined to one
food family.

Game Meat Stew with Carrots: Substitute elk,
moose, or beaver for the venison.

Chunky Lamb Stew

This versatile stew can accommodate itself to any food allergies. You can easily omit the peppers and tomatoes for a Nightshade-free stew. For a meal without foods from the Mint family, replace the herbs listed with herbs of your choice or Pizzazz Seasoning (page 210). This dish is nice served over potatoes, brown rice, or sweet potatoes.

1 pound lamb, cut into cubes
1 large Spanish onion, chopped
1 large green bell pepper, chopped
2 carrots, sliced into 1" chunks
2 celery ribs, sliced into 1" chunks
1–2 cloves garlic, minced
2 cups stewed tomatoes (optional)
2–4 cups water
1 teaspoon dried oregano
¼ cup arrowroot (optional)
½ cup cool water (optional)
2 tablespoons minced fresh or
  2 teaspoons dried basil
2 tablespoons minced fresh parsley

BROWN THE LAMB in a Dutch oven over moderate heat. Drain off all but a thin film of fat. Add the onions, peppers, carrots, celery, and garlic and cook for 5 minutes.

Add the tomatoes and 2 cups water (or use 4 cups water if you omit the tomatoes). Stir in the oregano. Cover and cook for 1½ to 2 hours, or until the lamb is tender.

For a thickened sauce, combine the arrowroot with the ½ cup cool water, stir until smooth, and stir into the stew. Cook, stirring, for 5 minutes or until the stew thickens and becomes clear. Remove from the heat and stir in the basil and parsley just before serving.

Makes 4 servings

Variation

Lamb-Shank Stew: Use 1 large or 2 smaller lamb shanks instead of lamb stew meat. Have your butcher cut them into 1–2" pieces and trim off the fat—but keep the bone to toss into the stew for flavor.

Turkey-Pumpkin Stew

Pumpkin is one of the least allergenic vegetables.
This stew is a good way to utilize leftovers from your holiday bird.

2 tablespoons vegetable oil

2 cups cooked turkey, cubed

1 green bell pepper, chopped

1 red pepper, chopped

½ Spanish onion, chopped

1 cup pumpkin puree

4 cups turkey or chicken stock or broth

Pinch of ground red pepper (optional)

3–4 cups cubed pumpkin or winter squash

4 medium red potatoes, cubed

4 fresh sage leaves, minced

Minced cilantro leaves or parsley (optional)

HEAT THE OIL in a Dutch oven or large pot over medium-high heat. Add the turkey and cook for 3 minutes, or until brown. Remove to a bowl. In the same pot, cook the peppers and onions for 5 minutes, or until crisp-tender.

Mix the pumpkin puree with the stock or broth and ground red pepper if using. Add to the pot and bring to a boil. Add the cubed pumpkin or squash and potatoes. Reduce the heat, and add the sage and turkey. Cover and cook for 30 to 40 minutes, or until the vegetables are tender. Top each serving with the cilantro or parsley if using.

Makes 4 servings

Kidney-Bean Vegetarian Stew

A tasty bean dish without tomatoes.
You can vary the beans or herbs to suit your diet or taste buds.

2 cups chopped onions

3 tablespoons olive oil

7 cups water or vegetable broth

1½ cups kidney beans, soaked overnight

1½ cups brown rice

1 tablespoon Dijon mustard

2 cups chopped chard, spinach, or beet greens

3–4 cloves garlic, crushed

1 teaspoon salt

2 tablespoons minced basil or 2 teaspoons dried

1 teaspoon dried oregano

Grated peel of 1 lemon (optional)

HEAT THE OIL in a Dutch oven or stockpot over medium heat. Add the onions and cook for 10 minutes, or until soft. Add the water and bring to a boil.

Drain the beans, discard the water, and rinse well. Add to the water-onion mixture. Stir in the rice and mustard. Cover and cook for 1½ to 2 hours, until the beans are tender. Add the greens, garlic, salt, basil, oregano, and half of the lemon peel if using

during the last 10 minutes of cooking time. Season with the remaining lemon peel if you want more tang.

Makes 8 servings

Variation

Chili-Seasoned Kidney-Bean Stew: Replace the basil and oregano with 1 to 2 tablespoons chili powder. Omit the mustard if you wish.

Garbanzo Garden Stew

This is best made in summer and early fall with garden-fresh vegetables.
The secret to the wonderful flavors of this dish is timing; the sauce develops a
slow-cooked flavor that complements fresh vegetables, which are cooked just until tender.
Serve hearty portions plain or over brown rice or quinoa.

1 tablespoon vegetable oil
1 cup chopped onions or leeks
2½ pounds fresh tomatoes, chopped
2 cups cooked chickpeas
½ teaspoon salt
1½ teaspoons Pizzazz Seasoning
  (page 210) (optional)
1 cup thinly sliced carrots
1 cup thinly sliced celery
2 cups zucchini slices
1 small green bell pepper, chopped
2 tablespoons minced basil or
  1 tablespoon dried basil or tarragon
  Freshly ground black pepper or a
  pinch of ground red pepper (optional)
2 cloves garlic, minced
¼ cup minced parsley

HEAT THE OIL in a 5-quart pot over medium heat. Add the onions or leeks and cook for 5 minutes, or until soft. Add the tomatoes, chickpeas, salt, and seasoning if using. Cook, uncovered, for 25 minutes, stirring occasionally.

Add the carrots and celery, and cook for 10 to 15 minutes. Add the zucchini, peppers, basil or tarragon, pepper if using, and garlic and cook for 10 minutes or just until crisp-tender. Stir in the parsley and serve.

Makes 4 servings

Pork and Pepper Stew with Beans

In this delightful stew, the focus is on sweet peppers and beans.
Feel free to use leeks or shallots instead of the onions. Serve over brown rice, quinoa, or pasta.

1–2 **tablespoons vegetable oil**

1½ **pounds lean pork, cut into bite-size cubes**

1½ **cups chopped onion**

¾ **teaspoon dried thyme**

½ **teaspoon salt**

⅛ **teaspoon ground red pepper or freshly ground black pepper**

2 **cans (14–19 ounces each) kidney beans, rinsed and drained**

1 **can (14½ ounces) diced tomatoes**

3–4 **cups vegetable or chicken stock or broth**

1 **large green bell pepper, cut in cubes**

1 **large red bell pepper, cut in cubes**

1 **large clove garlic (optional)**

⅓ **cup rye flour**

HEAT THE OIL in a 5-quart pot over medium heat. Add the meat and onions, and cook for 12 minutes, or until the meat is no longer pink and the onions are soft. Add the thyme, salt, and red or black pepper and cook, stirring, for 1 minute. Stir in the beans, tomatoes, and 3 cups of the stock or broth. Cover and cook for 2 to 4 hours, or until the meat is tender.

About 15 minutes before the end of the cooking time, combine the rye flour and ½ cup of the remaining stock or broth, whisking until smooth.

Add the green and red pepper to the meat-bean mixture and increase the heat to medium. Stir in the garlic. Stir in the flour mixture and cook, stirring, for 5 minutes, or until thickened. (For a thinner stew, stir in the remaining ½ cup stock or broth.)

Makes 4 servings

COOK'S TIPS

* This recipe works nicely with a variety of beans: pinto, black, white, roman. Or you might try Westbrae Natural salad beans, which come with three varieties of beans in one can: kidney, chickpeas, and pintos.

* In place of the tomatoes, you can use 1 can (15 ounces) pumpkin puree plus 2 tablespoons lemon or lime juice, cider vinegar, or ½ teaspoon unbuffered vitamin C crystals. Omit the rye flour.

Catfish Chowder

You might call this milk-free stew Manhattan-style fish chowder.
Catfish are especially good in this chowder, but you can substitute any mild-flavored fillets.
The tomato puree has a heavier tomato taste than the diced tomatoes.

1 tablespoon olive oil

1 cup diced onions or leeks

2 cups tomato puree or diced tomatoes
   in tomato juice

2 cups water

1 cup sliced celery

4 small potatoes or 2–3 small turnips,
   diced

2 carrots or 1 parsnip, sliced

2 bay leaves

½ teaspoon salt

1 teaspoon honey

¼ teaspoon fennel seeds

¼ teaspoon dried tarragon

   Pinch of ground red pepper
   (optional)

¾–1 pound catfish fillets, whole

1 medium zucchini, chopped

1 clove garlic, crushed (optional)

HEAT THE OIL in a 3-quart saucepan over medium heat. Add the onions or leeks and cook for 5 minutes, or until soft. Add the tomato puree or diced tomatoes, water, celery, potatoes or turnips, carrots or parsnip, bay leaves, salt, honey, fennel, tarragon, and ground red pepper if using. Cook for 10 minutes.

Add the fish, zucchini, and garlic if using, and cook for 10 to 15 minutes, or until the fish flakes easily. Discard the bay leaves and break the fish into bite-size pieces.

Makes 2 quarts

Rice and Wheat-Free Pasta

I love brown rice and whole-grain pastas for several reasons: For starters, they're complex carbohydrates—starchy foods that digest slowly and help us feel satisfied for as long as four hours after we've eaten. They provide many of the B vitamins, minerals, and fiber we need to stay healthy. With all this going for them, rice and pasta fill an important spot in my diet, especially when I don't have time to bake breads.

But I've learned to be cautious about using prepared mixes and eating restaurant foods containing rice or pasta. The reason: These time-saving meals usually contain white rice and white pasta that lack fiber and some trace elements. As a result, they just don't measure up nutrient-wise.

RICE

Rice is a grain. Although a few people with allergies react to rice, it's considered by most experts to be the least allergenic of the grains. Of all the rice varieties available, my favorite is brown rice, and I especially like the long-grain variety, which I suggest using in my recipes. Here are a few of my suggestions for making rice nice—every time.

Plan on using ¼ cup to ⅓ cup uncooked rice for each adult serving. Rice will expand during cooking and if you end up with leftovers, that's okay. I've discovered that cooked rice keeps very nicely in the refrigerator for several days. You can also freeze it for months and reheat it in the microwave.

Wash rice to eliminate dirt. Washing isn't recommended by most domestic suppliers because it removes some thiamin (vitamin B_1), but I like to rinse rice anyway. Rinsing reduces exterior starch so cooked rice is less sticky and has fluffy separate grains. I'm also happy knowing my rice is clean. You decide for yourself. To rinse rice: Place it in a saucepan of cool water, then swish it with a spoon several times. Quickly pour the mixture into a strainer. The first rinse water almost always appears gray and cloudy. Rinse a few more times until the water is clear.

Use almost twice as much liquid as rice. In other words, to cook 1 cup of brown rice, use about 1¾ cups of liquid.

Combine the rice, liquid, and seasonings in a large saucepan. Then bring the mixture to a boil. (Many cookbooks direct you to add the rice slowly to rapidly boiling water, but I don't do that and I have good results every time, anyway.) Reduce the heat to low, cover, and cook for 45 to 55 minutes, or until the liquid has been absorbed. (Brown basmati rice, an imported Indian variety, takes about 35 minutes to cook.) Remember: Use a *large* saucepan and lower the heat quickly because rice foams as it cooks and tends to "boil over." What a mess when it does.

Don't peek and don't stir. This is a place where other cooks and I agree: Lifting the pot lid and stirring after the liquid has come to a boil results in gummy sticky grains.

Remove rice from the heat as soon as it's done. After the liquid has been absorbed, rice will stick to the pan, become tough, and scorch if left over the heat. Fluff with a fork before serving.

PASTA

Today, people with allergies have wonderful pasta choices including Kamut brand, whole-grain and white spelt, rice (including rice vermicelli and rice sticks), rye, quinoa, and wild-rice pastas as well as bean thread noodles and 100 percent buckwheat soba noodles. Most of these pastas are distributed nationally and should be available in almost any health food store. I've also found the bean thread noodles and rice sticks in Asian markets as well as the Asian section of large supermarkets. When shopping, take the time to look over the selections; new wheat-free varieties are available with increasing frequency (hurray!). I love trying the new pastas—it's fun and can be quite rewarding—and I encourage you to give them a try, too. (See "Wheat and Grain Alternatives," page 5.)

When cooking pasta, you should always follow package directions because some pastas have unique instructions. For example, bean thread noodles must be soaked in very hot water for anywhere from 5 to 20 minutes instead of the usual boiling routine. Of course, the results are unique, too. These delightful noodles are clear after soaking and readily pick up the colors and flavors of accompanying sauces. But because they're slippery, they also can be difficult to toss and serve. So, I suggest cutting them into approximately 2" pieces after soaking.

Here's another creative approach to replacing wheat pasta: Use vegetable alternatives—spaghetti squash, shredded zucchini, bean sprouts, and others. It's an extra-easy solution and eliminates worries about gluten and other grain sensitivities. You'll find these special recipes grouped with the pastas.

Basic Rice

Allow plenty of time for cooking rice—and for letting it rest before serving.

1 cup brown rice
1¾ cups cold water
½ teaspoon salt

COMBINE THE RICE, water, and salt in a 2- or 3-quart saucepan. Bring to a boil. Immediately reduce the heat to low, cover, and cook for 45 to 55 minutes, or until the liquid is absorbed. Remove from heat and fluff with a fork. Cover and let rest for 5 to 10 minutes before serving.

Makes 2 cups

Rice Pilaf with Chicken

This main dish packs plenty of flavor—thanks to chopped nuts and sesame seeds. My favorite serving suggestion: Stir in lima beans, peas, or green beans and serve with baked acorn or butternut squash for added nutrients and color.

1 tablespoon vegetable oil
⅓ cup chopped cashews or walnuts
2 tablespoons sesame seeds or 3 tablespoons sunflower seeds
2 cups Basic Rice (above)
1 cup chopped cooked chicken or salmon
2 tablespoons tamari, sulfite-free white wine, or water
6–8 drops dark oriental sesame oil (optional)
2–4 scallions, thinly sliced (optional)

HEAT THE OIL in a large nonstick skillet over medium-low heat. Add the nuts and seeds and cook for 5 minutes, or until lightly brown. Add the rice; chicken or salmon; tamari, wine, or water; and sesame oil if using. Cook, stirring, for 2 to 3 minutes, or just until heated through. Divide among 4 dinner plates and top each portion with the scallions if using.

Makes 4 servings

Rice and Sweet Potato Patties

Here, two familiar foods combine to make a very pleasant dish. You get the flavor
of sweet potatoes with the chewy texture of rice. Both rice and sweet potatoes are thought
to be hypoallergenic foods. I like to serve this simple and quick side dish with chicken or turkey.

1 cup **Basic Rice (page 158)** or cooked
   brown basmati rice

1 cup **mashed cooked sweet potato**
   (about 1 medium)

2–3 tablespoons **quinoa flakes, amaranth**
   flakes, or soy flour or flakes

   Pinch of grated nutmeg

   Pinch of salt

1 tablespoon **vegetable oil**

IN A MEDIUM BOWL, combine the rice;
sweet potatoes; quinoa or amaranth flakes,
or soy flour or flakes; nutmeg; and salt. The
mixture will seem dry. Shape into 4 patties
that are ¾" thick.

Heat the oil in a large nonstick skillet
over medium heat. Add the patties and
cook for 3 minutes on a side, or until brown
on both sides. Serve immediately.

Makes 6 servings

Festive Pecan Rice

A simple but fancy side dish made with foods from just two food families.
Serve with fish or poultry.

1 cup **brown rice**

½ cup **wild rice**

3 cups **water**

⅓ cup **coarsely chopped pecans**

1 tablespoon **ghee or walnut oil**

In a small skillet, heat the ghee or oil
over medium-low heat. Add the pecans and
cook for 1 to 2 minutes, or just until fragrant. Add to the rice and toss lightly to
combine. Serve immediately.

Makes 6 servings

IN A 3-QUART SAUCEPAN, combine the
brown rice and wild rice. Add the water and
bring to a boil. Reduce the heat, cover, and
cook for 45 to 55 minutes, or until the
liquid has been absorbed. Remove from the
heat and let stand for 5 to 10 minutes.

COOK'S TIP

✳ To make ghee (or clarified butter): Melt butter in a
saucepan over low heat, then pour the liquid into a
jar, taking care to leave the milk solids in the bottom
of the pan. Discard the solids. Ghee will keep frozen
for up to 1 year.

Mushroom-Rice Casserole

*A wonderful dish for a picnic or potluck supper. Wrap the casserole in a huge beach towel
or several layers of newspapers for insulation. It will stay warm for two hours.*

  1 **cup brown rice**
2¾ **cups Mushroom Brown Sauce
(page 204)**
  ¼ **cup water or sulfite-free white wine**
¼–½ **teaspoon salt**

PREHEAT THE OVEN to 350°F. Oil a
2-quart baking dish. Place the rice in the
dish. Stir in the mushroom sauce, water or
white wine, and salt. Cover and bake for
1¼ hours, or until the rice has absorbed the
liquid and is tender.

Makes 4 servings

Variations

Brown Rice with Tuna Casserole: Add 1 can of
no-salt-added water-packed tuna to the rice
mixture. Finish cooking according to the directions.

Rice and Poultry Casserole: Add 1½ cups of
diced cooked chicken or turkey to the rice
mixture. Finish cooking according to the directions.

Mushroom-Rice and Vegetable Casserole: Add 1
cup lightly steamed broccoli florets or 1 cup
frozen peas to the rice mixture. Finish
cooking according to the directions.

Southwestern Rice and Meat Casserole

*This casserole is tomato-free but has plenty of intriguing flavor from chili powder,
sweet peppers, garlic, and other Tex-Mex seasonings.*

  1 **tablespoon vegetable oil**
  1 **pound ground turkey, chicken,
or buffalo**
1½ **cups chopped onions**
  ¾ **cup chopped red or green bell
pepper (optional)**
1½ **tablespoons mild chili powder**
1½ **cups brown rice**
  3 **cups boiling water**
  1 **can mild chopped chile peppers
(optional)**

  2 **cans (14–19 ounces) no-salt-added
kidney, black, or pinto beans, rinsed
and drained**
  ¾ **teaspoon salt**
  2 **large cloves garlic, minced (optional)**
  1 **cup grated Cheddar-style goat's-milk,
soy, or almond cheese**
    **Goat's-milk or soy yogurt or sour
cream (optional)**
    Black or green olives (optional)

PREHEAT THE OVEN to 350°F. Oil a 13" × 9" baking dish.

Heat the oil in a 4- or 5-quart heavy pot over medium heat. Add the turkey, chicken, or buffalo; onions; and bell peppers. Cook, stirring, for 10 minutes, or until the meat is crumbly and no longer pink. Add the chili powder and cook, stirring for 1 minute. Add the rice and cook, stirring, for 3 minutes. Stir in the water, chiles if using, beans, and salt. Bring to a boil. Remove from the heat and stir in the garlic if using.

Place in the prepared baking dish. Cover with foil and bake for 45 minutes. Remove from oven, and sprinkle with the cheese. Bake, uncovered, for 10 to 15 minutes, or until the cheese is melted and bubbly. Top each serving with the yogurt or sour cream and olives if desired.

Makes 6 servings

COOK'S TIPS

---

* If you have home-cooked beans on hand, you can use them instead of the canned variety. You'll need about 3½ to 4 cups.

* Sometimes, I like to substitute 1 seeded and minced mild dried chile pepper (wear plastic gloves when handling) for the chili powder. I also omit the canned chile peppers when I want a little different flavor.

Kale-Sausage Risotto

This extra-easy, unique dish packs tons of flavor, fiber and nutrients—thanks to kale, brown rice, and wild rice. It takes me a little more than an hour to prepare and cook it.

¾ cup brown rice

½ cup wild rice

3 cups vegetable or chicken stock or broth or water

½ teaspoon salt

4–5 cups chopped kale

¾ pound pork or turkey sausage

4–6 shallots, finely chopped

2 oranges, chopped (optional)

IN A 3-QUART SAUCEPAN, combine the rice, stock, and salt. Bring to a boil over high heat. Reduce the heat to low, cover, and cook for 10 minutes. Add the kale, but do not stir. Cover and cook for 25 minutes.

Meanwhile, in a large nonstick skillet, cook the sausage over medium heat for 15 minutes, or until crumbly and no longer pink, stirring often to crumble. Using a slotted spoon, place the sausage on a plate lined with three layers of paper towels. Pour excess fat from the skillet and return it to the heat. Add the shallots. Cook, stirring often, over medium-low heat for 5 minutes, or until the shallots are soft. Stir in the sausage. Stir in the rice-kale mixture. Cover and cook for 20 minutes, or until the rice is tender and the liquid has been absorbed.

Divide among 4 plates and top each portion with the orange if using.

Makes 4 servings

COOK'S TIPS

---

* If you want, you can mail-order preservative- and MSG-free sausage.

* To save time, I occasionally use store-bought vegetable or chicken broth.

Spaghetti Squash Italian-Style

Here's the perfect grain pasta substitute—and it's a snap to prepare.
Speed tip: I make the sauce ahead and keep a supply in the refrigerator or freezer.

1 large spaghetti squash (about 3½ pounds)

2 cups Fresh Tomato Sauce (page 198), Italian Spaghetti Sauce (page 200), or Tomato-Free Spaghetti Sauce (page 201)

PREHEAT THE OVEN to 375°F. Using a sharp knife, pierce the squash deeply in several places. Place on a jelly-roll pan. Bake for 25 minutes. Turn and bake 20 minutes more, or until the skin yields to gentle pressure. Allow to cool for 10 to 15 minutes.

Cut the squash in half. Using a large spoon, remove the seeds and strings from the center. Using a fork, separate the flesh into strands.

While the squash is cooking, heat the sauce until heated through. Divide the squash among 4 dinner plates and top each portion with the sauce.

Makes 4 (main dish)
or 6 (side dish) servings

COOK'S TIP

＊ Cooked spaghetti squash freezes nicely. To use, thaw in a colander to drain off excess water.

Variation

Spaghetti Squash Italian-Style with Meatballs: Prepare and serve 8 medium-size Versatile Meatballs (page 230) with the squash and sauce. Reserve remaining meatballs for another use.

Zucchini Pasta

Miss savoring your favorite tomato-based sauce—even more than you miss the wheat pasta it topped? I did. So, I created this super simple recipe.

1 medium zucchini, shredded

⅔ cup Fresh Tomato Sauce (page 198), Italian Spaghetti Sauce (page 200), or Tomato-Free Spaghetti Sauce (page 201)

STEAM THE ZUCCHINI over boiling water for 1 minute, or until heated through. While the water is heating, heat the sauce for 4 minutes, or until heated through. Place the zucchini on a plate and top with the sauce.

Makes 1 serving

COOK'S TIP

✳ When I'm not in the mood for cooking, I serve the squash raw instead of steamed. The flavor and texture are perfectly delightful.

Variations

Cabbage Pasta: Substitute 1 cup cooked spaghetti squash and 1 cup steamed finely shredded cabbage for the zucchini.

Bean-Sprout Pasta: Substitute 1 cup cooked spaghetti squash and 1½ cups blanched bean sprouts for the zucchini.

Zucchini Pasta with Meatballs: Prepare and serve Versatile Meatballs (page 230) with the zucchini and sauce.

Zucchini Lasagna with Lamb

In this no-noodle lasagna variation, I layer vegetables—
zucchini, to be specific—with sauce and ground meat.
You'll never miss the wheat pasta because the flavors here meld so nicely.

3 cups Fresh Tomato Sauce (page 198),
  Italian Spaghetti Sauce (page 200),
  or Tomato-Free Spaghetti Sauce
  (page 201)

3 medium zucchini, cut into
  ¼" lengthwise strips (about 1 pound)

8 ounces spinach

1 tablespoon lemon juice or
  ⅛ teaspoon unbuffered vitamin C
  crystals

½ teaspoon salt
  Pinch of freshly grated nutmeg

½ pound ground lamb

¾ cup chopped onion or leek
  Freshly ground black pepper
  (optional)

1 teaspoon Italian Seasoning (page 210)

PREHEAT THE OVEN to 350°F. Oil an
8" × 8" baking dish and spread ¼ cup of the
sauce over the bottom of the prepared dish.
Arrange ⅓ of the zucchini strips over the
sauce.

Steam the spinach over boiling water
for 3 minutes, or until wilted. Drain in a
colander, gently pressing with a large
spoon to remove excess water. Place on a
cutting board and chop. Distribute over
the zucchini. Season with the lemon juice
or vitamin C, salt, and nutmeg. Top with
2 to 3 tablespoons of the sauce. Arrange

another layer of zucchini over the spinach.

In a large nonstick skillet, cook the lamb
and onions or leeks for 7 minutes, or just
until the lamb is no longer pink. Drain off
the fat. Season with the salt, Italian Seasoning, and pepper if using. Arrange over
the zucchini and top with 2 to 3 tablespoons
sauce and the remaining zucchini. Pour in
the remaining sauce, spreading to cover.

Bake for 40 minutes, until the top is brown
and sauce is bubbly. Cut into large squares.

Makes 4 servings

Variations

Wheat-Free Lasagna with Lamb: Replace the
zucchini with one of the following: ½ to 1
cooked spaghetti squash, 4 ounces cooked
bean-thread noodles, or 8 ounces cooked
rice vermicelli (toss with olive oil to coat).

Zucchini Lasagna with Poultry: Replace the
lamb with ½ pound ground chicken or
turkey.

Vegetarian Lasagna: Replace the lamb with
one of the following: 1 can (14–19 ounces)
rinsed and drained chickpeas, 8 ounces
lightly browned cubed tofu, or 4–6 ounces
crumbled Soft Goat's-Milk Cheese (page
262) or 2 ounces grated dried Myzithra (a
hard Cheddar-style goat's-milk cheese).

* Myzithra is a traditional Greek cheese made from the whey of ewe's, goat's, or cow's milk. It's available fresh, which resembles ricotta cheese, or dried, which is much like Parmesan and Romano cheeses. Look for it in health food stores, cheese shops, and large supermarkets.

* This dish is very saucy, which is the way my family likes it. But if you prefer a thicker lasagna, here's what to do: Sprinkle ½ cup brown rice over the sauce in the bottom of the baking dish. Finish layering the ingredients, cover, and bake for 50 to 60 minutes.

* Busy? Then assemble the lasagna ahead and refrigerate it until you're ready to bake and serve. Add 15 minutes to the usual cooking time.

* To serve 6 to 8 people, double the recipe and bake in a lasagna pan or a 13" × 9" baking dish.

Pesto Pasta

A fragrant, colorful change from tomato-sauced pasta.
Makes a great side dish with fish or poultry.

3¾ ounces bean-thread noodles or 8 ounces rice vermicelli

1 cup Pesto Dip (page 274)

⅓ cup coarsely chopped walnuts or pine nuts, lightly toasted

PREPARE THE PASTA according to package directions. Drain well, place in a large bowl, and coarsely cut. Add the dip and toss gently to coat. Divide among 4 plates and sprinkle each portion with some of the nuts.

Makes 4 servings

COOK'S TIP

* To toast small nuts and seeds, spread them in a small nonstick skillet. Cook, stirring often, over medium-low heat for 5 minutes, or until lightly browned.

* Try substituting 8 ounces spelt or Kamut brand and quinoa gemelli pasta for the noodles or vermicelli.

Pasta Primavera Alfredo

*Lighter than a traditional Alfredo, this innovative dish
showcases tender asparagus and baby carrots. It's delicious—I think you'll agree.
Serve with a Marinated Sicilian Salad (page 182).*

SAUCE

- 8 ounces extra firm tofu, drained and crumbled
- ½ cup 1% soy or goat's milk or ¼ cup milk + ¼ cup sulfite-free white wine
- 2 tablespoons olive oil
- 1½ tablespoons chopped fresh tarragon, or ½ teaspoon dried
- ½ teaspoon Hungarian sweet paprika
- ¼ teaspoon turmeric (optional)
- ½ teaspoon salt
- 4 drops hot-pepper sauce

VEGETABLES

- 5 ounces spelt rotini or rice macaroni (about 1¼ cups)
- 12 stalks fresh asparagus, cut into ¾" pieces
- 12 baby carrots, thinly sliced
- 4 scallions, thinly sliced
- 2–4 tablespoons grated dried Myzithra or crumbled feta cheese (optional)

TO MAKE THE SAUCE: In a blender or food processor, combine the tofu, milk or wine and milk, oil, tarragon, paprika, turmeric if using, salt, and hot-pepper sauce. Process for 2 minutes, until very smooth.

To make the vegetables: Prepare the pasta according to package directions. During the last 5 minutes of cooking time, add the asparagus and carrots. Cook until the pasta and vegetables are tender. Drain and divide between 2 plates. Top each portion with the sauce (either warmed or at room temperature), scallions, and cheese if using.

Makes 2 servings

COOK'S TIP

* Myzithra is a traditional Greek cheese made from the whey of ewe's, goat's, or cow's milk. It's available fresh, which resembles ricotta cheese, or dried, which is much like Parmesan and Romano cheeses. Look for it in health food stores, cheese shops, and large supermarkets.

Kamut Spaghetti with Sage Cream Sauce

Lovely and luscious, this quick-and-easy pasta dish is one of my favorites.
It offers an opportunity to use a variety of delightful summer herbs,
many of which I grow in my garden.

SAUCE

8 ounces firm or extra-firm low-fat tofu, crumbled

½ cup 1% soy or goat's milk or ¼ cup milk + ¼ cup sulfite-free white wine

1 teaspoon vegetable oil

6–10 fresh sage leaves

¼–½ teaspoon salt

4 drops hot-pepper sauce or a few gratings white or black pepper

VEGETABLES

5 ounces Kamut brand or brown rice spaghetti

2 tablespoons olive oil

1 cup coarsely chopped onions or leeks

¾ cup chopped red bell pepper

1½ cups sliced mushrooms

1 cup chopped cooked turkey or chicken (optional)

2 sprigs sage (optional)

TO MAKE THE SAUCE: In a blender or food processor, combine the tofu, milk or wine and milk, oil, sage leaves, salt, and hot-pepper sauce or pepper. Process for 2 minutes, or until very smooth.

To make the vegetables: Prepare the pasta according to package directions. Drain the pasta and return it to the pot.

While the pasta is cooking, heat the oil in a large skillet over medium heat. Add the onions or leeks, bell peppers, mushrooms, and turkey or chicken if using. Cook, stirring occasionally, for 5 minutes, or just until tender. Stir in the sauce. Bring just to a boil and remove from the heat.

Divide the pasta between 2 plates. Top each portion with the sauce and sprigs of sage if using.

Makes 2 servings

COOK'S TIP

✱ Sage isn't the only herb that's well-suited to this dish. These are others that I often use: tarragon, rosemary, basil, or summer savory. (Use one variety at a time.)

Gemelli with Leek-Pepper Sauce

*Cashews and steamed broccoli and carrots give this quick-to-prepare dish
plenty of color and crunchy texture. If you prefer, you can leave out the bell peppers.*

8 ounces Kamut brand and quinoa
  gemelli pasta, spelt rotini, or rice
  macaroni

2 tablespoons olive oil

4 cups sliced leeks

1 cup chopped red or yellow bell
  peppers

2 cups broccoli florets

2 cups baby carrots, cut in thirds

1 cup hot water or vegetable broth

½ teaspoon salt

4–6 thin scallions, chopped (optional)

½ cup cashews, roasted (optional)

PREPARE THE PASTA according to
package directions. Add the broccoli and
carrots during the last 4 minutes of cooking
time. Drain and place in a large bowl.

Drizzle ½ tablespoon of the oil over the
pasta and gently toss to coat.

Meanwhile, heat the remaining 1½ tablespoons oil in a large skillet over medium
heat. Add the leeks and peppers. Reduce the
heat and cook, stirring often, for 5 minutes,
or until very soft. Do not brown. Place in a
blender or food processor. Pour in the hot
water or broth. Process until almost smooth.

Divide the pasta and vegetables among 4
plates. Top each with leek sauce and
sprinkle with scallions and cashews if using.

Makes 4 servings

COOK'S TIP

✳ To roast large whole nuts, spread them on a baking
  sheet. Bake at 300°F for 12 minutes, or until light
  brown.

Fettuccini with Spinach Pesto

*This superb pasta dish will please the entire family. Even my finicky
preschool granddaughters love it—and they profess not to like any food that's green!*

1 pound wheat-free fettuccini or kudzu
  and sweet potato pasta

1 pound package frozen spinach,
  thawed and squeezed dry

⅔ cup crumbled feta cheese

⅔ cup pine nuts

½ cup packed chopped fresh basil

⅓ cup olive oil

⅓ cup boiling water

½ teaspoon salt

1 clove garlic, crushed

½ teaspoon anise seeds

  Few grindings black pepper

PREPARE THE PASTA according to package directions. Drain and return to the pot.

Meanwhile, combine the spinach, cheese, ⅓ cup of the nuts, the basil, oil, water, salt, garlic, anise seeds, and pepper in a food processor. Process until smooth, scraping the bowl as needed. Sauce will be thick. Pour over the pasta and toss gently to coat.

Divide among 6 plates and top each portion with some of the remaining ⅓ cup nuts.

Makes 6 servings

COOK'S TIPS

* Some of my favorite wheat-free varieties of fettuccini include spelt, Kamut brand, rice, and 100 percent buckwheat (also called Soba noodles).

* Heat leftovers in the microwave oven or on the stove top, using medium-low heat. Do not boil.

Italian-Style Spaghetti and Meatballs

If you've been avoiding spaghetti and meatballs because the classic dish contains wheat (in the pasta) and cow's-milk cheese (Parmesan), it's time to put that all-time favorite back on your menu. This nicely spiced version calls for wheat-free pasta and cheeses made from goat's or sheep's milk. It's so delicious, I never miss the original version.

2 cups Italian Spaghetti Sauce (page 200), or Tomato-Free Spaghetti Sauce (page 201)

8 Versatile Meatballs (page 230)

10 ounces wheat-free spaghetti

2–4 ounces grated goat's-milk Cheddar or Myzithra or crumbled feta cheese (optional)

COOK'S TIPS

* Some of my favorite wheat-free varieties of spaghetti include spelt, Kamut brand, and rice. Other wheat-free pasta shapes and types that work well here include kudzu and sweet potato pasta, and Kamut brand and quinoa gemelli pasta.

* Myzithra is a traditional Greek cheese made from the whey of ewe's, goat's, or cow's milk. It's available fresh, which resembles ricotta cheese, or dried, which tastes similar to Parmesan and Romano cheeses. Look for it in health food stores, cheese shops, and large supermarkets.

PREPARE THE PASTA according to package directions.

While the pasta is cooking, heat the sauce and meatballs. Drain the pasta and divide among 4 plates. Top with the sauce, meatballs, and cheese. Sprinkle with cheese if using.

Makes 4 servings

RICE AND WHEAT-FREE PASTA

Creamy Pasta with Vegetables

A speedy mushroom sauce (it goes together while the pasta cooks)
flavors this pasta and vegetable dish.

8–10 **ounces rice or Kamut brand spaghetti**

2 **cups assorted chopped vegetables:**
carrots, broccoli, cauliflower, leek

2 **teaspoons olive oil**

2¾ **cups Mushroom Brown Sauce**
(page 204)

1 **cup chopped cooked lamb or chicken**
(optional)

PREPARE THE PASTA according to package directions. Add the carrots, cauliflower, and broccoli during the last 5 minutes of cooking time and cook just until the vegetables are tender. Drain and return to the pot. Add the oil and gently toss to coat.

While the pasta is cooking, prepare the mushroom sauce. Divide the pasta mixture among 4 plates. Top each portion with the lamb or chicken if using and the mushroom sauce.

Makes 4 servings

COOK'S TIPS

✳ Other wheat-free pasta shapes and types that work well here include kudzu and sweet potato pasta and Kamut brand and quinoa gemelli pasta.

✳ Onions, bell peppers, zucchini, and asparagus are other vegetables that I regularly use in this dish. Use singularly or in combination.

Variations

Creamy Cashew Pasta with Vegetables: Substitute Cashew Cream Sauce (page 198) for the mushroom brown sauce.

Mustard-Cashew Pasta with Vegetables: Substitute Creamy Mustard Sauce (page 197) for the mushroom brown sauce.

Chilled Pasta Salad with Cucumber-Dill Sauce

In the summer, I try to beat the dinner-hour heat (and survive those heat waves)
by making this fast salad in the morning. Let it chill until supper time.

1 cup Cucumber-Dill Sauce
(page 195)

8–10 ounces wheat-free spaghetti

2 teaspoons olive oil

2 cups assorted raw vegetables:
cucumbers, bell peppers, asparagus

1 cup chopped cooked lamb, chicken,
or turkey (optional)

¼ cup roasted cashews or pine nuts

PREPARE THE CUCUMBER SAUCE and
let chill for at least 30 minutes.

Meanwhile, prepare the pasta according
to package directions. Drain and place in a
large bowl. Add the oil and gently toss to
coat. Chill until ready to serve.

Divide the pasta among 4 plates. Top
each portion with the vegetables, meat or
poultry if using, and cucumber-dill sauce.
Top with the nuts.

Makes 4 servings

COOK'S TIPS

✳ Some of my favorite wheat-free varieties of
spaghetti include spelt, Kamut brand, and brown
rice. Other wheat-free pasta shapes and types that
work well here include kudzu and sweet potato
pasta and Kamut brand and quinoa gemelli pasta.

✳ Zucchini, scallions, tomatoes, and cooked beans of
all types are other vegetables that I regularly use in
this dish. Use singularly or in combination.

✳ To roast large whole nuts, spread them on a baking
sheet. Bake at 300°F for 12 minutes, or until light brown.

✳ Is that chilled pasta glued together in one big
clump? To de-clump it, place the pasta in a colander
and run hot water over it for a minute or two. Let
drain before dividing it among the plates.

Variations

Chilled Pasta Salad with Cucumber-Chive Sauce:
Substitute Cucumber-Chive Sauce (page
196) for the cucumber-dill sauce.

Chilled Pasta Salad with Tomato Sauce: Substitute Fresh Tomato Sauce (page 198) or
Fresh-Tomato Salad Dressing (page 193) for
the cucumber-dill sauce.

Vegetable Sides and Salads

With so many varieties to choose from, vegetables themselves aren't too much of a problem for people with food allergies. It's the sauces you have to watch for. But tasty options abound.

In this chapter, you'll find all sorts of side-dish vegetables and salads. Three of my favorites are the Vegetable Stir-Fry with Cashews, Spicy Jicama Slaw, and Spinach Salad. For more vegetable recipes, turn to Super Soups, Stews, and Chowders on page 135, Rice and Wheat-Free Pasta on page 156, and Vegetarian Main Dishes on page 247.

Here are a few suggestions for getting the most out of side dish vegetables.

Steam, roast, or stir-fry instead of boiling. Steaming, roasting, and stir-frying, as well as cooking vegetables in a microwave oven, are fairly kind to the food's nutrients. These cooking methods also retain more flavor. Boiling, on the other hand, tends to dilute flavors and many of the water-soluble nutrients in vegetables, such as vitamin C and the B vitamins.

Keep cooking times short. Overcooking vegetables, even with the gentlest of methods, destroys textures, colors, and nutrients. If you're eating vegetables plain—without even a misting of oil—go for a brief steaming, which leaves the vegetables crisp-tender and full of wonderful flavors. You'll barely miss saucy toppings. (See "Timetable for Cooking Vegetables," page 176.)

Use a baking dish with a tight-fitting lid. When cooking vegetables in the oven, I like to add a tablespoon or two of water to a baking dish and cover it tightly so the vegetables steam as they cook. Most vegetables cooked this way are ready in 45 to 75 minutes in a 375°F oven, depending on the size and variety of vegetable. My favorites for cooking this fuss-free way: asparagus, broccoli, cauliflower, turnips, and mixed carrots and celery.

Top vegetables simply. Cooked vegetables can taste great plain or with just a little spread or lemon juice. If you're avoiding citrus, you might try a light sprinkling of vitamin C crystals; the resulting taste is much like lemon juice.

Keep vegetables on the menu. Nutritionists recommend getting up to 5 servings a day. Make a point of going for the goal.

Golden Mashed Potatoes

*There's no butter, eggs, or milk, yet these potatoes
are just about the tastiest I have ever eaten.*

6 large Yellow Finn, Yukon gold, or red
  potatoes, peeled and quartered
1 carrot, sliced
1 cup water
½ teaspoon salt
1 tablespoon vegetable oil

COMBINE THE POTATOES, carrot, water,
and salt in a 2-quart saucepan with a tight-
fitting lid. Bring to a boil over high heat.
Reduce the heat, cover, and cook for 20
minutes, or until the vegetables are quite
soft.

    Remove from the heat. Add the oil, and
using a potato masher or hand-held electric
mixer set to high, whip until fluffy. Add
water as necessary.

Makes 4 servings

New Potatoes with Basil Vinaigrette

*This quick and easy dish tastes like hot potato salad.
Serve it with your favorite meat, fish, or poultry entree.*

12 new potatoes
  Basil Vinaigrette (page 191)
1–2 thinly sliced scallions or ¼ cup
  minced fresh parsley (optional)

STEAM THE POTATOES over boiling water
for 20 to 30 minutes, or until tender. Divide
among 4 dinner plates and quarter. Drizzle
the vinaigrette over the potatoes and top
each portion with the scallions or parsley if
using. Serve warm.

Makes 4 servings

Caramelized Leeks and Zucchini

Such a simple side dish and so delicious. Here, I've caramelized the vegetables
by cooking them very slowly. The results are superb.
Allow half an hour cooking time.

1–2 tablespoons olive oil

1 large leek, sliced ½" thick

1 large zucchini, quartered lengthwise and sliced ½" thick

2–3 tablespoons minced parsley, basil, or cilantro (optional)

HEAT THE OIL in a large nonstick skillet over medium heat. Add the leeks and cook for 1 minute. Add the zucchini and cook, stirring, for 2 minutes. Reduce the heat to medium-low, cover, and cook, stirring occasionally, for 30 minutes, or until very soft and lightly browned. Do not overbrown. Add 1 or 2 tablespoons of water if the vegetables start to brown too much.

About 5 minutes before the end of cooking, stir in the parsley, basil, or cilantro if using.

Makes 4 servings

Maple Carrots

Looking for something that's subtly sweet? Search no more.
The sweetness here is just right. Best of all, the kids will ask for seconds.

6 medium carrots, thinly sliced

1–2 tablespoons maple syrup

STEAM THE CARROTS over boiling water for 8 to 10 minutes, or until tender. Place in a serving bowl, and drizzle with the maple syrup. Toss gently to coat.

Makes 4 servings

Creamed Spinach

A popular side dish that I've adapted to be milk- and flour-free.

8 ounces spinach

⅓ cup cashews, very finely ground

¾ cup water

½ tablespoon Dijon mustard

2 tablespoons finely minced onions

½ teaspoon salt

3–4 drops of hot-pepper sauce
or ¼ teaspoon freshly ground black
pepper

STEAM THE SPINACH over boiling water for 3 minutes, or just until it wilts. Drain in a colander, pressing out and reserving the excess liquid. Place on a cutting board and chop coarsely. Measure the liquid and add water to equal ¾ cup.

Place the cashews and ¼ cup of the water in a blender. Process until smooth. Add the mustard, onions, salt, hot-pepper sauce or pepper, and remaining ½ cup water. Process until smooth. Pour into a 3-quart saucepan and bring to a boil, stirring constantly, over medium-high heat. Cook for 3 to 4 minutes, until thickened. Stir in the spinach and cook another 2 minutes to heat through.

Makes 2 servings

COOK'S TIPS

✳ To substitute other nuts, add 1 tablespoon of arrowroot or tapioca starch plus an additional ¼ cup water to the mixture in the blender.

TIMETABLE FOR COOKING VEGETABLES

People who are on a very limited diet may need to eat unadorned, plain vegetables. To conserve flavor and nutrients, steam vegetables lightly in a stainless steel steamer or wire basket over boiling water in a covered pot. Or cook them in a microwave oven following the manufacturer's directions. (You can also use this chart to cook potatoes and other vegetables for salads and combination dishes.)

VEGETABLE (1 LB. UNLESS NOTED)	STEAMING TIME	MICROWAVE OVEN TIME (HIGH)[†]
Artichokes		
1 whole	12–15 minutes	3–5 minutes
Asparagus		
Spears	7–10 minutes	3–5 minutes
2" pieces	4–6 minutes	3–5 minutes
Beans, Green*		
Whole	10–15 minutes	11–16 minutes
Cut	7–12 minutes	10–15 minutes
Beans, Wax (yellow)*		
Whole	10–15 minutes	8–9 minutes
Cut	7–12 minutes	6–7 minutes
Beets*		
Whole	25–60 minutes (varies with size)	12–20 minutes
¼" slices	10–15 minutes	10–15 minutes
Broccoli*		
Stalks	8–12 minutes	8–10 minutes
Florets	5–8 minutes	5–8 minutes
Brussels Sprouts*		
Whole	8–15 minutes	6–8 minutes
Cabbage*		
Quartered	10–15 minutes	6–8 minutes
Thinly sliced	5–10 minutes	4–8 minutes
Carrots*		
Whole baby	15–20 minutes	8–10 minutes
¼" slices	10–15 minutes	8–10 minutes

VEGETABLE (1 LB. UNLESS NOTED)	STEAMING TIME	MICROWAVE OVEN TIME (HIGH)†
Cauliflower*		
Florets	5–10 minutes	5–8 minutes
Celery*		
½" pieces	3–9 minutes	5–9 minutes
Chard, Swiss		
Coarsely chopped leaves	3–5 minutes	3–5 minutes
Corn*		
4 ears	7–10 minutes	5–6 minutes
Cut	4–5 minutes	4–5 minutes
Dandelion Greens		
Leaves	3–5 minutes	3–5 minutes
Endive		
Leaves	4–8 minutes	3–5 minutes
Escarole		
Leaves	4–8 minutes	3–5 minutes
Fennel*		
½"–1" slices	5–8 minutes	9–10 minutes
Green Pepper*		
¼" slices	5–7 minutes	6–8 minutes
Kale		
Leaves	4–8 minutes	3–5 minutes
Kohlrabi*		
¼" slices or ½" cubes	5–10 minutes	8–9 minutes
Leeks*		
½" slices	5–10 minutes	5–10 minutes
Okra		
Sliced	5–7 minutes	5–6 minutes
Parsnips*		
¼" slices	7–10 minutes	7–9 minutes
Pearl Onions*		
Whole	6–15 minutes	7–10 minutes

(continued)

TIMETABLE FOR COOKING VEGETABLES (cont.)

VEGETABLE (1 LB. UNLESS NOTED)	STEAMING TIME	MICROWAVE OVEN TIME (HIGH)†
Peas*		
Shelled, green	5–8 minutes	5–7 minutes
Potatoes, Sweet		
Whole	40–45 minutes	10–12 minutes
½" slices*	18–20 minutes	5–10 minutes
Scallions*		
½" pieces	3–5 minutes	3–5 minutes
Snow Peas*		
Whole	3–5 minutes	4–5 minutes
Spinach		
Leaves	3–5 minutes	3–5 minutes
Squash, Summer*		
½" slices or cubes	5–10 minutes	6–8 minutes
Squash, Winter		
Halved	20–30 minutes	7–9 minutes
½" cubes*	7–10 minutes	4–8 minutes
Turnips*		
½" cubes	5–7 minutes	7–9 minutes
Zucchini*		
½" slices or cubes	5–10 minutes	6–8 minutes

†Allow to stand for 2 minutes before serving.
*Add ⅛–¼ cup water when cooking in the microwave oven.

Vegetable Stir-Fry with Cashews

This quick dish makes a perfect accompaniment for baked fish or roasted poultry.
Serve over brown rice for a flavorful vegetarian main dish.

2 tablespoons vegetable oil

1 cup sliced mushrooms

1 cup thinly sliced celery or Chinese cabbage

1 cup bean sprouts or snow peas

½ cup sliced scallions

½ cup thinly sliced jicama

½ cup unsalted cashews or almonds

1–2 tablespoons wheat-free tamari sauce (optional)

HEAT THE OIL in a large skillet over high heat. Add the mushrooms and celery or Chi-nese cabbage and cook for 2 minutes. Add the bean sprouts or snow peas and cook for about 1 minute. Add the scallions and jicama and cook for 1 minute. Add the cashews or al-monds and cook for 2 minutes. Add the tamari if using and toss to coat. Serve immediately.

Makes 4 servings

COOK'S TIPS

✳ If you're avoiding soy products, sprinkle salt instead of tamari sauce over your stir-fry.

✳ For a successful stir-fry, cook the food *quickly* over high heat, constantly tossing the ingredients. Don't overcook; the vegetables should be crisp-tender.

Saucy Carrots

The sweet yet tangy sauce in this recipe is thick—somewhat like a glaze.

¾ pound carrots, thinly sliced

⅔ cup unsweetened apple or pineapple juice

1 teaspoon vegetable oil

1½ teaspoons arrowroot

COMBINE THE CARROTS and ⅓ cup of the apple or pineapple juice. Bring to a boil. Reduce the heat, cover, and cook for 12 to 15 minutes, or until tender, adding a little water if necessary to prevent sticking. Add the oil.

In a cup, combine the arrowroot and the remaining ⅓ cup juice. Stir into the carrot mixture. Cook, stirring, for 2 minutes, or until the sauce is thick and clear.

Makes 4 servings

Variations

Saucy Carrots with Mint: Add 1 tablespoon chopped fresh mint to the apple juice-arrowroot mixture.

Saucy Carrots with Dill: Add 1 teaspoon dried dillweed to the apple juice-arrowroot mixture.

Eggplant Pizzas

Serve as an appetizer, side dish, or evening snack.
Top with grated or crumbled hard goat's-milk cheese, if desired.

1 medium eggplant (about 1¼ pounds),
  peeled and sliced ½" thick
  Olive oil cooking spray
1 tablespoon olive oil
1 large sweet onion, chopped
1 green bell pepper, chopped
2 cups chopped tomatoes
1 clove garlic, minced
1½ teaspoons Italian Seasoning
  (page 210)

PREHEAT THE OVEN to 350°F. Line a
baking sheet with parchment paper. Mist
both sides of each eggplant slice with the
cooking spray. Arrange slices on the pre-

pared baking sheet. Bake for 15 to 20 minutes, or until tender.

Heat the oil in a skillet over medium
heat. Add the onion, pepper, tomatoes, and
seasoning and cook for 15 minutes, or until
the vegetables are soft. Stir in the garlic.

Place a heaping teaspoonful on each eggplant slice.

Bake for 10 minutes, or until heated
through.

Makes 4 (side dish or appetizer) servings

COOK'S TIP

* You can make this recipe ahead. Simply refrigerate
the topped eggplant slices, then when ready to serve,
bake for 12 to 15 minutes, or until heated through.

Cauliflower with Cashew Spread and Scallions

Good hot or cold. A tasty alternative to cauliflower with cheese sauce.

1 small head cauliflower, cut into
  florets
2–4 scallions, sliced
4–6 tablespoons Cashew Spread (page
  195) or Tofu-Dijon Spread (page 194)
  Savory Seed Seasoning (page 209)
  (optional)

STEAM THE CAULIFLOWER over boiling
water for 8 to 10 minutes, or until tender.
Place in a serving dish, and add the scallions and cashew spread. Toss to coat.
Season with the savory seasoning if using.

Makes 6 servings

20-Minute Sweet Potatoes

This extra-easy side dish is ideal for speedy meals.
Vary the seasoning to suit your mood.

1 large moist sweet potato, peeled and sliced ½" thick

1 large apple, peeled and sliced

¼ teaspoon cinnamon or pumpkin pie spice

ARRANGE THE SWEET POTATO and apple in a steamer. Sprinkle with the cinnamon or pumpkin pie spice. Steam over boiling water for 18 to 20 minutes, or until tender.

Makes 2 servings

Easy Roasted Vegetables

These vegetables are a big hit in my home. I recommend preparing extras because they'll go fast.
Use one or two of the suggested vegetables or all of them.

6 small new potatoes, halved

10–12 baby carrots

4 small beets, halved

2 slender parsnips, cut into 1" pieces

2 small turnips, quartered

2 sweet potatoes, cut into 1½" pieces

8 small onions, quartered

2 red bell peppers, cut into 2" strips

Hummus Bean Spread (page 271) or Pesto Dip (page 274)

PREHEAT THE OVEN to 450°F. Arrange the new potatoes, carrots, beets, parsnips, turnips, sweet potatoes, onions, and peppers on baking sheets with cooking spray. Place the sheets on 2 oven racks. Bake for 40 to 50 minutes, switching the positions on the racks when cooking is half done. Divide vegetables onto 4 plates. Serve along with a small cup of the bean spread or pesto dip for dipping for each diner.

Makes 4 servings

COOK'S TIP

* Other dip options include Curried Tofu Dip (page 275), Tofu-Dijon Spread (page 194), and Cashew Spread (page 195).

Summer Salad Bowl

*Salads are perfect for people with food allergies
because they can pick and choose the foods that agree with them.*

4 cups chopped mesclun, spinach, or romaine lettuce

4 cups assorted thinly sliced vegetables: carrots, zucchini, cucumbers

2 cups cubed cooked turkey, chicken, or lamb

¾ cup Sweet and Sour Salad Dressing (page 191) or Fresh-Tomato Salad Dressing (page 193)

PLACE THE MESCLUN, spinach, or lettuce in individual small bowls. Top with the assorted vegetables and turkey, chicken, or lamb. Drizzle with the Sweet and Sour or Fresh-Tomato Salad Dressing.

Makes 4 servings

COOK'S TIPS

✳ Bell peppers, celery, scallions, radishes, and jicama are other vegetables that I regularly use in this salad. Use singularly or in combination.

✳ Other protein sources that work nicely here include 2 cups of cooked salmon, two 6-ounce cans of salt-free tuna or 2 cans (14–19 ounces) rinsed and drained salad beans.

✳ If you want, serve this salad-bar style, allowing diners to construct their own salads.

Marinated Sicilian Salad

*This marinated salad makes perfect company fare.
It can be made a day ahead, so there's no last-minute hassle.*

1 can (12–14 ounces) artichoke hearts, drained and quartered

1 cup frozen peas

12 mushrooms, thinly sliced

¼ cup Basil Vinaigrette (page 191) or Tarragon Vinaigrette (recipe variation, page 191)

1 teaspoon dried oregano (optional)

IN A BOWL, combine the artichokes, peas, and mushrooms. Drizzle the vinaigrette over the vegetables and toss to coat. Sprinkle on the oregano if using. Cover and refrigerate for at least 2 hours.

Makes 4 servings

Spinach Salad

A welcome change from sandwiches at lunchtime.
Serve with muffins or tortillas.

6 cups spinach, chopped

6 scallions, sliced

8 radishes, diced

4–6 mushrooms, sliced

4 hard-cooked eggs, sliced (optional)

1 can (14–19 ounces) chickpeas, rinsed and drained

2 small cooked beets, sliced

2–4 tablespoons sunflower seeds, toasted

½ cup Sesame-Lime Salad Dressing (page 193)

2 tablespoons sesame seeds (optional)

DIVIDE THE SPINACH between 4 salad bowls. Top with the scallions, radishes, mushrooms, eggs if using, chickpeas, beets, and sunflower seeds. Drizzle with dressing. Sprinkle with the sesame seeds if using.

Makes 4 servings

COOK'S TIP

* To toast small nuts and seeds, spread them in a small nonstick skillet. Cook, stirring often, over medium-low heat for 5 minutes, or until lightly browned and fragrant.

Pesto Pasta Salad

A real treat on a hot summer day.
And, like conventional pasta salads, it's delightfully versatile.

1 cup Pesto Dip (page 274)

2 cups chilled cooked spelt spaghetti, cut into 2" lengths

12 cherry tomatoes, quartered (optional)

½ cup chopped sweet onion or 4 scallions

COOK'S TIPS

* Other wheat-free pastas work well here. Try Kamut brand pasta, rice vermicelli, or bean thread noodles.

* When preparing pasta several hours ahead to chill, mist the pasta with olive oil cooking spray.

Variation

Pesto Spaghetti Squash Salad: Substitute spaghetti squash for the pasta.

PLACE THE PASTA in a large bowl, add the dip, and gently toss to combine. Divide among 4 plates. Arrange the tomatoes if using around the outer edges of each salad. Top with the onions or scallions.

Makes 4 servings

Kidney-Bean Salad

Dressed with either mayonnaise or oil and vinegar, this salad is a winner.
Serve it with muffins or a dessert that contains nuts or seeds for a high-protein meal.

2 cups cooked kidney beans, or 1 can (14–19 ounces), rinsed and drained

½ cup thinly sliced celery

½ cup chopped green peppers

½ cup sliced scallions

2–3 tablespoons chopped dill pickles or honey-sweetened pickle relish

Dash of ground red pepper or hot-pepper sauce

⅓ cup Tofu-Dijon Spread (page 194) or Cashew Spread (page 195)

IN A LARGE BOWL, toss together the beans, celery, peppers, scallions, pickles or relish, and ground red pepper or hot-pepper sauce. Add the spread and toss gently to combine. Chill at least 2 hours before serving.

Makes 2 (main dish)
or 6 (side dish) servings

Variation

Sweet and Sour Kidney-Bean Salad: Replace the spread with ⅓ cup Sweet and Sour Salad Dressing (page 191) or 2 tablespoons oil, 2 tablespoons vinegar, and ½ teaspoon agave nectar or honey.

Four-Bean Salad

A traditional sweet and sour favorite. By making this salad yourself,
you avoid the corn syrup and sugar almost always present in commercial products.
Great for picnics and potluck suppers and it keeps well in the refrigerator.

1 cup cooked green beans

1 cup cooked kidney beans

1 cup cooked chickpeas

1 cup cooked wax beans

1 cup thinly sliced celery

¾ cup chopped green or red bell peppers

½ large sweet onion or 1 bunch scallions, sliced

¼ cup vegetable oil

⅓ cup balsamic or cider vinegar

¼ cup honey

2 cloves garlic, crushed (optional)

¼ teaspoon salt

⅛ teaspoon ground red pepper (optional)

IN A LARGE BOWL, combine the green beans, kidney beans, chickpeas, wax beans, celery, peppers, and onions or scallions.

In a small bowl, whisk together the oil, balsamic or cider vinegar, honey, garlic if using, salt and ground red pepper if using. Pour over the beans. Toss well to coat. Refrigerate several hours or overnight before serving.

Makes 8 servings

Hold the Lettuce

Lettuce is related to ragweed, so many hay fever sufferers can't eat it. Fortunately, it's very easy to make a tasty tossed salad without lettuce. (You can even make this at a restaurant salad bar!) To put this combination together, you'll need 1½ to 2½ cups of assorted vegetables for each serving. Choose as few or as many of the following ingredients as you can eat freely. Then drizzle with Creamy Zucchini Salad Dressing (page 192) or another dressing of your choice and toss gently to coat.

✳ Celery, thinly sliced

✳ Carrots, shredded

✳ Red or green bell peppers, chopped

✳ Scallions or onion rings, thinly sliced

✳ Zucchini, thinly sliced

✳ Cucumbers, thinly sliced

✳ Tomatoes, sliced

✳ Radishes, thinly sliced

✳ Kohlrabi, chopped

✳ Jicama, chopped

✳ Chickpeas, cooked

✳ Sunflower seeds, raw or toasted

✳ Nuts, raw or roasted

✳ Mushrooms, thinly sliced

✳ Avocado, chopped

✳ Beets, cooked and diced

✳ Green beans, cooked and cut into 2" pieces

✳ Broccoli, raw or blanched, chopped

✳ Cauliflower, raw or blanched, chopped

Fruit Salad

Fruit makes delightful cold salads. And with a little help, children can help pull this fast version together. It goes exceptionally well with wedges of goat's-milk cheese and Grain-Free Banana-Nut Muffins (page 111).

½ cup frozen pineapple or white grape juice concentrate, thawed

4 large leaves romaine or leaf lettuce

2 large bananas

1 large pear or apple, sliced

2 kiwifruits, peeled, sliced

40 red or white grapes

12 macadamia nuts, chopped (optional)

ARRANGE THE LETTUCE on 4 individual salad plates. Cut each banana in half cross-wise, then again lengthwise. Arrange on the outer edges of the plates. Arrange the pear or apple, kiwi, and grapes between the bananas.

Drizzle each salad with 2 tablespoons of the juice concentrate and top with the nuts if using.

Makes 4 servings

COOK'S TIP

✳ Other good fruit choices include melons, berries, peaches, nectarines, and apricots.

Cauliflower-Dill Salad

A salad without lettuce, tomatoes, or cucumbers—and absolutely delicious.

1 small head cauliflower, cut into florets and blanched

1 cup fresh peas, blanched, or frozen peas, thawed (optional)

½ cup sliced scallions

½ cup Cashew Spread (page 195) or Tofu-Dijon Spread (page 194)

1–2 teaspoons dried dillweed

2 teaspoons lemon juice or ½ teaspoon vitamin C crystals dissolved in 1 tablespoon of warm water

½ teaspoon salt

Hot-pepper sauce (optional)

IN A LARGE BOWL, combine the cauli-flower, peas if using, and scallions. In a small bowl, whisk together the spread, dill-weed, lemon juice or vitamin C crystals, salt, and hot-pepper sauce to taste if using. Stir spread mixture into cauliflower mixture. Chill several hours or overnight.

Makes 6 servings

COOK'S TIP

✳ To blanch vegetables: Pour 2 quarts boiling water over the vegetable in a large bowl. Let stand for 30 seconds; drain. Return to the bowl and add a trayful of ice cubes. Fill with cold water. Drain when the vegetable is cool.

Tangy-Sweet Slaw

A refreshing change from traditional mayonnaise-based slaws. Great with fish or chicken.

1 small head cabbage, chopped

2 cups chopped apples

1 cup chopped fresh or canned
unsweetened pineapple

½ cup raisins or ¼ cup currants

½ cup chopped onions

½ cup Cashew Spread (page 195)
or Tofu-Dijon Spread (page 194)

¼ cup rice vinegar or 2 tablespoons
cider vinegar

3 tablespoons frozen pineapple
or apple-juice concentrate

1 tablespoon lemon juice or water plus
¼ teaspoon unbuffered vitamin C
crystals

¼ teaspoon salt

IN A LARGE BOWL, combine the cabbage, apples, pineapple, raisins or currants, and onions.

In a small bowl, whisk together the spread, vinegar, juice concentrate, lemon juice or water, and salt. Pour over salad and toss to coat. Serve at room temperature or chilled.

Makes about 8 cups

Pickled Beets

Most commercially pickled beets contain corn syrup or sugar. These don't.

¼ cup water

¼ cup honey

¼ cup rice, cider, or white wine vinegar

3 cups sliced cooked beets

BRING THE WATER, honey, and vinegar to a boil in a saucepan. Reduce the heat and cook for 2 minutes. Stir in the beets and cook until heated through. Serve hot, warm, or cold.

Makes 4 servings

COOK'S TIPS

✳ If you're avoiding vinegar, try replacing it with 3 tablespoons water plus ¾ teaspoon unbuffered vitamin C crystals.

✳ For a thicker sauce or glaze: Add 1 tablespoon of arrowroot dissolved in ¼ cup of water to the honey mixture as it cooks. Cook for 1 minute, or until thickened. Add the beets and cook until heated through.

Variation

Spicy Pickled Beets: Add ¼ teaspoon ground cinnamon and a pinch of ground cloves to the honey mixture.

Spicy Jicama Slaw

Jicama is an unsung hero in the vegetable world. It has deliciously tender, sweet, and juicy flesh. An average jicama measures 5" or 6" across, which means that this recipe will use only part of one vegetable. Slice the remainder and sprinkle with lime juice and ground red pepper for a refreshing snack.

2–3 **cups coarsely shredded jicama**

1 **carrot, shredded**

6 **radishes, thinly sliced**

½ **large green bell pepper, diced**

½ **cup minced parsley**

3–4 **scallions, thinly sliced**

½ **cup Cashew Spread (page 195) or Tofu-Dijon Spread (page 194)**

1 **tablespoon lime or lemon juice**

1 **teaspoon chili powder**

¼ **teaspoon salt**

IN A LARGE BOWL, toss together the jicama, carrot, radishes, pepper, parsley, and scallions.

In a small bowl, whisk together the spread, lime or lemon juice, chili powder, and salt. Pour over the salad and toss gently to coat. Chill for 1 hour.

Serves 4

COOK'S TIP

* This slaw can be prepared quickly and easily with a food processor. Cut the jicama, carrot, and pepper into 1" chunks and place in the food processor. Add the parsley and process until coarsely chopped. Place in a bowl and add the scallions, radishes, and dressing.

Pineapple Gel Salad

A wonderfully yummy, firm gel without sugar or artificial coloring.
Don't substitute fresh pineapple—an enzyme in it prevents the mixture from gelling.

1 can (20 ounces) unsweetened
  crushed pineapple

4½ teaspoons unflavored gelatin

¾ cup frozen pineapple-juice
  concentrate

¾ cup water

½ cup Cashew Spread (page 195) or
  Tofu-Dijon Spread (page 194)

2 tablespoons agave nectar or honey
  (optional)

1–2 tablespoons minced parsley
  (optional)

LIGHTLY OIL an 8" × 8" baking dish or a 6-cup gelatin mold. Drain the pineapple, reserving the juice. Measure ¼ cup of reserved juice into a small saucepan. Sprinkle the gelatin over the juice and allow to soften for 5 minutes. Stir in the juice concentrate, water, and reserved pineapple juice. Bring to a boil, reduce the heat, and simmer for 5 minutes.

Remove from the heat. Add ¼ cup of the spread and the agave nectar or honey if using, whisking until smooth. Chill until slightly thick and syrupy. Stir in the pineapple by hand (for a lighter, fluffier gel, beat in with an electric mixer).

Pour into the prepared dish or mold. Chill until firm. Unmold, cut into serving pieces, and top each piece with some of the remaining ¼ cup spread and a sprinkling of parsley if using.

Makes 9 servings

COOK'S TIP

✳ For a less creamy version, replace the spread with ¼ cup water.

Salad Dressings, Sauces, and Condiments

For most folks with food allergies, home-made toppings make the most sense because the cook controls the ingredients. I dress salads with allergy-free Creamy Zucchini Salad Dressing or Sweet and Sour Salad Dressing. This chapter includes two versions of mayonnaise—one based on ground cashews, the other on tofu. Both will flavor your favorite sandwich or serve as the base for a dip or spread.

In place of dairy-based cream sauces, try Cashew Cream Sauce, Susan Dart's Blender Sauce, and Creamy Mustard Sauce—all excellent over cooked vegetables or fish. When fresh tomatoes are available, use the Fresh Tomato Sauce recipe. It goes so well with wheat-free pasta, potatoes, and most anything!

The fruit sauces here were designed for pancakes and waffles but are also terrific on breakfast breads, such as Breakfast Short-cake; pudding; or plain cakes. When fresh fruit is in season, I make plenty of Uncooked Fruit Sauce. And I've learned to stock my freezer so I can whip up a quick Blueberry Sauce, Cherry Sauce, or Peach Sauce from frozen fruit.

When it comes to seasonings, I prefer to make them myself too. Commercial blends often combine a little bit of a lot of things, involving many potential allergens and too many food families for people on a Rotary Diversified Diet. Instead, I use Pizzazz Seasoning and Italian Seasoning, each made from a single food family. These get rave reviews whenever I serve them. For something salty-tasting without a lot of sodium, turn to Savory Seed Seasoning. For those who tolerate seeds and soy, this seasoning is a winner.

Basil Vinaigrette

*A simple dressing that's very aromatic. Use fresh basil, if possible; it tastes heavenly.
This vinaigrette goes well with salads, but also try it over cooked vegetables,
such as broccoli, cauliflower, beans, cabbage, and spinach.*

½ cup olive oil

¼ cup cider vinegar or ⅓ cup lemon
   or lime juice

6–8 large basil leaves, minced,
   or 1½ to 2 teaspoons dried

½ teaspoon mustard powder

1 clove garlic, crushed (optional)

IN A BLENDER, combine the oil; vinegar, lemon, or lime juice; basil; mustard; and garlic if using. Process for 1 minute. Store in a tightly covered glass jar in the refrigerator.

Makes ¾ cup

Variations

Oregano Vinaigrette: Substitute 1½ to 2 teaspoons dried oregano for the basil.

Tarragon Vinaigrette: Substitute ¾ to 1 teaspoon dried tarragon for the basil.

Sweet and Sour Salad Dressing

*This delightful dressing is made with an all-fruit jam, which makes it thick
so you can use less oil than you would in a typical oil-and-vinegar dressing.*

½ cup apricot or plum all-fruit jam

¼ cup cider vinegar

¼ cup vegetable oil

½ teaspoon dried oregano (optional)

IN A BLENDER, combine the all-fruit jam, vinegar, oil, and oregano if using. Process for 1 minute, or until smooth. Pour into a jar with a tight-fitting lid. Refrigerate and use within a week.

Makes 1 cup

COOK'S TIPS

✻ If you want, you can use other flavor jams and different herbs.

✻ Want a thinner dressing? Add up to 2 tablespoons of water.

Creamy Zucchini Salad Dressing

This dressing gives you an oil-and-vinegar taste without the vinegar.
Dress it up with your favorite herbs.

1 zucchini (8 ounces), chopped

¼ cup water

¼ cup olive or canola oil

½ teaspoon unbuffered vitamin C crystals

1 small clove garlic (optional)

¼ teaspoon salt

2 teaspoons Italian Seasoning (page 210)

Pinch of Peppy (page 211) or a few drops hot-pepper sauce (optional)

IN A BLENDER, combine the zucchini, water, oil, vitamin C, garlic if using, salt, seasoning, and peppy or hot-pepper sauce if using. Process for 2 minutes, or until smooth. Adjust vitamin C to taste.

Serve immediately or chill a few hours.

Makes 1½ cups

COOK'S TIPS

* For a green salad dressing, do not peel the zucchini; for a cream-colored dressing, peel it.

* Increase the vitamin C for more tang.

* Best when used within 3 days.

Flax and Garlic Salad Dressing

This one is best when freshly made. Fortunately, it's quick and easy.

¼ cup lemon juice

2 tablespoons olive, avocado, or walnut oil

2 tablespoons flax oil

1 large clove garlic, crushed

IN A SMALL BOWL, whisk the juice, oil, flax oil, and garlic. Pour into a small jar and chill until needed. Use within 2 days.

Makes ½ cup

COOK'S TIPS

* Flax oil is fairly perishable, so check the freshness date and buy small quantities at a time.

* If the flavor of flax oil is new to you, use 3 tablespoons of the olive, avocado, or walnut oil and only 1 tablespoon of flax oil. Then as you become used to the taste of flax oil, increase the amount to 2 tablespoons as in the recipe.

Sesame-Lime Salad Dressing

This is my favorite dressing for spinach salads.

⅓ cup canola oil

3–4 tablespoons lime juice

2 tablespoons finely chopped onions

1 tablespoon agave nectar or maple syrup

2 teaspoons sesame seeds

Few drops dark sesame oil

3–4 mint leaves, minced (optional)

IN A BLENDER, combine the oil, lime juice, onions, agave nectar or maple syrup, sesame seeds, sesame oil, and mint leaves if using. Process until smooth.

Makes ¾ cup

COOK'S TIP

＊ You can also sweeten this dressing with honey or thawed apple juice concentrate.

Fresh-Tomato Salad Dressing

A low-fat dressing without sugar. Although this dressing will keep a few days in the refrigerator, it's best when used fresh.

1 cup Fresh Tomato Sauce (page 198), chilled

1 tablespoon olive oil

1 tablespoon unseasoned rice vinegar

1 teaspoon minced tarragon, basil, or rosemary (optional)

IN A SMALL BOWL, combine the sauce, oil, and vinegar. Adjust the oil and vinegar to taste. Top with the herb.

Makes about 1 cup

Tofu-Dijon Spread

A versatile soy-based, egg-free mayonnaise-style spread—
creamy and totally convincing as a stand-in for classic spread.

1½ tablespoons lemon juice or vinegar

1 teaspoon Dijon-style mustard

½ cup vegetable oil

1 teaspoon agave nectar or honey

¼ teaspoon salt

¼ teaspoon dark sesame oil (optional)

8 ounces firm, low-fat tofu, drained
and crumbled

IN A BLENDER or food processor, combine
the lemon juice, mustard, vegetable oil, agave
or honey, salt, sesame oil if using, and half
the tofu. Process until smooth, stopping and
scraping the sides of the container as necessary. Add the remaining tofu and process
until smooth. Adjust the seasonings to taste.

Pour into a glass container with a tight-
fitting lid and use within 1 week.

Makes 1½ cups

Dairy-Free "Sour Cream"

This nondairy "sour cream" has a smooth, creamy texture, and an appropriately
sharp tang. It's delightful on baked potatoes and in dips, toppings,
and other dishes where you'd use regular sour cream.

½ cup cashews

⅔ cup water

2 tablespoons lemon juice

2 tablespoons canola, avocado,
or walnut oil

1 teaspoon agave nectar, maple syrup,
or honey

½ teaspoon grated lemon peel

¼ teaspoon salt

Process for 1 minute more. Add the water
and process for 2 minutes, stopping to
scrape the bottom and sides of the container. Add the lemon juice; oil; agave
nectar, maple syrup, or honey; lemon peel;
and salt and process briefly. Adjust the seasonings to taste.

Pour into a saucepan and bring to a boil,
stirring often. Chill for 1 hour before serving.

Makes about 1 cup

PLACE THE CASHEWS in a blender, and
process until they become a fine powder.
Stop the blender and scrape the bottom.

COOK'S TIP

---

* Stick with cashews for this recipe. Other nuts don't
work well.

Cashew Spread

Here's a versatile egg-free, soy-free spread for sandwiches, dips, vegetables, and fish.

½ cup cashews

¾ cup water

2 tablespoons lemon juice
or ½ teaspoon unbuffered vitamin C crystals

2 tablespoons walnut or avocado oil

1 teaspoon agave nectar or honey

1½ teaspoons Dijon mustard

¼ teaspoon salt

Dash of ground red pepper (optional)

PLACE THE NUTS in a blender and process until they become a fine powder. Add ¼ cup of the water and process for 1 minute. Stop the blender and scrape the bottom. Add the lemon juice or vitamin C, oil, agave nectar or honey, mustard, salt, ground red pepper if using, and the remaining ½ cup water. Process until very smooth.

Pour into a saucepan and cook, stirring, for 5 minutes, or until thick. Allow to cool 10 to 15 minutes. Store in a tightly covered jar in the refrigerator for up to 1 week.

Makes about 1¼ cups

COOK'S TIPS

* Only ground cashews will thicken the spread without adding starch. If you want to substitute Brazil or other nuts, add 1 tablespoon arrowroot or tapioca starch flour to the mixture in the blender so it will thicken when you cook it.

* If you want to keep this spread for up to 2 weeks, you may want to use scalded jars. (See "Scalding Canning Jars and Lids," page 303.)

Cucumber-Dill Sauce

Here is a creamy sauce to top broiled fish or dress up fish salad.

½ cup Cashew Spread (above)
or Tofu-Dijon Spread (page 194)

½ cucumber, peeled, seeded, and finely chopped

1 teaspoon minced onion

1–2 teaspoons fresh dill
or ½ teaspoon dried dillweed

1 tablespoon lemon juice
or ¼ teaspoon unbuffered vitamin C crystals

IN A SMALL BOWL, combine the spread, cucumber, onion, dill, and lemon juice or vitamin C. Chill for at least 30 minutes.

Makes about 1 cup

Variation

Tartar Sauce: Omit cucumber, onion, and dill. Add 2 tablespoons of honey- or fruit-sweetened pickle relish. Lemon juice is optional. Makes about ¾ cup.

SALAD DRESSINGS, SAUCES, AND CONDIMENTS

Cucumber-Chive Sauce

Ground nuts make this sauce nearly as rich as versions that use sour cream.
It's terrific with cooked fish or as a dip for raw vegetables.

- 1 **cup cashews**
- ¾ **cup boiling water**
- ½ **cucumber, peeled, seeded, and finely chopped**
- 2–3 **tablespoons lemon juice**
- 1 **tablespoon minced onion or 1 thinly sliced scallion**
- ¼ **teaspoon salt**
- 1 **tablespoon snipped chives**

IN A BLENDER, grind the cashews in 3 batches (to prevent clumping). For each batch, place ⅓ cup cashews in the blender, grind to a powder, then remove to a bowl. Return all the ground cashews to the blender. With the blender running, slowly add the water. Process at highest speed for 3 minutes. Pour into a stainless steel bowl and let cool.

Fold in the cucumber, lemon juice, onion or scallion, salt, and chives. Process and adjust the seasonings to taste. Chill for at least 20 minutes.

Makes about 1¼ cups

COOK'S TIPS

✳ To make the sauce as smooth as possible, don't skimp on the blending time.

✳ To boost the flavor, add 6 drops of hot-pepper sauce, 1 tablespoon chopped chives, and/or a pinch of garlic powder.

✳ To cool the sauce as rapidly as possible, place in the freezer for 15 minutes.

Orange Sauce

This sauce is perfect for fish and duck. We loved it. Its flavor is intense, so you don't need much.

- 1 **tablespoon ghee or vegetable oil**
- ⅓ **cup thawed orange juice concentrate**
- 2 **tablespoons sulfite-free white wine or water**

COMBINE THE GHEE, juice concentrate, and wine or water in a small skillet. Cook over medium-low heat for 7–10 minutes or until slightly thickened. Serve immediately.

Makes 4 servings

COOK'S TIP

✳ To make ghee (clarified butter): Melt butter in a saucepan over low heat; then pour the liquid ghee into a jar, leaving the milk solids in the bottom of the pan. Discard the solids. Ghee will keep frozen for up to 1 year.

SALAD DRESSINGS, SAUCES, AND CONDIMENTS

Susan Dart's Blender Sauce

I've adapted this white sauce from a recipe developed by a friend.
It works well with chicken, mushrooms, peas, and pimientos; steamed celery;
and other foods that customarily take a cream sauce.

½ cup Zucchini Milk (page 302) or
Sweet Nut Milk (page 302)

½ cup chicken broth

2 tablespoons rolled oats

Pinch of Curry Powder (page 211)

Pinch of salt

IN A BLENDER, combine the milk, broth, oats, curry powder, and salt. Process until smooth.

Pour into a saucepan. Heat to a boil and cook, stirring, until thick.

Makes 1⅛ cups

COOK'S TIP

✳ If using Zucchini Milk, peel the zucchini twice for a whiter milk. You can also substitute soy, rice, or goat's milk in this recipe.

Creamy Mustard Sauce

This sauce thickens in the blender. It's a natural for topping members
of the mustard family, like cabbage, broccoli, cauliflower, or Brussels sprouts.
It's also excellent on fish, turkey, and chicken.

⅓ cup cashews

2 tablespoons quick-cooking oats

1 cup boiling vegetable broth

1 tablespoon Dijon mustard

1 tablespoon lemon juice

¼ teaspoon salt

IN A BLENDER, combine the cashews and oats and process until they're a fine powder. Add the broth and process for 30 seconds. Add the mustard, lemon juice, and salt. Process to blend. Let stand for 2 to 3 minutes to thicken. Serve warm.

Makes 1 cup

Cashew Cream Sauce

*This simple sauce is based on just three ingredients. Cashews thicken it without
added flour or starch. Unroasted cashews have a mild flavor, which creates
a perfect base for other seasonings to shine. I use this sauce in many
guises in my own cooking (see the Cook's Tip below).*

⅔ cup cashews
1⅓ cups water
¼ teaspoon salt
Few drops of hot-pepper sauce

PLACE THE CASHEWS in a blender, and
process until they become a fine powder.
Stop the blender and scrape the bottom.
Add ⅓ cup of the water and blend for 2
minutes, or until smooth. Add the salt, hot-
pepper sauce, and remaining 1 cup water
and process for 1 minute.

Pour into a saucepan and bring to a boil
over medium heat, stirring constantly. The
sauce thickens quickly as it boils. Continue
cooking and stirring for 1 to 2 minutes, or
until the sauce is pleasantly thick. Remove
from heat. (If using seasonings, add them
now; see Cook's Tip.) Use as a topping or
stir into a casserole.

Makes 1½ cups

COOK'S TIP

❋ Add any of these seasonings to taste: ½ teaspoon
Curry Powder (page 211), 1 teaspoon Pizzazz
Seasoning (page 210), 1 tablespoon Savory
Seed Seasoning (page 209), ¾ teaspoon Italian
Seasoning (page 210), 2 tablespoons chopped
parsley, or 2 tablespoons chopped fresh cilantro.

Fresh Tomato Sauce

*A lightly seasoned fresh-tomato puree to serve over fish, pasta,
marinated or fried tofu, chicken, lamb, eggs, rice, or vegetables.*

3 large tomatoes, peeled, seeded, and
   chopped
6 basil leaves (optional)
1 tablespoon olive oil
2 tablespoons finely chopped onions

1 small clove garlic, crushed
Pinch of salt
Sliced olives, snipped chives,
   or rinsed capers (optional)

IN A BLENDER or food processor, combine the tomatoes and basil if using. Process for 30 seconds. Chunks are fine. (Do not overprocess.)

In a saucepan, heat the oil over medium heat. Add the onions and cook for 2 minutes, or until soft. (Do not brown.) Add the garlic and cook for 1 minute. Add the tomato mixture and salt and heat just until warm throughout.

Serve over your favorite dish and top with the olives, chives, or capers if using.

Makes 1½ to 2 cups

COOK'S TIPS

* To peel and seed a tomato, dip it into boiling water for 30 seconds. With a sharp knife, remove the stem end. Slip off the skin.

* To seed tomatoes, cut them in half crosswise. Squeeze gently to remove seeds and juice.

Tomato Sauce

A simple, flavorful tomato sauce that's packed with rich, robust flavor.

  1 **tablespoon olive oil**
 ½ **cup chopped onions**
  1 **clove garlic, minced**
1½ **cups water**
  1 **can (6 ounces) tomato paste**
  1 **teaspoon light agave nectar or honey**
 ¼ **teaspoon salt**

IN A SAUCEPAN, heat the oil over medium-high heat. Add the onions and cook for 4 minutes, or until soft. Add the garlic and cook for 1 minute. Add the water, tomato paste, agave nectar or honey, and salt. Cook for 5 minutes. Serve warm.

Makes about 2 cups

Variations

Tomato Sauce with Basil: Add 1 tablespoon minced fresh basil or 1 teaspoon dried.

Tomato Sauce with Shallots: Replace the onions and garlic with 2 shallots, minced.

Italian Spaghetti Sauce

Enjoy this traditional favorite over any wheat-free pasta-rice flour, spelt or Kamut brand grain, Oriental bean-thread noodles, or steamed spaghetti squash or shredded zucchini.

2 tablespoons olive oil

2 cups chopped onions

1 cup sliced celery (optional)

½ cup chopped green or red bell peppers

2–3 cloves garlic, crushed (optional)

2 teaspoons dried oregano

½ cup minced parsley

1 can (28 ounces) tomato puree

1 can (6 ounces) tomato paste

½ cup sulfite-free red wine or water

1 large bay leaf

1 teaspoon light agave nectar or honey

1 teaspoon balsamic wine vinegar

½ teaspoon salt

⅛ teaspoon ground red or freshly ground black pepper

1–2 tablespoons minced fresh basil or 1 teaspoon dried basil

IN A LARGE SAUCEPAN, heat the oil over medium heat. Add the onions and cook for 5 minutes. Add the celery if using and the bell peppers, and cook for 8 minutes, or until soft. Add the garlic, oregano, and ¼ cup of the parsley and cook for 1 minute.

Add the tomato puree, tomato paste, wine or water, bay leaf, agave nectar or honey, salt, and red or black pepper. Bring to a boil. Reduce the heat, cover, and cook, stirring occasionally, for 1 to 3 hours. If sauce becomes too thick, thin it with a little water. Discard the bay leaf. Stir in the basil and the remaining ¼ cup parsley.

Makes about 4 cups

Variations

Italian Spaghetti Sauce with Meat: Brown 1 pound ground pork, lamb, buffalo, or venison along with the onions and celery.

Italian Spaghetti Sauce with Poultry: Brown 1 pound ground turkey or chicken along with the onions and celery.

Italian Spaghetti Sauce with Rabbit: Brown 1 pound cubed rabbit along with the onions and celery.

Italian Spaghetti Sauce with Tofu: Brown 8 ounces cubed tofu along with the onions and celery.

Italian Spaghetti Sauce with Beans: Add 1½ cups cooked pinto or roman beans to the tomato mixture.

Tomato-Free Spaghetti Sauce

While not quite the same as a tomato-based sauce, the Italian Seasoning lends spaghetti-sauce flavor to this hearty pasta topping. Ideal for people who can't eat tomatoes.

2 tablespoons olive oil

2 cups chopped onions

1 cup chopped red bell peppers

¾–1 pound ground pork, turkey, or chicken

½ pound mushrooms, sliced (optional)

⅓ cup chopped flat-leaf Italian parsley

2 tablespoons sweet paprika

1½ tablespoons Italian Seasoning (page 210)

¾ teaspoon salt

2 cups water

1 can (14 ounces) pumpkin puree

¾ teaspoon unbuffered vitamin C crystals

1 can (4 ounces) diced mild chiles

1–2 cloves garlic, minced (optional)

IN A LARGE SKILLET, heat the oil over medium heat. Add the onions, red peppers, and ground pork or poultry. Cook, stirring often, for 15 minutes, or until the meat is brown and crumbled. Add the mushrooms if using, parsley, paprika, Italian seasoning, and salt. Cook for 5 minutes, stirring often. Add the water, pumpkin puree, vitamin C, and chiles. Reduce the heat, cover, and cook for 1 hour, stirring occasionally.

About 10 minutes before serving, stir in the garlic if using. Serve over pasta.

Makes about 4 cups

COOK'S TIPS

❋ Other meats that you can add to this sauce include lamb, buffalo, ostrich, emu, or wild game.

❋ For a richer sauce, use chicken stock or broth in place of the water.

Variation

Tomato-Free Spaghetti Sauce with Wine: Replace ½ cup of the water with sulfite-free red wine or nonalcoholic wine.

Pizza Sauce

Here's a traditional sauce that's really easy to make.
It takes about 30 minutes to cook to the right thickness
and it's one instance where I prefer using dried herbs.

1 **can (6 ounces) tomato paste**
¾ **cup water**
1 **tablespoon olive oil**
¼ **teaspoon salt**
1 **teaspoon dried minced onion**
1 **teaspoon dried oregano**
½ **teaspoon dried thyme**
   Black pepper (optional)
1 **teaspoon dried basil**
1 **clove garlic, crushed**

IN A SAUCEPAN, combine the tomato paste, water, oil, salt, onion, oregano, thyme, and black pepper if using. Bring to a boil. Reduce the heat to medium-low, and cook, stirring occasionally, for 30 minutes, or until thickened. Stir in the basil and garlic and cook, stirring, for another 3 to 5 minutes. Remove from the heat.

Makes about 1 cup
(enough for one 12" pizza)

Plum Ketchup

A tomato-free condiment that's a breeze to make and really dresses up a burger!

1 **pound Italian plums, pitted**
2 **tablespoons finely chopped fresh ginger**
⅓ **cup finely chopped onion (optional)**
⅓ **cup light agave nectar or honey**
1 **tablespoon wheat-free tamari or a pinch of salt**
⅔ **cup pineapple juice or water**

IN A BLENDER or food processor, combine the plums and ginger. Process for 1 to 2 minutes, or until smooth.

Pour into a saucepan. Add the onion if using, the agave nectar or honey, tamari or salt, and juice or water. Cook, stirring occasionally, for 20 minutes, or until thickened. Adjust the seasonings to taste.

Makes about 1½ cups

COOK'S TIP

✳ This ketchup freezes nicely for up to 6 months.

SALAD DRESSINGS, SAUCES, AND CONDIMENTS

Pineapple Salsa

A welcome change from tomato salsa, this tasty condiment has plenty of zing.
For the best flavor, make it at least an hour ahead so the flavors can blend.

3 cups chopped pineapple

⅓ cup lightly packed cilantro leaves

½ red bell pepper, finely chopped

¼ cup thinly sliced scallions or finely chopped red onion

1 tablespoon finely chopped jalapeno chile pepper (wear plastic gloves when handling)

1 tablespoon grated fresh ginger

4 drops hot-pepper sauce

¼ teaspoon unbuffered vitamin C crystals

Dash of salt

PLACE 1½ CUPS of the pineapple in a blender and process until pureed. Add the cilantro and process for 10 to 15 seconds. Place in a bowl.

Stir in the remaining 1½ cups pineapple. Stir in the bell pepper, scallions or red onion, chile pepper, ginger, hot-pepper sauce, vitamin C, and salt.

Will keep up to a week covered and refrigerated.

Makes about 2 cups

Turkey Gravy

This tasty gravy is made with alternative flours, but you'll never miss the wheat flour.
And guests won't suspect a thing.

1–2 tablespoons drippings from Roast Turkey Breast (page 223)

3 tablespoons brown rice, rye, or teff flour

1⅞ cups water or chicken stock or broth

½ teaspoon salt

minutes, or until the flour is light brown. Stir in the water, stock, or broth. Cook, stirring, until thickened. Reduce the heat, add the salt and cook for 10 minutes. Adjust the salt to taste.

Makes about 2 cups

IN A SAUCEPAN or the roasting pan, combine the liquid and flour, whisking until smooth. Cook over medium heat for 3 to 5

COOK'S TIP

∗ If you prefer, you can thicken this gravy with 4 tablespoons Kamut brand grain or spelt flour or 6 tablespoons barley flour.

Mushroom Brown Sauce

This is especially good with vegetable entrees, such as Zesty Loaf (page 248),
that don't have meat drippings to make conventional gravy.

2½ cups Basic Stock (page 136) or broth
3 tablespoons olive oil
½ pound mushrooms, minced
2 tablespoons minced onions
3 tablespoons brown rice flour
¼ teaspoon salt
2 teaspoons wheat-free tamari sauce
(optional)

BRING THE STOCK or broth to a boil in a small saucepan. Cook, uncovered, until reduced to 1½ cups. Set aside.

In a large skillet, heat 1 tablespoon of the oil over medium-high heat. Add the mushrooms and onions and cook, stirring often, for 7 minutes, or until the moisture from the mushrooms evaporates. Place in a small bowl.

Place the remaining 2 tablespoons oil in the skillet. Heat over medium heat for 30 seconds. Whisk in the rice flour and salt and cook for 3 minutes, whisking constantly. Pour in the stock or broth, whisking constantly. Cook until thick and bubbling. Reduce the heat to low.

Stir in the mushroom mixture and tamari if using and cook for 1 minute. Adjust the seasonings to taste. Serve immediately.

Makes about 2¾ cups

COOK'S TIPS

✻ You can mince mushrooms in a food processor.

✻ Without the tamari sauce, the sauce will have a light color.

Savory Marinade

Use this pungent marinade for stir-fried chicken, meat, tofu, or vegetables.
The recipe makes enough sauce to marinate
half a pound of food and can be doubled easily.

½ cup water
2 tablespoons lemon juice
2 tablespoons white grape juice or
2 teaspoons light agave nectar or honey

⅛ teaspoon powdered ginger
⅛ teaspoon ground red pepper
½ teaspoon dark sesame oil

SALAD DRESSINGS, SAUCES, AND CONDIMENTS

IN A BOWL or jar, combine the water; lemon juice; grape juice, agave nectar, or honey; ginger; red pepper; and oil.

Makes ¾ cup

COOK'S TIPS

✳ If you want, you can make the sauce with ¼ cup white wine and ¼ cup water instead of ½ cup water.

✳ To marinate food, place marinade and food in a shallow bowl. Toss to coat pieces; marinate,

covered, at room temperature for 30 minutes or in the refrigerator for up to 24 hours. Drain food before cooking. Reserve marinade if you want to use as a sauce. Boil it for 10 minutes before serving.

Variation

Savory Stir-Fry Sauce: Dissolve 1 tablespoon arrowroot in ¼ cup cool water and stir into the marinade. Add to stir-fried dishes during the last 2 minutes of cooking, stirring constantly.

Tender-Meat Marinade

Papaya contains papain, an enzyme that can tenderize meat. And it's a good alternative to commercial meat tenderizers for people who react to monosodium glutamate (MSG). This marinade is especially useful with game and other lean meats that tend to be chewy.

1 **papaya**
  Peppy (page 211) (optional)
1½ **cups water**
1–2 **tablespoons vegetable oil**
  ½ **teaspoon vitamin C crystals**
  ½ **teaspoon crushed dried rosemary or oregano**

CUT THE PAPAYA in half. Scoop out the seeds and use them to make the peppy seasoning.

Scoop the flesh into a small bowl and mash with a fork. Add the peppy, water, oil, vitamin C, and rosemary. Mix well.

Makes about 3 cups

COOK'S TIPS

✳ Papain works on exposed surfaces of meat, so it will tenderize small pieces of meat faster than it will whole roasts. To use, place cubed pieces of meat in a shallow dish. Cover with the marinade and stir to coat all surfaces. Refrigerate, covered, for at least 1 hour. Drain, reserving the marinade to use in the recipe, if you want.

✳ To marinate roasts and poultry, reduce the water to ½ cup. The marinade will be the consistency of thick jam. Spread over the meat and refrigerate. Marinate poultry and small roasts for 1 hour. Marinate cuts of meat weighing more than 3 pounds for at least 2 hours.

Quick Applesauce

Delicious warm or cold, this dish makes a great topping for pancakes or waffles.
Use your favorite apples, but steer clear of Red Delicious for cooking;
they tend not to be as flavorful. This applesauce freezes very well.

3 pounds apples, peeled and chopped

1 can (6 ounces) frozen apple-juice concentrate, thawed

IN A LARGE saucepan, combine the apples and juice concentrate. Bring to a boil over medium heat. Reduce the heat, cover, and cook, stirring often, for 15 to 30 minutes, or until the apples are tender. Add water as necessary to prevent sticking.

Makes about 1½ quarts

COOK'S TIP

* Some apple varieties such as McIntosh will be tender in about 15 minutes; others such as Jonathan apples will take about 40 minutes.

Blueberry Sauce

This fruit sauce goes well with pancakes and waffles. Because you can use
arrowroot and tapioca starch flour interchangeably, it's especially helpful
if you're following a Rotary Diversified Diet.

¼ cup light agave nectar, honey, or maple syrup

2 cups fresh or frozen blueberries

1¼ cup water

4¼ teaspoons tapioca or arrowroot

⅛ teaspoon unbuffered vitamin C crystals (optional)

IN A SAUCEPAN, combine the agave, honey, or maple syrup; blueberries; and 1 cup of the water. Bring to a boil over medium high heat. Reduce the heat and cook for 7 minutes.

In a small bowl or cup, mix the tapioca starch or arrowroot with the remaining ¼ cup water, stirring until the starch dissolves. Stir into the blueberry mixture. Cook, stirring for 1 minute, or until the liquid is clear and slightly thickened. Remove from heat. Add the vitamin C if using. Serve warm.

Makes 3½ cups

COOK'S TIP

* For a sauce containing whole uncooked berries, prepare the recipe using only 1 cup of the blueberries, reserving the remainder. Let the sauce cool for 15 to 20 minutes. Just before serving, stir in the remaining blueberries.

SALAD DRESSINGS, SAUCES, AND CONDIMENTS

Peach Sauce

*Peaches are available in the frozen food section of most supermarkets,
so you can make this sauce year-round. Use it to top pancakes and waffles.*

1 **pound frozen peaches, thawed and chopped**

1¼ **cups water**

¼ **cup light agave nectar, maple syrup, or honey**

1½ **tablespoons tapioca or arrowroot**

IN A LARGE SAUCEPAN, combine the peaches and 1 cup of water. Bring to a boil. Reduce the heat to medium and cook for 4 minutes. Stir in the agave nectar, maple syrup, or honey and cook for 4 minutes, or until the fruit is tender.

In a small bowl, dissolve the tapioca or arrowroot in the remaining ¼ cup water. Stir into the peach mixture. Cook, stirring constantly, for 1 to 2 minutes, until thick and clear. Remove from heat.

Makes about 3 servings

Variation
Cherry Sauce: Substitute frozen sweet cherries for the peaches.

Quick Cranberry-Pineapple Sauce

A quick, easy, sugar-free sauce to accompany chicken, turkey, or pork.

12–16 **ounces fresh cranberries**

1 **can (20 ounces) crushed unsweetened pineapple in juice**

IN A 3-QUART SAUCEPAN, combine the cranberries and crushed pineapple with juice. Bring just to a boil, stirring occasionally. Reduce the heat to low. Cover, leaving the lid ajar, and cook for 15 minutes, or until most of the cranberries have popped and the sauce has thickened slightly. (For a thicker sauce, cook for 5 minutes more.) Serve warm or cold.

Makes 1 quart

Uncooked Fruit Sauce

*Here's a one-ingredient topping that's especially helpful if you're limiting
your intake of honey or maple syrup. The flavor of this uncooked sauce depends entirely
upon the sweetness of the fruit chosen, so pick fruits at peak ripeness.*

1 peach or pear, chopped
**1 tablespoon thawed fruit juice
    concentrate (optional)**

PLACE THE FRUIT and juice concentrate
if using in a blender. Process for 20 seconds
for a chunky sauce, 2 minutes for a smooth
sauce. Serve immediately.
Makes 1 serving

COOK'S TIPS

* If you want, combine fruits from the same food
family. For example, plums, nectarines, or apricots
can be added to the peaches. Or combine
mangoes, bananas, and pineapple.

* Apples, citrus, and melons aren't well-suited to this
uncooked blender technique.

Variation
Simple Berry Fruit Sauce: Substitute 1 cup
blueberries, blackberries, strawberries, or
raspberries for the peach or pear.

Mint Sauce

Try this with lamb. It also goes well with Indian dishes.

⅓ cup packed mint leaves
1⅛ cups water
¼ cup light agave nectar or honey
4 teaspoons arrowroot

IN A SMALL SAUCEPAN, combine the
mint and 1 cup of the water. Cook for 10
minutes and remove and discard the mint
leaves with a slotted spoon. Stir in the agave
nectar or honey.

In a cup, combine the arrowroot and remaining ⅛ cup water, whisking until the arrowroot dissolves. Stir into the mint mixture.
Cook, stirring, over medium heat for 5 minutes, or until slightly thickened and bubbly.
Serve warm.
Makes about 1¼ cups

COOK'S TIP

* If you want to give the sauce a little tang, add a
pinch of unbuffered vitamin C crystals after the
sauce thickens.

SALAD DRESSINGS, SAUCES, AND CONDIMENTS

Savory Seed Seasoning

Fill a large-hole saltshaker with this customized flavor booster. It contains only 43 milligrams of sodium per teaspoon, compared to 2,132 milligrams in a teaspoon of salt.

½ **cup sesame seeds or sunflower seeds**

1 **tablespoon wheat-free tamari sauce**

1 **teaspoon dried basil**

1 **teaspoon dried oregano**

¼ **teaspoon onion powder (optional)**

⅛ **teaspoon garlic powder (optional)**

PREHEAT THE OVEN to 250°F.

In a blender, process the sesame seeds or sunflower seeds until coarsely ground. Add the tamari and process for 3 seconds or until mixed.

Spread in an 8" × 8" baking pan. Bake for 30 minutes or until dry and very fragrant. Allow to cool.

Return to a dry blender and process to a fine powder. Stop the blender and scrape the bottom of the container. Add the basil, oregano, onion powder if using, and garlic powder if using. Process until well-blended and finely ground.

Makes ½ cup

Variations

Savory Seed Seasoning with Paprika: Substitute 2 teaspoons Hungarian paprika for the basil and oregano.

Savory Seed Seasoning with Kelp: Substitute 1 to 2 teaspoons kelp (unless you are allergic to iodine) for the basil and oregano.

Savory Seed Seasoning with Herbs: Substitute one or two of the following herbs for the basil and oregano: 1 teaspoon dried tarragon, 1 teaspoon dried dillweed, 1 teaspoon dried savory, 1 teaspoon dried marjoram, ½ teaspoon crushed dried rosemary or ¼ teaspoon dried sage.

Spicy Savory Seed Seasoning: Replace the tamari with ¼ teaspoon salt and 1 tablespoon of water. Add a few drops of hot-pepper sauce.

Italian Seasoning

Shake this tasty blend of Mint-family foods over salads, dips, soups or stews. It's especially nice when you're using tomatoes. Feel free to omit any herbs that bother you.

2 tablespoons dried basil
1 tablespoon dried marjoram
1 tablespoon dried oregano
1½ teaspoons dried rosemary
1½ teaspoons dried savory
1½ teaspoons dried thyme
1 scant teaspoon dried sage

COMBINE THE BASIL, marjoram, oregano, rosemary, savory, thyme, and sage in a small bowl or cup. Store in a tightly covered jar.

Makes about ⅓ cup

COOK'S TIP

* For maximum flavor, crush the herbs in your hand immediately before using them.

Pizzazz Seasoning

Eight interesting flavors from the Parsley family combine to make an ideal seasoning for cooked carrots, celery, meatloaf, soups, or stews.

1 small carrot
1 tablespoon caraway seeds
1 tablespoon cumin seeds
1 tablespoon coriander seeds
1 tablespoon fennel seeds
½ tablespoon dried celery leaves or ½ teaspoon celery seeds
2 tablespoons dried dillweed
2 tablespoons dried parsley

In a blender or spice mill, combine the carrots, caraway seeds, cumin seeds, coriander seeds, fennel seeds, and celery leaves or seeds. Process until finely ground. Sieve into a small bowl. Return large pieces to the blender and process again. Sieve into the bowl. Stir in the dill, parsley, and celery leaves if using. Store in a tightly covered spice jar.

Makes about ¾ cup

PREHEAT THE OVEN to 200°F. Using a vegetable peeler, pare the carrot, removing long, paper-thin slices (as if making carrot curls). Arrange the carrot strips on a baking sheet, and bake for 1 hour, or until very brittle and crumbly.

COOK'S TIP

* To dry parsley, celery, or lovage, wash and pat the leaves dry. Place them on a baking sheet and bake at 200°F for 30 minutes, or until very dry.

Variation

Pizzazz Seasoning with Lovage: Substitute dried lovage for the celery leaves.

Curry Powder

Traditionally, curry is made from a skillful blending of many flavors—often more than 30 spices. Even so, this one is limited to only two or three food families, depending on whether or not you include ground red pepper.

1 tablespoon coriander seeds

4 teaspoons turmeric powder

1½ teaspoons powdered ginger

1½ teaspoons cardamom seeds

1½ teaspoons celery seeds

2 teaspoons cumin seeds

½ teaspoon ground red pepper (optional)

1 tablespoon Pizzazz Seasoning (page 210)

IN A BLENDER or spice mill, combine the coriander seeds, turmeric, ginger, cardamom seeds, celery seeds, cumin seeds, and ground red pepper if using. Process until finely ground. Pour into a small bowl or cup and add the Pizzazz Seasoning. Mix well. Store in a tightly covered spice jar.

Makes about ⅓ cup

COOK'S TIP

✳ For more intense flavor, toast the coriander, cardamom, celery, and cumin seeds in a small nonstick skillet. Cook, stirring often, over medium-low heat for 5 minutes, or until lightly browned and fragrant.

Peppy

Here's an innovative use for papaya seeds. It's especially useful if black pepper bothers you.

1 papaya

PREHEAT THE OVEN to 200°F.

Cut the papaya in half, and scoop the seeds into a strainer, reserving the flesh for another use. Wash under running water and drain.

Spread in a single layer on a baking sheet or jelly-roll pan. Bake for 1½ hours, or until the seeds are brittle, shriveled, and look

like peppercorns. (Test one by biting on it.)

Place in a pepper mill. Use as you would dried peppercorns.

Makes about ¼ cup

COOK'S TIP

✳ An alternate method for using the dried seeds: Grind them to a fine powder in a seed mill or clean coffee grinder, and store them in a spice jar. Use within a few weeks.

SALAD DRESSINGS, SAUCES, AND CONDIMENTS

Corn-Free Baking Powder

Many brands of baking powder contain corn or potato starch; this one doesn't. For best results when baking with homemade baking powder, always combine the dry and liquid ingredients separately, then combine them quickly, pour batter into prepared pans, and bake promptly.

2 teaspoons cream of tartar
2 teaspoons arrowroot
2 teaspoons baking soda

SIFT TOGETHER the cream of tartar, arrowroot, and baking soda and mix well. Store in a tightly covered spice jar.

Makes 2 tablespoons

COOK'S TIPS

✳ For best results, make only small batches and use within a couple of weeks.

✳ Be sure to use fresh baking soda; old baking soda can give disappointing results in baking, yet can still be used for cleaning and deodorizing kitchen work areas.

Egg Substitute

This mixture has the binding properties of eggs, making it a useful alternative for patties and meat loaves. Note that it doesn't have the leavening properties of eggs necessary for quickbreads, soufflés, or other baked goods. This recipe makes enough to substitute for one egg; you can easily double or triple it.

½ cup water
1 tablespoon whole flaxseed

use high heat or the mixture will become thick and gummy.

Makes about ⅓ cup

IN A SMALL SAUCEPAN, combine the water and flaxseed. Bring to a boil. Reduce the heat to low and cook for 5 minutes, or until the consistency of egg whites. Don't

---
COOK'S TIP

✳ Don't try to strain out the flaxseeds. They don't have much flavor and won't detract from whatever you're making.

Meat, Poultry, and Game Dishes

Since beef sometimes triggers a reaction, no beef recipes appear in this chapter. Instead, I offer recipes for lamb, pork, rabbit, venison, chicken, turkey, Cornish game hens, and duck—often with the option to substitute buffalo, ostrich, emu, or other game meats you may have access to. Many of these game meats are extremely lean (and healthful). To help tenderize lean meats, I usually marinate them with acidic liquids and stew them with long, slow cooking.

Though related to beef, lamb is generally less allergenic. Try it in the Moussaka-Style Casserole, Cassoulet, and Easy Curry in this chapter, and in the Lamb Stew and Chunky Lamb Stew in the Super Soups, Stews, and Chowders chapter. Roast Lamb with Mint Sauce appears in Holiday Foods, page 350.

Pork is another good alternative to beef. Pork tenderloin and lean parts of the shoulder and leg are relatively low in fat. As an added benefit, pork is our best nongrain source of thiamin (vitamin B_1). In this chapter, Versatile Meatballs is one of my favorite recipes using pork. Check out Roast Pork in Holiday Foods on page 350 and Pork and Pepper Stew in Super Soups, Stews, and Chowders on page 135.

Rabbit is now widely available in supermarket freezer cases, and some farmers' markets carry it fresh. Check the source of any rabbit; farm-raised animals may be safer than wild. Rabbit-Vegetable Stew in Super Soups, Stews, and Chowders on page 135 is a good introduction to this less-allergenic meat. You can also substitute rabbit in almost any recipe calling for bone-in chicken.

Venison and other game can be ordered from suppliers listed in Resources for Foods, Supplies, and Information on page 379, but check your local suppliers first. Marjorie Fisher's Venison Stew with Carrots in the Super Soups, Stews, and Chowders chapter on page 135 is one of my favorite recipes using these game meats.

Because poultry is so popular, available, and versatile, I've developed several allergy-free chicken and turkey recipes. Roast Turkey Breast and Turkey Rollups with Asparagus are excellent all year round. However, note that some ground turkey and chicken contain additives, such as monosodium glutamate (MSG), spices, and other flavorings. Be sure to check labels or call the brand's consumer hotline (usually toll-free) if necessary.

Quick Fresh-Tomato Strata

Wonderful cold dish for when fresh tomatoes are overrunning the garden.
Also a good way to use leftover meat and cooked rice.

1½ cups cold cooked brown rice

1 cup diced cooked chicken, turkey, or lamb

¾ cup Fresh Tomato Sauce, chilled (page 198)

1–2 tablespoons minced fresh basil
   Salt

6–8 green or black olives, sliced (optional)

ON A SERVING PLATTER, layer the rice and chicken, turkey, or lamb. Top with the sauce and basil. Top with the olives if using.
Makes 2 servings

Variations

Fresh-Tomato Strata with Tuna: Replace the chicken, turkey, or lamb with 1 can (6 ounces) tuna, flaked.

Fresh-Tomato Strata with Egg: Replace the chicken, turkey, or lamb with 2 hard-cooked eggs, sliced.

Fresh-Tomato Strata with Tofu: Replace the chicken, turkey, or lamb with diced fried, marinated tofu.

Polynesian Chicken Dinner

A sugar-free sweet-and-sour dish that packs tons of flavor.

1½ cups raw brown rice

3 cups water

½ teaspoon salt

2 boneless, skinless chicken breasts, cut in half (1¼–1½ pounds)

¼ cup Basil Vinaigrette (page 191) or Sweet and Sour Salad Dressing, (page 191)

1 can (8 ounces) pineapple tidbits packed in juice

2 tablespoons arrowroot

1 cup chicken stock or broth

2 tablespoons wheat-free tamari sauce or ¼ teaspoon salt

1 tablespoon lemon juice or ¼ teaspoon unbuffered vitamin C crystals

2 tablespoons sesame oil

6 ounces snow pea pods

1 red bell pepper, cut into thin strips

1 green bell pepper, cut into thin strips

6–8 scallions, cut into ¼" slices

½ cup cashews, toasted

2 tablespoons shredded unsweetened coconut (optional)

COMBINE THE RICE, water, and salt in a 2-quart saucepan with a tight-fitting lid. Bring to a boil. Reduce the heat to low, cover, and cook for 45 minutes, or until the rice is tender and the water has been absorbed.

While the rice is cooking, preheat the oven to 400°F.

In a shallow bowl, dip the chicken into the vinaigrette or dressing. Place in a single layer in a baking dish and marinate for 10 to 30 minutes. Bake, uncovered, for 15 minutes.

Combine the pineapple with juice and arrowroot, stirring until smooth. Add the stock or broth, tamari or salt, and lemon juice or vitamin C.

In a skillet, heat the oil over medium heat. Add the pea pods and peppers, and cook, stirring, for 4 minutes. Add the scallions and cook for 1 minute. Stir in the pineapple mixture. Stir and heat for 1 to 2 minutes, until the sauce is thick and clear. Remove from the heat.

Divide the rice among 4 plates. Top with the chicken and vegetable mixture. Sprinkle with the cashews and coconut if using.

Makes 4 servings

COOK'S TIP

＊ To roast large whole nuts, spread them on a baking sheet. Bake at 300°F for 12 minutes, or until light brown and fragrant.

Stir-Fried Jicama Chicken Dinner

A simple meal involving only three food families, and it takes just 30 minutes to prepare.

2–3 tablespoons avocado or canola oil

  1 pound boneless, skinless chicken breasts, cut into ¾" cubes

  3 dark orange sweet potatoes, peeled and sliced

  1 pound jicama, cut into matchsticks

HEAT 2 TABLESPOONS of the oil in a large skillet or wok over medium-high heat. Add the chicken and cook for 5 minutes, or until cooked through and no longer pink. Add the sweet potatoes and cook for 7 minutes, or until tender-crisp, adding more oil as needed.

Add the jicama and cook and stir for 2 minutes.

Makes 4 servings

Morning-Glory Chicken

Sweet potatoes and jicama both belong to the Morning-Glory family. Combine them with chicken for a simple dish that's perfect on a Rotary Diversified Diet.

1 frying chicken, cut up (about 3 pounds) or 4 boneless, skinless chicken breast halves

3 dark orange sweet potatoes, peeled and cut into 1" chunks

¼ teaspoon salt (optional)

1 pound jicama, cut into matchsticks

PLACE THE CHICKEN pieces in a 5-quart pot. Add water to cover. Cook, uncovered, for 20 minutes. Add the sweet potatoes and salt if using and cook for 10 to 15 minutes, or just until the sweet potatoes are tender. Add the jicama and cook for 5 minutes, or just until the jicama is tender-crisp and liquid is slightly reduced.

Makes 4 servings

Slow-Cooked Chicken Dinner with Gravy

Chicken and gravy good enough for company.
The broth is thickened without flour.

3 carrots, sliced or 2½ cups baby carrots, whole

1 large onion, sliced

3 celery stalks, thickly sliced

½ cup chicken stock or broth, sulfite-free white wine, or water

¼ teaspoon dried basil

¼ teaspoon dried thyme

1 frying chicken, skinned and cut-up (3–3½ pounds)

2 tablespoons lemon juice or ½ teaspoon unbuffered vitamin C crystals

¼ cup rolled oats

Salt

ARRANGE TWO-THIRDS of the carrots, onions and celery in the bottom of a slow cooker. Add the stock, broth, wine, or water and sprinkle with a third of the basil and thyme.

Place the chicken pieces in a single layer atop the vegetables. Sprinkle with 1 tablespoon lemon juice or ¼ teaspoon vitamin C and a third of the basil and thyme. Add remaining chicken pieces and sprinkle with the remaining lemon juice or vitamin C, basil, and thyme.

Cover the pot and cook on the low setting for 5 to 8 hours. Place the chicken and vegetables on a serving platter. Cover with foil to keep them warm.

Pour the cooking juices into a 2-cup measure. Add the water, stock, or broth to measure 2 cups.

Place the oats in a blender and process to a fine powder. Add the cooking juices and process for 20 seconds. Pour into a saucepan and bring to a boil, stirring constantly until thick. Season with the salt. Pass the gravy separately.

Makes 4 servings

COOK'S TIPS

✻ If you prefer, you can thicken the gravy with 3 tablespoons oat, spelt, Kamut brand, or other flour or oat bran instead of the oat flakes.

✻ In the slow cooker, you can cook this dinner for up to 10 hours. The chicken will be so tender, it'll fall off the bones.

Variation

Slow-Cooked Chicken Dinner with Grain-Free Gravy: Omit the oats and dissolve 2 tablespoons tapioca starch or arrowroot in ¼ cup cold water. Whisk into 1¾ cups hot liquid. Cook, stirring, for 2 minutes, or until the gravy thickens.

Chicken Cacciatore

This popular entree is traditionally served over spaghetti. I serve it over Kamut brand grain spaghetti, spelt spaghetti, rice vermicelli, or spaghetti squash.

2 tablespoons olive oil

2 whole boneless, skinless chicken breasts, cut into thin strips (about 1¼ pounds)

1 cup chopped onions

½ cup chopped green bell peppers

1–2 cloves garlic, minced

3–4 cups Tomato Sauce (page 199)

1½ teaspoons dried oregano

1½ teaspoons dried basil or 2 tablespoons fresh, minced

HEAT THE OIL in a 5-quart pot over medium heat. Add the onions and cook for 5 minutes, or until soft. Add the chicken, peppers, and garlic, and cook until the chicken is lightly browned and no longer pink. Add the tomato sauce, oregano, and basil. Cook for 10 to 20 minutes. Serve over your favorite pasta.

Makes 4 servings

Chickburgers

Serve on pancakes instead of bread and accompany with
Tofu-Dijon Spread (page 194) or Cashew Spread (page 195) and sprouts.

4 **boneless, skinless chicken breast halves (about 1–1¼ pounds)**

¼ **cup fruit juice or tomato juice**

¼ **cup water**

1½ **tablespoons wheat-free tamari sauce, Worcestershire sauce, or steak sauce (optional)**

½ **teaspoon poultry seasoning**

¼ **cup spelt or Kamut brand flour**

½ **teaspoon salt**

1–2 **tablespoons vegetable oil**

USING A MEAT MALLET or heavy skillet, pound each piece of chicken to a uniform ½" to ¾" thick.

In a bowl, combine the juice, water, sauce if using, and ¼ teaspoon of the poultry seasoning. Add the chicken, cover, and marinate in the refrigerator for at least 15 minutes. Drain on paper towels.

In a shallow bowl or on waxed paper, combine the flour, salt, and remaining ¼ teaspoon poultry seasoning. Add the chicken, turning to coat both sides of each piece.

Heat the oil in a large nonstick skillet over medium heat. Add the chicken and cook for 7 minutes. Turn and cook for 5 minutes, or until lightly browned and cooked through.

Makes 4 servings

Variation

Chickburgers with Herbs: Substitute dried rosemary, tarragon, oregano, or basil for the poultry seasoning.

COOK'S TIPS

✳ The chicken can marinate for as long as 24 hours.

✳ If you have space in the freezer, prepare a few pounds of these Chickburgers at a time. Separate the burgers with waxed paper, wrap well, and freeze the uncooked breaded patties.

Quick Chickburgers

The flavor of these burgers is so good, we don't even add condiments.

1 egg or ⅓ cup Egg Substitute (page 212)

½ cup finely chopped onion, leeks, or shallots

1–3 teaspoons prepared mustard

¼ teaspoon salt

½ teaspoon five-spice powder or ground cinnamon

4–5 drops hot-pepper sauce (optional)

1–1¼ pounds preservative-free ground chicken

⅓ cup quinoa flakes or oat bran

IN A BOWL, combine the egg or egg substitute, onions, mustard, salt, five-spice powder or cinnamon, and pepper sauce if using. Add the chicken, stirring with a fork to crumble. Add the quinoa flakes or oat bran, and mix well. Allow to rest 5 to 10 minutes.

Heat a nonstick skillet over medium heat. Mist with cooking spray and spoon four mounds of the chicken mixture into the skillet. Using a spatula, flatten and shape the patties. Cook for 8 minutes, or until brown. Turn and cook for 8 minutes, or until cooked through and no longer pink and nicely brown on the exterior.

Serve between 2 pancakes.

Makes 4

Variation

Turkey Burgers: Substitute ground turkey for the chicken.

Baked-Chicken Salad with Apricots

My favorite company luncheon dish, and it's wonderful for buffets, too.

1 pound boneless, skinless chicken breasts

¼ cup Sweet and Sour Salad Dressing (page 191) or Basil Vinaigrette (page 191)

¾ cup chopped dried apricots

¾ cup sliced celery

½ cup chopped toasted almonds

⅓ cup Cashew Spread (page 195) or Tofu-Dijon Spread (page 194)

¼ teaspoon poultry seasoning
Salt (optional)

4 teaspoons toasted sesame seeds (optional)

2 cups mixed salad greens or mesclun

COMBINE THE CHICKEN and dressing in a baking dish, turning each piece to coat. Cover and marinate in the refrigerator for at least 1 hour.

Meanwhile, preheat the oven to 400°F. In a small bowl, soften the apricots in boiling water for 10 minutes; drain. Bake the chicken for 15 minutes, or until no longer pink and the juices run clear. Allow to cool.

Cut the chicken into ¾" chunks. In a large bowl, combine the chicken, apricots, celery, almonds, spread, and poultry seasoning. Season with salt and more poultry seasoning to taste. Chill for at least 1 hour.

Serve over the greens and top with the sesame seeds if using.

Makes 4 servings

COOK'S TIPS

✳ To toast small nuts and seeds, spread them in a small nonstick skillet. Cook, stirring often, over medium-low heat for 5 minutes, or until lightly browned and fragrant.

✳ To roast large whole nuts, spread them on a baking sheet. Bake at 300°F for 12 minutes, or until light brown and fragrant.

✳ If you want, you can marinate the chicken for as long as 8 hours.

Variations

Baked-Chicken Salad with Pineapple: Replace the apricots with 8 ounces drained unsweetened pineapple tidbits.

Baked-Chicken Salad with Apple: Replace the apricots with 1 apple, chopped.

Baked-Chicken Salad with Grapes: Replace the apricots with 1 cup red or white grapes.

Baked-Chicken Salad with Pecans: Replace the almonds with pecans.

Baked-Chicken Salad with Cashews: Replace the almonds with cashews.

Quick Chicken Salad: Use 2 cups cubed roasted chicken instead of the chicken breasts. Omit the marinating and baking.

Quick Turkey Salad: Use 2 cups cubed roasted turkey instead of the chicken breasts. Omit the marinating and baking.

Turkey Rollups with Asparagus

A wonderful way to use leftover turkey.

16–20 asparagus stalks, trimmed
4 large, thin slices cooked turkey breast
1 cup Creamy Mustard Sauce (page 197)

PREHEAT THE OVEN to 350°F and oil an 8" × 8" (or 9" × 9") baking dish.

Steam the asparagus stalks over boiling water for 5 minutes, or just until tender-crisp. Divide into 4 bundles.

Wrap 1 turkey slice around each bundle, secure with a toothpick, and place in the prepared baking dish. Or place the asparagus bundles directly in the prepared baking dish and drape the turkey over them.

Pour the sauce over the turkey, and bake for 15 minutes. Remove the toothpicks before serving.

Makes 4 servings

COOK'S TIP

＊ To save time, use store-bought roast turkey. Be sure, however, to check the label for ingredients.

Variations

Turkey Rollups with Green Beans: Substitute 32 whole, long green beans for the asparagus.

Turkey Rollups with Broccoli: Substitute eight 4" broccoli stalks for the asparagus.

Mix-and-Match Stir-Fry

Because the ingredients for stir-fried meals can be so varied, there's always lots you can eat—
no matter what you're allergic to. The cardinal "rule" for a successful stir-fry
is to keep the food moving by constant stirring over high heat.

¾ **pound boneless turkey breast, cut into ½" cubes**

¾ **cup Savory Marinade (page 204)**

1 **tablespoon arrowroot or tapioca starch**

2 **tablespoons wheat-free tamari or ½ teaspoon salt**

2–3 **tablespoons vegetable oil**

½ **cup cashews**

¾ **cup thinly sliced water chestnuts**

¾ **cup thinly sliced bok choy**

½ **cup thinly sliced nappa cabbage**

2 **cups hot cooked brown rice**

IN A BOWL, combine the turkey and marinade. Cover and marinate at room temperature for 30 minutes. Drain, reserving the marinade, and place on a double layer of paper towels.

Bring the marinade to a boil and cook for 10 minutes. Remove from the heat and let cool. Add the arrowroot or tapioca starch and tamari or salt.

Heat 2 tablespoons of the oil in a large skillet or wok over high heat. Swirl to distribute the oil. Add the turkey and cook, stirring, for 2 minutes, or until cooked through and no longer pink. Using a slotted spoon, remove to a plate. Place the cashews in the skillet and cook, stirring, for 1 minute. Add to the turkey.

Place the water chestnuts in the skillet and cook, stirring, for 2 minutes. Add the bok choy and cook, stirring, for 30 seconds or just until heated through and still crisp. Add the nappa cabbage and cook, stirring, for 30 seconds or just until heated through and still crisp.

Return the turkey and cashews to the skillet. Add the marinade and cook for 1 minute, or until the turkey is heated through and the marinade is thickened.

Serve at once over the rice.

Makes 4 servings

COOK'S TIPS

✱ Cooking goes fast in a stir-fry, so have all the chopping done before you heat the skillet or wok.

✱ If you're in a hurry, you can use unsweetened pineapple juice instead of the marinade.

✱ Other ingredients for stir-fries include cubed or julienne pieces of drained and pressed tofu, whole or chopped shrimp, crab meat, julienne kohlrabi, sliced green beans, sliced green peppers, cauliflower florets, sliced celery, halved or quartered cherry tomatoes, whole or slivered almonds, or sunflower seeds.

Variations

Chicken Stir-Fry: Substitute boneless, skinless chicken breast for the turkey. And use halved snow peas, sliced mushrooms, sliced bamboo shoots, and shredded spinach instead of the water chestnuts, bok choy, and nappa cabbage. Replace the cashews with almonds.

Fish Stir-Fry: Substitute firm-fleshed fish, such as halibut or monkfish, or scallops for

---

the turkey. And use sliced scallions, sliced red peppers, broccoli florets, sliced carrots, and pine nuts instead of the water chestnuts, bok choy, nappa cabbage, and cashews.

Pork Stir-Fry: Substitute lean pork for the turkey. And use jicama matchsticks, sliced scallions, sliced zucchini, red pepper strips, sliced chard, and sliced apple instead of the bok choy, nappa cabbage, and cashews.

Lamb Stir-Fry: Substitute lean lamb for the turkey. And use broccoli florets; sliced scallions; sliced carrots; peeled, seeded, and chopped tomatoes; and sesame seeds instead of the water chestnuts, bok choy, nappa cabbage, and cashews.

Roast Turkey Breast

Roast turkey breast is simple, classic, and easy to dress up or down with trimmings.

1 turkey breast (allow ¼ pound per person)

PREHEAT THE OVEN to 325°F.

Mist the turkey with cooking oil and place, skin side up, on a wire rack in a 13" × 9" roasting pan. Bake for 1½ to 3 hours, or until done and a meat thermometer registers at least 180°F. (See "Turkey Timetable," below.)

COOK'S TIPS
---

* Let the turkey rest at room temperature for 10 minutes before carving. For very thin slices that are perfect for sandwiches, chill the roast for several hours or overnight before carving. Use a very sharp serrated knife.

* Some turkey breasts come with a pop-up timer to indicate when the meat is done. Don't rely solely on it; use a good thermometer to confirm the temperature.

* To use a meat thermometer, insert it in the thickest part of the meat, making sure it doesn't touch a bone. Insert a standard meat thermometer before starting to cook. Insert an instant-read variety near the end of the cooking time to check the meat's internal temperature, but don't expose it to oven heat or leave it in the meat for more than a minute.

Variation
Roast Turkey Breast with Waldorf Stuffing: Place the breast, skin side down, on a 3-foot length of cheesecloth. Lightly pack the cavity with 6 cups Waldorf Stuffing with Buckwheat (page 133) or Waldorf Stuffing with Quinoa (recipe variation, page 133). Bring the ends of the cheesecloth up and fold them over the stuffing. Tie kitchen string around the breast to hold the cheesecloth in place. Place the breast, stuffing side down, on a wire rack and bake according to the timetable. When done, the meat temperature should be at least 180°F and the stuffing at least 160°F.

Turkey Timetable

WEIGHT	TIME
3–5 pounds	1½–2 hours
5–7 pounds	2–2½ hours
7–9 pounds	2½–3⅓ hours

Turkey Meatloaf

Applesauce makes this meatloaf moist and delicious. If you have leftovers,
use them to create scrumptious sandwiches for lunch.

1 egg, lightly beaten

⅓ cup fruit or honey sweetened ketchup

1 tablespoon prepared mustard

½ cup unsweetened applesauce

1 cup chopped onion

½ teaspoon salt

¼ teaspoon black pepper or 4 dashes hot-pepper sauce

1½ pounds ground turkey or chicken

⅔ cup oat bran

PREHEAT THE OVEN to 350°F. Coat an 8" × 4" loaf pan with cooking spray.

In a large bowl, combine the egg, ketchup, mustard, applesauce, onion, salt, and pepper or hot-pepper sauce. Add the turkey and oat bran, and mix well.

Spoon into the prepared pan, smoothing the top. Bake for 1 hour, or until the loaf is firm to touch and cooked through and the top is brown. Remove from oven and let stand 10 minutes.

Turn out onto a platter or cutting board and thickly slice.

Makes 6 servings

COOK'S TIP

✳ Be sure to use ground turkey without MSG or other preservatives.

Variations

Egg-Free Meatloaf: Replace the egg with ⅓ cup Egg Substitute (page 212).

Meatloaf with Game: Substitute buffalo, venison, emu, or ostrich for the turkey.

Grain-Free Meatloaf: Substitute ⅓ cup of quinoa flakes and ⅓ cup of amaranth flakes for the oat bran.

Roasted Cornish Game Hens

Allergic to chicken, but wish you could enjoy it again? Then give this recipe a try. Cornish game hens are just different enough from chicken that you may be able to tolerate them. Look for these small birds in your supermarket's frozen foods case. Allow one hen for two people.

2 Cornish game hens, thawed

4 baby carrots

½ rib celery, halved

PREHEAT OVEN to 350°F.

Place the hens on a rack, breast side up, in a shallow roasting pan. Tuck 2 carrots and a piece of celery into the cavity of each bird.

Tie the legs together. Bake, uncovered, for 1 hour and 20 minutes, or until nicely brown, the juices run clear, legs move freely, and a meat thermometer registers at least 180°F.

Cut in half to serve.

Makes 4 servings

COOK'S TIPS

✳ Thaw the game hens in the refrigerator for 24 hours.

✳ If you find a pad of fat in the cavity, flatten it across the breast bone to provide moisture as the bird cooks. If there is no fat, mist the bird with cooking spray.

✳ Let the hens rest at room temperature for 10 minutes before carving.

✳ To use a meat thermometer, insert it in the thickest part of the meat, making sure it doesn't touch a bone. Insert a standard meat thermometer before starting to cook. Insert an instant-read variety near the end of the cooking time to check the meat's internal temperature, but don't expose it to oven heat or leave it in the meat for more than a minute.

✳ Save the bones for making stock, if you wish; keep them frozen until you're ready to use them, and use in place of chicken broth.

Roast Duckling with Sweet Potatoes

Widely available in the frozen food section of most supermarkets, duckling provides wonderful diversity for the allergy diet. This duckling is excellent with Orange Sauce (page 196) or Cherry Sauce (recipe variation, page 207).

5–6 **pound frozen duckling, thawed**
2 **ribs celery, cut in half**
½ **apple, quartered**
2 **dark orange sweet potatoes**

PREHEAT THE OVEN to 350°F.

Place the duck on a wire rack in a 13" × 9" roasting pan. Insert the celery and apple into the cavity and tie the legs together. Bake a 5-pound bird for 2 hours 15 minutes or a 6 pounder for 2 hours 45 minutes (about 28 minutes per pound), or until done and a meat thermometer registers at least 180°F.

While the duck is cooking, wrap the potatoes in foil. About 1 hour before the end of the cooking time, place the potatoes in the oven. Bake for 1 hour, or until tender.

Makes 2 servings

COOK'S TIPS

✳ Before cooking the duck, be sure to remove the giblets and thoroughly rinse the bird inside and out.

✳ If you want stuffing with the meal, prepare the recipe and bake the stuffing in a separate baking dish.

✳ Some ducks come with a pop-up timer to indicate when the meat is done. Don't rely solely on it; use a good thermometer to confirm the temperature.

✳ To use a meat thermometer, insert it in the thickest part of the meat, making sure it doesn't touch a bone. Insert a standard meat thermometer before starting to cook. Insert an instant-read variety near the end of the cooking time to check the meat's internal temperature, but don't expose it to oven heat or leave it in the meat for more than a minute.

✳ Let the duck rest at room temperature for 10 minutes before carving.

✳ Save the roasted duck wings, which have no meat on them, for flavoring soup. Keep them frozen until you're ready to use them.

Moussaka-Style Casserole

Traditional Greek moussaka calls for tomato sauce; this version is tomato-free.
People who are allergic to beef will have yet another delicious lamb dish
to add to their repertoire.

1 **eggplant (about 1 pound), sliced lengthwise ¼" thick**

½–1 **teaspoon Italian Seasoning (page 210)**

1 **tablespoon olive or canola oil**

½ **pound ground lean lamb, pork, or buffalo**

1 **cup chopped onions**

2 **cloves garlic, crushed (optional)**

1 **cup pumpkin puree**

1 **cup water**

½ **teaspoon salt**

¼ **teaspoon dried thyme**

¼ **teaspoon unbuffered vitamin C crystals**

Dash of salt (optional)

¾–1 **cup grated goat's-milk Cheddar cheese (optional)**

PREHEAT THE OVEN to 400°F. Line a baking sheet with parchment paper. Oil an 8" × 8" baking dish.

Mist both sides of each eggplant slice with cooking spray. Place on the baking sheet and sprinkle with ½ teaspoon of the Italian Seasoning. Bake for 12 to 15 minutes, or just until tender.

In a large skillet, heat the oil over medium heat. Add the lamb, onions, and garlic and cook for 8 minutes, or until the onions are soft and meat no longer pink. Add the pumpkin, water, salt, thyme, vitamin C, and remaining ½ teaspoon seasoning. Bring to a boil, stirring. Remove from the heat.

Arrange half of the eggplant slices in a single layer in the prepared baking dish and sprinkle lightly with salt if using. Spread with half the meat mixture. Top with another layer of eggplant and the remaining meat sauce.

Bake for 30 minutes. Top with the cheese if using. Bake for 10 minutes, or until the cheese is melted.

Makes 4 servings

COOK'S TIPS

* If you wish, substitute ½ cup sulfite-free white wine for ½ cup of the water.

* Eggplant can be bitter, and it's often a guessing game which one to buy. Some people, among them Julia Child, recommend selecting eggplants that have flat bottoms rather than dimpled ones.

Cassoulet

*This traditional bean stew originated among the peasants in southern France
and went on to win fans all over the world.*

1 meaty roasted lamb or wild game
  shank bone

1½ pounds white beans, such as Great
  Northern, navy, or lima, soaked for
  8 to 10 hours

8 cups water

1 bay leaf

1 pound preservative-free pork or
  turkey sausage

1½ cups coarsely chopped onions or leeks

3–4 cloves garlic, crushed

½ teaspoon dried thyme

1 cup diced cooked chicken or turkey
  (optional)

4 whole cloves

2 tablespoons lemon juice or
  ½ teaspoon unbuffered vitamin C
  crystals

1 cup sulfite-free white or red wine
  or water

½ teaspoon salt

  Freshly ground black pepper or few
  drops of hot-pepper sauce (optional)

Preheat the oven to 250°F. Oil a nonstick 13" × 9" baking dish.

Crumble the sausage into a large skillet 30 minutes before the beans are done cooking. Cook over medium heat, stirring often, for 15 minutes, or until light brown and no longer pink. Drain on 4 thicknesses of paper towels. Discard the fat in the skillet. Add the onions or leeks, garlic, and thyme to skillet, and cook for 8 to 10 minutes, or until the onions soften.

When the beans are tender, remove the bone and discard the bay leaf. Stir in the lamb, chicken or turkey if using, sausage mixture, cloves, lemon juice or vitamin C, wine or water, salt, and pepper if using. Place in the reserved baking dish. Add water if necessary to just cover the bean mixture.

Bake, uncovered, for 2 hours, adding water every 30 minutes as necessary to keep the beans moist.

Makes 8 servings

TRIM AS MUCH meat as possible from the bone. Discard visible fat. Dice the meat and set aside in the refrigerator.

Place the bone in a 5-quart pot. Drain and rinse the beans. Add the beans, water, and bay leaf to the pot. Bring to a boil. Reduce the heat and cook, partially covered, for 2 hours, or until the beans are very tender, adding water as necessary to keep the beans covered.

COOK'S TIPS

✳ If the baking dish is very full, place the dish in the oven, *then* add the extra water, if needed.

✳ To keep this dish hot for up to 2 hours, cover it with foil and reduce the heat to 150°F.

✳ To use an uncooked bone, cook the bone and meat along with the beans. About 30 minutes before the beans are done cooking, carefully remove the bone and cut the meat from the bone. Discard the bone and return the meat to the bean mixture.

Easy Curry

There are almost as many good curry recipes as there are cooks.
You can curry lamb, chicken, turkey, white or sweet potatoes, peas, cauliflower,
or a myriad of other foods. My favorite combination is curried lamb and vegetables over
baked sweet potatoes. When serving curries, be sure to serve something cool—
like cucumbers or chilled fruit—on the side to cool the palate.

2 tablespoons olive oil

½ cup chopped onions or leeks

1 tablespoon Curry Powder (page 211)

2 tablespoons brown rice flour

2–3 garlic cloves, minced

2 cups chicken, meat, or vegetable
stock or broth

¼–½ teaspoon salt (optional)

¼ cup raisins or dried cranberries

1 apple, chopped

½ teaspoon powdered ginger

¼ teaspoon dried thyme

3 whole cloves

1 bay leaf

2–3 cups cooked cubed lamb, turkey,
chicken, or mixed vegetables

2 tablespoons grated unsweetened
coconut (optional)

2 cups cooked quinoa or brown rice

HEAT THE OIL in a 3-quart saucepan over medium heat. Add the onions or leeks and cook for 5 minutes, or until soft. Reduce the heat. Sprinkle with the curry powder and cook, stirring, for 3 minutes. Add the flour and garlic and cook, stirring, for 3 minutes. Add the stock or broth and cook, whisking or stirring constantly, for 3 minutes, or until thick and smooth. Season with the salt to taste.

Stir in the raisins or dried cranberries, apples, ginger, thyme, cloves, and bay leaf and cook for 15 minutes. Add the meat or vegetables, and cook until heated through. Discard the cloves and bay leaf. Serve in bowls or over quinoa or brown rice. Top with coconut if using

Makes 4 servings

Variation

Grain-Free Curry: Replace the rice flour with amaranth, buckwheat, or quinoa flour or puree ½ cup cooked potatoes or sweet potatoes with stock or broth in a blender until smooth. Add to the cooked onions after the garlic.

Pork Chops with Apples and Sage

This makes a surprisingly festive meal.
Add a vegetable and salad for a tasty feast.

1 tablespoon canola oil
2 thick pork chops
2 ribs celery, thinly sliced
1 cup brown rice
2 apples, 1 chopped, 1 sliced
¼ teaspoon ground cinnamon
¼–½ teaspoon dry sage, crumbled
1 cup chicken stock or broth
¾ cup apple juice

PREHEAT THE OVEN to 350°F. Heat the oil in a large skillet with an oven-safe handle and lid over medium-high heat. Add the pork and celery and cook for 5 minutes, or until the pork is brown. Remove chops to a plate and cover with foil to keep warm.

Combine the rice, chopped apple, cinnamon, and sage in the skillet. Cook, stirring, for 3 minutes. Stir in the stock or broth and apple juice. Return the chops to the skillet and partially bury them in the rice. Top with the sliced apple. Dust with a little more cinnamon.

Cover and bake for 40 minutes. Remove the lid and bake for 10 minutes more, or until the rice is tender.

Makes 2 servings

Cowboy Beans

No tomatoes and no beef. But these beans are still red, saucy, meaty, and tasty.

1 pound pinto or kidney beans, soaked overnight

½ pound preservative-free pork sausage or Italian turkey sausage, casings removed

1½ cups chopped onions

2–3 cloves garlic, minced

3 tablespoons minced fresh basil or 1 tablespoon dried (optional)

1 tablespoon lemon juice or ¼ teaspoon vitamin C crystals

1 teaspoon Italian Seasoning (page 210) (optional)

½ teaspoon salt

DRAIN THE BEANS and discard the water. Place in a large saucepan, cover with fresh water, and cook partially covered for 2 hours.

Add water as needed to keep beans covered.

Crumble the sausage into a large skillet and cook, stirring, over medium heat for 15 minutes, or until no longer pink. Drain off all but 1 tablespoon of fat. Add the onions and cook for 5 minutes, or until soft. Add the garlic and salt, and cook for 1 minute.

Add to the beans and simmer for 1 hour, or until the beans are very tender. Stir in the basil, lemon juice or vitamin C, Italian Seasoning if using, and salt. Using a potato masher, mash some of the beans to thicken the sauce slightly. Cook for 10 minutes more, stirring.

Makes 4 servings

Variation

Tex-Mex Cowboy Beans: Replace the Italian Seasoning with 1 tablespoon mild or hot chili powder.

Versatile Meatballs

You can season these meatballs any way you like: Italian, Swedish, Mexican, or "all-American" (a little of this, a little of that).

½ pound ground chicken, turkey, or pork loin

½ pound preservative-free pork or turkey sausage, casings removed

⅔ cup water

¾ cup Easy Bread Crumbs (page 134) or quinoa flakes

¼ cup powdered goat's milk (optional)

½ cup finely chopped onions

¼ cup minced fresh parsley, lovage leaves, or cilantro

½ teaspoon salt

¼ teaspoon ground black pepper or ⅛ teaspoon red pepper (optional)

1 large clove garlic, minced

2 teaspoons olive oil

PREHEAT THE OVEN to 400°F.

In a large bowl, combine the chicken, turkey, or pork; sausage; and water. Add the bread crumbs; powdered milk if using; onions; parsley, lovage, or cilantro; salt; black or red pepper if using; garlic; and oil. Mix well.

Shape into 40 cherry-size meatballs. Place on a rack set over a broiler pan. Bake for 15 or 18 minutes or until done.

Makes 6 servings

COOK'S TIPS

＊ If you want, you can make larger meatballs: 25 golf ball–size ones (cook for 20 to 25 minutes) or 8 to 10 lemon-size ones (cook for 25 to 30 minutes).

＊ Placing the meatballs on a rack allows the fat to drain during cooking.

＊ Using unusual meats? You may have to grind them yourself. To do so, cut a lean roast, such as loin, into 1" cubes. Place in a meat grinder or food processor and process to the desired consistency. Package and freeze whatever you won't be using immediately.

＊ If you've ground your own meat in a food processor, you can then mix the meatballs right in the same bowl. Add the water first, then the vegetables and seasonings. Add the bread crumbs last.

＊ Safety hint: After using your processor to grind raw meat, wash it very well in hot sudsy water to destroy any harmful bacteria.

Variations

Venison Meatballs: Replace the ground pork and sausage with 1 pound ground venison (or if venison sausage is available, ½ pound of each).

Italian Meatballs: Add 1 teaspoon dried oregano and 1½ teaspoons dried basil. After baking, serve with Tomato Sauce (page 199) or Tomato-Free Spaghetti Sauce (page 201) and your favorite pasta.

Swedish Meatballs: Use the powdered goat's milk. (Or replace it and the ⅔ cup water with a nut milk: Blend ½ cup raw cashews to a fine powder in a blender. Add enough boiling water to bring the liquid level to ⅔ cup. Blend well for 2 minutes to make a liquid that's the consistency of frosting. Let cool before adding to the meat mixture.) Serve with a creamy gravy or sauce such as Mushroom Brown Sauce (page 204).

Mexican Meatballs: Replace the parsley with cilantro and add ¼ teaspoon ground red pepper. If desired, also add ½ can chopped green chiles. Serve in a spicy tomato sauce over rice or with tortillas to tear and use as a scoop.

Meatloaf: Shape into a loaf instead of meatballs and place in an oiled 8" × 4" loaf pan. Bake at 350°F for 50 minutes.

Venison Pepper Steak

Whether you're allergic to beef or not, you'll love this version of the ever-popular pepper steak. Here, the secret to tender venison is thin slicing and quick cooking.

2 tablespoons vegetable oil

1 venison loin roast, thinly sliced (1–1¼ pounds)

1 large Spanish onion, thinly sliced

2 large green bell peppers, thinly sliced

1 clove garlic, minced

2–3 scallions, sliced ½" thick

1 cup water

½ teaspoon salt

1 tablespoon arrowroot or tapioca starch

3 cups hot cooked brown rice

HEAT 1 TABLESPOON of the oil in a large skillet over medium to medium-high heat. Add the venison and cook, stirring, for 5 minutes, or until brown. Remove to a plate.

Add the remaining 1 tablespoon oil to the skillet. Add the onions, peppers, and garlic. Reduce the heat to medium-low and cook for 10 minutes, or until the vegetables are soft. Return the meat to the skillet, and add the scallions and ¾ cup of the water. Season with the salt to taste.

In a small bowl or cup, dissolve the arrowroot or tapioca in the remaining ¼ cup water, and add to venison mixture. Cook, stirring, for 2 to 3 minutes, or until thick.

Serve over the rice.

Makes 4 servings

COOK'S TIPS

∗ For tender slices, cut the meat very thinly across the grain. This is easiest to do if the meat is partially frozen, and you use a very sharp serrated knife.

∗ If you want, you can substitute ¼ cup sulfite-free white wine for ¼ cup of the water. Or make and use a venison stock.

Oven-Fried Rabbit

Here's a tender, juicy alternative to fried chicken. Use any flour you wish.
(See "Cooking and Baking with Alternative Flours," page 6.)

1 **young frying rabbit, cut into pieces (about 3 pounds)**
½ **cup arrowroot, amaranth, or buckwheat flour**
½ **teaspoon salt**
Pinch of ground red pepper (optional)
3 **tablespoons oil**
½ **cup hot water**

PREHEAT THE OVEN to 325°F. Rinse the rabbit under cold water. Shake off the excess water.

Combine the flour, salt, and pepper if using in a shallow dish. Dredge the rabbit in the flour to coat.

Heat oil in a large skillet over medium heat. Add the rabbit and cook for 5 minutes, or until browned. Place in a 13" × 9" baking dish. Add the water. Cover and bake for 50 minutes. Remove cover and bake 10 minutes more, or until tender.

Makes 4 servings

COOK'S TIP

✳ Other flours or starches that work well include oat, potato, and tapioca starch.

Catch of the Day

Fish has a lot going for it: It's full of flavor, packed with quality protein, and is an excellent source of heart-healthy omega-3 fats. Just as important is what it doesn't have—artery-clogging saturated fat. That's why more people than ever are eating fish.

For people with food allergies, fish has even more in its favor: There are at least 33 different families of fish from which to choose. That makes fish much less similar to each other than if there were just one big food family called "fish." It's quite likely, then, that a person who reacts to fish "A" can enjoy eating fish "B" and "C" with no reaction at all. Still, you've got to try them to know which will bother you and which won't. (See Planning a Rotary Diversified Diet, page 35.)

Reactions to fish vary. Let me explain: If three people all react to the same species of fish, one of those people might get a splitting headache, another might develop a rash on the forearms, and the third might get a belly-ache—all minor discomforts. However, a small percentage of allergics may have a life threatening anaphylactic reaction. Anyone with such a history should abstain from eating all fish and seafood and discuss the risks with a physician. Some doctors teach anaphylactic patients to use an injection, commonly referred to as a "bee sting kit," to abort an allergic reaction.

To help you put more fish on your menu, here are a few tips:

Go for variety. To diversify your diet, seek out monkfish, catfish, tilapia, butterfish, and other less-familiar fish. If you can, include fresh salmon once a week—or at least once or twice a month—to get good-for-you omega-3 fats. Mackerel and trout have them, too, but not quite as much.

As healthful as fish is, you should be aware that mercury, cadmium, and other toxic metals have been found in many fish, especially those from inland lakes. When buying fish, inquire about the source, and always choose deep-water ocean fish over those from inland lakes. Farm-raised fish is a mixed bag. If the fish are fed corn pellets (a common practice on inland fish farms), they may be more allergenic than the same species would be from the wild. That said, some fish farms along the coasts have their pens in the ocean water, and those fish are thought by some people to provide a fairly natural food. Since different species concentrate toxic metals at varying rates, we are well-advised to avoid eating only one or two favorite species of fish.

Buy the freshest fish you can find. While not odor-free, fish should smell fresh, like a sea breeze. An "off" odor is a dead giveaway that fresh fish is no longer fresh. When fish sits around for as little as two or three days, it deteriorates rapidly, even when refrigerated or displayed on ice. If fish is suspect, you're better off buying rock-hard packages of flash-frozen unbreaded, raw fish—preferably fish that was frozen the day it was caught, which may be stated on the label. (Never buy frozen fish that's mushy. And thaw frozen fish on a plate, so it doesn't drip onto other foods, in the refrigerator.)

Keep preparation simple. Basic poaching, baking, or broiling is best. I've provided directions for each method, as well as recipes for a few combination dishes. Not sure how to prepare a new type of fish? Ask questions before you buy it. Usually, the answer will be to cook it hot (perhaps 425°F to 450°F) and quick, to prevent drying.

When preparing salmon, swordfish, and other large fish, you will see areas of very dark flesh. This is called the "lateral line" and is where the mitochondria and the brown adipose tissue that the fish uses in its sensory system is concentrated. It is often removed because it doesn't taste as good as other parts of the fish. In salmon, the lateral line lies between the skin and the peachy-pink flesh, and is easily scraped off and discarded after cooking. In swordfish, the dark areas are more integrated into the muscle yet are well delineated and can be cut out easily after cooking.

Baked Fish Fillets

Many people enjoy eating fish in restaurants but shy away from cooking it at home.
But follow this recipe and you'll serve a perfect restaurant-style catch every time.
Use the recipe for almost any type of fillets.

1½ **pounds fish fillets**

   Cooking spray or 1 tablespoon
   vegetable oil or Cashew Spread
   (page 195)

4 **lemon or lime wedges (optional))**

   Cucumber-Dill Sauce (page 195) or
   Creamy Mustard Sauce (page 197)
   (optional)

PREHEAT THE OVEN TO 400°F. Line a baking sheet with parchment paper. Rinse the fillets under cold running water, and pat dry with paper towels. Lay the fillets in a single layer on the prepared baking sheet. Mist each with the cooking spray, or brush with the oil or spread.

Bake for 8 to 10 minutes, or just until the fish is cooked through, opaque, and flakes easily when probed with a fork. Do not overcook.

Serve plain, with lemon or lime wedges, or with a sauce.

Makes 4 servings

COOK'S TIPS

✳ If fillets are very thin (sole and flounder, for example), stack the oiled fillets by twos or threes to minimize drying.

✳ A general rule for baking fish: Allow 10 minutes for each inch of thickness. Fish is done if it flakes easily when probed with a fork. Tricky though this sounds, try to catch it just before it falls apart. (If it does, no harm done, and you'll know it's cooked through.)

Broiled Fish

This is probably one of the quickest and easiest entrees you can make for dinner.
Have all ingredients ready—as well as the rest of your meal—
before you start cooking the fish. Cooking is fast.

1½ **pounds swordfish, halibut, or other large fish steaks, cut ¾" to 1" thick**

Cooking spray or 1 tablespoon vegetable oil

3 **tablespoons minced fresh parsley (optional)**

Dash of paprika (optional)

4 **lemon or lime wedges (optional)**

PREHEAT THE BROILER. Rinse the fish under cold running water, and pat dry with paper towels. Coat the skin side with the cooking spray or half of the oil. Place skin-side down on the rack of a broiler pan. Mist with the cooking spray or brush with the remaining oil. Add a little water to the bottom of the broiler pan to provide steam during cooking to help keep the fish moist.

Broil 3" to 4" from the heat for 7 to 8 minutes, or just until the fish is cooked through, opaque, and flakes easily when probed with a fork. Do not overcook.

Sprinkle with the parsley and paprika, if using, and serve with the lemon or lime wedges, if using.

Makes 4 servings

COOK'S TIPS

✴ For really quick and easy cleanup, treat yourself to a nonstick broiler pan.

✴ A general rule for broiling fish steaks: Allow 9 to 10 minutes for each inch of thickness. Most fillets measure ¾" and will take 7 to 8 minutes.

Easy Sole

*Here's a delightful variation of plain baked fish. Serve it often for family and friends—
just don't tell anyone how easy it is to make.*

12 **sole fillets (about 1½ pounds of
2-ounce fillets)**

1 **tablespoon Cashew Spread
(page 195) or Tofu-Dijon Spread
(page 194)**

4–6 **scallions, thinly sliced**

2 **tablespoons grated dried Myzithra
or crumbled feta cheese (optional)**

PREHEAT THE OVEN TO 450°F. Line a
baking sheet with parchment paper. Rinse
the fish under cold running water, and pat
dry with paper towels.

Spread 1½ teaspoons of the spread over
one side of each of the fillets. Place four fillets on the prepared baking sheet. Spread ½
teaspoon of spread over the fish. Arrange
half of the scallions on top of the fillets. Top
each with another fillet. Spread ½ teaspoon
spread over the fillets and top with the remaining scallions. Top with the remaining 4
fillets and spread the remaining ½ teaspoon
spread over them. (You should have four 3-
deep stacks of fillets.) Sprinkle with the
cheese if using.

Bake for 20 to 22 minutes, or just until
the fish is cooked through, opaque, and
flakes easily when probed with a fork.

Makes 4 servings

COOK'S TIPS

✳ For 3-ounce fillets, make 4 stacks with 2 fillets each.

✳ Myzithra is a traditional Greek cheese made from
the whey of ewe's, goat's, or cow's milk. It's
available fresh, which resembles ricotta cheese, or
dried, which is much like Parmesan and Romano
cheese. Look for it in health food stores, cheese
shops, and large supermarkets.

Fish Fillets Florentine

Truly a classy way to dress up fish. And you can do it quickly on the stove top.

8 ounces spinach
1 tablespoon olive oil
⅓ cup chopped onions
   Salt
   Pinch of freshly grated nutmeg
½–¾ pound flounder, sole, or catfish
   Spritz of olive oil spray or 1 teaspoon olive oil
¼ teaspoon dried dillweed (optional)
   Paprika (optional)
2 tablespoons grated dried Myzithra or crumbled feta cheese
   Lemon or lime wedges (optional)

IN A SAUCEPAN over boiling water, steam the spinach for 5 minutes, or just until wilted. Drain in a colander, pressing with a spatula or spoon to remove most of the moisture. Place on a cutting board and chop coarsely.

Heat the oil in a large skillet over medium heat. Add the onions and cook for 6 to 7 minutes, or until soft. Add the spinach and season with the salt. Dust with the nutmeg. Cook, stirring, over medium heat for 1 minute.

Arrange the fish in a single layer over the spinach. Mist with the spray or brush on the 1 teaspoon of oil. Sprinkle with the dillweed if using or the paprika if using. Top with the cheese.

Cover the pan and cook for 6 to 9 minutes, or just until the fish is cooked through, opaque, and flakes easily when probed with a fork. Serve with lemon or lime wedges if using.

Makes 2 servings

COOK'S TIPS

✳ To use frozen spinach: Buy 1 package (10 ounces) and allow it to thaw. Squeeze dry and chop. Do not steam; simply add it to the pan after the onions have softened, and proceed with the recipe.

✳ Myzithra is a traditional Greek cheese made from the whey of ewe's, goat's, or cow's milk. It's available fresh, which resembles ricotta cheese, or dried, which is much like Parmesan and Romano cheese. Look for it in health food stores, cheese shops, and large supermarkets.

Fish Fillets with Almonds

This dish cooks in a flash, so have the rest of the meal well under way before starting it. And feel free to use other mild-tasting skinless fillets: I also like trout, snapper, flounder, and catfish.

1 tablespoon ghee, melted, or almond oil
⅓ cup slivered or chopped almonds
¼ cup whole grain flour
¼ teaspoon salt
1½ pounds scrod fillets
1 tablespoon almond oil

HEAT THE GHEE or oil in a small skillet over medium-low heat. Add the nuts and cook until lightly browned.

Rinse the fish under cold running water, and pat almost dry with paper towels. Combine the flour and salt if using in a shallow bowl or on waxed paper. Add the fish, turning to coat.

Heat the almond oil in a large nonstick skillet over medium-high heat. Add the fish and cook for 3 to 4 minutes on a side, or until the fish is browned, cooked through, opaque, and flakes easily when probed with a fork. Top with the almonds.

Makes 4 servings

COOK'S TIPS

* To make ghee (or clarified butter): Melt butter in a saucepan over low heat; then pour the liquid into a jar, taking care to leave the milk solids in the bottom of the pan. Discard the solids. Ghee will keep frozen for up to 1 year.

* For the breading, use any whole grain flour that agrees with you. (See "Wheat and Grain Alternatives," page 5.)

* Buy four 6-ounce small fillets such as scrod or two 12-ounce thick fillets such as snapper.

Variation

Fish Fillets with Lemon and Almonds: Drizzle 1 tablespoon lemon juice over the fish before coating it with the flour. Drizzle with additional lemon juice just before serving.

Avocado Stuffed with Tuna

Here's a dressy tuna salad that's free of onions and egg mayonnaise. It makes for a very special luncheon dish.

1 can (6 ounces) no-salt-added water-packed tuna, drained
½ cup thinly chopped celery
⅓ cup chopped walnuts or other nuts
¼ teaspoon salt

¼ cup Tofu-Dijon Spread (page 194)
4 leaves lettuce or 1 cup mesclun
1 large avocado, halved and peeled

IN A SMALL BOWL, combine the fish, celery, nuts, and salt. Add the spread and toss to coat.

Arrange the lettuce or mesclun on 2 plates. Spoon the tuna mixture into the avocado halves.

Makes 2 servings

Poached Salmon

Salmon is a mouthwatering break from the usual meat or poultry routine. And it's a delightful way to get the omega-3 oils we all need. I like to serve poached salmon with dishes I can prepare ahead (such as baked potatoes) so I can give all my attention to cooking the salmon and making a sauce for it.

1 quart water
1 bay leaf or sprig thyme (optional)
1½ pounds salmon fillets (two ¾-pound tail pieces) or other firm-fleshed fish
Orange Sauce (page 196) (optional)

BRING THE WATER TO A BOIL in a large skillet. Add the bay leaf or thyme if using. Add the salmon, immediately reduce the heat, cover, and simmer for 8 to 10 minutes, or until the salmon is cooked through and flakes easily when probed with a fork. Do not let the water boil. Cut down the midline of each piece and using a spatula, and place the pieces on a plate. Remove the skin and the dark gray layer immediately under it. Top each serving with the sauce if using.

Makes 4 servings

Salmon Salad

Makes a great main dish salad or a delicious sandwich filling.
Try serving the salad with pancakes left from breakfast or with rice crackers.

1 cup flaked poached salmon or other cooked fish

¼ cup Tofu-Dijon Spread (page 194) or Cashew Spread (page 195)

2 tablespoons chopped parsley

2 tablespoons minced onions

2 tablespoons honey-sweetened pickle relish (optional)

¼ teaspoon salt

4 leaves lettuce or 8 large leaves spinach

IN A LARGE BOWL, mix the salmon, spread, parsley, onions, relish if using, and salt. Cover and chill for at least 1 hour. When ready to serve, arrange the lettuce or spinach on 2 plates and top with the salad. Or spread on bread or pancakes and top them with the greens.

Makes 2 servings

Salmon Cakes

This is a quick and easy way to enjoy cooked salmon. I usually buy and cook enough fish
to make this dish a few days after enjoying Poached Salmon (page 241).

½ cup water

1 tablespoon flax seeds

3–4 drops hot-pepper sauce

1½–2 cups flaked cooked salmon or other fish

3 tablespoons finely minced onion (optional)

½ teaspoon dillweed (optional)

¼ teaspoon salt

2 tablespoons Cashew Spread (page 195) or Tofu-Dijon Spread (page 194)

2 tablespoons oat bran or quinoa flakes

1 tablespoon canola or other oil

COMBINE THE WATER, flax seeds, and hot-pepper sauce in a small saucepan. Bring to a boil, reduce the heat to low, and cook for 5 minutes, or until the mixture has thickened. (Don't let it boil dry.) Let cool.

In a bowl, combine the salmon, onion if using, dillweed if using, and salt. Stir the spread into the flaxseed mixture and add to the salmon. Toss to moisten. Add the oat bran or quinoa flakes and mix. Mixture will be stiff.

Heat the oil in a nonstick skillet over medium heat. Divide the salmon mixture into 4 portions. Place in the skillet. Using a rubber spatula, flatten to form cakes.

Cook for 5 minutes or until the bottoms are brown. Turn and cook for 5 minutes more, or until the second side is brown. Serve at once.

Makes 4

Baked Sole with Asparagus Spears

A perfect marriage of subtle flavors. For an attractive color contrast,
serve with baked sweet potatoes.

1¼ **pounds sole fillets or other mild-flavored fish**

1 **teaspoon vegetable oil or a spritz of cooking spray**

24 **thin asparagus stalks, trimmed**

Creamy Mustard Sauce (page 197), warmed

2 **teaspoons chopped chives or ½ teaspoon paprika (optional)**

PREHEAT THE OVEN to 400°F. Line a 13" × 9" (or 9" × 9") baking dish with foil and oil or coat with cooking spray.

Rinse the fish under cold running water, and pat dry with paper towels. Arrange in a single layer in the prepared baking dish. Brush with the oil or mist with the cooking spray. Bake for 10 to 12 minutes or just until the fish is cooked through, opaque, and flakes easily when probed with a fork.

While the fish is cooking, steam the asparagus over boiling water for 7 to 10 minutes, or just until the stems are tender.

To serve, arrange 6 stalks in the middle of each dinner plate. Top with the fish and sauce. Sprinkle the chives or paprika if using over the sauce.

Makes 4 servings

COOK'S TIP

✳ Fresh asparagus spears will break at the point where the tough stems end and the tender portions begin. Your best bet then is to give asparagus spears a quick snap instead of cutting them.

Baked Tuna Steak

For me, fresh tuna is a real treat. I like to buy enough for dinner
as well as a special tuna salad lunch the next day.

1–1¼ **pounds yellowfin (ahi) or albacore**
     tuna steaks (about 1" thick)
  ⅓ **cup Brazil nuts**
     Pinch of salt
1–2 **tablespoons lemon juice or water**
     Cooking spray

PREHEAT OVEN to 450°F. Line an 8" square pan with foil. Rinse the fish under cold running water, and pat dry with paper towels.

Combine the nuts and salt in a blender and process until the mixture becomes nut butter. Add 1 tablespoon of the lemon juice or water and process, stopping as needed to scrape down the sides of the container. Add the remaining 1 tablespoon lemon juice or water only if needed for a spreadable consistency.

Mist the fish on 1 side with the cooking spray. Arrange in the prepared baking pan, sprayed side down. Spread the nut mixture over the fish.

Bake for 15 minutes, or just until the fish is cooked through, opaque, and flakes easily when probed with a fork.

Makes 4 servings

Tuna Burgers

Serve as an entree with vegetables. Or place burgers between pancakes
or slices of any wheat-free bread for sandwiches. Dress them up
with ketchup, relish, mustard, lettuce, and tomato slices.

1 can (6 ounces) no-salt-added water-packed tuna, drained

¼ cup minced onions

2 tablespoons honey-sweetened or fruit-sweetened ketchup

1 tablespoon prepared mustard (optional)

2 tablespoons mayonnaise

2 tablespoons minced parsley or cilantro (optional)

¼–½ teaspoon salt

1 starch: 1 small cooked white potato or ¼ cup defatted toasted amaranth flakes or ⅓ cup quinoa flakes or ¼ cup oat bran

1–1½ tablespoons vegetable oil

IN A FOOD PROCESSOR combine the tuna, onions, ketchup, mustard if using, mayonnaise, parsley or cilantro if using, salt, and the starch (potato, amaranth, quinoa or oat bran). Process for 10 to 20 seconds, or until well mixed, stopping once to scrap down the sides of the container. Mixture should be chunky. Do not overprocess.

Heat 1 tablespoon of the oil in a large skillet over medium-low heat. Using a spatula or spoon, drop the tuna mixture, in 4 mounds, into the skillet. Using a knife and spatula, flatten and shape the mounds into ¾"-thick patties. Cook for 5 to 7 minutes, or until brown. Turn and cook for 5 minutes more, or until brown. Add the remaining ½ tablespoon of oil if needed to prevent sticking. Don't let the patties overbrown.

Makes 4

COOK'S TIP

✱ No-salt-added canned tuna is the only variety in which the tuna isn't bathed in a broth of MSG-laden flavorings.

Oven-Fried Fillets with Cashews

Love the flavor of breaded, deep-fried fish—but want something healthier?
This version is not only good for you, but it's quick and easy to prepare, too.

½ cup raw cashews

   Basil, dill, or tarragon (optional)

   Salt and pepper (optional)

2–3 whitefish fillets (about 1½ pounds)

1–1½ teaspoons melted ghee or vegetable oil

PREHEAT THE OVEN to 500°F. Line a baking sheet with parchment paper. Combine the nuts and the basil, dill, or tarragon if using in a blender or food processor. Add the salt and pepper if using. Process until finely ground. Do not overprocess or nut butter will form. Place on a plate.

Rinse the fish under cold running water, and pat dry with paper towels. Dip into the nut mixture to coat. Arrange on the prepared baking sheet. Drizzle with the ghee or oil.

Bake for 10 to 12 minutes, or just until the fish is cooked through, opaque, and flakes easily when probed with a fork. Serve at once.

Makes 4 servings

COOK'S TIP

* To make ghee (or clarified butter): Melt butter in a saucepan over low heat; then pour the liquid into a jar, taking care to leave the milk solids in the bottom of the pan. Discard the solids. Ghee will keep frozen for up to 1 year.

Vegetarian Main Dishes

We can all benefit from eating a meat-free meal once or twice a week. For one thing, it's a great way to reduce our intake of animal fats. And if you or someone in your family is allergic to meat, poultry, or fish, vegetarian dishes give you a much wider choice of meals to prepare.

I've purposely avoided relying too heavily on soybeans and soy foods in this section because of potential reactions to that legume. And only two recipes use egg: Zesty Loaf and Egg Foo Yong with Ginger Sauce. Most of the recipes in this section offer a choice of beans to meet individual needs and tastes. Savory Skillet Supper, Better Burgers, and Vegetarian Chili have all been enthusiastically received by vegetarian guests at my house, and the Savory Skillet Supper has been a big hit at potlucks.

If you are allergic to either grains or legumes, which are often combined in vegetarian dishes, here are a few alternatives: Zesty Loaf, Veggie Nut Burgers, Cashew-Zucchini Patties, Grain-Free Stuffed Peppers, and Egg Foo Yong with Ginger Sauce. These recipes do not include grains or legumes.

Savory Skillet Supper

So simple, fast, and satisfying. Use any beans you like.

- 1 cup brown rice
- 2 tablespoons olive oil
- 1 cup chopped onions
- 1 large rib celery, thinly sliced
- 2 carrots, thinly sliced
- 1 tablespoon wheat-free tamari sauce or ½ teaspoon salt
- 2 teaspoons dried basil
- 1 teaspoon dried oregano
- 2 cloves garlic, crushed
  Dash of ground red pepper (optional)
- ½ cup chopped parsley
- 2 cups cooked pinto or kidney beans, or 1 can (14–19 ounces), rinsed and drained
- 2 tablespoons water
- 1 cup cherry tomatoes, halved

COOK THE RICE according to the directions in Basic Rice (page 158).

In a large skillet, heat the oil over medium heat. Add the onions, celery, and carrots and cook for 12 minutes, or until tender. Stir in the tamari or salt, basil, oregano, garlic, red pepper if using, and ¼ cup of the parsley. Add the beans and water. Cover and cook for 10 minutes or until heated through.

Reduce the heat to low and gently stir in the rice. Arrange the tomatoes, cut side down, in a circle around the outer edges of the pan. Sprinkle with the remaining ¼ cup parsley. Cover and cook for 2 minutes.

Makes 4 servings

Zesty Loaf

Cold slices make wonderful sandwiches.

- 2 tablespoons olive oil
- 1 cup finely chopped onions
- 1 cup finely chopped celery
- 1 cup finely chopped carrots
- 1 clove garlic, crushed
- ¾ cup finely chopped cashews
- ¾ cup oat bran, quinoa flakes, or Easy Bread Crumbs (page 134)
- 2 eggs or ⅔ cup Egg Substitute (page 212)
- ¼ cup Plum Ketchup (page 202) or Cashew Spread (page 195)
- 2 tablespoons wheat-free tamari sauce or ½ teaspoon salt
- ½ teaspoon dried basil
- ½ teaspoon dried oregano
- ⅛ teaspoon ground red pepper (optional)
  Plum Ketchup or Mushroom Brown Sauce (page 204) (optional)

PREHEAT THE OVEN to 350°F. Oil a 7" × 3" nonstick loaf pan. In a large skillet, heat the oil over medium-high heat. Add the onions, celery, and carrots and cook for 5 minutes, or until tender. Add the garlic and cook for 1 minute, stirring. Remove from the heat. Stir in the nuts and oat bran, quinoa flakes, or bread crumbs.

In a large bowl, beat together the eggs or egg substitute, ketchup or spread, tamari or salt, basil, oregano, and red pepper if using

until well combined. Add the onion-nut mixture and mix well. Let rest for 10 minutes.

Spoon into the prepared pan and press firmly. Bake for 50 minutes, or until brown and set. Allow to stand at room temperature for 10 minutes before slicing.

Serve plain or with the ketchup or brown sauce.

Makes 6 servings

Tostadas Improvised

The Rodale Test Kitchen staff served a version of this at an open house party, and everyone raved about it! There's no corn, cheese, or sour cream, yet its flavor is very Mexican.

2 cups cooked brown rice
1 cup South-of-the-Border Sandwich Spread (page 272)
1 cup Guacamole (page 273)
1½ cups shredded lettuce
8 scallions, thinly sliced
6 tablespoons sliced black olives

PREHEAT THE OVEN to 300°F. Place ½ cup of the rice on each of 4 heat-proof plates. Press into a round about ½" or less thick. Put the plates in the oven for 8 to 10 minutes, or until the rice is hot.

Meanwhile, heat the sandwich spread in

a nonstick skillet over medium heat. Spoon over each portion of the rice and top with the Guacamole. Top with lettuce, scallions, and olives.

Makes 4 servings

Variations
Tostadas with Cheese: Add a dollop of Goat's-Milk Yogurt (page 266) and 1 to 2 tablespoons shredded goat's-milk Cheddar cheese to each serving.

Tostadas with Chili-Beans: Substitute chili-flavored beans (puree and cook for 10 minutes, or until thick) for the South-of-the-Border Sandwich Spread.

Veggie-Nut Burgers

Here's a scrumptious alternative to traditional hamburgers.

1 cup Brazil nuts or hazelnuts
  or ½ cup of each
½ cup coarsely chopped celery
½ cup coarsely chopped carrots
½ cup coarsely chopped onions
½ cup packed cilantro leaves
½ teaspoon salt
¼ cup sesame seeds (optional)
½ teaspoon fennel seeds (optional)
⅓ cup Egg Substitute (page 212)
½ teaspoon ground cumin (optional)

PREHEAT THE OVEN to 400°F. Line a baking sheet with parchment paper and coat with cooking spray.

In a food processor, combine the nuts, celery, carrots, onions, cilantro, salt, sesame seeds if using, and fennel seeds if using. Process for 20 to 30 seconds, or until finely chopped. Add the egg substitute and cumin if using. Process for 10 seconds, or until well mixed and beginning to hold together.

Spoon 4 mounds of the mixture onto the prepared baking sheet. Using a rubber spatula, flatten and shape into round patties. Bake for 15 to 20 minutes, or until golden and crisp. Remove from oven and let stand for 5 minutes before serving.

Makes 4

COOK'S TIP

✳ I sometimes add two additional seasonings to the burger mix: ½ teaspoon dried dillweed and ½ teaspoon ground coriander.

Vegetarian Chili

Chili is one of life's great comfort foods—especially in winter.
This meat-free version incorporates all of the right flavors!

2 tablespoons vegetable oil
3 carrots, thinly sliced
3 ribs celery, thinly sliced
1 large green bell pepper, chopped
1 large Spanish onion, chopped
2–3 cloves garlic, crushed
1½ pounds tomatoes, chopped,
  or 1 can (14–16 ounces) diced
  tomatoes

2 cups cooked kidney beans, or 1 can
  (14–16 ounces), rinsed and drained
1 can (6 ounces) tomato paste
1 cup vegetable broth or water
2 tablespoons mild chili powder
½ teaspoon salt
⅛ teaspoon ground cinnamon (optional)
½ cup chopped olives (optional)
1 cup Guacamole (page 273) (optional)

HEAT THE OIL in a 5-quart pot over medium-high heat. Add the carrots, celery, peppers, and onions and cook for 10 minutes, or until the vegetables are soft. Add the garlic and cook for 1 minute.

Stir in the tomatoes, beans, tomato paste, broth or water, chili powder, salt, and cinnamon if using. Cook for 50 to 60 minutes, stirring occasionally. Thin with broth or water if necessary.

Serve topped with the olives if using and guacamole if using.

Makes 4 servings

Variation

Vegetarian Chili with Soy: Simmer 1 cup of soy flakes in 2 cups vegetable broth. When the liquid is mostly absorbed, stir into the chili and cook for 30 to 40 minutes. This will make 6 servings instead of 4.

Mexican Supper with Quinoa

Looking for spicy Mexican flavors free of wheat, corn, and milk?
This recipe and the buckwheat variation are totally dairy-free and grain-free.

2 tablespoons vegetable oil
1 cup chopped onions
½ cup chopped celery
¼ teaspoon red pepper flakes
1½ teaspoons mild chili powder
1–2 cloves garlic, crushed
1½ cups water
½ teaspoon salt
1 cup quinoa, washed 3 times
2 cups chopped tomatoes or 1 can (14–16 ounces) diced
2 cups cooked kidney beans, pinto beans, or chickpeas
¼ cup chopped green chiles
1 teaspoon dark agave nectar or honey
½ cup minced fresh cilantro
1½ cups Guacamole (page 273) (optional)

HEAT THE OIL in a skillet over medium-high heat. Add the onions, celery, pepper flakes, and chili powder and cook for 8 minutes, or until the vegetables are soft. Add the garlic and cook for 1 minute. Stir in the water, salt, quinoa, tomatoes, beans or chickpeas, chiles, and agave nectar or honey. Cook for 25 minutes, covered, stirring occasionally. Stir in the cilantro and cook for 5 minutes.

Top each portion with a dollop of Guacamole if you wish.

Makes 4 servings

COOK'S TIPS

✳ For more zing, add another ¼ cup chopped canned chiles.

✳ I sometimes top this dish with 6 thinly sliced scallions and/or ⅓ cup sliced black or green olives.

Variation

Mexican Supper with Buckwheat: Substitute 1 cup of unroasted buckwheat groats for the quinoa.

Confetti Rice Salad

A one-dish lunch meal. Ideal for brown-bagged lunches, too.

2 cups cooked brown rice

1 cup frozen green peas

4 scallions, thinly sliced

1 rib celery, thinly sliced

1 large carrot, chopped

6 radishes, chopped

⅓ cup parsley leaves, finely chopped

¼ cup toasted sunflower seeds

¼ cup vegetable oil

¼ cup lemon or lime juice

1 tablespoon prepared horseradish (optional)

1–2 tablespoons minced fresh tarragon or 1 teaspoon dried

½ teaspoon salt

¼ teaspoon celery seeds

IN A LARGE BOWL, combine the rice, peas, scallions, celery, carrot, radishes, parsley, and sunflower seeds.

In a small bowl, whisk the oil, lemon or lime juice, horseradish if using, tarragon, salt, and celery seeds. Pour over the salad. Toss lightly to combine. Cover and chill for at least 1 hour.

Makes 4 servings

COOK'S TIPS

＊ In place of the lemon or lime juice, you can use cider vinegar or 1 teaspoon unbuffered vitamin C crystals dissolved in 2 tablespoons warm water.

＊ To toast small nuts and seeds, spread them in a small nonstick skillet. Cook, stirring often, over medium-low heat for 5 minutes, or until lightly browned and fragrant.

Rice-Nut-Seed Croquettes with Almond-Wine Sauce

Lentils, quinoa, nuts, and seeds all complement rice in these high-protein croquettes. Serve with baked winter squash.

CROQUETTES

- 1½ **cups cooked short-grain brown rice**
- ½ **cup quinoa flakes**
- ¾ **cup chopped almonds**
- ½ **cup ground pumpkin or sunflower seeds**
- ⅔ **cup red lentils**
- 1½ **cups water**
- ½ **teaspoon salt**
- 1 **tablespoon Dijon mustard**
- ¼–½ **cup water**
- 4–6 **drops hot-pepper sauce (optional)**
  Olive-oil cooking spray

SAUCE

- 2 **tablespoons almond butter**
- ¼ **cup sulfite-free white wine or white grape juice**
- 1 **cup water**
- ¼ **teaspoon salt**

TO MAKE THE CROQUETTES: In a large bowl, combine the rice, quinoa, almonds, and pumpkin or sunflower seeds.

In a small saucepan, combine the lentils and water. Bring to a boil. Reduce the heat, cover, and cook for 20 to 30 minutes, or until very tender. Remove from the heat and stir in the salt and mustard. Beat with a fork for 1 to 2 minutes, or until pureed.

Preheat the oven to 400°F. Place a wire rack on a baking sheet.

Place half the lentil-water mixture in a bowl. To the portion in the bowl, stir in ¼ cup water and the hot-pepper sauce if using. Adjust the seasonings to taste. Stir into the rice mixture and let sit for 10 minutes.

Form into 12 balls, about the size of golf balls, rolling them between your palms to make them firm. Mist each with cooking spray. Place on the rack on the baking sheet. Bake for 20 minutes, or until crisp and brown.

To make the sauce: To the lentil mixture in the saucepan, add the almond butter, wine or grape juice, water, and salt. Stir until very smooth and add 1 to 2 tablespoons water if necessary. Adjust the seasonings to taste and cook for 10 minutes, or until heated through, stirring occasionally. Serve over the croquettes.

Makes 4 servings
(Sauce makes about 2 cups.)

COOK'S TIPS

---

* Be sure to use red lentils; the usual brown variety doesn't work nearly as well in this dish.

* Use a ¼-cup measure or a ¼-cup ice cream scoop to shape the croquettes.

* To flavor the sauce a bit more, I sometimes add one or a combination of the following seasonings: 1 tablespoon Dijon mustard, 1 tablespoon chopped fresh rosemary or tarragon or 1 teaspoon dried, or 3 to 4 drops hot-pepper sauce.

VEGETARIAN MAIN DISHES

Fancy Fried Rice

This is a little more elaborate than plain fried rice. It's just right for brunch, lunch, or supper and is especially good with Egg Foo Yong with Ginger Sauce (page 257).

2 tablespoons vegetable oil

3 thin slices fresh ginger

6–10 mushrooms, thinly sliced

4–6 scallions, thinly sliced

¼ cup pine nuts

¼ cup pumpkin or sunflower seeds

3 cups cooked brown rice

2 tablespoons tamari sauce or water

½ teaspoon sesame oil

⅛ teaspoon ground red pepper or
  4–6 drops hot-pepper sauce

⅓ cup minced parsley (optional)

IN A LARGE SKILLET, heat the oil over medium-high heat. Add the ginger and cook for 2 minutes. Add the mushrooms,

scallions, pine nuts, and pumpkin or sunflower seeds. Cook for 5 minutes, stirring often. Discard the ginger. Add the rice and cook for 5 minutes, stirring.

In a cup, whisk the tamari sauce or water, sesame oil, and red pepper or pepper sauce. Stir into the rice mixture. Cook over medium heat for 3 minutes or until heated through and fragrant. Top with the parsley if using.

Makes 4 servings

COOK'S TIPS

✳ Add ½ teaspoon salt if you omit the tamari.

✳ You can add any of these ingredients along with the mushrooms and scallions: 1 cup frozen peas, 1 cup bean sprouts, 1 cup thinly sliced carrots, 1 cup thinly sliced celery, or ½ chopped bell pepper.

Better Burgers

These vegetable burgers make for a great alternative to cold cuts in the lunch bag. Dress them up with your favorite condiments.

2 tablespoons olive oil

2 carrots, finely chopped

2 ribs celery, finely chopped

1 cup cooked mashed pinto
  or kidney beans

½ cup chopped pecans

½ cup toasted sunflower seeds

¼ cup toasted sesame seeds

⅓ cup Plum Ketchup (page 202) or
  honey- or fruit-sweetened ketchup

½ teaspoon salt

⅛ teaspoon ground red pepper (optional)

1–2 tablespoons amaranth, quinoa,
  or chickpea flour

6 Whole Grain Pancakes (page 88)
  or Grain-Free Pancakes (page 89)

PREHEAT THE OVEN to 350°F. Line a baking sheet with parchment paper. Heat the oil in a large skillet over medium heat. Add the carrots and celery and cook about 10 minutes, or until soft.

In a large bowl, mix the beans, pecans, sunflower seeds, sesame seeds, ketchup, salt, and red pepper if using. Add the carrot mixture and mix well. Stir in the flour, a tablespoon at a time, until the mixture is stiff enough to shape into patties.

Form 6 patties. Place on the prepared baking sheet. Bake for 18 to 20 minutes.

Serve as an open-faced sandwich on the pancakes.

Makes 6 servings

COOK'S TIPS

* Feel free to use your favorite cooked beans.

* These pancakes also make excellent breads for burgers: Rice-Flour Pancakes (page 93), Buckwheat Pancakes (page 90), and Grain-Free Pancakes (page 89).

Grain-Free Stuffed Peppers

For a brightly colored meal, use red bell peppers and serve with green beans or peas and baked sweet potatoes.

4 green bell peppers, cored, seeded, halved lengthwise, and blanched

2 cups Waldorf Stuffing with Buckwheat (page 133)

¼ cup minced parsley (optional)

Paprika (optional)

PREHEAT THE OVEN to 350°F. Oil a 13" × 9" baking dish. Fill each pepper half with the stuffing. Place in the prepared baking dish and bake for 30 to 40 minutes, or until the apples and celery in the stuffing are tender. Top with the parsley if using and paprika if using.

Makes 4 servings

COOK'S TIP

* To blanch vegetables: Pour 2 quarts of boiling water over the vegetable in a large bowl. Let stand for 30 seconds and drain in a colander. Return to the bowl and add a trayful of ice cubes. Fill with cold water. Drain when the vegetable is cool.

Eggplant with Feta and Tomatoes

This version of the classic Greek eggplant dish known as "moussaka"
contains no cow's milk, eggs, or wheat.

1 eggplant (1–1¼ pounds), sliced lengthwise ½" thick

3 zucchini, sliced lengthwise ¼" thick

Olive oil cooking spray

1 can (14–16 ounces) pinto beans or chickpeas, rinsed and drained

½ teaspoon salt

1 tablespoon olive oil

1 cup chopped onions

8 ounces mushrooms, sliced

2 cloves garlic, crushed

6 ounces feta cheese, crumbled (optional)

1 teaspoon dried oregano

2 cups Tomato Sauce (page 199)

PREHEAT THE OVEN to 400°F. Line 2 baking sheets with parchment paper and oil a 13" × 9" baking dish. Mist the eggplant and zucchini with the cooking spray. Arrange on the prepared baking sheets. Bake for 15 minutes.

Place the pinto beans or chickpeas in a bowl and season with the salt.

In a large skillet, heat the oil over medium-high heat. Add the onions and mushrooms and cook for 10 minutes, or until the liquid from the mushrooms evaporates. Add the garlic and cook for 1 minute.

Arrange the eggplant in a single layer over the bottom of the prepared baking dish. Top with the beans. Sprinkle ½ teaspoon of the oregano over the beans, and top with the mushroom mixture. Top with the cheese if using, zucchini, and remaining ½ teaspoon oregano. Pour the tomato sauce over the zucchini.

Bake for 45 minutes. Allow to stand for 10 minutes before serving.

Makes 6 servings

COOK'S TIP

✳ You can assemble the casserole ahead and refrigerate it until ready to bake. Increase baking time to 55 minutes.

✳ Look for imported sheep's-milk feta cheese for this dish.

Egg Foo Yong with Ginger Sauce

An Asian-style all-vegetable dish that's great for brunch, lunch, or a light supper.
Serve with Fancy Fried Rice (page 254).

EGGS

½ cup finely chopped carrots

½ cup finely chopped zucchini

½ cup finely chopped onion (optional)

½ cup bean sprouts

½ cup chopped walnuts (optional)

3 large eggs

1 tablespoon wheat-free tamari sauce
   or ¼ teaspoon salt (optional)

SAUCE

½ cup thawed apple juice concentrate

½ cup water

1 tablespoon arrowroot or tapioca
   starch flour

¼ teaspoon powdered ginger

Dash of salt or wheat-free tamari
   sauce (optional)

TO MAKE THE EGGS: Combine the carrots, zucchini, onion if using, sprouts, and walnuts if using in a small bowl.

In a bowl, mix the eggs and tamari or salt if using. Whisk for 2 minutes. Stir in the carrot mixture.

Coat a nonstick skillet with cooking spray and heat over medium heat. Scoop in ¼ cup of the egg mixture and press lightly to make ½"-thick patties. Cook about 5 minutes on a side, or until lightly browned. Place on a platter and keep warm in a 200°F oven until ready to serve. Repeat until all the egg mixture has been used. (The recipe should make 8 egg foo yong patties.)

To make the sauce: Combine the juice concentrate, water, arrowroot or tapioca starch flour, ginger, and salt or tamari if using in a small saucepan. Whisk until the starch is dissolved. Bring to a boil over medium heat, whisking constantly, until the sauce thickens and is clear.

Serve over the egg foo yong.

Makes 4 servings

COOK'S TIPS

✳ For a dish without legumes, omit the bean sprouts and increase the carrots and zucchini to ¾ cup each.

✳ Use your favorite nuts instead of the walnuts, if desired.

✳ To keep this dish warm for up to an hour, cover the egg foo yong completely with the sauce.

Cashew-Zucchini Patties

A delicious light entree! Serve on a pancake
or with a baked sweet potato or winter squash and a salad.

1 pound zucchini, finely chopped

½ pound raw cashews (1⅔ cups), finely ground

¼ teaspoon salt

2 tablespoons tapioca starch flour or arrowroot

2 tablespoons vegetable oil

COMBINE THE ZUCCHINI, cashews, salt, and tapioca starch flour or arrowroot in a bowl, tossing to mix well.

Heat the oil in a large skillet over medium heat. Drop, by the tablespoonfuls, 4 mounds of the zucchini mixture into the skillet. (You'll use about half the mixture.) Using the back of a spoon, press into flat patties. Cook for 5 minutes, or until brown. Turn and cook for 5 minutes more, or until brown. Place on a plate and cover with foil to keep warm while cooking the remaining zucchini mixture.

Makes 4 servings

COOK'S TIPS

✳ To speed preparation, use a food processor to chop the zucchini. Avoid using a blender, however, because it will puree the vegetable.

✳ The cooked patties freeze well for up to 1 month.

Tofu Salad

Much like traditional egg salad, this makes a nice luncheon dish, especially
if served with colorful fresh vegetables, such as carrot sticks, red or green pepper sticks,
and thin rice crackers. Or make a sandwich on Spelt Yeast Bread (page 128).

16 ounces firm tofu, rinsed, drained, and diced

⅓ cup chopped celery

4 scallions, thinly sliced

1 tablespoon canola oil

½ teaspoon salt

2 teaspoons tahini

2 teaspoons lemon juice or a scant ¼ teaspoon unbuffered vitamin C crystals

¼ teaspoon turmeric

3–4 drops hot-pepper sauce (optional)

IN A BOWL, combine the tofu, celery, and scallions.

In a small bowl, whisk together the oil, salt, tahini, lemon juice or vitamin C crystals, turmeric, and hot-pepper sauce if using. Pour over the tofu, and mix gently. Chill at least 1 hour before serving.

Makes 4 servings

Variation

Citrus-Free Tofu Salad: Replace the lemon juice with 2 tablespoons honey-sweetened pickle relish, available at most health food stores.

COOK'S TIP

✳ Tahini is ground sesame seeds, or sesame butter. It's available in almost any health food store or large supermarket.

Quinoa Tabbouleh-Style Salad

Easy to prepare, this salad is traditionally dressed with oil and vinegar. Instead, I've provided several vinaigrette suggestions. For the best flavor, allow at least an hour for the salad to chill and marinate before serving.

1 **cup quinoa, thoroughly rinsed and drained**

2 **cups water**

½ **teaspoon salt**

1 **cup finely chopped parsley**

⅓ **cup finely chopped mint leaves**

¾ **cup seeded and finely chopped tomatoes**

⅔ **cup thinly sliced scallions**

⅓ **cup chopped yellow bell pepper**

½ **cup Basil Vinaigrette (page 191) or Sweet and Sour Salad Dressing (page 191)**

IN A SAUCEPAN, combine the quinoa, water, and salt. Bring to a boil. Reduce the heat, cover, and cook for 20 minutes. Remove from the heat and let sit for 10 minutes. Fluff with a fork and place in a large bowl and let cool completely.

Add the parsley, mint, tomatoes, scallions, and pepper. Pour the dressing over the quinoa mixture and toss to mix well. Cover and chill at least 1 hour before serving.

Makes 6 servings

COOK'S TIPS

✳ Rinsing quinoa is essential because it removes the grain's naturally bitter saponin coating. To rinse quinoa, place it in a sieve and run under cool water, moving and shaking the sieve constantly, until the water runs clear.

✳ You can use half parsley and half cilantro, if you wish.

✳ Other salad dressings that go very well with this dish include Flax and Garlic Salad Dressing (page 192) and Sesame-Lime Salad Dressing (page 193).

✳ To peel and seed a tomato, dip it into boiling water for 30 seconds. With a sharp knife, remove the stem end. Slip off the skin.

✳ To seed tomatoes, cut them in half crosswise. Squeeze gently to remove seeds and juice.

VEGETARIAN MAIN DISHES

Spelt-Cashew Casserole

The secret to digestible whole-grain spelt dishes? Pre-soaking.
This casserole is dairy-free, yet creamy and satisfying.
Start this recipe a day ahead.

1⅓ cups whole grain spelt
⅔ cup small dried red kidney beans
3 cups water
1 teaspoon salt
2 tablespoons vegetable oil
2 cups chopped leeks or onions
1 turnip, diced
1 chopped red or yellow bell pepper
8–12 mushrooms, sliced
1½ cups Cashew Cream Sauce (page 198)
2 cloves garlic, pressed (optional)

COMBINE THE SPELT and beans in a 3-quart saucepan. Fill with water, cover and soak for 8 hours or overnight. Drain in a colander and rinse under cool running water. Return to the pan and pour in 3 cups of water. Bring to a boil. Reduce the heat, cover, and cook for 1½ hours. Remove from heat, stir in the salt, and let cool to luke-warm. Refrigerate for 4 to 6 hours.

Preheat the oven to 350°F. Oil a 3-quart baking dish.

Heat the oil in a 5-quart pot over medium heat. Add the onions or leeks, turnip, peppers, and mushrooms and cook for 10 minutes. Add the garlic if using. Cook for 2 minutes. Remove from the heat and stir in 2 tablespoons water.

Stir the spelt mixture into the vegetable mixture. Stir in the cashew sauce. Cook for 5 minutes, or until the sauce boils and thickens. Spoon into the prepared baking dish. Bake, covered, for 35 minutes. Uncover and bake for 10 minutes more.

Makes 10 servings

COOK'S TIPS

* Optional seasonings for this dish include 1 teaspoon oregano, 1 can (4 ounces) diced mild green chiles, and 2 tablespoons prepared mustard (or 2 teaspoons dry). Use singularly or in combination.

* When making the Cashew Cream Sauce, add ½ cup more water and omit all optional seasonings.

Goat's Milk and Goat's-Milk Cheese Dishes

Goat's milk and cow's milk are alike in some ways and different in others—different enough, in fact, that it is quite common to be allergic to cow's milk but not goat's milk. (Pediatricians have known that for some time, but adults with allergies don't always realize that it applies to them, too.) The fat globules in goat's milk are significantly smaller than those in milk from cows, making it easier to digest. But like cow's milk, goat's milk does contain the milk sugar lactose, a potential problem for lactose-intolerant people. Whether you tolerate goat's milk or not will probably depend on what specific factor in milk bothers you. If it agrees with you, it's a great dairy alternative.

Nutritionally, goat's milk stacks up very well next to whole cow's milk. Cup for cup, goat's milk has 3o5 milligrams more calcium, 144 International Units (IU) more vitamin A, more than three times as much niacin, nearly four times as much manganese, 129 milligrams more potassium, and 5 milligrams less cholesterol—and only 18 more calories. However, goat's milk is significantly lower than cow's milk in 2 nutrients: vitamin B_{12} and zinc. All other nutrient values are approximately equal, with the exception of vitamin D. Look for vitamin-D fortified goat's milk or get your vitamin D in a supplement.

As the popularity of goat's milk has increased, more supermarkets carry 1-quart cartons of full-fat and 1% versions. They are packaged in cans or aseptic boxes and are ultra-pasteurized so they have a fairly long shelf life. Look for these milks in the refrigerated dairy case. Of the two versions, the 1% has a lighter flavor, which some people prefer, especially children.

In health food stores, you can often find two other forms of goat's milk: evaporated in cans and powdered. Both have a somewhat stronger flavor than the fresh ultra-pasteurized version.

If you own goats, I suggest scalding the jars you use to store the milk. (See "Scalding Canning Jars and Lids," page 303.) And why not make your own cheese and ice cream, when you have an excess supply? It's fun and it's easy. My favorite recipes follow.

Soft Goat's-Milk Cheese

This delicate, sweet cheese tastes much like ricotta. It's perfect for lasagna, casseroles, or cheese spreads. Because this cheese isn't aged, it's a boon to people who are allergic to cheese mold—especially if you make the cheese with vitamin C crystals instead of vinegar, which is fermented.

3 quarts whole goat's milk

6 tablespoons vinegar or ¾ teaspoon vitamin C crystals

HEAT THE MILK in a large heavy pot over medium heat until it reaches 185°F, stirring often so it doesn't scorch. Slowly stir in the vinegar or vitamin C crystals.

Turn off the heat and allow to rest for 15 to 30 minutes. If the temperature begins to dip, turn the burner to the lowest heat for a few minutes.

After 15 to 30 minutes, the mixture should have separated into curds and whey. If it hasn't, add another tablespoon or two of vinegar, or ¼ to ½ teaspoon more of the vitamin C crystals. Stir, and allow to rest again until the solids and liquid separate.

Line a colander with about 1 yard of cheesecloth that you've folded into quarters. Place the colander in the sink, and pour boiling water through it. Gently pour the milk mixture into the colander. Gather up the corners, and tie securely with string. Suspend the bag from a faucet above the colander. Allow to drain for 1 to 2 hours, until it reaches a firmness that

you find pleasing. Scrape the cheese off the cloth, and shape into a ball or flatten it into a round. Place the cheese in a deep bowl and cover with plastic wrap. Chill at least 1 hour before eating.

Makes 1 pound

COOK'S TIPS

❋ For best results, use a stainless steel or enamel pot and colander for making this cheese, which is high in acid. (See "Cookware," page 61.) You'll also need a kitchen thermometer that registers between 100°F and 200°F. There are special floating thermometers sold for cheesemaking as well as standard candy thermometers to choose from. Make sure that all your equipment for cheesemaking, including the jars your goat's milk is stored in, is impeccably clean, perhaps even scalded. (See "Scalding Canning Jars and Lids," page 303.)

❋ If the temperature goes a little higher than 185°F, you'll have a firmer and drier cheese. Under no circumstances, however, should you allow the mixture to boil.

❋ If you have your own fresh goat's milk, you will find that it separates best when it's at least 3 days old. You're most likely to have trouble getting it to separate if the milk is first-day fresh.

❋ To make more or less cheese, use this general guide: Stir in 2 tablespoons vinegar or ¼ teaspoon vitamin C crystals for each quart of whole milk.

Onion Cheese Ball

Make this with cheese that is still soft enough to mix well. Then allow time for the flavors to ripen and the cheese to firm up. Serve with crackers or raw vegetables.

8 ounces Soft Goat's-Milk Cheese (page 262) or store-bought soft goat's milk cheese

1 clove garlic, crushed (optional)

1 tablespoon Savory Seed Seasoning (page 209)

2–3 teaspoons finely grated onions
  Pinch of salt (optional)

4 drops hot-pepper sauce

2 tablespoons Hungarian paprika

IN A MEDIUM BOWL, combine the cheese, garlic if using, seasoning, onions, salt if using, and hot-pepper sauce. Adjust the seasonings to taste.

Shape into a ball and put into a deep bowl. Cover with plastic wrap and chill for at least 1 day. Remove from the refrigerator 1 hour before serving. Roll in paprika to coat completely.

Makes 1

COOK'S TIPS

* If you want to buy the soft goat's-milk cheese, look for it in a natural foods store, which is more likely to have a wider variety of these cheeses than a supermarket. Choose a plain white cheese with a consistency similar to cream cheese.

* Here's my favorite trick for grating an onion: Run a sharp paring knife firmly across the cut surface of an onion, using the same motion you would if you were trying to hollow out a depression in the onion. Work directly over a bowl or measuring spoon to catch all the juice that's exuded. You can also use the fine holes on a cheese grater.

* The Savory Seed Seasoning can be replaced with your favorite herbs.

* This cheese can be wrapped in plastic wrap, waxed paper, or cellophane and refrigerated for up to 1 week.

Herbed Cheese Ball

8 ounces Soft Goat's-Milk Cheese (page 262) or store-bought soft goat's milk cheese

1 tablespoon Savory Seed Seasoning (page 209)

1 tablespoon snipped chives

1 clove garlic, crushed

2 teaspoons grated onions

½ teaspoon dried basil

½ teaspoon dried sage

¼ teaspoon dried tarragon

¼ teaspoon dried thyme

4 drops hot-pepper sauce

Pinch of salt (optional)

3 tablespoons minced parsley or cilantro

IN A MEDIUM BOWL, combine the cheese, seasoning, chives, garlic, onions, basil, sage,

tarragon, thyme, hot-pepper sauce, and salt if using. Adjust the seasonings to taste.

Shape into a ball and put into a deep bowl. Cover with plastic wrap and chill for at least 1 day. Remove from the refrigerator 1 hour before serving. Roll in the parsley or cilantro to coat completely, pressing firmly so the herb sticks.

Makes 1 ball

COOK'S TIPS

✳ If you want to buy the soft goat's-milk cheese, look for it in a natural foods store, which is more likely to have a wider variety of these cheeses than a supermarket. Choose a plain white cheese with a consistency similar to cream cheese.

✳ You can shape this cheese into a log instead of a ball, if desired. Roll in finely chopped pecans.

✳ This cheese can be wrapped in plastic wrap, waxed paper, or cellophane and refrigerated for up to 1 week.

Holiday Fun

This colorful—and flavorful—cheese is perfect for Christmas or Fourth of July festivities. Guests will rave over your creativity.

Two-Tone Cheese Balls

1 Onion Cheese Ball (page 263)

1 Herbed Cheese Ball (above)

CUT EACH BALL in half and form two new balls by gently pressing the con-

trasting halves together. Serve at room temperature.

Makes 2

Cook's Tips

✳ Wrapped in plastic wrap, this cheese will keep in the refrigerator for up to 1 week.

✳ For a red, white, and blue theme, omit the paprika on the Onion Cheese Ball. Incorporate minced parsley into the Herbed Cheese Ball and roll it in paprika. Cut and re-form these red and white balls. Serve on a blue plate.

Wheat-Free Pizza with Goat's-Milk Cheese

This pizza, free of wheat and cow's milk, is delicious and satisfying.

CRUST

- ¾ cup very warm water
- 2 teaspoons dry yeast
- 1 teaspoon honey or maple syrup
- 1½ cups spelt or Kamut brand flour, plus extra for kneading
- ½ teaspoon salt
- 1½ teaspoons xanthan gum

TOPPINGS

- 1 recipe Pizza Sauce (page 202), warmed
- ½ pound preservative-free pork sausage, cooked and crumbled (optional)
- ⅓ cup chopped onions
- ¼ cup chopped green bell peppers
- 4 ounces mushrooms, sliced
- Pinch of dried oregano or Italian Seasoning (page 210)
- 5–6 ounces goat's-milk Cheddar cheese, shredded, or feta cheese, crumbled

TO MAKE THE CRUST: Oil a baking sheet or 12" pizza pan. Combine the water, yeast, and honey or maple syrup in a cup. Set aside for 10 minutes, or until the yeast is foamy.

In a medium bowl, combine the flour, salt, and xanthan gum. Using a fork, stir in the yeast mixture and mix just until the dough gathers itself into a ball. Turn the dough out onto a floured work surface. With floured hands, knead for about 10 minutes, or until the dough forms a smooth elastic ball.

Place the dough in an oiled bowl and turn once to coat. Cover with a damp cloth and let rise in a warm, draft-free place for 30 to 60 minutes, or until doubled.

Preheat the oven to 425°F. Punch down the dough and place between 2 large sheets of oiled waxed paper. Pat into a flat circle and, using a rolling pin, roll out to 12" circle, about ¼" thick. Place on the prepared baking sheet or pizza pan; remove the waxed paper. Let rest for 10 minutes. Bake for 5 minutes.

Spread the sauce over the crust. Top with the sausage, onions, peppers, and mushrooms. Sprinkle with oregano or seasoning. Top with cheese. Reduce the heat to 400°F; bake for 18 minutes, or until the crust is brown.

Makes 8 slices

COOK'S TIPS

* In the winter, let the dough rise in a warm oven. Set the oven on a low setting (150° to 200°F); then turn it on for 1 minute—just until the air feels warm on your hand. Turn off the oven promptly; too much heat will inactivate the yeast.

* You can use any alternative grain flour and the dough will rise successfully because of the addition of xanthan gum. All flours (except barley, which requires 2 cups) can be used in equal measure.

Variation

Grain-Free Pizza with Goat's-Milk Cheese: Instead of the grain flour, use ½ cup *each* of amaranth flour, buckwheat flour, and quinoa flour. Or use ¾ cup each of two of those flours.

Goat's-Milk Yogurt

I love the mellow flavor of this yogurt. Making yogurt can be a little tricky,
but the following thermos method usually gives excellent results.

3 **cups hot water**
1⅓ **cups powdered goat's milk**
1 **tablespoon dairy-free freeze-dried**
Lactobacillus acidophilus

SCALD A STRAINER, wire whisk, mixing bowl, and 1-quart glass- or metal-lined, wide-mouthed thermos bottle with boiling water. (Scalding sterilizes the equipment and pre-heats the thermos so it can effectively incubate the yogurt. See "Scalding Canning Jars and Lids," page 303.)

In a bowl, whisk together the water and powdered goat's milk. Test the temperature of the mixture. It should be between 100°F and 110°F on a thermometer or feel quite warm yet comfortable if you place a drop or two on your forearm.

Sprinkle the lactobacillus over the milk mixture. Whisk to mix well. Pour, through a strainer, into the prepared thermos bottle

(which should be warm). Cap tightly and allow to stand *undisturbed* for 5 to 8 hours, or until the mixture is firm and has a thin layer of whey on top. Spoon into a jar or bowl. Cover tightly, and refrigerate until needed.

Makes about 1 quart

COOK'S TIPS

* Powdered goat's milk and a nondairy starter culture are available at health food stores. I've had wonderful success using the capsules of freeze-dried dairy-free *Lactobacillus acidophilus* culture, which also contain gelatin, pectin, and magnesium stearate. These have been specially formulated for milk-sensitive people. Look for them in the refrigerator case.

* When testing yogurt to see if it has firmed up, don't shake or jiggle the jar. You could disturb the culture and could prevent it from setting properly if the yogurt isn't done.

* If you have your own goat, you can make yogurt with fresh goat's milk. Use about 4 cups milk and heat it to 185°F (a skin will form on top of the milk); then let it cool to between 100°F and 110°F.

Maple-Pecan Ice Cream

Make this ice cream with the freshest goat's milk you can find. The flavor will be outstanding—it's a delicious way to enjoy goat's milk for the first time. And it's easy to make, too.

2 cups whole goat's milk
1 banana
⅓ cup chilled maple syrup
1½ teaspoons vanilla extract (optional)
⅓ cup chopped toasted pecans

PUT A MIXING BOWL and individual serving dishes in the freezer to chill. Pour the milk into an ice-cube tray. Freeze until solid.

In a blender, combine the banana, maple syrup, and vanilla if using. Process on high speed until smooth.

Turn the frozen milk cubes onto a sheet of waxed paper. (If necessary, loosen the cubes by placing the ice cube tray up to its rim in warm water for 30 to 60 seconds.) Working quickly with the blender running, add the cubes, 2 or 3 at a time, to the banana mixture, stopping as necessary to scrape the sides of the container. The mixture will be quite thick. When smooth and creamy, turn the mixture into the chilled bowl, and stir in the pecans.

For soft ice cream, serve at once in chilled dishes. Otherwise, place in the freezer for an hour or two.

Makes about 4 servings

COOK'S TIPS

✳ To toast the chopped nuts, spread them in a small nonstick skillet. Cook, stirring often, over medium-low heat for 5 minutes, or until lightly browned and fragrant. Be sure they're cool before using them in this recipe.

✳ The ice cream will keep for several days in a tightly covered container in the freezer.

Variation

Peach-Almond Ice Cream: Use 2 peaches or nectarines instead of the banana and replace the pecans with toasted almonds. Replace the vanilla extract with ½ teaspoon almond extract.

Strawberry Ice Cream

You can make this yummy ice cream with either evaporated or whole goat's milk.

2 cups whole goat's milk or 1 can (12½ ounces) evaporated + ½ cup water

1 small banana or 2 peaches, cut into chunks

½ cup light agave nectar or honey

1 tablespoon lime juice or ¼ teaspoon unbuffered vitamin C crystals

1½ teaspoons vanilla extract (optional)

1 cup quartered frozen strawberries

PUT INDIVIDUAL DISHES in the freezer to chill. Pour the milk into an ice cube tray and freeze until solid.

In a blender, combine the banana or peaches, agave or honey, lime juice or vitamin C crystals, and vanilla if using. Process until smooth.

Turn the frozen milk cubes out of the tray onto waxed paper. (If necessary, loosen the cubes by placing the ice cube tray up to its rim in warm water for 30 to 60 seconds.) Working quickly with the blender running, add the cubes, 2 or 3 at a time, to the banana mixture, stopping as necessary to scrape the sides of the container. The mixture should be thick, creamy, and smooth. Add the strawberries and process until coarsely chopped and evenly distributed.

For soft ice cream, serve at once in chilled dishes. Otherwise, place in the freezer for an hour or two.

Makes about 4 servings

COOK'S TIPS

* If using evaporated milk, submerge the unopened can in hot (not boiling) water for 5 minutes to slightly thin the contents. Shake well, open, and pour into the ice cube tray. Carefully add the ½ cup water to the tray.

* The ice cream will keep for several days in a tightly covered container in the freezer.

Blond Fudge

This easy-to-make confection is rich but nourishing. And I learned from my grandchildren that kids who are wary of "goat's-milk fudge" adore Blond Fudge!

1 **cup almond or cashew butter, at room temperature**

½ **cup light agave nectar, honey, or maple syrup**

½ **cup powdered goat's milk**

USING A STURDY FORK, blend the nut butter and agave nectar, honey, or maple syrup in a bowl. Stir in the powdered milk. The mixture will be very thick.

Place on a plate and press flat with a rubber spatula. Chill; then cut into squares.

Makes about 1 pound

COOK'S TIP

✳ You can find almond or cashew butter in most health food stores and many large supermarkets.

Variations

Blond Fudge with Sesame Seeds: Before chilling, scatter sesame seeds over the fudge. Press firmly into the fudge.

Blond Fudge with Raisins: Before chilling, scatter raisins over the fudge. Press firmly into the fudge.

Fudge-Filled Date Confections: Buy 1 pound of medjool dates. Cut a pocket in each date, remove the pit, and stuff with 1 rounded teaspoon of Blond Fudge. If you wish, put sesame seeds in a small cup and dip the top of each confection into the seeds (pat into place so they stick well). Arrange confections on a plate and serve. Or cover with plastic wrap, waxed paper, or cellophane and chill.

GOAT'S MILK AND GOAT'S-MILK CHEESE DISHES

Dips, Spreads, and More

At party time, I love to nibble. Don't we all? And I don't want my allergies to get in the way. That's why I created this chapter. It's packed with my favorite hypoallergenic treats, such as Hummus Bean Spread, South-of-the-Border Sandwich Spread, and Eggplant Appetizer. There's even a Guacamole. Avocado, guacamole's main ingredient, is just about the least allergenic base upon which to build a spread or dip.

These dishes will please everyone at the party. So don't tell guests that they're munching on special diet goodies. If they don't know, they'll never miss the usual party fare.

Another of my party secrets: Most dips and spreads are interchangeable. All you need to do is vary the amount of liquid used. Add more liquid and you have a dip; take it away for a spread.

Of course, you need something to dip or daub spreads on. You'll find crackers in the Snacks chapter on page 281 and tortillas in Better Breads on page 109. Raw vegetables also fill the bill—try to include more than one member of a food family, such as carrots and celery, or cauliflower, broccoli, radishes, thin slices or sticks of kohlrabi, and raw turnip. And don't hesitate to use matchstick-size pieces of jicama and other crisp vegetables. (See "Unusual Fruits and Vegetables," page 22.)

But why wait for a party to enjoy these tasty foods? They make terrific lunch and snack fare, too.

Hummus Bean Spread

*Basically pureed and seasoned chickpeas, this traditional Middle Eastern food
has been adopted by American cooks and makes a wonderful alternative to cheese spreads
for people who need to avoid dairy foods. It's customarily served with pita bread,
but you can improvise with crackers or tortillas.*

2 cups cooked chickpeas

¼ cup water

¼ cup lemon juice or ¾ teaspoon
unbuffered vitamin C crystals
dissolved in ¼ cup water

2 tablespoons tahini

2 small garlic cloves, crushed

½ teaspoon salt

Olive oil cooking spray

2 tablespoons minced fresh cilantro or
parsley

2–3 scallions, chopped, or 1 tablespoon
minced cilantro or parsley (optional)

COMBINE THE CHICKPEAS, water, lemon juice or vitamin C crystals, tahini, garlic, and salt in a blender or food processor. Process until smooth. Adjust seasonings to taste.

Spoon into a bowl and mist with the cooking spray. Top with the scallions, cilantro, or parsley if using. Chill for several hours. Bring to room temperature before serving.

Makes 2½ to 3 cups

COOK'S TIPS

* Tahini is ground sesame seeds, or sesame butter. It's available in almost any health food store or large supermarket.

* If the hummus is too thick, thin it with water or lemon juice. The juice will give it additional tang.

South-of-the-Border Sandwich Spread

Best if made a few hours ahead to allow flavors to blend fully.
See also the tomato-free variation.

- 2 **cups cooked pinto or kidney beans**
- ¼ **cup tomato paste or honey- or fruit juice-sweetened ketchup**
- ¼ **cup minced parsley**
- ¼ **cup minced celery leaves**
- ¼ **cup finely chopped onions**
- ½ **teaspoon salt**
- 2 **teaspoons mild or hot chili powder**
- ⅛ **teaspoon cayenne pepper**

IN A BOWL, mash the beans with a fork. Stir in the tomato paste or ketchup, parsley, celery, onions, salt, chili powder, and cayenne. Adjust seasonings to taste.
Makes about 2½ cups

Variations
South-of-the Border Dip: Add 2 to 4 tablespoons water until a dip consistency is reached.

Tomato-Free Bean Spread: Substitute ¼ cup Tofu-Dijon Spread (page 194) or Cashew Spread (page 195) for the tomato paste.

Sesame-Olive Pâté

A bean-based party pâté that doubles as a change-of-pace sandwich filling.

- 1 **can (14–19 ounces) chickpeas, navy beans, or soybeans, rinsed and drained**
- ¼ **cup fruit juice- or honey-sweetened ketchup or Tofu-Dijon Spread (page 194) or Cashew Spread (page 195)**
- ¼ **cup chopped onions**
- 1½ **tablespoons tahini or 2 tablespoons freshly ground sesame seeds**
- 2 **tablespoons lemon juice or ¼ teaspoon unbuffered vitamin C crystals + 2 tablespoons water**
- 1½ **tablespoons Dijon mustard**
- 2 **teaspoons wheat-free tamari sauce or ½ teaspoon salt**
- ⅓ **cup chopped Brazil nuts or walnuts**
- ½ **cup chopped olives**
- 2–3 **tablespoons snipped chives**
- 2 **tablespoons finely chopped pickles or honey-sweetened pickle relish**
- 2–3 **olives, sliced**
- 2 **tablespoons sesame seeds**

IN A FOOD PROCESSOR or blender, combine the beans, ketchup or spread, onions, tahini or ground sesame seeds, lemon juice or vitamin C crystals + water, mustard, and tamari or salt. Process until very smooth, stopping twice to scrape down the sides. Add the nuts, chopped olives, chives, and pickles or relish. Process just until mixed. (The texture should be chunky.) Top with the olives and sesame seeds.

Makes 2⅓ cups

COOK'S TIPS

✳ To serve as a pâté, turn onto a plate and smooth the top. Arrange the olive slices in a pattern on the top, and scatter the sesame seeds over the surface. Cover with plastic wrap and chill for 2 hours.

✳ To use as a sandwich spread, chill in a container with a lid. Spread on bread, savory pancakes, or tortillas and top with lettuce, sprouts, or tomato slices.

Guacamole

Many guacamole recipes call for sour cream or yogurt. But traditional versions don't, and neither does this one. Serve as a dip, a spread, a topping for Mexican casseroles, or as part of a salad.

2 large avocados, chopped

1–2 tablespoons lime or lemon juice, or ¼–½ teaspoon unbuffered vitamin C crystals

1 tablespoon water or olive oil

¼ cup finely chopped onions (optional)

1 tomato, seeded and finely chopped (optional)

Olive oil cooking spray

COOK'S TIPS

✳ To make a chunky version, mash the avocados with a fork and stir all ingredients together in a bowl.

✳ Other ingredients that you can add to this recipe include 2 tablespoons finely chopped green bell peppers; ½ teaspoon mild or hot chili powder; or 1 small clove garlic, crushed. Use singularly or in combination.

✳ For a dip or spread, serve with Grain-Free Saltines (page 283) or store-bought thin rice crackers and raw vegetables.

✳ To peel a tomato, dip it into boiling water for 30 seconds. With a sharp knife, remove the stem end. Slip off the skin.

✳ To seed tomatoes, cut them in half crosswise. Squeeze gently to remove seeds and juice.

PLACE THE AVOCADO in a food processor. Add the lime or lemon juice or vitamin C crystals and water or oil. Process until smooth.

Spoon into a small bowl and stir in the onions if using and tomato if using. Mist with the cooking spray. Cover with plastic wrap and chill for at least 1 hour.

Makes 1½ to 2 cups

DIPS, SPREADS, AND MORE

Pesto Dip

*This version of pesto is cheese-free. Use it to top pasta or serve
with raw vegetables, rice crackers, or tortillas.*

1 **large avocado, chopped**

1 **cup basil leaves**

1 **tablespoon lemon juice or ¼ teaspoon
unbuffered vitamin C crystals**

1 **clove garlic, chopped, or ⅛ teaspoon
powder**

¼ **cup pine nuts**

   Olive oil cooking spray

IN A FOOD PROCESSOR, combine the avocado, basil, lemon juice or vitamin C crystals, garlic, and pine nuts. Process for about
2 minutes, or until nearly smooth, stopping
twice to scrape the sides of the container.
Place in a small bowl and mist with the
cooking spray. Serve at once or chill and use
within 4 hours.

Makes 1 cup

Variations

Pesto Dip with Feta: Add 2 to 4 tablespoons
crumbled goat's or sheep's milk feta cheese.

Pesto Dip with Myzithra: Add 2 tablespoons
grated dried Myzithra cheese.

Spinach Dip

*This creamy dip is a cinch to make—especially if you have a food processor. Even youngsters
will go for it, if you don't tell them it's made with spinach.*

1 **package (10 ounces) frozen spinach,
thawed and squeezed dry**

⅓ **cup chopped scallions**

¼ **cup lightly packed parsley leaves**

¼ **teaspoon thyme (optional)**

¼ **teaspoon salt**

¼ **teaspoon white pepper or 4 drops
hot-pepper sauce**

¾ **cup Tofu-Dijon Spread or Cashew
Spread**

¾ **cup goat's-milk yogurt**

IN A FOOD PROCESSOR, combine the spinach, scallions, parsley, thyme, salt, pepper, spread, and yogurt. Process until coarsely chopped and well mixed. Chill for at least 1 hour. Adjust seasonings to taste.

Makes about 2¾ cups

Variations

Cilantro-Spinach Dip: Replace the parsley with ⅓ cup lightly packed cilantro leaves.

Garlic-Spinach Dip: Add 1 crushed small clove of garlic.

Curried Tofu Dip

Make this dip a few hours or a day ahead. Serve as a dip for raw vegetables or as a sauce for cooked broccoli, cauliflower, or green beans.

¼ cup olive or canola oil

1½ teaspoons Curry Powder (page 211)

½ teaspoon salt

½ teaspoon powdered ginger

½ teaspoon Hungarian paprika

½ teaspoon ground cumin (optional)

16 ounces tofu, rinsed, drained, and chopped

3 tablespoons lemon juice or ½ teaspoon unbuffered vitamin C crystals

2 tablespoons prepared horseradish

1 large garlic clove

¼ cup minced parsley

2 scallions, thinly sliced

HEAT THE OIL in a small skillet over medium heat. Add the curry powder, salt, ginger, paprika, and cumin if using. Cook, stirring, for 2 minutes, or until fragrant.

In a blender or food processor, combine the tofu, oil mixture, the lemon juice or vitamin C crystals, horseradish, and garlic. Process for 2 minutes, or until smooth, stopping and scraping the sides of the container as necessary.

Place in a bowl, stir in the parsley, and refrigerate for 2 hours. Top with scallions just before serving.

Makes 1¾ cups

Eggplant Appetizer

This creamy dip is known as baba ghanouj *in the Middle East.*
Mix it a few hours (or 1 day) in advance so flavors can meld.
Serve with rice crackers or tortillas cut into wedges.

1 **eggplant (about 1¼ pounds)**

2–3 **tablespoons lemon juice**
or ½–¾ teaspoon vitamin C crystals

1 **garlic clove, minced**

3 **tablespoons finely minced parsley**

¼ **teaspoon salt**

2–4 **tablespoons tahini**

1 **tablespoon chopped chives**
or 2 scallions, thinly sliced (optional)

1 **tablespoon olive oil**

PREHEAT THE OVEN to 375°F. Pierce the eggplant in several places with a fork or sharp knife. Place on an oven rack and bake for 50 minutes, or until so tender it appears to collapse. Place on a work surface and cut in half. Allow to cool enough to handle.

While the eggplant is cooling, combine 2 tablespoons of the lemon juice or ½ teaspoon vitamin C crystals + 2 tablespoons water, the garlic, parsley, salt, and 1 tablespoon of the tahini in a food processor or blender. Add the eggplant flesh, discarding the skin. Process until pureed. Adjust seasonings to taste.

Spoon into a bowl. Cover and chill for 2 hours. Bring to room temperature before serving and top with the chives or scallions if using and a drizzle of the oil.

Makes 2½ cups

COOK'S TIPS

✱ Tahini is ground sesame seeds, or sesame butter. It's available in almost any health food store or large supermarket.

✱ To serve as a vegetarian main dish, use a 1½-pound eggplant and serve with tortillas or pita bread and Easy Roasted Vegetables (page 181).

Pineapple Preserves

Here's a fresh fruit spread that's sweetened with juice concentrate.
You can't get much simpler than 2 ingredients.

3 cups fresh pineapple chunks
¾ cup thawed pineapple-juice
   concentrate

COMBINE THE PINEAPPLE and juice concentrate in a saucepan. Cook, covered with lid ajar, over low heat for 1 hour, stirring every 15 minutes. Let cool slightly.

Pour into a food processor or blender and briefly process. Don't puree; mixture should still be chunky. Return to the saucepan, and cook, uncovered, for 15 minutes more, or until thickened. Pour into a jar. Cover, cool, and store in the refrigerator. Use within 3 weeks.

Makes about 2 cups

COOK'S TIP

* To reduce or retard the formation of mold, store the preserves in scalded jars. (See "Scalding Canning Jars and Lids," page 303.)

Pumpkin Butter

A fragrant, spicy topping for biscuits, pancakes, flat breads, or muffins.

2 cups pumpkin puree or 1 can
   (16 ounces)
⅓ cup light agave nectar or honey
¼ cup water
1 teaspoon ground cinnamon
½ teaspoon grated nutmeg
½ teaspoon powdered ginger
⅛ teaspoon ground cloves
⅛ teaspoon salt

COMBINE THE PUMPKIN, agave nectar or honey, water, cinnamon, nutmeg, ginger, cloves, and salt in a saucepan. Cook, uncovered, over very low heat for 1 hour, or until very thick, stirring often. When thick, pour into a pint jar. Cover and refrigerate. Use within 1 month.

Makes 1 pint

COOK'S TIPS

* If you want, you can bake the pumpkin mixture in a 350°F oven, uncovered, for 1 hour, or until very thick, stirring every 15 minutes.

* You may want to store the butter in scalded jars. (See "Scalding Canning Jars and Lids," page 303.)

* If you don't want all of the suggested spices, use any 2 or 3 of them.

Pear Honey

This twice-pureed technique for making a smooth pear honey dates from colonial days.
The short cooking time preserves the delicate flavor of fresh juicy pears
much better than the usual fruit-butter recipes. I like to serve this puree the way
my grandmother did—with hot biscuits to complement the heavenly taste.

15 pears, quartered, cored, and peeled
½ cup water
½ cup light agave nectar or honey

COARSELY CHOP 12 of the pears and put them in a stainless-steel or enamel 5-quart pot. Coarsely chop the remaining 3 pears and place in a blender. Add the water and process until pureed. Pour into the pot.

Bring to a boil. Reduce the heat to medium-low and stir in the agave nectar or honey. Cook, covered with lid ajar, for 30 minutes, or until very tender. Let cool slightly.

Pour into a blender or food processor. Process until pureed. The puree should be about the consistency of honey. If it is too thin, return it to the pan and cook it down a bit. If it is too thick, thin with a little water.

Pour into a 3-pint jar, cover, and store in the refrigerator for up to 1 month.

Makes 3 pints

COOK'S TIP

* To store longer than 1 month, freeze the puree in tightly covered containers (leave about ¾" head space) and use within 1 year. (See "Scalding Canning Jars and Lids," page 303.)

* The flavor will be best when you use ripe, juicy pears.

Simple-Simon Jam

This jam is very easy to make, and the variations are almost endless.
To serve as a pancake or waffle topping, simply dilute with juice or water
to the desired consistency and warm the mixture slightly
so as not to chill your pancakes or waffles.

1 cup coarsely chopped dried dates,
figs, or apricots

1 cup unsweetened pineapple, apple,
or grape juice

COMBINE THE FRUIT and juice in a
saucepan. Cook over medium heat for 5
minutes, and pour into the blender. Process
until chunky. Return to the saucepan and
cook over medium heat for 5 minutes. The
mixture becomes firm as it chills. Serve
warm or cold. Refrigerate and use within a
few weeks.

Makes about 2 cups

COOK'S TIP
---

* Other tasty combinations include figs and
blended crushed pineapple; raisins and purple
grape juice; dried apples and apple juice and a
few drops of lemon juice; dried peaches or
prunes and prune juice; dried pineapple and
pineapple juice or strawberry puree; apricots
and apple juice, apricot nectar, or pineapple
juice; and dates and white grape juice and a
few drops of lemon juice or a pinch of vitamin C
crystals.

Kids' Delight Sandwich Spread

A great alternative to peanut butter and jelly.
Spread on warm flat bread or use in lunch box sandwiches.

½ cup almond, cashew, or sunflower
butter

½ cup Quick Applesauce (page 206)

2–3 tablespoons sunflower seeds
(optional)

¼ cup raisins or sugar-free cranberry-
raisins

IN A SMALL BOWL, combine the nut
butter and applesauce. Stir in the sunflower
seeds if using and raisins. Store in the refrigerator.

Makes 1¼ cups

Old-Fashioned Fruit Butter

*A yummy treat that's great for gifts, too. Use any fruits you like,
such as apples, pears, peaches, or plums. Combine any members of the Plum family,
or mix apples and pineapple. Or try berries and apples or pineapple. The choices
and combinations are endless. This recipe uses a slow cooker so the butter cooks
pretty much unattended and you needn't worry about it scorching.*

15 **cups chopped peeled fruit: apples or pears**

 4 **cups unsweetened apple juice or cider**

¼ **cup light agave nectar or honey (optional)**

PLACE THE APPLES or pears in a 4- or 5-quart slow cooker. Pour in the juice or cider. (Follow the manufacturer's directions on how high to fill your cooker.) Cover the cooker and cook on high for 2 hours. Reduce the heat to low and cook for 6 to 8 hours, stirring once.

Add the sweetener if using and cook for 2 hours more or until very thick. To test for doneness, drop a spoonful onto a cold plate. When done, it should remain in a mound and not develop a "halo" of watery liquid around it. If not done, cook for 1 to 2 hours more, testing every 30 minutes.

Ladle into freezer-safe containers with tight-fitting lids, leaving ¾" head space. Store in the refrigerator for up to 1 month or in the freezer for up to 1 year.

Makes about 3½ pints

Variation

Spiced Fruit Butter: Add 1 teaspoon ground cinnamon, ¼ teaspoon ground cloves, ¼ teaspoon ground allspice, and 2 to 4 tablespoons lemon juice.

Snacks

The great American pastime of snacking has come into its own. Research shows that several small "meals" throughout the day may be better for us than three big meals, assuming, of course, that we eat reasonable portions of healthy foods at each meal.

There are so many possibilities for great snack foods—savory as well as sweet. There is no reason for those with food allergies to feel deprived. To satisfy a sweet tooth, reach for Carob Crispy Crunch, Coconut-Date Confection, Stuffed Dates, or 11 kinds of cookies, among other treats. For kids, make the slightly sweet Fruit Gelatin Cutouts. You can even serve some snacks, such as Caramel-Coated Puffed Amaranth, for breakfast. Wholesome snacks like this come in handy if you have children who turn up their noses at breakfast food—or skip breakfast altogether.

When it's time for something crunchy, try Chili Seeds, Tamari Nut Mix, or 4 kinds of crackers. Grocery stores offer a few less-allergenic snacks too. Possibilities include rice cakes, rice crackers, all-rye crackers (Scandinavian flat breads), trail mix, nuts, wheat-free cookies (usually made with rice or barley flour), and a variety of rice and soy ice creams.

Chili Seeds

If you like Mexican food, you'll love this snack.
It's great for parties, Halloween treats, and trail food.

1 cup sunflower seeds

1 cup pumpkin seeds

¼ cup sesame seeds

1 tablespoon sunflower oil or light sesame oil

1 tablespoon chili powder

⅛ teaspoon garlic powder

⅛–¼ teaspoon ground red pepper

PREHEAT THE OVEN to 300°F. In a large bowl, combine the sunflower, pumpkin, and sesame seeds; sunflower or sesame oil; chili powder; garlic powder; and red pepper. Toss to mix well.

Spread in a jelly-roll pan. Bake for 20 minutes, stirring after 10 minutes, until seeds are light brown and fragrant. Cool and store in a tightly closed container. Use within 1 month.

Makes 2½ cups

Tamari Nut Mix

Golden brown and savory, these make a perfect party nibble.

¼ cup wheat-free tamari sauce

¼ cup water

Pinch of ground red pepper (optional)

1 cup almonds

1 cup pecans

1 cup cashews

1 cup hazelnuts or halved Brazil nuts

¾ cup sunflower seeds

PREHEAT THE OVEN to 325°F.

In a large bowl, combine the tamari, water, and red pepper if using. Add the almonds, pecans, cashews, hazelnuts or Brazil nuts, and sunflower seeds. Toss to coat.

Drain in a colander and spread, in a single layer, on a baking sheet. Bake for 18 minutes, stirring every 10 minutes, or until brown and fragrant. Let cool and store in a tightly covered container.

Makes 4¾ cups

Grain-Free Saltines

At last, not only wheat-free, but grain-free crackers!

1 cup buckwheat flour

½ cup quinoa flour

½ cup amaranth flour

1 teaspoon ground caraway seeds (optional)

½ cup cashews, almonds, or sesame seeds

¼ teaspoon onion powder (optional)

¼ teaspoon salt

¼ cup ghee or Spectrum Spread

1 tablespoon boiling water

¾ teaspoon baking soda

2 tablespoons thawed white grape or apple juice concentrate

⅓ cup cold water

2 tablespoons sesame seeds

PREHEAT THE OVEN to 400°F. Line 2 baking sheets with parchment paper. Cut 2 pieces of waxed paper, each to the size of a baking sheet. Coat each piece of waxed paper on 1 side with cooking spray.

In a food processor, combine the buckwheat, quinoa, and amaranth flour; nuts or seeds; caraway seeds if using; onion powder if using; and salt. Process for 30 to 45 seconds, or until well-mixed and the nuts are finely chopped. Add the ghee and process for 30 seconds.

In a small cup, combine the boiling water and baking soda, whisking until the baking soda dissolves. With the processor running, pour in the liquid ingredients in a slow steady stream in the order listed: baking soda mixture, juice concentrate, and cold water. As soon as the mixture forms a ball, stop the processor.

Place on 1 sheet of the prepared waxed paper and pat into a rectangle, ¾" thick. Top with the remaining waxed paper, sprayed side down. Using a rolling pin, roll out to ⅛" thick. Remove the waxed paper (but don't discard it). Sprinkle with the sesame seeds. Return the waxed paper and roll lightly to press in the seeds. Remove the top waxed paper.

Using a table knife, straighten the sides, pushing back any that are too thin (and likely to burn). Using a pizza cutter, cut into 1½" × 1½" pieces. Prick each with a fork. Using a spatula, place on the prepared baking sheets, separating the pieces by about ¼". Bake, 1 sheet at a time, for 12 minutes, or until lightly browned. Remove to a rack to cool.

Store in a tightly covered container.

Makes about 48

COOK'S TIPS

* To grind caraway, cumin, and other seeds, place them in a nut and seed grinder or a clean coffee mill and process for 1 to 2 minutes.

* To make ghee (clarified butter): Melt butter in a saucepan over low heat; then pour the liquid ghee into a jar, leaving the milk solids in the bottom of the pan. Discard the solids. Ghee will keep frozen for up to 1 year.

Teff-Rice Crackers

These teff and brown rice crackers are delicious when eaten alone or accompanied by dips and spreads such as Hummus Bean Spread (page 271).

Brown rice flour, for dusting

¾ cup brown rice flour

¾ cup teff flour

½ cup chickpea flour

1 tablespoon tapioca starch or arrowroot

1 teaspoon ground caraway seeds

½ teaspoon salt

⅜ teaspoon unbuffered vitamin C crystals

2 tablespoons boiling water

¾ teaspoon baking soda

3 tablespoons vegetable oil

¼ cup thawed white grape or apple juice concentrate

2–4 tablespoons boiling water

PREHEAT THE OVEN to 350°F. Line 2 baking sheets with parchment paper and dust with the rice flour. Cut 2 pieces of waxed paper, each to the size of a baking sheet. Coat each piece of waxed paper on 1 side with cooking spray.

In a food processor, combine the rice, teff, and chickpea flours; tapioca starch or arrowroot; caraway seeds, salt; and vitamin C crystals. Process until well mixed.

In a small cup, combine the boiling water and baking soda, whisking until the baking soda dissolves. With the processor running, pour in the liquid ingredients in a slow steady stream: the oil, juice concentrate, baking soda mixture, and 2 tablespoons water. Add remaining water 1 tablespoon at a time until the mixture forms a ball; stop the processor and discard any remaining water.

Place on 1 sheet of prepared waxed paper and pat into a rectangle, ¾" thick. Top with the remaining waxed paper, sprayed side down. Using a rolling pin, roll out to ⅛" thick. Remove the waxed paper (but don't discard it). Using a table knife, straighten the sides, pushing back any that are too thin (and likely to burn). Return the waxed paper and roll lightly to smooth. Remove the top waxed paper and using a pizza cutter or sharp knife, cut into 1½" × 1½" pieces. Prick each with a fork. Using a spatula, place on the prepared baking sheets, separating the pieces by about ¼".

Bake, 1 sheet at a time, for 8 minutes or until lightly browned and firm. Remove to a rack to cool. Crackers will become crisper as they cool. Store in a tightly covered container, and use within 2 weeks.

Makes 48

Oat Crackers

This is my version of traditional pie-shaped Scottish flat breads served at afternoon teas. They're light and quite simple to make. Good plain, with soup, or topped with Simple-Simon Jam (page 279). Best when served fresh and warm.

⅓ **cup rolled oats**

1½ **cups oat flour**

½ **cup soy grits, amaranth, or quinoa flour**

¼ **teaspoon salt**

¼ **teaspoon unbuffered vitamin C crystals**

3 **tablespoons boiling water**

¾ **teaspoon baking soda**

3 **tablespoons oil**

2 **tablespoons white grape or apple juice concentrate**

½ **cup cool water**

PREHEAT THE OVEN to 350°F. Line 2 baking sheets with parchment paper. Cut a piece of waxed paper the size of a baking sheet and spread the rolled oats over the waxed paper.

In a food processor, combine the oat flour; soy grits, amaranth, or quinoa flour; salt; and vitamin C crystals. Process until well mixed.

In a small cup, combine the boiling water and baking soda, whisking until the baking soda dissolves. With the processor running, pour in the liquid ingredients in a slow steady stream in the order listed: oil, juice concentrate, baking soda mixture, and cool water. As soon as the mixture forms a ball, stop the processor.

Place on the prepared waxed paper and roll in the oats. Cut in half and roll in the oats again. Working with 1 ball at a time, flatten to a 6" diameter circle. With a rolling pin, roll out to 10" diameter circle, ¼" thick.

Using a pizza cutter or sharp knife, cut into 8 wedges. Separate the wedges and place on the prepared baking sheets, separating the pieces.

Bake, 1 sheet at a time, for 12 minutes, or until lightly browned. Remove to a rack to cool. Store in a tightly covered container for up to a week.

Makes 16

COOK'S TIP

✳ The soy grits (or amaranth or quinoa flour) give these crackers a nice protein boost. If you don't have those on hand, substitute oat bran.

Grain-Free Graham Crackers

These tasty, grain-free graham crackers will delight snackers of all ages—
from toddlers to seniors. Enjoy them plain or spread with Old-Fashioned Fruit Butter
(page 280) or a store-bought spread.

¾ **cup quinoa flour**

¾ **cup amaranth flour**

½ **cup white buckwheat flour**

¼ **cup date sugar**

1 **teaspoon tapioca starch or arrowroot**

¼ **teaspoon salt**

⅜ **teaspoon vitamin C crystals**

2 **tablespoons boiling water**

¾ **teaspoon baking soda**

3 **tablespoons vegetable oil**

¼ **cup thawed white grape or apple juice**
concentrate

PREHEAT THE OVEN to 350°F. Line a baking sheet with parchment paper. Cut 2 pieces of waxed paper, each to the size of a baking sheet. Coat the waxed paper with cooking spray.

In a food processor, combine the quinoa, amaranth, and buckwheat flours; date sugar; tapioca starch or arrowroot; salt; and vitamin C crystals. Process to mix well.

In a small cup, combine the boiling water and baking soda, whisking until the baking soda dissolves. With the processor running, pour in the liquid ingredients in a slow steady stream in the order listed: oil, juice concentrate, and baking soda mixture. As soon as the mixture forms a ball, stop the processor.

Place on the prepared waxed paper and pat into a rectangle, ¾" thick. Top with the remaining waxed paper, sprayed side down. Using a rolling pin, roll out to ⅛" thick. Remove the top waxed paper.

Using a table knife, straighten the sides, pushing back any that are too thin (and likely to burn). Using a pizza cutter or a sharp knife, cut the dough into 3" × 3" pieces. Prick the dough with a fork. Using a spatula, place on the prepared baking sheet, separating the pieces slightly.

Bake for 10 minutes, or until light brown. Remove to a rack to cool. Crackers will become crisper as they cool. Store in a tightly covered container, and use within 1 week.

Makes 14 to 18

COOK'S TIP

* To make white buckwheat flour, grind ½ cup white, unroasted whole groats at a time in a blender for 1 to 2 minutes. Pour into sieve. Repeat grinding, adding any groats that didn't go through the sieve.

Caramel-Coated Puffed Amaranth

My inspiration for this recipe comes from alegria,
*a Mexican confection that calls for butter, honey, and molasses to be cooked together
and used to coat puffed amaranth. Here's my adaptation.*

1 tablespoon ghee or canola oil

**2 tablespoons light or dark agave
nectar or honey**

**1½ cups puffed amaranth or quinoa or a
mixture of the two**

MELT THE GHEE in a 3-quart saucepan
over medium heat. Stir in the agave nectar
or honey, and reduce the heat to medium-
low. Cook, stirring, until bubbly. Reduce the
heat to low and cook for 10 minutes. Remove from the heat and stir in the puffed
amaranth or quinoa.

Makes 1½ cups

COOK'S TIP

* To make ghee (clarified butter): Melt butter in a
saucepan over low heat; then pour the liquid ghee
into a jar, leaving the milk solids in the bottom of the
pan. Discard the solids. Ghee will keep frozen for up
to 1 year.

Glazed Puffed Amaranth

This uncooked version of alegria *is quick to make, though the coating isn't caramelized.
It uses flax oil, which is rich in beneficial omega-3 fatty acids. If the flavor of flax oil
is new to you, start by using half canola, or another mild-tasting oil.
Over time, you can increase the amount of flax oil.*

1 tablespoon flax oil

**2 tablespoons light or dark agave
nectar or honey**

**1½ cups puffed amaranth or quinoa or a
mixture of the two**

COMBINE THE OIL and agave nectar or
honey in a bowl. Add the amaranth or
quinoa, and stir to coat.

Makes 1½ cups

Rice "Popcorn" Balls

*A fun-to-make caramel snack for Halloween, birthday parties, or snow days
when the kids just need something to do—and eat. These rated a top score with my young testers!*

¼ cup honey

¼ cup sorghum, dark agave nectar, or
    molasses

5 cups crisp brown rice cereal

LINE A JELLY-ROLL PAN with waxed
paper. Combine the honey and sorghum,
agave nectar, or molasses in a 3-quart
saucepan. Cook over low heat for 10 minutes. Remove from the heat and add the cereal. Stir to coat well. Drop 10 large mounds

of the rice mixture on the prepared pan
and let cool.

Place each mound in the center of a
piece of plastic wrap. Fold in the corners of
each piece of plastic, wrapping snugly and
pressing to form tight balls.

Store at room temperature for up to 3 days.
Makes 10

COOK'S TIP

* Use a crisp, popped rice cereal, not a soft, puffed
  one. Look for the crisp cereals in health food stores.

Carrot Cookies

Delicious cookies, high in vitamin A.

¼ cup light agave nectar or honey

3 tablespoons vegetable oil

3 tablespoons apple juice concentrate

1 teaspoon vanilla extract (optional)

1 cup amaranth flour

⅓ cup tapioca starch or arrowroot

½ teaspoon cream of tartar
    or ¼ teaspoon unbuffered vitamin C
    crystals

½ teaspoon baking soda

½ teaspoon ground cinnamon (optional)

¼ teaspoon salt

¾ cup grated carrots

⅓ cup raisins or dried cranberries

PREHEAT THE OVEN to 325°F. Line 2
baking sheets with parchment paper.

In a saucepan, combine the agave or
honey, oil, and juice concentrate. Heat for 2
minutes over medium-low heat, or just until
the sweetener has melted. Remove from the
heat and let cool slightly. Stir in the vanilla
if using.

In a large bowl, whisk the amaranth
flour, tapioca starch or arrowroot, cream
of tartar or vitamin C crystals, baking soda,
cinnamon if using, and salt. Add the carrots and raisins or cranberries, and toss to
combine.

Add the agave nectar mixture and mix just until combined. Drop by rounded teaspoonfuls onto the prepared baking sheets. Bake 15 minutes, or until light brown. Remove to a rack to cool.

Store in a paper bag and use within a few days.

Makes 30

Cookies on Parade

A very basic cookie that's grain-free.

- ¼ **cup dark or light agave nectar or honey**
- 3 **tablespoons vegetable oil**
- 3 **tablespoons apple, white grape, or pineapple juice**
- ½ **cup white buckwheat flour**
- ½ **cup quinoa flour**
- ½ **cup amaranth flour**
- ¼–½ **teaspoon freshly grated nutmeg (optional)**
- ½ **teaspoon cream of tartar or ¼ teaspoon unbuffered vitamin C crystals**
- ½ **teaspoon baking soda**
- ¼ **teaspoon salt**
- ⅓ **cup chopped walnuts or hazelnuts (optional)**

PREHEAT THE OVEN to 350°F. Line 2 baking sheets with parchment paper.

In a saucepan, combine the agave nectar or honey, oil, and juice. Heat for 2 minutes over medium-low heat, or just until the sweetener has melted. Remove from the heat and let cool slightly.

In a large bowl, whisk the buckwheat flour, quinoa flour, amaranth flour, nutmeg if using, cream of tartar or vitamin C crystals, baking soda, and salt. Add the nuts if using and toss to combine.

Add the agave nectar mixture and mix just until combined. Drop by rounded teaspoonfuls onto the prepared baking sheets. Bake for 12 minutes, or until puffed and light brown. Remove to a rack to cool.

Serve warm or at room temperature. Store in a paper bag and use within a few days.

Makes 24

Dream Cookies

*If you rotate your foods, you'll really find
these two-ingredient cookies to be a dream.*

1 cup ground walnuts
¼ cup maple syrup or honey
Pinch of salt (optional)

PREHEAT THE OVEN to 300°F. Line a
baking sheet with foil, shiny side up, and
coat lightly with cooking spray.

In a bowl, combine the nuts and maple
syrup or honey and salt if using. Drop by
rounded half-teaspoonfuls onto the prepared baking sheet, placing about 2" apart.

Bake for 12 minutes, or just until light
brown. Remove foil and cookies to racks
and let cool completely. Peel foil from the
cookies.

Makes about 20

COOK'S TIPS

✳ Use any nuts you like in this recipe.

✳ These cookies burn easily, so start checking them
after 9 minutes.

Variations

Almond Dream Cookies: Substitute almonds
for the walnuts and add ½ teaspoon of almond extract if you wish.

Lace Cookies: Add ¼ cup water and space
3" apart on the baking sheets. Allow to
cool on the baking sheets for 1 minute.
Remove, still on the foil, to racks to cool
completely. Carefully peel off the foil.
Makes about 30.

Quinoa Date Doodles

These sweet treats, which are wheat-, sugar-, and egg-free, are made with quinoa.

¼ cup light or dark agave nectar or
honey
¼ cup water
¾ cup pineapple juice
8 medjool dates, chopped (about ¾ cup)
1½ cups quinoa flour
1 teaspoon pumpkin pie spice
(optional)

½ teaspoon cream of tartar
or ¼ teaspoon unbuffered vitamin C
crystals
½ teaspoon baking soda
¼ teaspoon salt
3 tablespoons vegetable oil
1–2 teaspoons grated orange or lemon
peel (optional)

PREHEAT THE OVEN to 350°F. Line 2 baking sheets with parchment paper.

In a saucepan, combine the agave nectar or honey, water, juice, and dates. Bring to a boil and cook for 2 minutes. Remove from heat and cover.

In a large bowl, whisk the flour, pumpkin pie spice if using, cream of tartar or vitamin C crystals, baking soda, and salt.

Stir the orange or lemon peel if using

and oil into the pineapple juice mixture. Add to the flour mixture and mix just until combined.

Drop by rounded teaspoonfuls onto the prepared baking sheets. Bake for 12 minutes, or until light brown. Remove to racks to cool. Store in a paper bag and use within a few days.

Makes about 24

Ginger Gems

A wheat-free answer to ginger snaps.

⅓ **cup light or dark agave nectar or honey**

3 **tablespoons vegetable oil**

⅓ **cup apple juice or thawed apple juice concentrate**

½ **cup amaranth flour**

½ **cup white buckwheat flour**

½ **cup quinoa flour**

½ **teaspoon cream of tartar or ¼ teaspoon unbuffered vitamin C crystals**

1 **teaspoon powdered ginger**

½ **teaspoon ground cinnamon (optional)**

½ **teaspoon baking soda**

¼ **teaspoon salt**

PREHEAT THE OVEN to 350°F. Line 2 baking sheets with parchment paper.

In a saucepan, combine the agave nectar

or honey, oil, and juice. Heat for 2 minutes over medium-low heat, or just until the sweetener has melted. Remove from the heat and let cool slightly.

In a large bowl, whisk amaranth flour, buckwheat flour, quinoa flour, cream of tartar or vitamin C crystals, ginger, cinnamon if using, baking soda, and salt. Add the agave mixture and mix just until combined.

Drop by rounded teaspoonfuls onto the prepared baking sheets. Bake for 12 minutes, or until light brown. Remove to racks to cool. Store in a paper bag and use within a few days.

Makes about 24

COOK'S TIP

❋ To make white buckwheat flour, grind ½ cup white, unroasted whole groats at a time in a blender for 1 to 2 minutes. Pour into sieve. Repeat grinding, adding any groats that didn't go through the sieve.

Spicy Date Drops

These amaranth cookies are moist, chewy, and spicy.
If you don't want all the suggested spices, choose one and double it.

1 cup chopped dates

1 cup raisins

1¼ cups apple, white grape, or orange juice

¾ teaspoon powdered ginger

¾ teaspoon ground cinnamon

¼ teaspoon ground cloves

1¼ cup amaranth flour

¼ cup tapioca starch or arrowroot

¾ teaspoon baking soda

¼ teaspoon salt

½ cup chopped walnuts (optional)

⅓ cup vegetable oil

1 tablespoon grated orange or lemon peel or ¼ teaspoon unbuffered vitamin C crystals

PREHEAT THE OVEN to 350°F. Line 2 baking sheets with parchment paper.

Combine the dates, raisins, juice, and spices in a 2-quart saucepan and bring to a boil. Reduce the heat and cook for 3 minutes. Remove from the heat and let cool. Add the oil and orange or lemon peel or vitamin C crystals and mix well.

In a large bowl, whisk the amaranth flour, tapioca starch or arrowroot, baking soda, salt, and nuts if using. Add the date mixture and stir until well combined. The mixture will be stiff. Drop by rounded teaspoonfuls onto the prepared baking sheets. Bake for 13 to 15 minutes, or until lightly browned. Remove to racks to cool.

Makes about 60

COOK'S TIPS

✳ Other juices that you can use in these cookies include pineapple and prune. Or you can use 1 cup of water plus ¼ cup thawed juice concentrate.

✳ If you prefer other nuts, feel free to use them instead of the walnuts.

✳ If you're following the Rotary Diversified Diet, you can coordinate the oil and nuts (or seeds); for example, walnut oil with walnuts, sunflower oil with sunflower seeds, or almond oil with almonds.

Variation

Spicy Apricot Cookies: Replace the dates with 1 cup chopped dried apricots and the raisins with 1 cup chopped prunes.

Carob Fudgies

Children love these chocolaty-tasting cookies.

⅓ cup light agave nectar or honey

3 tablespoons vegetable oil

⅓ cup white grape juice or thawed concentrate

¼ cup water

1 teaspoon vanilla extract (optional)

⅔ cup amaranth flour

⅔ cup quinoa flour

⅓ cup carob powder

½ teaspoon cream of tartar or ¼ teaspoon unbuffered vitamin C crystals

¾ teaspoon baking soda

¼ teaspoon salt

⅓ cup chopped almonds (optional)

PREHEAT THE OVEN to 325°F. Line 2 baking sheets with parchment paper.

In a saucepan, combine the agave nectar or honey, oil, and juice. Heat for 2 minutes, or until the sweetener is melted. Remove from the heat and let cool slightly. Stir in ¼ cup water and the vanilla if using.

In a large bowl, whisk the amaranth flour, quinoa flour, carob, cream of tartar or vitamin C crystals, baking soda, and salt. Stir in the nuts if using.

Add the agave nectar mixture and mix just until combined. Drop by rounded teaspoonfuls onto the prepared baking sheets. Bake for 15 minutes. or until lightly browned. Remove to racks to cool. Store in a paper bag and use within a few days.

Makes about 24

COOK'S TIP

✳ You can use walnuts or other favorite nuts in these cookies.

Variation

Pecan-Topped Carob Fudgies: Omit nuts from the batter and press a pecan half into the top of each cookie before baking.

Easy Macaroons

*Start these special egg-and-almond sweet treats at least 6 hours
before you want to bake them.*

- 3 **cups instant rolled oats**
- 1 **cup date sugar**
- ¾ **cup vegetable oil**
- ½ **cup sorghum, dark agave nectar,
  or molasses**
- ½ **cup amaranth or quinoa flour**
- 2 **eggs, lightly beaten**
- ¼ **teaspoon salt**
- 1 **teaspoon pure almond extract**

PREHEAT THE OVEN to 350°F. Line 2
baking sheets with parchment paper.

In a bowl, combine the oats and date sugar.

In a small saucepan, combine the oil and
sorghum, agave nectar, or molasses. Heat over
low heat, stirring, for 2 minutes, or until the
sweetener is fluid. Pour over the oat mixture,
and mix to combine. Cover, and let stand at
room temperature for at least 6 hours.

Stir in the flour. In a small bowl, combine
the eggs, salt, and almond extract. Stir into
the oat mixture.

Drop by rounded teaspoonfuls onto the
prepared baking sheets. Bake for 15 minutes, or until brown. Cookies will be crisp on
the outside and soft inside. Store loosely covered or in a paper bag.

Makes about 60

COOK'S TIPS
---

* These cookies soften if stored in a tightly covered
  container.

* For a milder flavor, replace ¼ cup of the sorghum,
  dark agave nectar, or molasses with ¼ cup light
  agave nectar or honey. Or you can use all honey.

High-Fiber Cookies with Sesame Seeds

*These easy cookies pack fiber, protein, complex carbohydrates,
vitamins, minerals—and great taste. They're wonderful anywhere, any time.*

- ½ **cup thawed apple or white grape juice
  concentrate**
- 1 **tablespoon whole flaxseed**
- 1¼ **cups rolled oats**
- ¾ **cup quinoa flakes**
- ⅓ **cup amaranth or white buckwheat flour**
- ¼ **teaspoon salt**
- ½ **teaspoon baking soda**
- ½ **cup raisins or dried cranberries**
- 3 **tablespoons sesame seeds**
- ½ **teaspoon ground cinnamon
  (optional)**
- ½ **cup Spectrum Spread**
- ⅓ **cup light agave nectar or honey**

PREHEAT THE OVEN to 350°F. Line 2 baking sheets with parchment paper.

In a small saucepan, combine the juice concentrate and flaxseeds. Cook over medium-low heat for 5 minutes, or until thickened to the consistency of unbeaten egg whites. Remove from the heat, and let cool.

In a large bowl, combine the oats, quinoa flakes, amaranth flour, salt, baking soda, raisins or cranberries, sesame seeds, and cinnamon if using. Stir in the spread.

Stir the agave nectar or honey into the flax seed mixture. Add into the oat mixture, stirring to combine. Allow to stand a few minutes.

Drop by rounded teaspoonfuls onto the prepared baking sheets. Bake for 10 minutes, or until light brown. Cool on the baking sheets on racks for 2 or 3 minutes. Remove to the racks to cool completely. The cookies will become crisper as they cool. Store in a paper bag.

Makes about 36

Variation

High-Fiber Cookies with Nuts: Replace the sesame seeds with ⅓ cup chopped nuts.

No-Bake Cookies

Children love to help shape these cookies—and eat them, too!

½ cup thawed pineapple juice concentrate

¼ cup water

2 tablespoons honey

2¾ cups bread crumbs

1 cup ground almonds

½ cup date sugar

¼ cup grated unsweetened coconut

IN A 2-QUART SAUCEPAN, combine the pineapple juice concentrate, water, and honey. Cook for 5 minutes. Remove from the heat. Stir in the bread crumbs, ground almonds, and date sugar. Mix until well combined.

Shape into 1" balls and roll in the coconut in a small bowl. Place on waxed paper and let stand for 3 hours. Store in a tightly covered container.

Makes 30

COOK'S TIPS

✽ To make bread crumbs, process dry pancakes, crackers, muffins, bread, or cake in a food processor or blender until fine crumbs form.

Variations

No-Bake Date Cookies: Halve crosswise and pit 10 dates. Wrap a teaspoonful of dough around each date half and roll in coconut. Chill a few hours. Makes 20.

No-Bake Pecan Cookies: Wrap a rounded teaspoonful of dough around each of 20 pecan halves and roll in coconut or ground pecans. Chill a few hours. Makes 20.

Buckwheat-Ginger Cookies

Be sure to use unroasted groats to make these tasty cookies.
Their flavor is mild enough to let the ginger dominate.

- ⅔ **cup agave nectar or honey**
- ⅓ **cup Spectrum Spread or canola oil**
- 1½ **tablespoons fresh ginger, finely chopped**
- ¼ **cup water**
- 1½ **cups white buckwheat flour**
- ¾ **cup unroasted whole buckwheat groats**
- ⅓ **cup tapioca starch flour or arrowroot starch**
- ¾ **teaspoon baking soda**
- ¾ **teaspoon cream of tartar**
- ½ **teaspoon salt**

PREHEAT THE OVEN to 350°F. Line 2 baking sheets with parchment paper.

Combine the agave nectar or honey, spread or oil, ginger, and water in a blender and process for 3 minutes.

In a bowl, whisk the buckwheat flour, whole groats, tapioca or arrowroot starch, baking soda, cream of tartar, and salt. Add the honey mixture and mix just until combined.

Drop by rounded tablespoonful onto the prepared baking sheets. Bake for 10 minutes, or until light brown and firm. Remove to racks to cool. Serve immediately or store in a paper bag.

Makes about 25

COOK'S TIPS

* To make white buckwheat flour, grind ½ cup white, unroasted whole groats at a time in a blender for 1 to 2 minutes. Pour into sieve. Repeat grinding, adding any groats that didn't go through the sieve.

* Use either dark or light agave nectar, or ⅓ cup each of the light and dark.

* Spectrum Spread is available in health food stores. (See Nutrition Basics in Brief, page 52.)

Apricot-Almond Crispy Crunch

A nutritious snack for the after-school crowd.
Great for breakfast, too. This recipe contains only three food families,
so it's a good choice for people on a Rotary Diversified Diet.

- ⅓ **cup almond butter**
- ¼ **cup light or dark agave nectar or honey**
- 1 **tablespoon almond oil**
- ¾ **cup diced dried apricots, peaches, or prunes**
- 2½ **cups crisp brown rice cereal**

OIL A PIE PLATE or 8" × 8" baking pan.

In a saucepan, combine the almond butter, agave nectar or honey, and oil. Cook, stirring, over medium heat until blended. (Do not boil.) Remove from the heat. Stir in the fruit and cereal.

Press into the prepared pan, smoothing with a rubber spatula or wooden spoon.

Chill for 2 hours and cut into wedges or bars. Cover with foil and refrigerate. Will remain crisp for 2 to 3 days.

Makes 8 wedges or 16 bars

Carob Crispy Crunch

Adapted from a recipe my mother made frequently when I was a child.
This confection delights kids of all ages and is a favorite with my grandchildren.

⅔ **cup light agave nectar or clover honey**
½ **cup almond or cashew butter, room temperature**
1 **teaspoon vanilla extract (optional)**
¼ **cup carob powder**
4 **cups crisp brown rice cereal**

OIL AN 11" × 7" BAKING PAN.

In a 3-quart saucepan, combine the agave nectar or honey and nut butter. Cook, stirring, over medium-low heat until the honey melts and the nut butter visibly softens and is easy to mix. (Do not boil.) Remove from the heat.

Quickly stir in the vanilla if using, carob, and rice cereal. The mixture will be stiff. Press firmly into the prepared pan. Chill for 1 hour before cutting into bars. Cover with foil and keep refrigerated. Will stay crisp for up to 3 days.

Makes 24 bars

COOK'S TIPS

✳ Crisp brown rice cereal is available in many health food stores and supermarkets. Do not substitute puffed rice cereal.

✳ Serve chilled. At room temperature, this confection is soft and sticky.

Coconut-Date Confection

This sweet treat combines members of the Palm family.
It's ideal for serving at birthdays and holidays.
For best flavor, prepare at least a day ahead.

½ **pound pitted dates**
¾ **cup finely grated unsweetened**
   coconut

IN A FOOD PROCESSOR, combine the dates and ½ cup of the coconut. Process until well mixed. Shape the mixture into ¾" balls. Roll in the remaining ¼ cup coconut. Store in a tightly covered container and use within 2 weeks.

Makes ½ pound

Variation

Coconut-Date Confection with Nuts: Press an almond or half a walnut or pecan into each ball. Roll in either ground nuts or coconut.

Stuffed Dates

A simple snack that children can make. To pack in lunch boxes,
wrap two dates facing each other, so the nut butter doesn't stick to the wrapper.

24 **large dates, pitted**
½ **cup almond, cashew, or sunflower**
   butter
24 **walnuts, pecans, or almonds**

WITH A SHARP KNIFE, cut each date lengthwise along 1 side. Fill each with a teaspoonful of nut butter. Press a walnut, pecan, or almond into the nut butter.

Makes 24

COOK'S TIPS

✻ For less sticky confections, omit the whole nuts and roll the stuffed dates in ⅓ cup of seeds or ground nuts.

✻ Look for nut and seed butters in health food stores.

Fruit Gelatin Cutouts

*Here's a colorful, sweet-tasting fun food that's free of sugar and artificial colors
and flavors. After the gelatin sets, the kids can cut out animals, stars, and other playful
shapes using cookie cutters. These are firm enough to eat out of hand.*

3 tablespoons unflavored gelatin
12 ounces thawed purple grape juice
   concentrate
1½ cups boiling water

OIL A 13" × 9" BAKING DISH.

In a saucepan, sprinkle the gelatin over
the juice concentrate and let soften for 5 to
10 minutes. Add the water and stir until the
gelatin dissolves.

Pour into the prepared dish and chill for
1 hour, or until firmly set. Cut into cubes or
fancy shapes. Gel can stand at room temperature for up to 4 hours. Store in a covered
container.

Makes about 24

Ice Pops

*Here's a sugar-free, additive-free version of a favorite summertime frozen snack.
I make these in July through October when melons are really good. You'll need four
5-ounce paper cups and 4 wooden Popsicle sticks.*

3 cups chopped watermelon, honeydew
   or cantaloupe
1 teaspoon lemon or lime juice
   (optional)

IN A BLENDER, combine the melon and
lemon or lime juice if using. Process until
very smooth. Divide mixture among 4 paper
cups, leaving a little room at the top for expansion. Place the cups in an 8" × 8"
baking pan. Insert a wooden stick in each
cup. Place in the freezer for 30 minutes and

straighten the sticks if they've moved off
center. Freeze for 1 hour, or until solid.

Makes 4

COOK'S TIPS

✳ Puree the melon in a blender; you'll need nearly 3
  cups of chopped melon.

✳ Look for the Popsicle sticks in supermarkets and
  craft and hobby shops.

✳ These ice pops are best when used within a few
  days. For slightly longer storage, place the cups in
  cellophane or plastic bags.

Drinks, Milks, and Smoothies

Shakes, sodas, smoothies, mocha latte—any of these drinks can be a healthful and low-allergen treat if it contains the right ingredients.

Over the years, I've discovered that a little imagination can go a long way toward avoiding the high-allergen beverages, especially those made with cow's milk, citrus juices, and artificial flavors (like fruit drinks and soda). In this chapter, you'll find more than a dozen of my favorite beverage creations. I hope they'll help you in two ways: give you recipes that agree with you and spark your imagination for creating even more delicious drinks.

With fruits and fruit juices, sometimes combined with nuts, goat's milk, or tofu, you can create countless milk-free shakes and smoothies like Peach Ice Cream Soda or Peach Smoothie with Mint. And you can make sparkling beverages—such as Cranberry Soda or Ginger Ale from homemade concentrates. You can also stir together a Berry Good Tea Punch without citrus or ar-

tificially flavored soda. (For more punch recipes, turn to Holiday Foods on page 350.)

For cooking and baking, your beverage choices will be somewhat different than the common cow's milk varieties, of course. I've found that soy milk, rice milk, Sweet Nut Milk, Pineapple Milk, and Zucchini Milk are especially useful alternatives. Look for soy and rice milks, as well as goat's milk, in health food stores and supermarkets. I'm particularly enthusiastic about discovering Zucchini Milk, which uses a prolific garden vegetable in a new and exciting way and is easily made at home. Both Zucchini Milk and Pineapple Milk are helpful options for people who are allergic to soy or nuts, as well as cow's milk. Of the two, zucchini has a more neutral flavor. Pineapple Milk is best suited to baking (in muffins and quick breads) and cooking (in puddings) where pineapple is a welcome flavor.

I can't forget to mention my all-time favorite hot-weather beverage: Melon Cooler. Be sure to give it a try when honeydew is in season.

Zucchini Milk

Zucchini milk is a versatile liquid that's ideal for making bread, cakes, and cream soups.
Make the milk when zucchini is in season and freeze it in one-cup containers. For a pale, off-white
milk, peel the zucchini thickly (or double peel). Unpeeled zucchini will result in green milk.

2½ pounds firm zucchini, peeled and cut into chunks

PLACE ENOUGH ZUCCHINI in a blender to fill it about one-quarter full. Process to a thick, smooth liquid. Pour into a large saucepan. Repeat to puree all the zucchini.

Heat to boiling over medium-high heat and cook for 1 minute. Cool briefly and pour into four 1-cup canning jars.

Makes about 1 quart

COOK'S TIP

＊ This versatile milk can be stored in the refrigerator for up to 1 week or in the freezer for up to 1 year.

Sweet Nut Milk

Enjoy this milk as a beverage, in a cream sauce, or as a cooking ingredient. Or use it on cereal.
Cashews, almonds, filberts, and Brazil nuts all make delightful milks, and you can vary the
proportions of nuts and water to achieve whatever richness and thickness you desire.

¼–⅔ cup raw or toasted cashews or almonds
1 cup water
¼ teaspoon pure vanilla extract (optional)
1 teaspoon light agave nectar, honey, or maple syrup (optional)

PLACE THE NUTS in a blender. Process for 1 to 2 minutes, or until a fine powder forms. Turn off the blender. Using a narrow spatula or blunt knife, loosen the nuts in the bottom of the blender jar. Add ½ cup of the water, the vanilla if using, and the agave nectar, honey, or maple syrup if using. Process for 2 min-

utes, or until very smooth. Add the remaining ½ cup water and process for 10 seconds more.

Makes about 1 cup

COOK'S TIPS

＊ For a silky, smooth consistency, strain the milk through a sieve.

＊ To roast large whole nuts, spread them on a baking sheet. Bake at 300°F for 12 minutes, or until light brown and fragrant.

Variation
Savory Nut Milk: Omit the vanilla and sweetener. Use this savory version for creamy sauces, soups, or gravies.

Scalding Canning Jars and Lids

When preparing milks or concentrates for the refrigerator or freezer, I usually scald the canning jars and lids. This step isn't essential, but I've found that it increases the length of time foods will keep before molds become a problem. If you're mold-sensitive, consider taking this extra precaution. Here's what I do:

To scald the jars: Place them in the sink; then pour boiling water into each one. Fill to overflowing. Let sit for a few minutes.

To scald the lids (and other items such as the funnel to be used for filling): Place them in a pot; then pour in enough boiling water to cover. Let sit for a few minutes. Use tongs to remove from the water.

Pineapple-Nut Shake

A thick, refreshing, dairy-free shake for snacking—or dessert.

1 cup Sweet Nut Milk (page 302)
2 cups chopped pineapple
1 tablespoon light agave nectar or honey
1–2 teaspoons lemon juice (optional)

POUR THE NUT MILK into a blender. Add the pineapple, agave or honey, and lemon juice if using. Process until smooth. Serve at once.

Makes 2 servings

COOK'S TIP

✳ For this recipe, I use fresh, frozen, or stewed fruit. On occasion, I also use 1 cup frozen fruit plus 1 cup fresh.

Variations

Peach-Nut Shake: Substitute peaches for the pineapple.

Banana-Nut Shake: Substitute bananas for the pineapple.

Berry-Nut Shake: Substitute raspberries or blueberries for the pineapple.

Melon-Nut Shake: Substitute cantaloupe or honeydew for the pineapple.

Banana-Orange Milk-Free Shake

Another sunny-tasting beverage for people
who are allergic to both milk and soy.

1 **very ripe, large banana, sliced**

1 **tablespoon light agave nectar, maple syrup, or honey**

1 **cup chopped oranges**

¼ **cup water or 3 ice cubes**

2 **teaspoons lemon juice or ⅛–¼ teaspoon unbuffered vitamin C crystals (optional)**

COMBINE THE BANANA and agave nectar, maple syrup, or honey in a blender. Process for 30 seconds, or until blended. Add the oranges, water or ice cubes, and lemon juice or vitamin C crystals. Process for 1 minute, or until smooth. Serve over ice cubes.

Makes about 1 cup

Variations

Minted Fruit Shake: Add 2 or more mint leaves along with the oranges. Garnish with a mint sprig.

Pineapple-Banana Milk-Free Shake: Substitute canned or fresh pineapple for the oranges.

Peach-Banana Milk-Free Shake: Substitute peaches (or nectarines) for the oranges.

Berry-Banana Milk-Free Shake: Substitute blueberries or raspberries for the oranges.

Apricot-Banana Milk-Free Shake: Substitute fresh or stewed apricots for the oranges.

Blender or Food Processor?

Which is best for whipping up a shake or smoothie? I favor the blender. It handles swirling liquids much better than processors, which have shallow bowls and often leak. Plus, blenders excel at creating the classic milkshake froth (the design of food processors doesn't allow them to incorporate enough air for this effect).

Pineapple Milk

This "milk" is great over puffed rice, granola, or other breakfast cereals or for use in muffins or quick breads.

2 **small ripe bananas, chopped, or 1 can (8 ounces) unsweetened crushed pineapple in juice, chilled**

3 **cups unsweetened pineapple juice, chilled**

IN A BLENDER, combine the banana or undrained pineapple and ½ cup of the pineapple juice. Process until smooth. Add the remaining 2½ cups of the juice and process for 30 seconds, or until frothy.

Makes about 1 quart

COOK'S TIP

✳ To keep Pineapple Milk for up to a week, add ¼ teaspoon unbuffered vitamin C crystals to the mixture and process until the crystals are dissolved and well-blended. Store in the refrigerator or freezer.

Grape Fizz

Here's a sweet carbonated juice drink without added sugar or artificial ingredients.

¾ **cup sparkling water, chilled**

¼ **cup white or purple grape juice concentrate**

FILL A GLASS with ice cubes. Pour in the sparkling water and juice concentrate and stir.

Makes 1 cup

Variations

Apple Fizz: Substitute apple concentrate for the grape juice concentrate.

Orange Fizz: Substitute orange concentrate for the grape juice concentrate.

Pineapple Fizz: Substitute pineapple concentrate for the grape juice concentrate.

Freezing Hint

All foods—especially liquidy ones—expand as they freeze. Here's the best way to compensate for that expansion when freezing beverages: Fill each jar to 1 inch from the top. If you're using a two-piece canning lid, place the flat lid on the jar. Chill in the refrigerator for several hours; then transfer to the freezer. When the contents are frozen, add the screw-bands.

Melon Cooler

Frosty glasses are a nice touch for this cool, refreshing beverage.
It's thick and creamy like a milkshake but light as a feather and not too sweet.

4 cups chopped ripe honeydew melon, chilled

1 tablespoon lime juice

Mint sprigs (optional)

PLACE THE MELON in a blender and process until liquified. Add the lime juice and stir. Pour into 2 tall, chilled glasses. Garnish with the mint if using.

Makes 2 servings

Variations

Melon-Mint Cooler: Add 4 or more mint leaves to the mixture before processing.

Cantaloupe Cooler: Substitute cantaloupe for the honeydew melon and replace the lime juice with lemon juice.

Old-Fashioned Lemonade

Every summer, I make this sweet-tart treat. It's a hit at our house.

¼ cup light agave nectar or honey

¼ cup boiling water

3 cups very cold water

½ cup lemon juice

POUR THE SWEETENER in a heat-safe glass jar or stainless steel bowl. Pour in the boiling water and stir until the sweetener dissolves. Whisk in the cold water and lemon juice. Pour into 2 to 4 tall, ice-cube-filled glasses.

Makes about 1 quart

COOK'S TIPS

* If you don't have light agave nectar on hand, use the lightest, mildest honey you can find (otherwise, the honey's flavor may dominate the lemonade).

* Add any additional honey before the mixture has cooled so it mixes in well.

Berry-Good Tea Punch

A pretty party punch that's based on foods of the Rose family. Serve and enjoy!

2 cups boiling water

6 rosehips tea bags

⅓ cup light agave nectar or honey

1¼ cups raspberries, blackberries, or strawberries

Pinch of unbuffered vitamin C crystals (optional)

2 cups sparkling water

PLACE THE TEA BAGS in a heat-safe glass or stainless steel bowl. Pour in the boiling water, and allow the tea to steep for 10 minutes. Using a strainer and spoon, press the liquid from the tea bags and discard the bags. Stir in the agave nectar or honey. Refrigerate until needed.

Just before serving, combine the tea mixture, 1 cup of the berries, and vitamin C if using in a blender. Process on high speed for 1 minute. Pour into a small punch bowl, add the sparkling water, and briefly stir. Slice the strawberries if using. Float the remaining raspberries, blackberries, or sliced strawberries in the tea mixture. Serve immediately.

Makes about 5 cups

COOK'S TIP

* You can use a carbonated-water dispenser to make your own sparkling water if you wish. (See "Food Storage and Equipment," page 383.)

Peach Ice Cream Soda

Here's a milk-free treat that can rival soda-fountain drinks. It's a favorite with my grandkids.

1 scoop Peach-Almond Ice Cream (page 338) or Soft Sherbet (page 340)

1½–2 cups chilled sparkling water

PLACE THE ICE CREAM or sherbet in a tall glass. Add the sparkling water to fill.

Makes about 2 cups

COOK'S TIP

* You can use a carbonated-water dispenser to make your own sparkling water if you wish. (See "Food Storage and Equipment," page 383.)

DRINKS, MILKS, AND SMOOTHIES

Herbal Iced Tea

This tea is cool, refreshing, and free of caffeine.
It's ready to drink in 15 minutes and keeps for several days.

10–12 herbal tea bags
   3 cups boiling water
3–4 tablespoons light agave nectar or honey
   1 lemon, thinly sliced (optional)
   6 ice cubes
   Mint sprigs (optional)

PLACE THE TEA BAGS in a teapot or heat-safe glass bowl. Pour in the boiling water and stir in the agave nectar or honey. Allow to steep for 5 minutes. Add the lemon if using and steep for 5 to 7 minutes more.

Place the ice cubes in a 2-quart glass pitcher. Using a sieve, strain the tea into the pitcher, pressing the tea bags with the back of a spoon to extract all the tea and lemon juice. Add enough cold water to fill the pitcher. Refrigerate until needed.

To serve, pour over ice cubes in tall glasses. Garnish with mint sprigs if using.

Makes about 2 quarts

Variation
Mint Tea: Add 8 to 12 mint leaves or 1 peppermint tea bag to the steeping tea.

Hot Carob Drink

Here's a delightful chocolate-free version
of everyone's favorite hot comfort-beverage.

2½ cups goat's milk
   1 tablespoon light agave nectar or honey
   2 tablespoons carob powder
   ½ teaspoon vanilla (optional)

COMBINE THE MILK, agave nectar or honey, and carob in a 2-quart saucepan. Warm over medium-high heat, whisking or stirring for about 7 minutes, or until heated

through and just barely simmering. Do not let the mixture boil. Stir in the vanilla if using. Divide between two mugs and serve immediately.

Makes about 2½ cups

Variation
Mocha Latte: Add 1 rounded teaspoon decaffeinated instant coffee to each mug before pouring in the hot carob mixture. Stir to mix well and serve immediately.

Sparkling Beverages

These fizzy drinks make great alternatives to soda. I often whip up a couple on a moment's notice. To do just that, keep 1 to 2 liters of chilled sparkling (or carbonated) water on hand. Use the water and the beverage concentrates below to make Ginger Ale, Cranberry Soda, Strawberry Soda, and Strawberry Ice Cream Soda.

Ginger Ale Concentrate

2 tablespoons minced fresh ginger
1¼ cups hot (not boiling) water
¾ cup honey

COMBINE THE GINGER, water, and honey in a blender. Process for 1 minute, or until pureed. Strain into a canning jar and refrigerate for at least 2 hours and up to 10 days.

To make Ginger Ale: Pour ¼ cup of the ginger mixture (more or less, to taste) into a glass. Add sparkling water and ice cubes.

*Makes about 2 cups
(enough for about 8 servings of Ginger Ale)*

Strawberry Concentrate

1¼ cups whole strawberries
⅓ cup light agave nectar or honey

PLACE THE STRAWBERRIES in a blender and process until smooth. With the blender running, pour in the agave nectar or honey in a thin stream. Process until well-blended. Pour into a canning jar and store in the refrigerator for up to 10 days.

To make Strawberry Soda: Pour ¼ cup of the strawberry mixture (more or less, to taste) into a glass. Add sparkling water and ice cubes.

Makes about 1½ cups (enough for about 6 servings of Strawberry Soda)

Variation
Strawberry Ice Cream Soda: Add a scoop of Strawberry Ice Cream (page 268).

Cranberry Soda

To make this soda, you'll need cranberry juice concentrate. Be sure to get a bottled unsweetened brand at a health food store; the frozen variety contains sugar.

3 tablespoons light agave nectar or honey
2 tablespoons cranberry juice concentrate
2 cups sparkling water

MIX THE AGAVE NECTAR or honey and juice concentrate in a 16-ounce glass (use less sweetener and juice concentrate in a smaller glass). Add the sparkling water and ice cubes and stir.

Makes about 2 cups

Peach Smoothie with Mint

Peach season is short, but this smoothie works well with unsweetened frozen peaches,
so you can get a taste of summer's best any time of the year.

1 pound peaches, peeled and sliced

½ cup white grape juice concentrate

½ cup water

1½ tablespoons lemon juice or
   ¼ teaspoon unbuffered vitamin C
   crystals

1 cup plain goat's- or sheep's-milk
   yogurt

6 fresh mint leaves

2 sprigs fresh mint (optional)

PLACE 2 GLASSES in the freezer to chill. Combine the peaches, grape juice concentrate, water, lemon juice or vitamin C crystals, yogurt, and mint leaves in a blender. Process for 1 minute, or until very smooth. Pour into the frosted glasses and garnish each with a sprig of mint if using.

Makes 3 to 4 cups

COOK'S TIPS

✳ In the off-season, I purchase 1-pound bags of frozen unsweetened peaches for making this treat. Let the fruit thaw for an hour before making the smoothie.

✳ You can make this smoothie sweeter or mintier by adding more white grape juice concentrate or a few more mint leaves.

Desserts

Next to breads, desserts probably pose the most difficulty for people with food allergies. Commercial mixes and standard recipes invariably contain wheat, milk, eggs, sugar, corn syrup, or other highly allergenic ingredients. But desserts taste so good! That's why I've made this the largest chapter in the book. It will help you make pies, cakes, and other sweets that your whole family and your friends will enjoy. Recipes range from quick and easy Carob Fudge Cake and Apple-Berry Tapioca Pudding to the more elaborate English Trifle and everything in between.

Thanks to the food processor, my favorite dessert is now pie, particularly Peach Streusel Pie, made with Spelt-Kamut Pie Crust. If you're scared off by pie-making, give this one a try. It comes together easily and is oh-so-satisfying.

You can also make grain-free versions of many baked goodies from amaranth, buckwheat, or quinoa flours, alone or in combination with each other. The combination produces baked goods far superior in flavor and texture to those baked with any of those flours alone. If you react to one of those flours, but do well with the other two, experiment with the grain-free recipes and create your own customized recipes.

Don't limit yourself to this chapter when searching for desserts. For cookies and other lunch-box fare, see the Snacks chapter on page 281. And check out Holiday Foods on page 350 for a special occasion Party Sponge Cake, Plum Pudding, Elegant and Easy Fruitcake, and two great (and easy) pumpkin pies. Also, you will find some terrific ice cream recipes in Goat's Milk and Goat's-Milk Cheese Dishes on page 261.

Carob Fudge Cake

In answer to America's love affair with chocolate desserts, I'm including
more than one version of this universal favorite. This one is grain-free.

⅔ cup white buckwheat flour

½ cup quinoa flour

½ cup amaranth flour

½ cup carob powder

2 tablespoons tapioca starch or
  arrowroot

1½ teaspoons baking soda

¼ teaspoon salt

1 cup thawed white grape juice
  concentrate

½ cup canola oil

1 teaspoon vanilla extract (optional)

PLACE AN OVEN RACK just below the
middle position, and preheat the oven to
350°F. Coat a 9" round pan with cooking
spray or oil and flour it.

In a large bowl, whisk the buckwheat
flour, quinoa flour, amaranth flour, carob,
starch, baking soda, and salt.

Combine the grape juice concentrate,
oil, and vanilla if using. Pour into the flour
mixture and mix well.

Pour into the prepared pan. Bake for
27 to 30 minutes, or until the edges are
brown, small cracks appear on top, and a
cake tester inserted in the center comes
out clean. Don't overbake. Cool in the pan
on a rack.

Serve warm or cold, plain or with Carob
Fudge Glaze (page 342).

Makes 8 servings

COOK'S TIP

＊ Freeze pieces that won't be used within a day or two.

Carob Cake with Teff

Rich and delicious—a must-have for your sweet tooth.

1½ cups teff flour

½ cup carob powder

2 tablespoons tapioca starch or
  arrowroot

2 teaspoons baking soda

¼ teaspoon salt

½ teaspoon unbuffered vitamin C
  crystals

⅔ cup lukewarm water

⅔ cup maple syrup

⅓ cup canola oil

PREHEAT OVEN to 350°F. Coat a 9" round pan with cooking spray or oil and flour it.

In a bowl, whisk the flour, carob, starch, baking soda, and salt.

In a 2-cup measure, dissolve the vitamin C in the water. Add the maple syrup and oil, stirring until blended. Quickly pour into the flour mixture, and mix well.

Pour into the prepared pan. Bake for 22 to 26 minutes, or until the top springs back when touched in the center. Cool in the pan on a rack.

Serve warm or cold, plain or topped with Carob Fudge Glaze (page 342).

Makes 8 servings

Fudge Brownies

These exceptionally moist fudgy-tasting brownies have won rave reviews.

⅔ **cup carob powder, rubbed through a strainer**

⅓ **cup quinoa flour**

½ **teaspoon baking soda**

½ **teaspoon salt**

½ **teaspoon xanthan gum**

½ **teaspoon white stevia powder**

2 **tablespoons instant espresso or coffee (optional)**

⅔ **cup chopped walnuts (optional)**

1 **can (15 ounces) unseasoned black beans, rinsed and drained**

½ **cup Spectrum Spread**

⅔ **cup light agave nectar**

2 **teaspoons vanilla extract**

PREHEAT THE OVEN to 325°F. Coat a 9" × 9" baking pan with cooking spray. Line with parchment paper and spray with the cooking spray.

In a bowl, whisk the carob powder,

quinoa flour, baking soda, salt, xanthan gum, white stevia powder, and espresso or coffee if using. Stir in the nuts if using.

In a food processor, combine the beans, Spectrum Spread, agave nectar, and vanilla. Process for 3 minutes, or until very smooth. Pour the bean mixture into the flour mixture and mix just until combined. Batter will be thick.

Spread in the prepared pan and smooth with a spatula, being sure to fill the corners. Bake for 30 to 33 minutes, until a cake tester inserted into the center comes out almost clean. Cool in the pan on a rack.

Makes 16 servings

COOK'S TIPS

* Here's an easy way to cut the brownies: Turn the uncut brownies out on a cutting board, remove the parchment, and cut into 16 squares.

* Feel free to substitute any other unseasoned beans for the black beans.

Grain-Free Fudge Brownies

Egg-free, wheat-free, moist, and delicious—need I say more?

⅔ cup white buckwheat flour

½ cup amaranth flour

½ cup quinoa flour

½ cup carob powder

¼ cup maple or date sugar

2 tablespoons tapioca starch or arrowroot

½ teaspoon baking soda

¼ teaspoon salt

½ cup thawed white grape or apple juice concentrate

½ cup canola or sunflower oil

1½ teaspoons vanilla extract (optional)

PLACE AN OVEN RACK just below the middle position, and preheat the oven to 350°F. Coat an 11" × 7" baking dish with cooking spray or oil and flour it.

In a large bowl, whisk the buckwheat flour, amaranth flour, quinoa flour, carob, maple or date sugar, starch or arrowroot, baking soda, and salt.

In a 2-cup measure, combine the grape juice, oil, and vanilla if using. Quickly pour into the flour mixture and mix just until combined. Batter will be quite thick.

Spread in the prepared pan and smooth with a spatula, being sure to fill the corners. Bake for 13 to 14 minutes, or until the edges are brown and small cracks appear on top. Don't overbake.

Makes 16 servings

COOK'S TIP

✳ To make white buckwheat flour, grind ½ cup white, unroasted whole groats at a time in a blender for 1 to 2 minutes. Pour into sieve. Repeat grinding, adding any groats that didn't go through the sieve.

Kamut-Maple Cake

Topped with Maple-Nut Frosting (page 342), this delightful cake borders on the wicked!
Pears keep it moist—even without eggs.

2½ cups Kamut brand flour

2 teaspoons baking soda

2 teaspoons cream of tartar

½ teaspoon salt

½ teaspoon white stevia powder

½ cup Spectrum Spread

1 jar (4 ounces) baby food pears

¾ cup maple syrup

PREHEAT THE OVEN to 325°F. Coat a 9" round pan with cooking spray or oil and flour it. Line with parchment paper.

In a small bowl, whisk the flour, baking soda, cream of tartar, salt, and white stevia powder.

In a bowl, combine the Spectrum Spread and pears. Beat with an electric mixer for 30 to 60 seconds, and slowly pour in the maple syrup. With the mixer set to low, add the flour mixture, ⅓ at a time, beating after each addition.

Quickly pour into the prepared pan. Bake for about 22 minutes, or until brown and a cake-tester inserted in the center comes out clean. Cool in the pan on a rack for 10 to 20 minutes. Remove to the rack to cool completely.

Makes 8 servings

COOK'S TIPS

✳ Frost when slightly warm or completely cool.

✳ Egg-free cakes such as this one become dry quickly, so prepare and enjoy on the same day.

✳ Store leftover pieces wrapped in plastic wrap.

Two-Step Carrot Cake

This festive dessert is dense and moist, almost like fruitcake. But unlike most cakes, it doesn't contain eggs. I call it a two-step cake because you prepare the carrot mixture the night before and finish the cake the next day.

STEP ONE

1½ **cups packed grated carrots**

1 **cup raisins or dried cranberries**

½ **cup shredded unsweetened coconut (optional)**

1 **teaspoon ground cinnamon**

½ **teaspoon grated nutmeg**

¼ **teaspoon ground cloves**

1¼ **cups pineapple juice**

1 **can (8 ounces) crushed pineapple in juice**

⅔ **cup light or dark agave nectar or honey**

¼ **cup oil**

STEP TWO

⅔ **cup chopped walnuts or pecans**

2 **cups rye flour**

2 **teaspoons baking soda**

½ **teaspoon salt**

STEP ONE: Combine the carrots, raisins or cranberries, coconut if using, cinnamon, nutmeg, and cloves in a saucepan. Stir in the juice, pineapple with juice, and agave nectar or honey. Bring to a boil over medium-low heat. Cook for 10 minutes. Allow to cool to room temperature and stir in the oil. Refrigerate, covered, for at least 4 hours (can store for up to 10 hours).

Step Two: Preheat the oven to 300°F. Coat a 13" × 9" baking dish or oil and flour it.

Remove the carrot mixture from the refrigerator, and allow to warm to room temperature. Stir in the walnuts or pecans.

In a large bowl, whisk the flour, baking soda, and salt. Add the carrot mixture, and mix just until combined. Don't overmix.

Pour the batter into the prepared baking dish. Bake for 1 hour, or until a cake tester inserted in the center comes out clean. Cool completely in the pan on a rack before cutting.

Makes 24 servings

COOK'S TIPS

✱ When well-wrapped, this cake freezes nicely for up to 1 month.

✱ If you want to avoid pineapple, substitute white grape juice or apple juice for the pineapple juice. Omit the crushed pineapple and increase the grated carrots to 2 cups.

Grain-Free Gingerbread

*It still surprises me how great-tasting something can be when made
with alternative ingredients: different flours, no egg, no milk, and in this case,
no powdered spice off the shelf. This cake disappears fast around our house.
We especially like it topped with Peach Sauce (page 207).*

¾ **cup white buckwheat flour**

½ **cup amaranth flour**

⅓ **cup quinoa flakes or ¼ cup quinoa flour**

2 **tablespoons tapioca starch or arrowroot**

1½ **teaspoons baking soda**

1½ **teaspoons cream of tartar**

½ **teaspoon salt**

⅓ **cup maple or date sugar**

½ **cup water**

1½ **tablespoons minced fresh ginger**

1 **jar (4 ounces) baby food winter squash**

¼ **cup dark agave nectar, sorghum, or honey**

3 **tablespoons vegetable oil**

PREHEAT THE OVEN to 350°F. Coat a 9"
pie plate or an 8" round pan with cooking
spray or oil and flour it.

In a large bowl, combine the buckwheat
flour, amaranth flour, quinoa flakes or flour,
starch or arrowroot, baking soda, cream of
tartar, salt, and maple or date sugar.

In a blender, combine the water; ginger;
winter squash; agave nectar, honey, or
sorghum; and oil and process until smooth.
Pour into the flour mixture and mix just
until combined.

Pour into the prepared pan and lightly
shake the pan to level the batter. Bake for
20 to 22 minutes, or until the edges are
brown, little cracks appear across the top,
and a cake-tester inserted into the center
comes out clean. Cool completely in the
pan on a rack.

Makes 8 servings

COOK'S TIPS

✳ To make white buckwheat flour, grind ½ cup white,
unroasted whole groats at a time in a blender for 1
to 2 minutes. Pour into sieve. Repeat grinding,
adding any groats that didn't go through the sieve.

✳ Other baby food options that work well include
sweet potato, green peas, applesauce, pears,
prunes, and carrots.

Plum-Good Coffee Cake

This absolutely delicious upside-down cake is not only wheat-free, but milk-free and egg-free as well. We like this well enough that I pit and freeze a couple of baking sheets full of small Italian plums when they're in season so I can make this treat the following winter.

1½ tablespoons date sugar

12 small purple plums, halved (about 10 ounces)

¾ cup buckwheat flour

½ cup quinoa flour

½ cup amaranth flour

¼ cup tapioca starch or arrowroot

1½ teaspoons baking soda

½ teaspoon unbuffered vitamin C crystals

½ teaspoon salt

½ teaspoon freshly grated nutmeg

½ teaspoon white stevia powder

1 or 2 herbal tea bags, such as Peach Passion

½ cup boiling water

½ cup light agave nectar or honey

⅓ cup canola or sunflower oil

⅓ cup peach or apricot all-fruit preserves

PREHEAT THE OVEN to 325°F. Coat a 9" pie plate or an 8" round pan with cooking spray or oil and flour it. Line it with parchment paper and oil the parchment.

Spread the date sugar evenly over the bottom of the prepared pan. Arrange the plums, cut side down, in two concentric circles atop the sugar.

In a bowl, combine the buckwheat flour, quinoa flour, amaranth flour, tapioca starch or arrowroot, baking soda, vitamin C, salt, nutmeg, and white stevia powder.

In a 2-cup measure, steep the tea in the boiling water, let cool to warm, and discard the tea bags. Add water if necessary to make ½ cup. Add the agave nectar or honey, stirring until dissolved. Add the oil. Pour into a blender and add the preserves. Process for about 30 seconds. Pour into the flour mixture, and mix just until combined.

Pour over the fruit, taking care not to stir or disturb the fruit. Bake for 32 to 34 minutes, or until the top is lightly brown, springs back when touched, and a cake-tester inserted into the center comes out clean. Cool in the pan on a rack for 5 to 10 minutes. Turn onto a plate and serve warm or at room temperature.

Makes 8 servings

COOK'S TIP

✳ To remove the cake from the pan: Place a plate over the pan and flip the plate and pan as a unit. Peel off the parchment paper.

Fruit-Fluff Pie

A light, versatile dessert that contains no cream, sugar, or egg whites.
And it's both delicious and easy to make. My granddaughter, Brooke, apparently awestruck,
exclaimed between bites, "It's purple. I'm eating a purple pie!"

⅔ cup thawed purple grape or apple
    juice concentrate

⅓ cup water

2 envelopes unflavored gelatin

2 cups fresh raspberries

2 cups banana slices (about 3 large
    bananas)

1 can (8 ounces) crushed pineapple in
    juice

2 tablespoons canola or sunflower oil

1 baked Oat and Barley Pie Crust
    (recipe variation, page 325)

    Whipped Tofu Topping (page 346) or
    Nutty Crème Topping (page 345)

IN A SMALL SAUCEPAN, mix the juice concentrate and water. Sprinkle the gelatin over concentrate, and allow to soften for 5 minutes. Heat briefly, stirring, to dissolve the gelatin.

Place the raspberries in a blender. Process for 1 minute, or until smooth. Pour through a sieve, pressing lightly and scraping the puree from the bottom of the sieve. Discard the seeds. Return to the blender and add 1 cup of the banana slices, the crushed pineapple, and oil. With the blender running on low speed, pour in the gelatin mixture. Process for 30 seconds.

Pour into a bowl and refrigerate for 1 hour, or until the mixture is partially set and forms mounds when dropped from a spoon. Whip with an electric mixer for 2 minutes, or until light and fluffy. Spread about one-third of the mixture in the bottom of the pie crust.

Arrange remaining 1 cup banana slices over the raspberry mixture in a single layer. Spoon the raspberry mixture into the crust, and chill at least 1 hour before serving.

Spoon a dollop of topping onto each serving.

Makes 8 servings

COOK'S TIP

✳ Can't find any fresh raspberries? Then use 1 package (10 ounces) frozen unsweetened raspberries, thawed instead.

Variations

Fruit-Fluff Gel: Omit the pie crust. Pour whipped fruit mixture into individual custard cups or a small ring mold. Submerge remaining banana slices. Chill until firm. Unmold before serving, or spoon into small dishes.

Fruit-Fluff Parfaits: In parfait glasses, alternate layers of fruit-gelatin mixture (just after whipping it), banana slices, and chilled Whipped Tofu Topping (page 346) or Nutty Crème Topping (page 345), ending with the topping. Chill and top each parfait with 5 whole raspberries just before serving.

Double-Apple Pie

Everyone will love this version of America's most traditional dessert.
Use baking apples that will hold their shape, such as Yellow Delicious, Fuji, Greening,
and Jonathan. Don't use McIntosh apples, which disintegrate as they cook.

6 cups peeled, sliced apples

¾ cup thawed apple juice concentrate

3 tablespoons quick-cooking tapioca
granules

1 teaspoon ground cinnamon
(optional)

1 unbaked Spelt-Kamut Pie Crust
(page 324)

1 cup Spelt-Kamut Streusel Crumbs

PREHEAT THE OVEN to 350°F.

In a large bowl, mix the apples, juice concentrate, tapioca granules, and cinnamon if using. Let stand for 15 minutes. Pour into the crust.

Bake for 20 minutes. Remove to a baking sheet. Sprinkle with the streusel crumbs, pressing lightly. Return, on the baking sheet, to the oven for 15 minutes, or until the fruit is tender, crumbs are brown, and the juices bubbly.

Makes 8 servings

COOK'S TIPS

✳ Shape the edge of the pie crust so that it's about ½" above the pie plate. This will help prevent the juices from running over; a baking sheet is still recommended.

✳ When checking for doneness, use the tip of a knife to separate the streusel crumbs to see if the fruit mixture is bubbling.

Variations

Apple Pie with Nut Crust: Replace the Spelt-Kamut Pie Crust with Nut and Seed Crunch Crust (page 327).

Apple-Raisin Pie: Add ¼ cup raisins, dried cranberries, or currants to apple mixture.

Peach Streusel Pie

Peach season is all too short—but thanks to frozen unsweetened peaches we can enjoy this treat year round. I find a streusel topping easier and faster than fussing with lattice strips or even a top crust. But feel free to double the crust and roll out a top crust (be sure to cut slits in the top to release steam) if you want.

2 bags (1 pound each) frozen sliced peaches, thawed

¾ cup light agave nectar or honey

½ teaspoon unbuffered vitamin C crystals

Pinch of salt

½ teaspoon powdered ginger

⅛ teaspoon ground cinnamon

⅛ teaspoon freshly ground nutmeg

3½ teaspoons tapioca starch

1 unbaked Spelt-Kamut Pie Crust (page 324)

1 cup Spelt-Kamut Streusel Crumbs (page 328)

PREHEAT THE OVEN to 400°F.

In a large bowl, toss together the peaches, agave nectar or honey, vitamin C, salt, ginger, cinnamon, nutmeg, and tapioca.

Pour into the prepared pie crust and put on a baking sheet. Bake for 12 minutes, and reduce the heat to 350°F. Bake for 25 minutes. Sprinkle the streusel crumbs over the peach mixture. Pat the crumbs gently into the filling. Bake for 15 minutes, or until the crust and crumbs are brown and the filling is bubbly.

Allow to cool for at least 30 minutes before cutting.

Makes 8 servings

COOK'S TIPS

* If you want to sweeten your pie with fruit juice, omit the agave nectar or honey. Pour ¾ cup thawed white grape juice or apple juice concentrate into a small saucepan. Bring to a boil over medium heat and cook until reduced to ½ cup. Combine the peaches, tapioca, and spices, and pour the fruit juice concentrate over all.

* Shape the edge of the pie crust so that it's about ½" above the pie plate. This will help prevent the juices from running over; a baking sheet is still recommended.

* When checking for doneness, use the tip of a knife to separate the streusel crumbs to see if the fruit mixture is bubbling.

Banana Chiffon Pie

Fruit and nuts are the main ingredients in this light-as-a-feather dessert.
It's naturally sweet yet not terribly rich.

   2 **very ripe bananas, sliced**
   1 **baked Spelt-Kamut Pie Crust**
      (page 324)
1½ **cups Lime Bavarian (page 335)**

ARRANGE THE BANANAS in the bottom of the pie crust. Beat the lime Bavarian until light and fluffy and pour over the bananas. Chill for at least 1 hour before serving.

Makes 8 servings

COOK'S TIP

---

* To allow room for the bananas, shape the edge of the pie crust so that it's about ½" above the pie plate.

Pear Streusel Pie

Pears are one of nature's least allergenic fruits.
They make great pies in fall and winter when they're sweetest.

   5 **cups peeled, sliced pears**
  ¼ **cup quick-cooking tapioca granules**
  ¼ **cup light agave nectar or honey**
   2 **tablespoons lemon juice or**
      ½ teaspoon unbuffered vitamin C
      crystals
1–2 **tablespoons water (optional)**
   1 **baked Grain-Free Pie Crust**
      (page 326)
   1 **cup Grain-Free Streusel Crumbs**
      (page 329)

PREHEAT THE OVEN to 350°F. In a large bowl, mix the pears, tapioca, agave nectar or honey, lemon juice or vitamin C, and water. If pears aren't particularly juicy, add 1 to 2 tablespoons more water; if fruit isn't as sweet as expected, add another tablespoon or two of honey. Let stand for 15 minutes.

Pour into the crust. Bake for 15 minutes. Sprinkle streusel crumbs over the pear mixture, pressing lightly. Place on a baking sheet and bake for 15 to 20 minutes, or just until the fruit is tender and crumbs are brown.

Makes 8 servings

Hawaiian Pineapple Pie

*A friend came back from a Hawaiian vacation determined to re-create a pie
that she had tasted in Lanai. This delightful blend of tropical ingredients is what
we came up with. It's lighter than most pies, yet very flavorful.*

1 **can (20 ounces) crushed pineapple
with juice**

⅔ **cup mashed ripe banana (about
2 medium)**

2 **tablespoons thawed pineapple juice
concentrate (optional)**

¼ **cup unsweetened coconut**

2 **tablespoons small, quick-cooking
tapioca granules**

1 **Spelt-Kamut Pie Crust (page 324)**

PREHEAT THE OVEN to 350°F.

Combine the pineapple with juice, bananas, pineapple juice concentrate if using, coconut, and tapioca.

Pour into the prepared pie crust. Bake for 40 minutes, or just until the edges of crust are golden brown. The pie will continue to become firmer as it cools.

Serve at room temperature or slightly chilled. Refrigerate leftovers.

Makes 8 servings

COOK'S TIPS

✳ If you want, you can use light agave nectar or clover honey instead of the pineapple juice concentrate.

✳ You can add 2 tablespoons of date sugar to the crust if you want.

Spelt-Kamut Pie Crust

Now you can enjoy pastry again—thanks to spelt and Kamut brand flours, together with Spectrum Spread for shortening. And making the crusts is quick and easy with a food processor. Please note that you can make satisfactory pie crust with either Kamut brand or spelt flour alone, but the combination of the two makes the best wheat-free pie crust I've ever tasted.

⅔ cup white spelt flour
⅔ cup Kamut brand flour
½ teaspoon salt
⅓ cup Spectrum Spread
3½ tablespoons ice water

PREHEAT THE OVEN to 400°F for a baked crust or use the temperature called for in a filled pie recipe. Mist a 9" pie plate with cooking spray and wipe it with a paper towel, leaving just a thin film coating the pan.

In a food processor, combine the spelt flour, Kamut brand flour, and salt and process for 10 to 20 seconds. Add the spread and process for 1 minute, or until the mixture resembles cornmeal.

With the processor running, pour in 3 tablespoons of the ice water in a thin, steady stream. Add the remaining ½ tablespoon water slowly, stopping as soon as the dough gathers itself into a ball.

Cut 2 pieces of waxed paper, each about 18" long. Mist one side of each with cooking spray. Place the dough between the sheets, sprayed sides facing the dough. Pat into a 6" circle. Roll out to a 12" circle.

Remove the top paper and carefully flip the bottom paper and crust into the prepared pie plate. Remove the waxed paper. Adjust the crust and crimp the edges. Fill and bake according to a recipe.

Or crimp the edges, prick the bottom and sides with a fork, and line with parchment and a single layer of dry beans. Bake for 10 minutes and remove the parchment and beans. Bake for 4 to 5 minutes more, or until light brown. Allow to cool before filling.

Makes one 9" pie crust

COOK'S TIPS

* I like the lighter texture of white spelt flour, but you can use the whole grain variety. Or you can rub whole grain flour through a sieve to remove the bran, saving the bran for muffins or pancakes.

* Store the beans used to keep the pie crust flat in a plastic bag; reuse again and again. Don't cook for eating.

Variations

Sweet Spelt-Kamut Pie Crust: Add 2 tablespoons of date sugar before mixing the dry ingredients.

Kamut Pie Crust: Omit the spelt flour and use 1⅓ cups Kamut brand flour and increase the water to 4 tablespoons.

Spelt Pie Crust: Omit the Kamut brand flour and use 1⅓ cups spelt flour and ¼ cup arrowroot or tapioca starch and 3 to 3½ tablespoons of water.

Oat and Barley Pie Crust: Use ¾ cup each oat and barley flours, 2 tablespoons arrowroot or tapioca starch, and 3½ to 4 tablespoons water.

Rice-Flour Pie Crust

A no-roll, press-in-place crust. Fill it before or after baking.

⅓ **cup whole almonds**
¾ **cup brown rice flour**
¼–½ **teaspoon salt**
¼ **teaspoon ground cinnamon (optional)**
3 **tablespoons water**
2 **tablespoons almond oil**
2 **tablespoons honey**

PREHEAT THE OVEN to 350°F. Grind the almonds to a fine powder in a blender. Place in a 9" pie plate. Add the flour, salt, and cinnamon if using. Mix well with a fork.

Combine the water, oil, and honey in a small saucepan. Heat over low heat just until honey liquefies. Pour into the flour mixture. Stir with a fork until well blended. Let stand a few minutes for rice flour to absorb the liquid.

Press the mixture firmly into place with your fingers, spreading to cover the bottom and sides of pie plate. Pat top edge of crust into a straight edge.

For a baked crust, bake for 18 minutes, or until lightly brown and marked with a few small cracks. Cool before filling.

For an unbaked crust, bake 5 minutes. Add desired filling, and finish baking as the recipe directs.

Makes one 9" pie crust

Grain-Free Pie Crust

A versatile crust featuring amaranth, buckwheat, and quinoa flours.

½ cup amaranth flour

½ cup white buckwheat flour

½ cup quinoa flour

2 tablespoons arrowroot or tapioca starch

½ teaspoon salt

⅓ cup Spectrum Spread

3–4 tablespoons ice water

PREHEAT THE OVEN to 400°F.

In a food processor, combine the flours, arrowroot or starch, and salt, and process for 15 to 20 seconds. Add the spread and pulse a few times until mixture looks like coarse cornmeal.

With the processor running, pour in 3 tablespoons of the ice water in a thin steady stream. Add the remaining water slowly, stopping as soon as the dough gathers itself into a ball.

Cut 2 pieces of waxed paper, each about 18" long. Mist one side of each with cooking spray. Place the dough between the sheets, sprayed sides facing the dough. Pat into a 6"-diameter circle. Roll out to a 12"-diameter circle. Remove the top paper and carefully flip the bottom paper and crust into the prepared pie plate. Remove the waxed paper. Adjust crust and smooth edges.

For a baked crust, prick all over with a fork and line with parchment paper and dry beans in a single layer. Bake for 8 minutes, and remove the parchment and beans. Return to oven for 4 to 5 minutes more, or until light brown. Allow to cool before filling.

For an unbaked crust, bake for 3 minutes. Add desired filling, and finish baking as the recipe directs.

Makes one 9" pie crust

COOK'S TIPS

* To make white buckwheat flour, grind ½ cup white, unroasted whole groats at a time in a blender for 1 to 2 minutes. Pour into sieve. Repeat grinding, adding any groats that didn't go through the sieve.

* A gluten-free crust like this one tends to tear easily and may seem to be falling apart. It's nothing you're doing wrong—it's the nature of these flours. However, this isn't much of a problem because the dough patches easily. Don't try to crimp the edges. Just fold the extra dough under, making a double-thick, flat, straight edge about ½" higher than the pie plate edge.

Nut and Seed Crunch Crust

Excellent flavor, with crunch—a great alternative to graham cracker crust.

½ **cup brown rice flour**

½ **cup ground nuts**

¼ **cup ground sunflower or pumpkin seeds**

1 **tablespoon arrowroot**

½ **teaspoon ground cinnamon**

2 **tablespoons water**

2 **tablespoons vegetable oil**

1 **tablespoon honey**

PREHEAT THE OVEN to 350°F.

In a bowl, combine the flour, nuts, seeds, arrowroot, and cinnamon.

In a small saucepan, combine the water, oil, and honey. Heat over low heat just until the honey liquefies. Pour over the flour mixture, and stir with a fork until well combined.

Place in a 9" pie plate. Press firmly into place with your fingers, spreading to cover the bottom and sides of the pie plate. Pat top into a straight edge.

For a baked crust, bake for 18 to 20 minutes, or until lightly brown. Cool before filling.

For an unbaked crust, bake for 8 minutes. Add desired filling, and finish baking as the recipe directs.

Makes one 9" pie crust

Nut Streusel Crumbs

These crumbs are a delicious and easy way to top pies and fruit crisps.

½ **cup brown rice flour**

½ **cup ground or finely chopped walnuts**

1 **tablespoon arrowroot**

¼ **teaspoon salt**

¼ **teaspoon ground cinnamon (optional)**

1–2 **tablespoons walnut oil**

1–2 **tablespoons honey**

IN A BOWL, mix the flour, nuts, arrowroot, salt, and cinnamon if using. Drizzle with 1 tablespoon each of the oil and honey. Toss until evenly distributed. Add more oil and honey as needed for a good crumb texture.

Makes about 1 cup
(enough for an 8" or 9" pie or fruit crisp)

COOK'S TIP
---

* To use this topping on a pie or fruit crisp: Prebake an empty pie crust for 5 minutes. Add the filling, and bake as the filling recipe directs, except remove the pie (or fruit crisp) from the oven 15 minutes before the end of the cooking time. Sprinkle on (and pat gently) the streusel crumbs. Return it to the oven and bake for the last 15 minutes of cooking time.

Spelt-Kamut Streusel Crumbs

*These are quick and easy to prepare and perfect
for topping a coffee cake, fruit crisp, or pie.*

⅓ cup **Kamut brand flour**

⅓ cup **spelt flour**

¼ teaspoon **salt**

¼ cup **date or maple sugar**

¼ cup **Spectrum Spread**

IN A FOOD PROCESSOR, combine the Kamut brand flour, spelt flour, salt, date or maple sugar, and spread, and process for 30 seconds, or until the texture resembles coarse cornmeal.

Makes about 1 cup
(enough for an 8" or 9" pie or fruit crisp)

COOK'S TIPS

✳ If you want, you can cut the spread into the flour by using a rubber spatula.

✳ To use this topping on a pie or fruit crisp: Prebake an empty pie crust for 5 minutes. Add the filling, and bake as the filling recipe directs, except remove the pie (or fruit crisp) from the oven 15 minutes before the end of the cooking time. Sprinkle on (and pat gently) the streusel crumbs. Return it to the oven and bake for the last 15 minutes of cooking time.

Variations

Kamut Streusel Crumbs: Omit the spelt flour and use ⅔ cup Kamut brand flour.

Spelt Streusel Crumbs: Omit the Kamut brand flour and use ¾ cup whole grain or white spelt flour.

Oat and Barley Streusel Crumbs: Replace the Kamut brand and spelt flours with ⅓ cup oat flour and ⅓ cup barley flour.

Rice-Flour Streusel Crumbs

½ cup brown rice flour

¼ cup ground almonds

2 tablespoons tapioca starch or arrowroot

¼ teaspoon salt

¼ teaspoon ground cinnamon (optional)

1–2 tablespoons vegetable oil

1–2 tablespoons honey

IN A BOWL, mix the flour, almonds, starch or arrowroot, salt, and cinnamon if using. Drizzle with 1 tablespoon each of the oil and honey. Toss until evenly distributed, adding more oil and honey as needed for a good crumb texture.

Makes about ¾ cup
(enough for an 8" or 9" pie or fruit crisp)

COOK'S TIP

✳ To use this topping on a pie or fruit crisp: Prebake an empty pie crust for 5 minutes. Add the filling, and bake as the filling recipe directs, except remove the pie (or fruit crisp) from the oven 15 minutes before the end of the cooking time. Sprinkle on (and pat gently) the streusel crumbs. Return it to the oven and bake for the last 15 minutes of cooking time.

Grain-Free Streusel Crumbs

¼ cup amaranth flour

¼ cup buckwheat flour

¼ cup quinoa flour

1 tablespoon arrowroot

⅓ cup ground walnuts

½ teaspoon ground cinnamon

2 tablespoons honey

2–3 tablespoons vegetable oil

IN A BOWL, mix the amaranth flour, buckwheat flour, quinoa flour, arrowroot, nuts, and cinnamon. Drizzle with 2 tablespoons each of the honey and oil. Toss until evenly distributed. If crumbs seem dry, add the remaining oil and toss again.

Makes about 1 cup
(enough for an 8" or 9" pie or fruit crisp)

COOK'S TIPS

✳ Feel free to use any of your favorite nuts in this recipe.

✳ To use this topping on a pie or fruit crisp: Prebake an empty pie crust for 5 minutes. Add the filling, and bake as the filling recipe directs, except remove the pie (or fruit crisp) from the oven 15 minutes before the end of the cooking time. Sprinkle on (and pat gently) the streusel crumbs. Return it to the oven and bake for the last 15 minutes of cooking time.

Blueberry Cobbler

*This is a favorite at our house. It may appear for dessert after dinner
or it may be featured for a weekend brunch.*

4 cups fresh or 1 pound frozen
blueberries

½ cup thawed purple or white grape
fruit juice concentrate

⅓ cup water or grape juice

1½ tablespoons tapioca starch

½ recipe Country-Style Quick Bread
(page 121) or Spelt Drop Biscuits
(page 119)

PREHEAT THE OVEN to 400°F. Mist a 2-quart or 9" × 9" baking dish with cooking spray or oil it.

Drain fresh berries on cotton or paper towels. If using frozen fruit, do not thaw. In a saucepan, combine the blueberries and the fruit juice concentrate. Bring to a boil. Reduce the heat.

In a cup, combine the water or fruit juice with the tapioca. Stir into the blueberries and return to a boil. Cook, stirring, for 1 minute after it reaches a boil. Remove from the heat. Pour into the prepared dish.

Drop the bread or biscuit dough, by rounded tablespoonfuls, onto the blueberries, forming six mounds. Bake for 20 minutes, or until the berries are bubbly and biscuits are brown.

Cool for 15 to 30 minutes, and serve warm.

Makes 6 servings

COOK'S TIPS

✳ Other fruit juice concentrates and juices that can be used in this recipe include apple, pineapple, and lemonade.

✳ The Country-Style Quick Bread or Spelt Drop Biscuits recipe will be used as the cobbler topping so you'll need only *half* the ingredient amounts. Follow this recipe (Blueberry Cobbler) for combining the liquid and dry ingredients and baking instructions.

✳ The Kamut Drop Biscuits (page 119) or Rye and Barley Drop Biscuits (page 118) also work nicely in the recipe instead of the Country-Style Quick Bread or Spelt Drop Biscuits.

Apple-Sweetened Apple Crisp

A delightful fruit and whole grain dessert everyone can enjoy.

TOPPING

- ¼ cup melted ghee or walnut oil
- 2 tablespoons apple juice concentrate
- ⅔ cup rolled oats
- ½ cup oat bran
- ⅓ cup chopped walnuts
- 1 teaspoon ground cinnamon
- ¼ teaspoon freshly grated nutmeg
- ¼ teaspoon salt

FRUIT

- ½ cup thawed apple juice concentrate
- 2 tablespoons quick-cooking tapioca granules
- 6 cups peeled, sliced apples

TO MAKE THE TOPPING: Preheat the oven to 350°F. Mist a 9" × 9" baking dish with cooking spray or oil it.

In a 2- or 3-quart saucepan, combine the ghee or oil and 2 tablespoons apple juice concentrate. Heat over low heat until the ghee melts. Remove from the heat and stir in the rolled oats, oat bran, nuts, cinnamon, nutmeg, and salt. Mixture will be dry and crumbly.

To make the fruit: In a large bowl, combine the apple juice concentrate and tapioca granules, and let soak for 15 minutes. Add the apples, stirring to coat. Pour into the prepared pan and distribute the crumbs evenly over the top. Cover loosely with foil and bake for 20 minutes.

Reduce the heat to 325°F and remove the foil. Bake for 12 to 15 minutes, or until the crumbs are brown. Cool for 20 to 30 minutes and serve warm.

Makes 6 servings

COOK'S TIP

* To make ghee (clarified butter): Melt butter in a saucepan over low heat; then pour the liquid ghee into a jar, leaving the milk solids in the bottom of the pan. Discard the solids. Ghee will keep frozen for up to 1 year.

Rhubarb-Buckwheat Crumble

*A crumble is a fruit crisp made with honey. Rhubarb and buckwheat
are a natural combination because they're members of the same family.*

TOPPING

- ¼ **cup oil**
- 2 **tablespoons honey**
- ½ **cup white buckwheat flour**
- ¼ **cup arrowroot**
- ⅓ **cup chopped walnuts (optional)**
- 1 **teaspoon ground cinnamon**

FRUIT

- 5 **cups sliced rhubarb**
- 3 **tablespoons arrowroot**
- ½ **cup honey**
- ⅓ **cup water**

TO MAKE THE TOPPING: Preheat the
oven to 350°F. Oil an 8" × 8" baking dish.

In a saucepan, combine the oil and
honey and warm over low heat until the
honey melts. Stir in the flour, arrowroot,
walnuts if using, and cinnamon. The mixture should be dry and crumbly.

To make the fruit: Place the rhubarb in a
3-quart saucepan. Add the arrowroot, and
toss to coat. Add the honey and water. Bring
to a boil over medium heat, stirring constantly. Boil for 30 seconds. Pour into the
prepared dish.

Sprinkle the topping over the rhubarb.
Bake for 35 to 40 minutes. Allow to cool
for 30 minutes before serving.

Makes 6 servings

COOK'S TIP

✳ To make white buckwheat flour, grind ½ cup white,
unroasted whole groats at a time in a blender for 1
to 2 minutes. Pour into sieve. Repeat grinding,
adding any groats that didn't go through the sieve.